Land Legislation in
Mandate Palestine

Land Legislation in Mandate Palestine

VOLUME 6

OFFICIAL REPORTS AND MEMORANDA, PART II

Editor: Martin Bunton

an imprint of

CAMBRIDGE UNIVERSITY PRESS

Cambridge, New York, Melbourne, Madrid, Cape Town, Singapore, São Paulo

Cambridge University Press
The Edinburgh Building, Cambridge CB2 2RU, UK

Published in the United States of America by Cambridge University Press,
New York

www.cambridge.org
Information on this title: www.archiveeditions.co.uk

© Copyright in this edition including research, selection of documents, arrangement,
contents lists and descriptions: Cambridge Archive Editions Ltd 2009

Cambridge Archive Editions is an imprint of Cambridge University Press.

Facsimiles of original documents including Crown copyright material are published
under licence from The National Archives, London, England. Images may be used only
for purposes of research, private study or education. Applications for any other use
should be made to The National Archives Image Library, Kew, Richmond, Surrey
TW9 4DU. Infringement of the above condition may result in legal action.

Subject to statutory exception and to the provisions of relevant collective licensing
agreements, no reproduction of other parts of the work may take place without written
permission of Cambridge University Press.

Every reasonable effort has been made to contact all copyright holders; in the event of
any omission please contact the publisher.

First published 2009

Printed and bound by CPI Group (UK) Ltd, Croydon, CR0 4YY

British Library Cataloguing in Publication Data
Land Legislation in Mandate Palestine.
  1. Land tenure–Law and legislation–Palestine–History–
  20th century. 2. Land tenure–Law and legislation–
  Palestine–History–20th century–Sources. 3. Palestine–
  Politics and government–1917-1948.
  I. Bunton, Martin P.
  346.5'6940432-dc22

ISBN-13:   978-1-84097-260-3 (set) (hardback)
           978-1-84097-305-1 (volume 6)

Land Legislation in Mandate Palestine

CONTENTS

VOLUME 6:

OFFICIAL REPORTS AND MEMORANDA, PART II

Section 5: Memoranda on Land Taxation, 1927–1933	1
5.01 C.H.F. Cox, Office of the Chief British Representative Trans-Jordan, Amman, Trans-Jordan, to Chief Secretary, Jerusalem, 13 February 1927, regarding Sir E. Dowson's recommendations for land taxation reform in Trans-Jordan [CO 733/140/7]	
5.02 Sir E. Dowson, 'Notes on the abolition of the tithe and the establishment of a land-tax in Palestine', April 1928 [CO 733/152/1]	11
5.03 Despatch No. 289, Lord Plumer, High Commissioner for Palestine, Jerusalem, to L.S. Amery, Secretary of State for the Colonies, 23 March 1928, enclosing a proposal by A. Abramson, Commissioner of Lands, Jerusalem, to introduce a new land tax [CO 733/152/1]	51
5.04 Request from A.N. Strong, 15 February 1928, and reply: Colonial Office minute by J.T. Hall, 16 April 1928, regarding labour [CO 733/152/1]	63
5.05 Sir E. Dowson, Kent, to Commissioner of Lands, Jerusalem, 18 April 1928, regarding land tax reforms [CO 733/152/1]	73
5.06 Despatch No. 311, J.R. Chancellor, High Commissioner for Palestine, Jerusalem, to Lord Passfield, Secretary of State for the Colonies, London, 17 April 1930, on the appointment of a committee to investigate the economic conditions of farmers in Palestine and enclosing a memorandum by A. Abramson, Commissioner of Lands, 21 February 1930, on the economic condition of the Arab farmer [CO 733/185/2]	81
5.07 W. Davis, Officer Administering the Government, Jerusalem, to Lord Passfield, Secretary of State for the Colonies, 5 July 1930, forwarding 'Report of Committee on the Economic Condition of Agriculturalists and the Fiscal Measures of Government in Relation Thereto' [Johnson–Crosbie Report] (Jerusalem, 1930)' [CO 733/185/4]	87

5.08 A. Wauchope, High Commissioner for Palestine, Jerusalem, to Sir P. Cunliffe-Lister, Secretary of State for the Colonies, 13 August 1932, forwarding the 'Report of the Rural Taxation Committee' by C.H. Ley, Director of Surveys, Jaffa 1931 [CO 733/216/7] — 201

5.09 A. Wauchope, High Commissioner for Palestine, Jerusalem, to Sir P. Cunliffe-Lister, Secretary of State for the Colonies, 15 September 1932, forwarding the 'Report of Committee on Arrears of Werko, Tithes and Agricultural Loans' [CO 733/227/5] — 253

5.10 A. Wauchope, High Commissioner for Palestine, Jerusalem, to Sir P. Cunliffe-Lister, Secretary of State for the Colonies, 23 February 1934, on the subject of rural taxations, with four enclosures including: Report of the Committee Appointed by His Excellency to Give Further Consideration to the Draft Ordinance on Rural Property Tax; Observations of Committee on Sir John Campbell's Note on the Report of the Rural Taxation Committee; short Rural Property Tax Ordinance (Schedule 1, with table); and Report of the Rural Taxation Machinery Committee [CO 733/267/1] — 275

5.11 A. Wauchope, High Commissioner for Palestine, Jerusalem, to P. Cunliffe-Lister, Secretary of State for the Colonies, London, 11 February 1935, regarding Rural Property Tax Ordinance, with four enclosures; A. Wauchope to P. Cunliffe-Lister, 11 February 1935, forwarding extract from *Palestine Gazette*, published by Palestine Authority, regarding Rural Property Tax Ordinance [CO 733/279/7] — 361

Section 6: Memoranda on the Settlement of Title to Land, 1927–1934

6.01 Lord Plumer, High Commissioner for Palestine, Jerusalem, to L.S. Amery, Secretary of State for the Colonies, London, 8 April 1927, enclosing a memorandum by Sir E. Dowson on the appointment of a land commissioner, and notes on same by Lord Plumer [CO 733/136/8] — 415

6.02 'Explanatory Note on the Land Settlement Ordinance,' by N. Bentwich, Attorney General, Jerusalem, June 1927 [CO 733/142/11] — 433

6.03 Sir E. Dowson, 'Report on the Progress of Land Reforms in Palestine, 1923–1930', Submitted November 1930 [CO 733/221/4] — 443

6.04 'O'Donnell Commission, Chapter 5: "Lands Department, Commission of Lands, and Survey Department"' [CO 733/208/5] — 495

6.05 Young, Officer Administering the Government, Jerusalem, to J.H. Thomas, Secretary of State for the Colonies, 24 October 1931, regarding the report of the O'Donnell Financial Commission, with two enclosures: 'Observations on the recommendations on Land Settlement in the Report of the O'Donnell Commission, Chap. 5, Middle East No. 43 Confidential', and 'Memorandum on the Recommendations of the Financial Commission in paragraph 48 of the report' [CO 733/208/5] — 511

6.06 Extract from semi-official letter from Sir E. Dowson to Mr. Hall, 24 May 1932, regarding the system of land registration in Palestine; A. Abramson, Commissioner of Lands, Jerusalem, to Chief Secretary, Jerusalem, 14 September 1932, responding to concerns expressed by Sir E. Dowson [CO 733/217/5]   547

6.07 H.H. Trusted, Officer Administering the Government, Jerusalem, to Sir Philip Cunliffe-Lister, Secretary of State for the Colonies, 13 May 1933, enclosing draft ordinance to provide for the partition of musha'a lands in advance of settlement, and memorandum on same by Lloyd Blood, Solicitor General, Jerusalem, 22 April 1933 [CO 733/245/1]   553

Section 5: Memoranda on Land Taxation, 1927–1933

5.01

COPY.

Office of the Chief British Representative.
Trans-Jordan.

II-90/28. Amman, 13th February, 1927.

The Chief Secretary,
    Government Offices,
        Jerusalem.

        Miri Land in Trans-Jordan is subject by law to the payment of a Land Tax and to a tithe of the actual produce of the land. The assessment of Land Tax is out of date and was badly done and the records thereof have been maintained as badly here as in other parts of the Turkish Empire.

        As regards "Tithe", the annual assessment of the crops is only carried out in the sub-districts of Salt and Amman, and in the sub-district of Madeba excluding the land occupied by the Beni Hameida, and in a limited area of State Domains which are leased to the people at an annual rental of 10% of the gross value of the products. In the remainder of the country, the Government collect a fixed sum per annum from each village or tribe in lieu of tithe and leave the villagers or tribesmen to arrange for the apportionment of this payment amongst themselves. The sums fixed are based on the previous similar Turkish levy except in the case of Kerak where the sum was increased by 20% in 1925. The amount payable to Government under this arrangement is very much less than is the Government's due and the division of the amounts payable by each village or tribe amongst the individual villagers or tribesmen varies in the manner of its division and is entirely uncontrolled by the Government. Roughly speaking, in the Northern District, it is divided amongst the villagers according to the land they cultivate, whilst in the Kerak district it is divided amongst the tribesmen irrespective of whether they hold land or not, and irrespect of the area they hold.

        Although the Government would immediately increase its revenue by the introduction of a tithe estimation throughout, it is obviously undesirable to attempt to adopt this method, firstly because it is very doubtful if Government would be strong enough to enforce it, and secondly because of the very many defects inherent in the tithe system.

        The better method, and the method which Sir Ernest Dowson recommends is to commence without delay to improve the method of dividing the present fixed amounts and to obtain reliable statistics which would justify an increase in these fixed amounts. Steps are immediately being taken to ascertain more clearly the manner of dividing the fixed sums which at present obtain, and to work out an arrangement under which it can be ensured that the division will be equitable, properly controlled and recorded.

                              Statistics/

-2-

Statistics on which to base the increase of these fixed amounts can only be obtained by valuing the land and for this purpose it is proposed to employ Mr. Hughes for a part of each year, firstly as a valuer himself and instructor of other valuation officers, and later as an inspector of these valuation officers.

For the purpose of arriving at a valuation, village boundaries must first be determined and the land of each village be divided into sections of even value within themselves. This determination of village boundaries and division of village lands into sections is also a necessary preliminary step to the Survey and to the Reorganisation of the Land Registers.

Sir Ernest Dowson, in his report, insists on the entire inadequacy of the present system of Land Registration. He points out that although Land Registers cannot be properly kept without the aid of continuous cadastral survey, yet a topo survey based on a reliable triangulation, indicating village and other administrative boundaries, the boundaries of cultivated blocks and the natural features of the terrain, and incorporating a sufficiency of ground marks is very much better than no survey at all, and that such a survey is the next best thing to a cadastral survey and should not be rejected if a continuous cadastral survey proves impracticable in Trans-Jordan on financial grounds.

I have discussed these questions at length with Sir Ernest Dowson who now definitely recommends that the Government should adopt the alternative to the cadastral survey mentioned above, that the Ajloun district should first be dealt with and that the topo survey thereof should be on a scale of 1/10,000.

We are fully agreed that an Englishman who is an expert in Survey should be engaged to supervise and take part in the work and that if the man chosen proves to be capable of it, he should also assume general charge of the reorganisation of the Land Registers, and the reassessment of land tax and tithe equivalent as well.

Thinking that Major T. Haycraft, R.E. would be a man well suited to carry out this difficult task, I wrote to him explaining the situation and asking whether he would accept the appointment on secondment at £.1,000 a year should the offer of it be made to him, and have heard from him that he is ready to accept it.

The Amir and the Trans-Jordan Government, to both of whom I have spoken, express their readiness to employ Major Haycraft, and, with me, realise to the full that it is only by employing an expert whose whole time will be devoted to it that there is any hope of bringing about these most important reforms for the full consideration of which neither they nor I have sufficient time or knowledge.

Major Ley who has been asked by Sir Ernest Dowson to make an estimate of the cost of a Triangulation and

Topo/

quare/

Topo Survey of Northern Trans-Jordan has, on the assumption that it comprises an area of 4000/kilometres furnished the attached figures. These figures which of course are extremely rough, include demarcation and the salary of the Officer in Charge but do not include cost of computation or reproduction. Major Ley estimates that if the whole of Trans-Jordan were taken, the estimate could be doubled, but I am of opinion that for the present and until more experience has been gained in the North, the extension of the Survey over the rest of Trans-Jordan should be limited to triangulation.

In the Ajloun District, the sum payable to Government on account of Werko is £.8114 and on account of the <u>fixed</u> tithe assessment is £.22,255. During 1927/28, no increase in these rates could be made and perhaps not in 1928/29 either. But commencing from 1929/30 it is estimated that the introduction of taxation on the new valuation would justify an increase of perhaps £.15,000.

In view however of the difficulties of imposing a very large increase of taxation all at once, it might not be possible to realise this increase, but it is considered safe to estimate for an increase of £.8,000 in 1929/30 and succeeding years with a further rise after a period of from 5 to 10 years.

Bad as the Land Registers at present are, the increased confidence of the people in the stability of the Government is reflected in an encouraging increase in the Land Registry receipts and it is confidently anticipated that the cost of the improvement in the Registers will be covered by the additional fees which will accrue as more confidence is gained and greater use made of the Registers. Furthermore the Government will become increasingly able to take control of and profit by the very large areas of State Domains of which its records are at present entirely inadequate.

I attach hereto three schedules shewing:-

——— (a) The estimated cost of the Triangulation and Topo Survey of the Northern District.

——— (b) The estimated cost of the Survey party for the year 1927/28. In this I have calculated that Major Haycraft will not arrive in Trans-Jordan until the end of June and that since he will need perhaps three months to study the situation, to discuss ways and means with the Director of Surveys of the Palestine Government and to choose his personnel, this personnel need only be provided for six months.

——— (c) An estimate of the cost of the valuation party which should commence operations on the 1st April next.

The total/

-4-

The total of the estimated expenditure on account of schedules (b) and (c) is £5,140, whilst in the 1927/28 estimates the sum of £2,000 only is provided for Land Demarcation, Settlement and Survey. A sum of £3,140 thus remains to be found. No re-appropriation from other Heads of Expenditure can be suggested, but since the Budget was framed, the Government has approved in principle the sale of an area of 6000 dunums of land in the Jordan Valley to the Palestine Electric Corporation which should realise not less than £10,000 since Mr. Rutenberg has expressed his readiness to pay £3,112 for some 1280 dunums thereof.

It is legitimate therefore that permission should be granted to set off this unforeseen and ultimately profitable additional expenditure against this unforeseen additional receipt.

I beg therefore that the estimates contained in schedules (b) and (c) may receive approval at the earliest possible date and that in forwarding them to the Secretary of State a request may be made for the secondment of Major T. Haycraft, R.E., to the Trans-Jordan Government for a period of two years which may be extended on further demand.

(Sgd) C. H. F. COX.

Chief British Representative.

SCHEDULE (4).

Rough Estimate.

Northern Trans-Jordan (Trig. & Topo Survey).

Year	Classn.	TRIG. Main	Minor	1/10,000	Marks	O. i/c	Total
First	Initial	500	500	750	750		2500
	Recc. t	1200	300	-	-	1000	2500
Second	Recc. t	2500	1200	2400	800	1000	7900
Third	"	-	1300	3800	500	1000	6600
Fourth	-			3500		1000	4500
Total		4200	3300	10450	2050	4000	24000

SCHEDULE (B).

(1) **Personal Emoluments**:

Major Haycraft, 9 months	£750	
1 Surveyor £26-31, 6 months	156	
1 " £21-25, 6 months	126	
4 " Apprentices @ £12, 6 months	288	
8 Carriers @ £4, 6 months	192	£1512
(2) Transport and Travelling		300
(3) Camp Equipment		200
(4) Instruments		400
(5) Animals		300
(6) Marks		350
(7) Computation and Drawing		500
		£ 3,562

SCHEDULE (C).

(1) **Personal Emoluments:**

Mr. Hughes, 4 months @ £60	£ 240	
2 Valuers £26-31 @ £26	624	
1 Surveyor £17-20 @ £17	204	
Labourers	100	£ 1168

(2) Transport and Travelling   300

(3) Equipment   50

(4) Lighting and Heating   10

(5) Printing and Stationery   30

(6) Contingencies   20

                                       £ 1,578

5.02

Wrotham,

Kent.

April, 1928.

Commissioner of Lands.

Notes on the abolition of the tithe and the establishment of a land-tax in Palestine.

The greater part of the accompanying notes was written in the winter of 1926-27 and formed the basis of discussions with District Commissioners, the members of the Average Tithe Committee and others. The notes were not finally communicated to Government as intended, because I found great difficulty in doing justice to some of the objections of the Chairman of the Average Tithe Committee to the majority scheme, and by the time that I felt that I had surmounted this difficulty after several discussions with the Chairman a general line of policy had been decided, while my views on the subject seemed to me to have been sufficiently recorded in the interval in the minutes of various meetings and in official correspondence. Among such papers may be mentioned:

(i) Memo of conference held on the 21st. February 1927 on settlement and registration of rights to immovable property and taxation of such property.

(ii) Letter to C.S. dated 18th. March on the majority scheme of the Average Tithe Committee.

(iii) Letter to C.S. dated 28th. March on the valuation of immovable property for fiscal purposes.

(iv) Letter to C.S. dated 9th. April on the action to be taken on the report of the Average Tithe Committee.

(v) Letter to C.S. dated 23rd. April on the draft Commutation of Tithes Ordinance 1927.

In accordance with your request of the 21st. January last I have, however, now completed and had my original draft notes typed in the hope that they will still prove of use. But I feel that the addition of this explanation is necessary, since at least so far as the majority scheme is concerned, the situation is viewed as it appeared in 1926-27 before it had been decided to give effect to the main provisions of the majority scheme of the Average Tithe Committee.

(Signed)   ERNEST M. DOWSON.

NOTES on the abolition of tithe and the establishment of a land tax in Palestine.

----

§§ 1-12. Replacement of tithe by commuted tithe scheme.
§ 13.   Untrustworthy character of commuted tithe as basis of assessment.
§ 14.   Necessity to replace werko as well as tithe.
§ 15.   Block land tax.
§ 16.   Character of land tax.
§ 17.   Stereotyped assessment.
§ 18.   Basis and methods of assessment.

CORRIGENDA.

p.16, bottom line, for "considerable" read "considered".

p.23, line 6 from bottom, insert "tax" after "land".

p.24, line 10., for "equivalent" read "equivalence".

NOTES on the ABOLITION OF TITHE AND THE ESTABLISHMENT
OF LAND TAX IN PALESTINE.

REPLACEMENT OF
TITHE BY COM-
MUTED TITHE SCHEME.

The divergent views expressed in the majority and the minority report of the Average Tithe Committee reflect a difference of opinion that has been the outstanding feature of all discussions relating to the tithe during the last four or five years. It can broadly be said that the officers more directly responsible for the conduct of district and village affairs, as also the Director of Agriculture, have throughout been so impressed with the evils of the existing tithe system that they have held its prompt abolition to be imperative; while the officers principally concerned with administering the Government as a whole from the Capital have considered those evils to be exaggerated and that it was better to perpetuate a defective system to which people were accustomed until a thorough-going reform could be made.

A composition of the views thus crudely expressed and the adoption of a policy which will commend itself to all responsible officers of Government is possible without any important sacrifice of conviction. Thus I suggest that the two findings that follow provide the basis of a common policy and practice which can be subscribed to by everyone:-

(i) that the tithe is a seriously objectionable tax which should be replaced as soon as possible by some less injurious measure.

(ii) that such replacement should be carried out with sufficient caution and knowledge of the actual operation of the projected alternative to ensure that the anticipated improvement is realized in practice.

2. My own frequently expressed opinion of the grave objection to the tithe and the necessity to sweep it away at the earliest possible moment need not for the most part be repeated in view of the strong indictments of the tithe by the Commissioners of the Northern and Southern Districts set forth in their minutes supporting the main recommendations of the majority report. But there are two evil features of the existing tithe system which I think still require emphasis.

Thus in the minority report and elsewhere the virtue of elasticity is claimed for the tithe. The claim merits careful consideration if only because it represents the feature that is superficially most attractive; although elasticity may be too dearly bought if it connotes great variation in public revenues from year to year and ever present uncertainties for the taxpayer. And the fact that a regular land tax is the accepted objective of Government in due course, shows that the qualities of certainty and stability are in practice preferred. But if by elasticity is meant that the tithe accommodates itself to a cultivator's circumstances, this is not so except when applied to the primitive husbandry of primitive societies, conditions which no doubt linger in Palestine but which it is contrary to public interest to foster. For the tithe is levied on the gross production of a man's holding without any regard to his effort or expenditure; and consequently far from being elastic in any equitable or beneficial way it penalises the progressive cultivator who puts money into his holding and seeks to improve it. Consequently the tithe is in principle a thoroughly bad tax, even if it could be purged of the gross errors and defects which characterize its application in practice.

The following two extracts may perhaps be usefully quoted to show that elsewhere the tithe has proved, and is recognized to be, a vicious fiscal instrument. Mr. J. A. Venn, tracing

the history of the tithe in England,+ says, "By the
"seventeenth century its incidence had become a mill-stone
"round the neck of those who wished to improve their methods
"of farming. It was not the cost of the charge itself - whe-
"ther paid in money or in kind.........; but it was rather
"the knowledge that there was always present a sleeping partner
"to share in the gains of husbandry but never to risk any
"capital - one who appeared and claimed a tenth of all the
"results accruing from improved methods and from the growth of
"new crops." And the Mission appointed in 1925 by the Secretary of State for the Colonies to enquire into the financial
position and prospects of 'Iraq, in § 25 of their report say,
"Speaking quite generally, we were advised that corrupt prac-
"tices were extremely widespread in 'Iraq....... and that they
"permeated the whole system of revenue assessment and collec-
"tion. If this is so, it furnishes a conclusive argument in
"favour of the substitution of a system of fixed assessment
"which would eliminate many of the opportunities for fraud.
"In any case, it may be pointed out that the levying, as tax,
"of a share of the gross produce is a method which is economic-
"ally unsound. It definitely penalizes any extra expenditure
"which the taxpayer puts into the land, and therefore penal-
"izes that intensive cultivation, for the spread of which any
"real development of agricultural conditions in 'Iraq must
"wait. A fixed assessment, based on the natural productiveness
"of the land under normal conditions would offer inducements
"to keener effort, increased expenditure on tools and equipment,
"and improvement of property. A proportionate tax on the gross
"produce discourages them all."

+"Foundations of Agricultural Economics" by J.A.Venn,M.A.,
Gilbey Lecturer in the History and Economics of Agriculture in
the University of Cambridge; Economic Advisory Officer to the
British Ministry of Agriculture. Camb. Univ. Press 1923. p.100.

3. The second evil feature of the existing tithe system which appears to need further emphasis is the inequitable variation in individual assessments.

The District Commissioner of the Northern District says, "Even with the cleverest and most careful estimator the process "(of estimation) can only be described as guessing at the quan- "tity of grain in a particular heap of sheaves........ Not only "is estimation merely guess-work, but an estimator's guesses "are deliberately increased or decreased" (on interested grounds of which the writer gives instances). The District Commissioner of the Southern District expresses the same defect forcibly in arithmetical form in his second minute (No.821); and concludes his observations by saying, "it would be perfectly easy to demon- "strate practically by actual experiment with the most reliable "estimators and inspectors on a given threshing floor or grove "that the whole system as a means of physical measurement is "worthless and as a basis of taxation grossly immoral."

And it should be added that the incidence on the individual taxpayer of the wide divergences from the truth, which are inseparable from any attempt to determine the total yield of each successive crop of every individual cultivator in every village in Palestine, is accentuated by the subsequent compulsory cash commutation of these untrustworthy quantitative assessments. A single cash value is assigned over wide districts to each of some seventy to eighty varieties of agricultural produce; whereas it is evident that the quality of any given variety of produce (e.g. wheat or Jaffa oranges) harvested in innumerable holdings all over the country must vary widely with situation and circumstances, as must also the cost of marketing such product and the price obtained for it.

4. I have drawn attention again to the vicious character of the tithe as a modern fiscal instrument and the wide range

of arbitrariness in its incidence on individuals, because the belief still lingers that this tax is at least in principle sound and operates in practice with a rough measure of fairness. And to viciousness in principle and arbitrariness in practice are added the continuous interference with agriculture and marketing, the deterioration and depredation of crops retained on the threshing floor for assessment, the increasing deflection of District Staff from other duties and the innumerable opportunities for corruption and oppression to which District Officers and the Department of Agriculture have unceasingly called attention for a number of years.

Therefore it is surely not an over-statement that the tithe is a seriously objectionable tax which should be replaced as soon as possible by some less injurious measure? It has already survived nine years of British rule in Palestine. Is it also to survive the further ten or fifteen years that must be expected to pass before the completion of the settlement of rights to land and the establishment of a sensible system of registration of such rights ultimately provide an unimpeachable substitute? This is the critical question to be answered, and by the answer to which policy must be governed.

If it is agreed that it is wrong to perpetuate the existing tithe system for another ten or fifteen years, or indeed a day longer than can be helped, it follows that some provisional substitute for the ultimate land tax is needed which will remedy the graver evils of the tithe without introducing others equally serious. Such a substitute is bound in important respects to be imperfect, because of the prevailing absence of intelligible and reliable records of rights to land, which only the slow march of settlement of such rights can remedy. But the imperfections consequently inseparable from any provisional measure of reform do not justify the condemnation of such a measure if it may reasonably be expected to effect an appreciable amelioration of existing conditions and practice. Nor can it be admitted that human knowledge and experience is so barren that no such provisional substitute for the ultimate land tax can be devised, and that the perpetuation of the crying defects of the existing tithe system for another ten or fifteen years is inevitable.

5. Now since it is evidently unreasonable to apply to the recommendations of the majority report comparisons with ideals, or even with the proposed land tax, seeing that the latter is admittedly unattainable in advance of the settlement of rights to land, what criteria may be fairly and usefully applied? These criteria should I suggest be:

(i) Will these recommendations, if brought into successful operation, remove or considerably mitigate, the graver evils of the existing tithe system?

(ii) will they introduce other comparably serious evils?

(iii) can their successful operation be ensured?

Let us now apply these three criteria in turn to the main recommendations of the majority report.

But before doing so it may be convenient to re-state these recommendations as far as possible briefly in the words of the authors.

(i) An average tithe in money on cereals and other rotation crops shall be calculated for each village, and the total amount for each village shall be distributed among the individual tithe payers of the village in proportion to the potential productivity of their lands estimated in wheat (§ 18 majority report).

- 6 -

(ii) This distribution shall be carried out in the first instance by the villagers themselves and shall then be inspected and (where necessary) revised by the local District Officer assisted by suitable assessors (Loc. cit.).

(iii) Average tithes in money on fruits shall be calculated direct for individual tithe payers (loc. cit.).

(iv) The basis of the fixed assessment shall be the average of tithes in money for the four years 1922/23 to 1925/26 (§ 9).

I understand from subsequent discussion that the term "individual tithe-payers" in recommendation (i) should more precisely be "individual possessors of arable land", and that in essence the majority scheme is the introduction of a crude land-tax on land that is held for cultivation (miri wa mevqufè land), whether such land is actually cropped during a given season or not. Mulk land is, I believe, ordinarily not liable for tithe.

The principal evils of the existing tithe system are briefly summarized in §4 above. Let us consider seriatim whether these defects would be removed or mitigated by the successful operation of the majority scheme.

(i) Defective fiscal principle. The main characteric of the majority scheme is the substitution of a crude land tax for a crude tithe. As the substitution of a land tax for the taxation of gross agricultural production is accepted as an ultimate object of reform, the application of the majority scheme would be a move in the direction of an accepted and sound principle in place of a condemned and faulty one.

(ii) <u>Arbitrary individual assessment</u>. Village communities undoubtedly have the knowledge both (a) of the persons in effective possession of the cultivated lands of the village and (b) of the value of those lands, which would enable them to distribute an aggregate village assessment equitably among individuals. This is so in all countries, and is expressly affirmed to be so in Palestine by the District Commissioners in the minutes already mentioned. They also point out that judicial notice is continually taken of this local knowledge and that settlement of rights to land will be dependent upon it. Similar local knowledge constituted the basis of at least the earlier revenue settlements in India, of the re-assessment of the land tax in Egypt, and is being used for corresponding work in Nigeria. And actually throughout the villages of Palestine itself in respect of both shifting ('mesha') and stable holdings, whenever there is no known connection between the existing land tax (werko) and the land that is supposed to be taxed (as is often the case), the sums claimed are distributed by the villagers themselves in the very way that the majority report recommends that the aggregate average tithe levy should also be distributed.

It may be objected that the werko is admittedly as often as not levied in an arbitrary and illegitimate manner, and that to model the distribution of an average tithe on bad methods practised in collecting the werko would merely be piling wrong upon wrong. To such an objection it can be answered that the defects of the existing werko are due to other and deeper causes (i.e. faulty land registration and neglect of re-assessment) and that when the distribution of verko follows local recommendations, such distribution is probably the soundest part of the proceeding.

There is in my opinion no doubt at all that a broadly equitable distribution of the proposed aggregate tax among individuals that is now conspicuously lacking, can be secured (and in advance of land settlement can only be secured) by successfully enlisting the co-operation of the villagers concerned.

(iii) Interference with agriculture and marketing, and

(iv) Deterioration and depredation of crops retained on the threshing floor for assessment would both cease under the majority scheme.

(v) Deflection of District staff from other duties would, in my opinion, for some years to come be as great as at present; but should steadily diminish as the proposed measures became familiar.

(vi) Opportunities for corruption and oppression, so far as exercised by outsiders, and more particularly by salaried officials of Government, should cease under the operation of the majority scheme. Opportunities for corruption and oppression within village communities would not I think be appreciably affected one way or the other. The District Commissioners report that under the existing tithe system the former type of abuse is general and do not think that under the proposed scheme the latter form is to be feared. And if the former is not in itself the more objectionable, it is that for which the Government is directly responsible and which injures its reputation the more. As against the above I am inclined to think that occasions for internal quarrels (hareqat) and intrigue (fasad) in villages would increase, since any relief from taxation would be at the expense of a neighbour instead of the Government.

On a general review of the conclusions reached under the six heads examined it is clear that the successful operation of the majority scheme would go a long way towards removing or mitigating the grave evils of the existing tithe system.

8.   Let us next consider whether the application of the majority scheme would introduce any serious defects of its own. And here our most useful guide should evidently be the minority minute of dissent by the Chairman of the Committee. He gives seven grounds for his inability to agree with his fellow-members. It is better to examine these objections seriatim, although this involves some repetition. The numbers which follow refer to the seven objections as set out in Section 2 of the minute of dissent itself, and to three other objections in the paragraph which follows.

> (i) The attribution of elasticity to the existing tithe system has been discussed above (see §2). There is nothing in the majority scheme which excludes modification of distribution of the commuted tithe to meet subsequent changes in the possession of land. But I understand that the changes primarily meant are the changes in the gross production of a village due to shrinkage or extension of the village population and of the village lands, and/or to changes in the character of the crops. Objection on these grounds is valid and weighty to any lengthy application of a

- 10 -

commutation based on the returns of a few past
years, but loses its force if such commutation
is only to operate for a few years, (see §13 below).

(ii) Neither the proposed commutation nor the existing
tithe system can be regarded as attempts to arrive
at the true value of the land as the object of taxation. In both cases the tax levied is based upon
the value of produce only. The conformity of either
system to the ability of taxpayers to pay is unascertainable; but the power of an agriculturalist to
carry over from a good to a bad season is mainly determined by his prosperity, thrift and freedom from debt.
The existing tithe system by its interference with
agriculture and marketing and by its discouragement
of enterprise is an obstacle to both prosperity and
thrift. The majority scheme would remove this obstacle.

(iii) It is indisputable that "the identification of par-
"ticular holdings in villages and the registration of
"owners or cultivators......are impracticable in the
"absence of reliable data", if identification by
Government and data in its possession are meant. It
is also recognized that no unimpeachable system of
taxing land directly or indirectly can be brought
into operation until the absence of such reliable
data is remedied. But the absence of information
in the hands of Government concerning the parcellation and the possession of land does not mean that
such information does not exist. It means, as already
represented, that it only exists in any reliable degree
or to any adequate extent among the villagers directly concerned. No reform is possible now or ever
except through the medium of this local knowledge.

The basis of the majority scheme is that this knowledge can, and should, be used to obtain an immediate escape from the evils of the tithe.

Absentee landholders and changes in holdings are for the most part as well known to the village community as other material facts.

(iv) Villagers play an essential part in the assessments of the existing tithe. If the villagers as a body connive, individuals can under the existing system readily use or conceal a part of their crops; and as the Government alone is the loser no villager has any economic incentive to prevent such losses. Under the majority scheme the Government cannot unwittingly be the loser, and one or more villagers would always be interested in resisting any improper assessment. Whether the existing system or the majority scheme affords greater opportunities for corruption and abuse is doubtful. (see §7.).

(v) I understand the majority scheme to apply to all land that is normally cultivated, irrespective of the kind of crop. Only temporary exemptions to allow plantations to come into bearing appear to be proposed (see §§18, 20, 23-25 of Majority Report).

(vi) The amalgamation of the existing land tax (werko) assessments with the commuted tithe is not an intrinsic part of the majority scheme. I agree that it is undesirable. The proposal is discussed separately later (see §14 below).

(vii) It is surely misleading to characterize the existing tithe system as long established in distinction to the majority scheme. Ottoman application of the tithe varied. Distribution of aggregate

(x) The majority scheme involves a tax on unimproved values - or more precisely on neglected land - and a surtax on land cultivated with inferior crops to exactly the same extent as the regular land tax, which is accepted as the Government's ultimate objective. The essence of a land tax is that land is taxed in proportion to its extent and value regardless of the nature or existence of any crop thereon. The majority scheme does exactly the same.

No serious objections other than those that have now been considered have been suggested or to the best of my belief exist, to the essential features of the majority scheme as the purely provisional measure it is intended to be. There is consequently in my opinion no doubt that the graver evils of the tithe can be removed or greatly mitigated without risk of counterbalancing evils by bringing the majority scheme into succesaful operation. It remains to consider how such successful operation can be reasonably ensured.

Now although village communities undoubtedly possess the local knowledge that would enable them to distribute the aggregate commuted tithe fairly among the actual holders of the cultivated lands of their villages, the Government should be assured before putting the proposals into force that such local knowledge for the most part can and will be used in a businesslike and equitable way.

The signatories of the majority report and the District Commissioners of the Northern and Southern Districts are confident that these conditions can substantially be satisfied. I agree with them, but I think that both the amount and the duration of the control that would be needed is under-estimated, and that it would consequently be unwise to apply the majority scheme to the whole country without any preparation or trial.

[Page 13 is missing in the original file.]

It would perhaps be justifiable to do so if (as might be understood from § 12 of the majority report) a mere reversion was intended to the practice common under Ottoman administration (and still practised in Transjordan and apparently in Syria) of fixing the aggregate contribution required from a village and leaving its apportionment to the leading members of the village community. But the majority scheme departs from the Turkish original in several important particulars. In the first place it requires that the apportionment of the aggregate village payment among individual taxpayers shall be subject to external control (see §§ 12 and 21). So long as Palestine is under a British Mandate this means ultimately that such apportionment must be readily open to investigation and revision by British Supervising Officers and be conducted throughout on lines that will stand such scrutiny. To permit of the above all village apportionments must be systematically recorded and be effected in a manner that is intelligible to such British Officers and that commends itself to them and to Government as broadly equitable. These conditions do not merely have to be satisfied once at the outset, but also regularly afterwards: for a detailed amendment of each village apportionment roll and the incorporation therein of all subsequent changes in the de facto holders of the village lands will be needed annually.

I have no doubt that the village authorities can (with suitable assistance) be taught to fulfil the above requirements: but I think that they will need teaching in the first place and constant supervision for some time thereafter. Such training and supervision would be a moderate price to pay for the abolition of the tithe alone, whereas the operation of the majority scheme will also steadily assist in the definition of the ownership of land: but it is my view that if the introduction of the scheme (so far as it applies to rotation crops) is undertaken without previous preparation and thorough subsequent control for some years to come the risk of a serious muddle is to be apprehended. If my apprehension is at all well founded no such risk should be run, both on general grounds and because no greater set back to the abolition of the existing tithe system or to the cause of land reform as a whole could occur than the failure of measures taken after such detailed and lengthy consideration.

10. A second important respect in which the majority scheme is a departure from the Turkish original is that it proposes to shift the incidence of the commuted tax from the produce to the land, and from the cultivator to the landholder. This would be unimportant when a landholder cultivated his holding himself; but in the numerous cases in which landholders either (i) leave land untilled or (ii) enter into arrangements with other parties to cultivate it, redistributions of tax and re-adjustments of customary relations would be necessitated. Although the taxation of untilled land is desirable, it would make the distribution of commuted tithe by the village authorities more difficult. And while there seems no reason to fear that the general re-adjustment of relations between landholders and cultivating partners or tenants will present any serious difficulty, it is an additional complication which must take a little time and discussion to settle satisfactorily, and which may have unexpected reactions. Both the considerations mentioned appear to me to reinforce the arguments for the advisability of more careful preparation for and more sustained control of, the majority scheme than I understand the authors themselves to suggest.

11. The advisability of some single specific criterion of land value for investigatory purposes is considered (Majority

Report § 13). It is suggested that the potential productivity of land in terms of wheat should be adopted as a general criterion of land value in imitation, it was erroneously believed, of the English commutation of tithe. The English tithes expressed in kind were commuted directly into terms of money; but the prices of the three principal products (wheat, barley and oats at specified dates and markets) were used as factors to re-adjust the commuted value each year.

The adoption of a single arbitrary criterion of land values throughout Palestine appears to me inadvisable, and is certainly not needed for the application of the majority scheme. Under that scheme each village is dealt with as an independent unit and only an expression of the relative values of the various blocks of land within the perimeter of the particular village concerned is in each case needed. The members of each village community know within close limits the relative values of every portion of the village lands; and they are accustomed regularly to weigh these relative values and to express them in simple arithmetical terms when dividing land. In many cases an expression of relative values in terms of potential wheat production might be welcome to villagers and adjustable to facts. In other cases such an expression of values might be entirely unreal and therefore suspect. Since no such common measure is needed or will fit the facts throughout Palestine why impose it? Any officer who is competent to supervise the apportionment of a commuted village tithe at all, will be able to control the values allotted to the various blocks of village land more readily and more acceptably by weighing local factors and applying familiar standards than by the imposition of a single, rigid and often artificial formula everywhere.

12.   At first sight there appears no reason why the recommendation to levy an average tithe on individual fruit plantations should not be immediately applicable: but I understand that in fact the past records of such payments even in recent years are not sufficiently complete or precise to enable the sums paid in tithe on the production of individual plantations to be determined. Nor is any complete record available of the ownership, position, extent or value of existing plantations.[+]

13. UNTRUSTWORTHY CHARACTER OF COMMUTED TITHE AS A BASIS OF ASSESSMENT.   It will be remembered that one of the grounds of dissent of the Chairman of the Average Tithes Committee from the majority scheme was that it took no cognisance of successive changes, by which changes in the gross production of a village was primarily meant (see § 8 (i) above). The District Commissioner of the Northern District in his minute on the findings, says that "it must be admitted that the majority proposal would perpetuate for an indefinite period the payment .... of a tax which has been based mainly on guesswork." But the gross sums levied on villages in accordance with the scheme may be fairer between village and village than the individual assessments from which they are derived are between cultivator and cultivator, For no grounds appear for assuming any accumulative error in either direction in the individual assessments. But figures that have been derived from a number of individual assessments taken during a few past years in a manner so open to criticism are evidently an untrustworthy basis of village taxation and will become more and more so as the population, the nature and quality of the crops, the means of transport and marketing, the prices of produce and other conditions affecting the gross value of the agricultural production of each village change.

[+] After this note was drafted the imposition of an advance land tax on orange groves was discussed in a letter to the Chief Secretary dated 27th. June, 1927.

So that, although the adoption of the average tithe commutations of the last four years as gross tax levies on villages can be justified as an immediate means of escape from the greater evils of the tithe system itself, these untrustworthy figures should be replaced as soon as possible by some systematic and dependable assessment.

14. NECESSITY TO REPLACE WERKO AS WELL AS TITHE. The majority scheme has been described earlier as the replacement of the existing tithe by a crude land-tax, since it proposes to substitute taxation of the possession of land for taxation of gross agricultural production. But there is already a statutory land-tax (werko) in being. There would perhaps be no serious objection to two land-taxes running concurrently if their incidence was comparable and consistent. But far from this being probable, it can hardly be doubted that radical discrepancies would appear between the two. And it would be difficult to maintain two widely discrepant land-taxes in Palestine for any length of time. The signatories of the majority report say that "many of the fundamental werko registers are missing and those that exist are inaccurate and out of date," and the correctness of the statement is not challenged by anyone. They thereupon recommend the amalgamation of (a) the aggregate sum now claimed in werko from each village, with (b) the proposed average tithe, as a single consolidated land-tax to be distributed by the villagers themselves in the manner proposed in the report.

This proposal is objected to by the Chairman of the Tithes Committee in his minute of dissent because he considers that it would be inequitable owing to the different nature of the systems and inequalities in assessments. The District Commissioner of the Northern District in his minute says that he does not consider the proposal practicable, since "the incidence of werko is so irregular, the values of property have altered so considerably since the country was last assessed ....., the original assessment and application .... was so unjust, that the whole country requires to be revalued and reassessed, and .... all the information required (for these purposes) will be obtained automatically as land settlement proceeds."

The proposed consolidation of the two taxes would have the great advantage of obviating the concurrent existence of two discrepant land-taxes. And if the inequities of the werko are otherwise to be perpetuated in separate form, it may be thought that they might as well be merged in the average tithe. But whereas the adoption of the average tithe as a basis for taxation of villages will be understood and will probably not be considered unfair if independently maintained, the proceeding would take on much of the arbitrary and fortuitous characteristics of the existing werko if the two were combined.

It would therefore seem the lesser of two evils to maintain the existing werko for a time side by side with the average tithe. But the admitted inequities and fiscal defects which characterize the werko evidently make it a pressing matter to put this tax also on to a completely revised footing without waiting for the completion of land settlement.

15. BLOCK LAND TAX.   Thus while the majority scheme has the great virtue of providing the quickest practicable escape from the existing tithe system it would both (i) perpetuate (and gradually aggravate) a series of untrustworthy village assessments derived from the tithe system itself, and (ii) leave untouched the parallel evils of the Ottoman land tax (werko). The

majority scheme is in short an immediately useful, but unavoidably faulty, fiscal measure that should be promptly replaced in its turn by a sounder measure, free from the two serious objections just mentioned.

The Block land tax suggested in §14 of my report of December 1925, would finally substitute a single sound - although necessarily incomplete - land tax for both the existing tithe and werko. It cannot be put into operation as quickly as the majority scheme, since it must be preceded by survey and valuation; but its establishment throughout Palestine (northward of Beersheba) within the next few years is quite feasible. And it would constitute a solid instalment of permanent reform very rapidly achieved.

The Block survey recommended in the same passage of my report is now in progress. It is expected that this survey will be completed throughout the plain area of Palestine (northward of Beersheba) in 1928-29, and throughout the additional hill area by about the end of 1931. (See §§9 and 10 of memorandum of conference held at Government Offices on the 21st. February 1927).

The Blocks or cultivation groups of village territories which are being defined, demarcated and surveyed will form a system of pigeon holes extending over the surface of the country into one or more of which all landed properties will fall. They will constitute a permanent framework for purposes of both (i) land tax and (ii) registration of rights to land as opposed to the unstable ever-fluctuating jig-saw puzzle of property units. With occasional and minor exceptions the boundaries - and consequently the content - of each block will be invariable in contrast to the highly unstable boundaries and contents of property holdings traversing it. And, in conformity

- 21 -

both with common village practice and with the present fiscal objective, the land included within the boundaries of any given block will broadly be similarly situated and homogeneous; so that ordinarily the whole extent of a block can be reasonably assessed for fiscal purposes at a uniform economic value. Actually of course no parcel of land is identical in situation and structure throughout; but the unavoidable divergences in value from the rough general average will be relatively unimportant within the limits of a block, if blocks are reasonably well selected. Moreover the effect of such divergences on the fairness of the annual tax rates should be negligible, seeing that such rates will be small fractions (say 1/100 or 1/200) of the capital value of the land, and although the economic value of blocks will change with changing agricultural, transport and market conditions, such changes will for the most part be gradual particularly in relation to corresponding changes in neighbouring blocks. So that for fiscal purposes the land comprised within a block can ordinarily be reasonably assessed for an appreciable term of years as well as at a uniform rate. I have on several occasions suggested that this term should be ten years for agricultural land, and five years for urban property.

Valuation, or assessment, of blocks for land tax should follow on the heels of the Block Survey. While Block Survey and such valuation are proceeding experience will be being gained, through the application of the majority scheme, as to the best methods of distributing aggregate tax claims among groups of landholders. So that the necessary data and experience should be available for the replacement of both the existing tithe and the existing werko by a Block land tax (a) throughout the plain area of Palestine by about the end of next year, and (b) throughout the additional hill area by the middle of 1932.

The principles and methods of valuation on assessment are considered below. They should in any case be identical with those adjudged proper for the full land tax that is to follow the settlement of rights to land. Indeed the same valuation should be used for both the provisional, and the ultimate, measures, subject merely to amendments in procedure indicated by experience. For the Block land tax need, and should, only fall short of the ultimate full land tax, because the incidence of any such tax among individual tax-payers cannot be determined and recorded by Government until the defects of the existing land registers have been purged by the progress of systematic settlement and registration of rights.

These processes have no concern with, and they will add nothing to the means and information available for, the assessment of land for purposes of land-tax. There is consequently no reason to postpone, and it seems to me no justification for postponing, this readily realizable portion of a greatly needed reform, until the complementary determination and record of individual taxpayers can be simultaneously effected in a proper and formal manner. And if the Block land tax is put into operation without delay, it can be smoothly and easily converted into an officially distributed land tax, village by village, as fast as the settlement of rights permits.

16. CHARACTER OF LAND TAX.   By a land tax is meant a tax annually levied on the ownership or occupation of

- 83 -

land. The English land tax appears to have originated in 1692 as part of a general tax of four shillings in the pound on the income derived from three main forms of property, viz. (i) profits and salaries, (ii) interest on the value of goods, merchandise and other personal property, and (iii) the full annual value of all forms of real estate. A payment of twenty-four shillings for every £100 of the capital value of property in the second category was laid down as equivalent to four shillings in the pound of its annual value. The same equivalent between annual and capital value (6%) is laid down in the Turkish Musaqafat Law and re-adopted in Section 5 (4) of the Palestine Urban Property Tax Ordinance 1928. The English land tax still lingers although now unimportant in amount and arbitrary in its incidence. Its intended place in national taxation has been taken by Schedules A. and B. of the Income Tax.

Various views prevail as to the principles which should govern the assessment for land tax that should be adopted in Palestine and as to the utilization of such taxation as an economic weapon. Without entering here into the general merits of such expedients as taxation of unimproved values, of unearned increments, &c., it may be observed:

    (i) that the more closely the methods of assessment in Palestine conform to what the bulk of the peasantry understand and consider fair the more readily the land tax will be introduced, the greater satisfaction will it give and the more smoothly will it work.

    (ii) that whatever the theoretical bases or economic objectives of a land tax in Palestine may be, it will appear to the mass of landholders merely as an annual item of expenditure over and above working costs which has to be paid to Government from the profits derived from the land. In other words a land tax will for the most part operate and be considered merely as an income tax on incomes obtained, or obtainable, annually from the ownership or use of land.

(iii) that, if this is so and if payments are to be governed by ability to pay, the income-producing capacity of the land - or what is sometimes termed the economic value as distinct from the unimproved value, the market value, the speculative value - should be the basis of assessment. This is the statutory basis of assessment for the existing land tax (werko) and is in principle familiar. And no other basis of assessment is so demonstrably reasonable and equitable, and so likely on all grounds to commend itself to the people at large.

(iv) that although it may be just and politic in advanced communities to penalize poorly developed land and poor husbandry fiscally, any such deliberate penalization of primitive practices would surely be unfair and impolitic in Palestine for some time to come.

(v) that encouragement can nevertheless be given to the planting of fruit trees and to expenditure on other agricultural improvements by remissions of taxation while such improvements are unproductive (e.g. for five years after trees are planted) and by discounting such improvements for a lifetime or for an amortization period (e.g. 15 years) when re-assessing the land.

(vi) that the early establishment of a land tax of the simple income tax variety in Palestine in place of the existing tithe and the existing werko is so greatly to the public advantage, both fiscally and economically, that no risk of failure or delay should be run by straining at supreme perfection or by pursuing courses that are not understood or are disliked, when courses that are understood and familiar are available.

17. STEREOTYPED ASSESSMENT. The assessment of land values for fiscal purposes by means of a chemical and physical soil survey must be considered, because it has received steady and weighty advocacy in Palestine. Although it would no doubt be extremely helpful to have definite determinations of such factors as the physical structure, the chemical composition, and the surface depth of the soil in each block, assessment should not be primarily attempted in this way. Our knowledge of the action and interaction of even the material factors (such as those instanced) which contribute to the economic value of land, and our capacity to measure such factors, are too imperfect to justify basing a system of national taxation on a soil survey alone. Moreover the reliance to be placed on all such observed data varies widely with the quantity and distribution of the observations, and the methods and personal equations of the observers, so that such observations would all have

to be weighed before use. And finally the influence of such critical factors as commercial enterprise, scientific invention, public taste, and fashion which combine to make, modify or mar the values of certain products, and consequently of land suited to their culture and marketing, may quite invalidate conclusions based merely on certain soil conditions. In short since economic values are far from being developed either by fully understood natural processes, or even by natural processes alone, it is a delusion to suppose that scientific determinations of such values can be ground out mathematically from a collection of material data. Since land values are mainly the product of human appraisement, human judgment must enter decisively at some stage into any just assessment of such values.

It is not suggested that assessment by stereotyped methods is impracticable. On the contrary it appears that classification of land for fiscal purposes by such methods has proved conspicuously successful in a number of Indian provinces, when it may be assumed more elastic methods might have failed. But the classification and procedure employed were necessarily empiric expressions of human experience and judgment. They make no pretence of following any natural law or scientific theory. In short it was found preferable under the conditions prevailing to embody human experience and judgment, so far as possible, in tables and prescribed criteria rather than permit of the wide exercise of these qualities by the field-staff. There is nothing to be gained by examining the methods mentioned more closely here, or in exploring the formidable difficulties which faced the revenue authorities concerned, to which no doubt the methods used were best adapted. For assessment of land for land tax in Palestine is a simple matter which (as already indicated) can be readily and best effected in the field in consultation with those primarily concerned and on lines which they understand. It would, I think, be most unwise in the absence of some imperative need, to endeavour instead to fix the groundwork of taxation by rigid methods elaborated in office or laboratory, which could be based on no accepted principle, which would be suspect because not understood, and the results of which could hardly fail to conflict widely with the current conceptions of the agricultural population.

18. BASIS AND METHODS OF ASSESSMENT OUTLINED.

It has already been observed that the block system provides the foundation for the permanent, as well as the provisional, land tax; and also that all land contained within the limits of a given block should ordinarily be assessable at a uniform rate for an appreciable term of years.

If the expedient of utilizing the block system for joint fiscal and land registry requirements had not been adopted, it would have been necessary to assess each property unit separately. Such individual assessment of all landed properties in Palestine would be an unjustifiably laborious and expensive undertaking; while the changes that unceasingly occur in the boundaries and areas of such properties would involve constant revision and readjustment of the assessments thus made.

Following previous reasoning it is in principle desirable that the valuation of blocks should be expressed in terms of net income derivable under average conditions from a representative unit (e.g. donum) of the block concerned. In Egypt the valuation of the land for the assessment of land tax carried out during the two years 1895 and 1896, was expressed nominally in terms of gross mean rental value per feddan (4200 sq. metres) of similar blocks. In England, for purposes both of income tax and of local rates, the assessment of houses and land is expressed in the terms of gross rental value, with statutory allowances for repairs, etc., intended roughly to reduce the figure to the net annual rental value or the net income derivable from the property. The draft Palestinian Urban Property Tax Ordinance adopts the same course.

Now throughout most of the rural areas of Palestine it would certainly be impolitic to seek, and probably impossible to obtain, a monetary statement of the incomes derivable from agricultural land. Villagers know the relative economic values of the various tracts of village land, but they can rarely know, even if they were willing to state, the absolute income value of the land in terms of money. Profits and costs of working only take the form of money partially if at all; so that desirable as it may be to assess the land tax on the average net incomes derivable from the parcels of land taxed, the fact must be faced that in practice no trustworthy return of such figures is likely to be obtainable. In Egypt the assessments of gross rental value mentioned, on which the land tax has for many years been paid without difficulty or complaint, were never more than relative indexes of such values, even at the time of original assessment. And in England where taxation of this character has been long in force and where great public honesty is combined with a rare wealth of the requisite data, it is admitted that the existing assessments are far from reliable as expressions of the absolute annual values they purport to be.

In brief although in principle the assessment of the actual income producing value of landed property is the natural fiscal objective, in practice such direct assessment is usually very difficult. Its pursuit is assuredly not a practicable policy at present in Palestine. Fortunately relative assessments of the income producing value of the various blocks present considerably less difficulty and will provoke less opposition and deception; and such assessments will meet all immediate practical needs.

If it is agreed that it is advisable, if not inevitable, to accept relative valuation of blocks as the immediate aim of assessment instead of absolute valuation, it becomes necessary to adopt some scale for the purpose. Such a scale should be applicable fairly to the whole country, be easy to understand and simple to use. Three forms of scale suggest themselves:

    (i) The current monetary scale of the country.
    (ii) The Classification of blocks in a series of arbitrary categories.
    (iii) The grading of blocks on a simple proportional scale.

The first should clearly be rejected - as the use of monetary units to express relative values would be misleading and confusing. The possibility is merely mentioned because monetary units are in practice frequently used to express what are really relative values (e.g. in Egypt as observed above) owing to the difficulties of absolute assessment.

The classification of land in a limited number of artificial categories (e.g. ten) is, I believe, generally utilized in India to express the results of the stereotyped methods of valuation developed there. And it can be understood that it would be difficult to express these results numerically, as readily or as fairly. But there appears to be neither need nor advantage and evident disadvantage in adopting this expedient to express the results of the simpler and more elastic methods of assessment possible in Palestine. There would be obvious difficulty in classifying all land in Palestine to the satisfaction of the people in one or other of a limited series of arbitrary categories. "Marginal" cases between a higher and a lower grade would be innumerable and would be a constant source of difficulty to the assessment authorities and probably of dissatisfaction to the public. For although the difference between two adjoining grades would doubtless not be great in terms of resulting taxation, it is well-known that in such circumstances the most trivial grievances if widely felt may arouse serious, if misguided, opposition to the best measures.

In my opinion it is both easier and better to grade blocks on a continuous proportional scale which enables differences of value to be expressed to any degree considered advisable, and avoids the entirely artificial creation of the marginal difficulty just mentioned. Thus land of the highest economic value might be graded 100, and land of absolutely no economic value be graded 0. Any shade of difference between the two could be expressed by its appropriate intermediate index number. There is of course no objection to adopting the higher figure to represent land of the highest existing economic value, as higher degrees (e.g. 120) can be added later if needed. At the other end of the scale no such need for expansion would arise.

The establishment of a set, or sets, of standards is recommended as one of the earliest duties of the assessment officers, if either of the last two expedients is adopted. The establishment of these standards should evidently be carried out with the greatest care since they will constitute the practical control points in either case; but it should be accepted at the outset that both experience and skill in assessment will grow and that some revision of early work (including some readjustment of initial standards) is to be anticipated and desired before finally satisfactory figures are obtained. Such revision and re-adjustment will be very readily effected if the work is done and recorded in an orderly way from the first. I suggest that ten standard blocks should be initially chosen ranging at approximately equal intervals of value from 10 to 100 on the proposed index scale. It is not necessary that the standards should represent values on that scale expressed by exact multiples of ten, but it will facilitate the work if they approximate as closely as possible to such multiples. With the assistance of such standards it will be possible after a little experience to grade any block with its appropriate index figure on the suggested scale. So far as feasible the initial set of standards should be easily accessible from the locality in which assessment starts; but ultimately standards should be repeated throughout the country. If classification in a series of arbitrary categories is preferred to grading on a continuous proportional scale standards should be chosen to indicate the mean or the extreme values of such categories or better still both mean and extreme values.

Now it has been shown by experience

(i) that villagers know the relative economic values of the blocks comprising the territory of their villages intimately.

(ii) that these values are not appraised by them merely by the fertility of the soil but by the general economic value, that is to say by a combination of fertility with other important factors such as the situation of the land, transport facilities, access to markets, public security, water and drainage conditions.

(iii) that such knowledge is put to practical use every day by villagers in their current dealings with the land. In other words villagers are regularly accustomed to assess the relative economic values of tracts of village land.

(iv) that a suitable officer in consultation with representatives of any village can without undue difficulty

(a) outline a satisfactory block system for such a village,

(b) grade these blocks according to their relative economic values so that the results are useful and acceptable in practice.

Little need has so far arisen to institute any comparison officially between the economic values of blocks in neighbouring villages; but the establishment of such comparison can certainly be effected with the assistance of local, or locally chosen, representatives. Such an undertaking should present no serious difficulty to any officer who has acquired experience and proved his aptitude in grading the component blocks of the same village. And if the series of standards recommended are established it will be merely a matter of patient labour and acquired experience to grade the relative economic values of all blocks throughout Palestine in a way that meets all fiscal needs equitably and satisfactorily and is understood by, and therefore is acceptable to, the people.

5.03

PALESTINE.

GOVERNMENT OFFICES,
JERUSALEM.

DESPATCH NO. 289

REFERENCE NO. 1234/28.

23rd March, 1928.

Sir,

(1)   I have the honour to refer to Lieutenant Colonel Symes' despatch No.121 of the 3rd of February regarding the basis of assessment of a tax on land values in Palestine, and to enclose copy of a memorandum prepared by the Commissioner of Lands on the subject.

2. I have discussed the memorandum in Executive Council but in the absence of reliable data regarding the practicability of applying locally the principles set out in the memorandum, I am unwilling at the moment wholly to endorse the opinions expressed therein.

3. It is obvious that the present tithe and werko taxes on land are unsatisfactory in their incidence and effect; and the commuted tithe is admittedly only a palliative measure which should be succeeded at an early date by a radical measure of reform of land taxation. The gradual substitution for werko and commuted tithe of a simple land

tax/

The Right Honourable L.C.M.S. AMERY, P.C., M.P.,
    His Majesty's Principal Secretary of State
        for the Colonies.

- 2 -

tax to produce equivalent revenue and based on the village block as the taxable unit, if practicable, would satisfactorily bridge the interim period until an exact valuation of individual plots can be made.

4. I have requested the Commissioner of Lands privately to obtain the views of Sir Ernest Dowson on his suggestions, and I should be glad to receive an expression of your views as to the soundness of the principles embodied in Mr. Abramson's recommendations. Meanwhile he has been instructed to conduct certain experiments with a view to testing the practicability of his proposals.

     I have the honour to be,
     Sir,
     Your most obedient,
     humble servant,

     [signature]

HIGH COMMISSIONER FOR PALESTINE.

Proposal
to substitute a Land Tax for the present
werko and tithe.

Demand for a Land Tax.

1. There has been for some time a general and steadily increasing demand by the public for a more equitable distribution of the incidence of taxation in rural areas.

Some of the vexatious delays and difficulties which attended the tithing of crops have been removed by the enactment of the Commutation of Tithes Ordinance, 1927, but the incidence of the tithe, which is represented by the commuted tithe, is still so inequitable, as is also that of the present assessment of werko, that it is the duty of the Government to find, as soon as possible, some means of replacing them by an equitably distributed tax.

Why the present tithe and werko distribution is inequitable.

2. The tithes on crops in Arab villages were assessed by estimators hazarding a guess that heaps of sheaves placed on threshing floors contained so many camel or donkey loads of sheaves, and after examining a number of layers of the sheaves, by estimating that a load of sheaves contained an assumed number of kilos of grain.

Experienced estimators were generally capable of arriving at a fair approximation of the quantity of grain, but they were not always experienced, and when they were, they were not infrequently careless, and sometimes even biassed in favour of, or against a cultivator. Also, in order that the heap may appear to be small and so deceive the estimator, the lower layers of sheaves were pressed closely together while the upper layers were laid on loosely, and unless he carefully examined the heaps which, because of their size, and because of lack of time, he could not do satisfactorily, the estimator either over-estimated the number of loads or estimated the heap to contain a smaller number than it actually did.

In the most favourable circumstances, the estimation was bound to be only approximate.

In Jewish villages where threshing machines were used, the estimator attended the threshing and weighed the grain itself.

In effect therefore, while Arab cultivators' crops were only approximately estimated, those of Jewish cultivators were usually correctly assessed.

Then after estimation work was completed, the authorities fixed, more or less arbitrarily, the price which the tithe-payer was supposed to receive for his crops and the tax payable was based on the price so fixed.

/Under

-2-

Under the Werko Law, other inequalities exist. Lands which were purchased and registered since 1921 were revalued for registration fees, and werko charged on the revaluation price, excluding the additional 41% on the tax which was imposed by Ottoman decrees for education and other purposes; while on lands which did not change hands or where they did and the transactions were not registered, the Werko tax, including the additional 41%, is paid on assessments made 25/30 years ago.

If a consolidated tax were imposed of the total of the present assessments of tithe and werko, the inequalities enumerated would be perpetuated, and while one section of the public would continue to pay a correct and high tax, the others would pay an incorrect and lower tax.

The existing system of taxation must be changed.

3. It is therefore obvious that the existing system must be replaced as soon as possible, and it is suggested that it be replaced by a land tax based on a revaluation of all immovable property.

Foundation for taxation records.

4. Taxation of land, however, cannot be put on to a sound footing until the foundation exists for the completion of a trustworthy record of property. The record should comprise :-

   a) Taxable units of immovable property;
   b) Taxable value of immovable property;
   c) A tax roll of persons legally liable, in virtue of ownership and other rights, for the taxation levied thereon.

Village blocks as taxable units of immovable property.

5. In the course of the 1/10,000 survey which is now proceeding, the Department of Surveys locates and provisionally adjusts village boundaries and demarcates, numbers and maps, blocks of land within each village for settlement and registration purposes, together with such topographical details as appear desirable.

The blocks are fixed in consultation with village elders and are generally the same as the divisions of land which villagers in musha' villages have always been using for their periodical partition of land for cultivation purposes.

These divisions, which will normally become the registration blocks, take into account the productivity of the land, the existence of water near the surface, facility of irrigation, relative position, and distance from water sources, towns, railway stations, etc.

Where official or unofficial partition of musha' land has already been made, the divisions are still known and named by villagers, who also know the productivity and the relative value of the land in them.

/These divisions

-3-

These divisions having been made after many years experience of the productivity of the soil, are based on so accurate a knowledge of the soil that there are not only main divisions but sub-divisions of those and minor divisions of the sub-divisions.

The expedient of constituting blocks of land of approximate equal value is therefore familiar to the people of Palestine. It has been used by them as an equitable basis for the apportionment of land shares, and it is one which cannot be bettered for simplicity of application.

Some elements for the valuation of land.

6. While the *musha'* system must be condemned because it has delayed the agricultural improvement of the country, it has one virtue which is of considerable benefit at this stage. As has already been explained, because of it villagers have elaborated and perpetuated the gradation of productivity values by blocks of land which will provide many of the elements for the valuation of land for a land tax, and those divisions, adapted as registration blocks, demarcated and mapped by the Department of Surveys, can be adopted with few modifications as fiscal blocks for a land tax.

Block tax plan.

7. If the 1/10,000 survey is accompanied by land valuation carried out systematically block by block, a first assessment of land in rural areas for fiscal purposes can be effected irrespective of individual property boundaries, by including all contiguous land of closely equal value in blocks of convenient size and shape. Each block can be assessed in turn and all land follow the assessment of the block in which it is situated.

The survey, thus accompanied by a block valuation, will provide at the shortest possible time the basis for a concrete, as opposed to an abstract, consideration of the present amalgam of tithe and werko, by a single fiscal instrument for the taxation of property.

Comparison for rates of tax.

8. This survey has already been completed in a number of village areas and a comparison can now be made between the yield of the tithe and werko and varying rates of a land tax.

Other elements for the valuation of land.

9. But it would be inequitable to assess on productivity alone since a dunum of land of similar productivity situated, e.g., respectively in the vicinity of Jaffa and of say the village of Yatta, south of Hebron, would bring in a very different monetary return to the possessor.

Regard must be had to locality, accesibility to markets, means of communication, variety of rainfall, proximity to water, etc.

Classification of soil is of use where it exists, but an elaborate soil survey is not so necessary for the purpose as to delay the

/introduction

-4-

introduction of a land tax until all the soil of Palestine has been surveyed.

Current market values for assessment.

10. Current market value should not necessarily be taken into consideration except as a means of checking relative values.

It will also be necessary to guard against a weakness to attribute to existing conditions a greater degree of stability than they actually possess, i.e., when high prices or low prices have ruled for a period, a permanent rise or a permanent fall must not be assumed, as it is common knowledge that in recent years abnormal prices have been paid for sentimental and other reasons for agricultural land.

The assessment should be moderate so as to encourage the prosperity and development of the land, to keep the country quiet and contented, and to encourage improvements; but it must not be so low as to encourage neglect and bad farming.

It will further be necessary to endeavour to find a measure of equality in different parts of the country.

Authorities should assess the land.

11. The authorities should make the assessment of land in order that the assessment should not be subjected to interested local pressure. The assessment lists should be open to public inspection and should be subject to appeal, in order to arrive at a uniform valuation and to avoid complaints and injustice.

Moderation of demand by Government is not only due morally and actually to the people, but is also conducive to the best interest of Government. When valuation lists are being prepared, care should therefore be taken not to over-assess. It is more fatal to over-assess than to under-assess; as over-assessments will prove a burden and a deterrent to agricultural progress.

Certain improvements should not be excluded from taxation.

12. It is not either practical or useful permanently to exclude improvements from taxation. All cultivated land has been improved and undergoes change from generation to generation, and as soon as the burden of an improvement has been discharged and an adequate reward garnered, there seems no reason why a modern improvement should be differentiated from the earlier improvements that have brought all civilized lands from wilderness to a cultivable state or from a cultivable state to a higher culture.

Land should be assessed at its capital value with prescribed deduction for beneficial improvements.

13. Land should therefore be assessed at its capital value as unimproved or improved, according to its condition when assessed, but prescribed percentages for deduction must be provided for specified cultivators' beneficial improvements, such as, fertilizers, farm-buildings, fences, drainage, silo, irrigation channels, etc. No deduction need ordinarily be made for the value of trees or of improvements which are in the nature of amenities

/for the

for the cultivator, e.g., dwelling houses, etc.

It is more difficult to assess the annual value of land.

14. It would be more difficult to assess the annual value of land and to prescribe percentages for deduction for annual expenditure on cultivators' beneficial improvements. Land in Palestine is not leased annually for a specific sum, and the system of leasing varies considerably.

One landlord leases his land to a single cultivator or to a group of cultivators and provides land, seed, animals for ploughing, ploughing instruments, etc., and after deduction of the tithe, takes 75% of the crop, the cultivator keeping the remaining 25%; another provides perhaps only the land and animals; or the land and seed; or only the land; and his share of the produce varies from 75% to as little as 20%.

Neither the majority of land-owners nor tenant-cultivators keep any record of their income, and they therefore could not state the accurate quantity of produce which is derived from any particular part of land during a given number of years. As the tithe registers do not contain correct quantities because the results of tithe estimation do not represent the actual produce derived from land, the registers would not provide data to find the gross produce of a village as a whole or of a block, and still less of an individually owned parcel.

Categories of standard block values.

15. The Land Valuer should first provide a category of standard block values, perhaps separately for each sub-district because of the variation of rainfall, of facility of communication, of accessibility to markets, etc.

It may also be necessary to distinguish between the additional advantages accruing to land-owners from irrigation supplied :-

   a) by their own exertions;
   b) at the cost of the State.

The fiscal blocks in each village would then be assessed and classified according to the categories of the standard blocks.

Temporary and final block values.

16. The blocks in each village should be assessed at :-

   a) a temporary value; and
   b) a final value.

The assessment of blocks containing unimproved land should be fixed at temporary values which should apply until the land contained therein has been improved when its value should be moved up to a final value, according to its standard block category. Blocks of improved land should at once be assessed at their final value according to their standard block categories.

/17.

Periodical re-assessment of land.	17. At the end of each period of say 12 years, a general re-assessment of land should be made. If the period of re-assessment is shorter, it is inconvenient to land-owners and to Government; if it is much longer, undesirable disparities of tax tend to develop and too abrupt changes of tax would be called for.
Revision of temporary value blocks.	18. Revision of the block temporary values should be made at intervals of four years, and if it is found at the quaternary revision that lands are deliberately left unimproved, they should be arbitrarily assessed at a higher temporary value on a prescribed rising scale, in order to discourage sloth and neglect; or, as an alternative to a rising scale, a prescribed undeveloped land tax might be added equal to say one-fourth of the previously assessed value of the land.
	If it is found at the quaternary revision that land is being improved, its temporary value, as originally assessed, should be retained until the improvements effected enable it to be assessed at one of the final values of the standard block categories.
Maximum and temporary rates of tax.	19. A maximum percentage rate of tax should be prescribed to apply permanently, i.e., until an amending ordinance is promulgated, to alter the maximum rate. Temporary rates within the maximum should be prescribed to apply for fixed periods of say five years. It will be necessary to fix both a maximum permanent rate and temporary rates for prescribed periods within the maximum, otherwise landowners will hesitate to spend money on improvements.
	If, however, a maximum and periodically fixed temporary rates are prescribed, landowners would know what amount of tax they would have to pay during the temporary rate period, and the amount which would be payable whatever rate within the maximum might be imposed. They would be assured therefore that, notwithstanding any improvements which they may put into their land, the amount of tax which they would have to pay would not exceed a definite sum.
Suggested first rate to be imposed.	20. The first rate to be imposed should not be required to produce more than the present total combined assessment of werko and tithe.
	Higher or lower rates would be imposed subsequently to provide for increased or reduced Treasury demands.
Taxable units and tax roll of persons liable for tax.	21. Under the block land tax system suggested, the amount of the tax would be distributed by Government on each block. These fiscal blocks would be the effective taxation units in each village, and pending the passage of land settlement and the compilation of a tax roll of property-owners,

/the amount

—7—

the amount of tax payable on a fiscal block would be distributed by the villagers among the reputed owners of parcels of land within each block.

As settlement of land proceeds, and the ownership, limits, and areas of parcels are determined, and the Schedules of Rights and Schedules of Partition completed in a village, the amount of the block tax would be redistributed among the owners of the parcels included in the schedules.

<u>Provision for partial or total remission.</u> 22. It may be necessary also to make provision for partial or total remission where failure of rain, or destruction by locusts, etc., has resulted in the partial or complete loss of crops.

<u>Assessment of houses in villages.</u> 23. Houses in villages should be taxed on a basis similar to that in the Urban Property Tax Ordinance.

(Sgd) A. ABRAHSON.

5.3.28. <u>COMMISSIONER OF LANDS.</u>

A/H.

5.04

57195/28

1. Oag. 121   3/2/28

  Requests copies of any legislation and reports on the subject framed by other administrations under control of C.O.

  ? Would you please let me have copies of the relevant legislation and reports.

      (Sgd.) A.M.Strong

      15/2/28.

  Copies of the following Dominion and Colonial laws and reports are annexed:-

Commonwealth of Australia
Land Tax Assessment Acts, 22/1910; 12/1911; 37/1912; 29/1914; [33/1916]; 29/1923; [32/1924] [50/1926].
Parliamentary Papers, Nos 9 and 11 of Session 1925; No. 7 of 1926; No.96 of 1926-27.

South Australia
Taxation Acts, Nos. 1787 and 1830.

New Zealand
Valuation of Land Acts, Nos. 31/1925; 71/1926; 52/1927.
Land and Income Tax Acts, Nos. 21/1923; 22/1924; 12/1925; 24/1926; 12/1927.
ˣReport on the form and practice of valuation of lands apart from improvements, and also on the taxation of land values in New Zealand.

British Honduras
Land and Property Tax Ordinance, Cap.24, Consolidated Laws 1924.
Report of Land Tax Commission, 1901(1902)

Cyprus
Immovable Property Registration and Valuation Law, 1907, No.12 of 1907, 1923 Revision.

Grenada
Taxes Management Ordinance, Cap.20 Revised Laws 1911, and amending Ordinances Nos. 5/1912 and 8/1925.

Trinidad and Tobago
Lands and Buildings Taxes Ordinance, Cap.204, Revised Edition of Laws 1925.

 ˣ In the event of it being decided to send the New Zealand report out to Palestine, the Librarian desires that it may be returned after perusal.

      29.2.28.

P.T.O.

? Send H.Cr. 4. ref. ① the documents
mentioned supra, except the 3
Commonwealth ones (bracketed) &
other than the N.Z. report marked ×
be returned in due course.

[signature]
25/2/28

Yes. Send a brief despatch, saying also as at A
enclose a schedule of the
documents.

[signature]
29/2 above

↙ To H.Cr. 249. (with docs) cons. 14/3/28.

~~CANCELLED~~ UNDER STATUTE

3   H.Cr. 289   ———   23/3/28

Treas., for observs., copy memo. on
the assessment of a tax on land values
prepared by the Commissioner of Lands

Mr Abramson is apparently
consulting Sir E. Dowson, but I see
no reason why we should not consult
him. Perhaps he would send us his
opinion on encls. or (3)?

[signature]
3/4/28

The main feature of Mr. Abramson's scheme is
that, pending an exact valuation of individual plots,
the carrying out of which will presumably involve
many years labour, a simple land tax should be
introduced in substitution for the Werko and
commuted

commuted title based, not upon individual ownership, but upon village blocks as the taxable units. The need for the early introduction of such a tax, as explained in Mr. Abramson's memorandum, is to be found in the inequalities of the present system under which land valuation has been carried out. In some cases the tax is paid on assessments made 25 or 30 years ago. In other cases, namely where properties have since changed hands and consequently have been revalued for the purpose of registration fees, tax is chargeable upon a more correct and consequently much higher assessment. The present system or lack of system is clearly productive of injustice in many cases and it would be difficult not to accept Mr. Abramson's view that so great are the inequalities at present that they call for an immediate remedy. The village blocks, which he proposes as the effective taxation units, are those which have been used for many years for the periodical partition of land for cultivation purposes. In these divisions account is apparently taken of the productivity of the land and other amenities such as the existence of water for irrigation and proximity to markets etc. As a further argument in favour of adopting these blocks, Mr. Abramson shows (in paragraph 5 of his memorandum) that the blocks of land adopted by the Department of Surveys for the purpose of the survey which is now proceeding are generally the village blocks which he proposes to adopt as fiscal units. Moreover,

by

by adopting this method/an elaborate soil survey. ~~would no longer be an urgent necessity~~.

Mr. Abramson suggests that the land should be assessed at its capital value with certain deductions for beneficial improvements. This would please Colonel Wedgwood who, in a recent letter complained that Palestine had adopted in the Urban Taxation Ordinance the basis of annual or rental value. ~~He~~/proposes that the fiscal blocks in each village should be assessed at a temporary value and a final value. The temporary valuation should apply only to undeveloped land, improved land being assessed at once at its final value. In the case of lands which are deliberately left unimproved he suggests, as a deterrent to neglect, the imposition either of an arbitrarily higher assessment or of a special penal tax and he proposes that temporary valuations should be subject to more frequent reassessment than final valuations.

Much the same problem has arisen in the case of Iraq and a great deal of correspondence on the subject has passed between the Iraq Revenue Officer Mr. Longrigg and Sir Henry Dobbs who has had both in India and Iraq, considerable experience in land settlement and taxation. You will see from Sir H. Dobbs' note on the Yusufyah leases, Flag A in 20739/26 below, that the same idea of fiscal blocks chosen irrespective of individual ownership

ownership appealed to him. In Iraq as well
as in Palestine there is the need for replacing
the present tithe by a tax based upon a quasi-
permanent assessment, but in the former case
the present intention appears to be to go more
slowly than is suggested in the case of
Palestine and to adopt a tax on the lines of
the present commuted tithe in Palestine. In
Iraq, of course, the difficulties are increased
by the fact that a comparatively small proportion
of the population is settled. In deciding
upon a revenue system in that country account
has to be taken of the special problems presented
by the presence of large nomad shepherd tribes.

The question of the form of taxation to be
adopted in settled areas in Kenya was considered
by the Feetham Commission (see pages 101 to 105
of Volume 2 of the Report below). Mr. Abramson's
proposals are similar to those numbered (3) and
(4) on page 102 of the Report.

On broad grounds of principle I can see
little to criticise in Mr. Abramson's scheme.
Experience will show whether it is practicable,
and, as you will see, it is proposed to
introduce it gradually by experimenting in
certain selected areas.   It is not
intended to be a final system of taxation, but ,
as the High Commissioner suggests, it may well
serve to bridge the gulf until it can be replaced
by taxation based upon an exact valuation of
individual

individual plots.

    I should be inclined to write to Sir E. Dowson as suggested by Mr. Strong and to inform him that we should be grateful to learn his views, but that on broad grounds of principle we see no objection to the proposals, provided that they are regarded as an experiment only and provided that, as is indeed proposed, they are introduced gradually and ~~admitted to be~~ are subject to such modification as experience shows to be necessary. In order to forestall criticism it might even be thought advisable to send a copy of this despatch and enclosure to Colonel Wedgwood, who professes to have made a close study of taxation problems in Palestine, and ask him whether he has any observations to make.

A.—

Hall 16/4/:8.

Mr Abramson's proposals seem to me distinctly sound in principle; and, as Sir E Dowson is being written to by the Comm^r of Lands, I don't think we had better write to him also. I would reply that, subject to anything Sir E Dowson may have to say, the S of S is inclined to approve Mr

Mr. ~~Cohen~~ Abramson's proposals.

A. J. Harding
24/4/28

Sir S. Wilson.

This is a matter of importance, and the S. of S. should perhaps see.

As regards the suggestion at **A.** in Mr. Hall's minute, I doubt the advantage of taking Colonel Wedgwood into our confidence. To consult him would mean in effect consulting the more extreme wing of the Zionists. The latter have no love for Mr. Abramson (he is a Christianised Jew who inclines to Arab sympathies) and would probably put up Colonel Wedgwood to send us in a string of carping criticisms, and to get up an agitation in advance of any action by the Palestine Government. That is all we should gain by our <u>beau geste</u>.

As proposed by Mr Harding ?.

H.J. 25/4/28

Sec. of State
 Yes. I think a reply as proposed by Mr Harding will meet the case.

S.H.G.
1.5.28.

JM 45

A. To H.C. 400 (3 ancd.) 7/5/28.

5.05

COPY.

Wrotham,
Kent.

18th April, 1928.

Commission of Lands.

As requested a few observations on your recent memorandum on the land tax follow. You will of course appreciate that I may not always have fully understood your proposals, also that I naturally confine my remarks to the points on which I am not in agreement. I posted to you a few days ago my Notes on the Abolition of the Tithe and the establishment of Land Tax in Palestine which you asked for previously.

Section 9. A soil survey is not necessary at all, nor would the cost and labour of such a survey be justifiable for purposes of land tax assessment.

Section 10. As an annual tax must be a charge on the annual return (whether in cash or in kind) from the land that is taxed, it is some index of such annual return that is needed as a measure of taxable capacity.

In all countries Market prices of land are frequently governed by other considerations than the return obtainable from the land. Market prices are consequently not only untrustworthy as a direct measure of the economic value of agricultural land, but also as a check upon assessments of such value based on other data.

Sections 10-11. Although fully concurring in the desirability of as light taxation of land as possible, I think that it should eventually be made clearer that the scale of taxation is a matter for the decision of the Government as a whole, not a matter to be influenced by the benevolence of individual assessment officers. If such

officers/

officers endeavour to be both lenient and fair, they must endeavour to be lenient to exactly the same degree in every case. Even if this was practicable, it would merely leave things ultimately unaffected, since the total revenue demand would be finally adjusted to suit. Those charged with the assessment of the taxable capacity of the land should evidently be required to work with strict scientific detachment and impartiality. It is their difficult duty to be rigorously discerning and just. Their greatest temptation will be to be lenient. For under-assessment in particular cases is much more to be apprehended and guarded against than over-assessment, because generosity at the expense of the public purse or of the bulk of other taxpayers is so much easier and pleasanter than unsentimental fair dealing between man and man, and between the nation and the individual. But the more severely fair the assessment of taxable capacity can be maintained throughout, the juster the incidence and probably the lower the rate, of the land tax will be.

Section 13. My views on the alternatives of a capital and an annual basis for assessment follow below.

My views on improved and unimproved land are briefly reproduced in your Section 12. In Palestine cultivated land shades imperceptibly from the barest scratching of the hillside to well developed scientific farming. Improvement of the land may begin with the roughest terraces and retaining walls and is necessarily imperfect on the best farms. Where and how is the line between improved and unimproved land to be drawn?

My opinion with regard to the taxation of "improvements" is probably sufficiently indicated in #16 of my accompanying "Notes on the abolition of the tithe, etc." It would I think be a mistake to go further, and more particularly to allow a

scale/

scale of actual remissions of current taxation as suggested in your memorandum. Such a scale would be most troublesome to apply, it would cause endless heartburnings and it would for the most part result in a multitude of petty reliefs which would reduce revenue (or shift its incidence) without really stimulating improvements. I think adequate encouragement of improvement can be accorded in the way I suggest, and that no remissions of actual taxation are necessary or advisable. But if such remissions are considered desirable they should at least be accorded only for works of a capital character that bring little or no immediate return.

Section 14. Confirms the views I express in §18 of my "Notes on the abolition of the tithe, etc." about the impracticability of determining absolutely the income producing value of agricultural land in Palestine: but the difficulty extends in exactly the same degree to any capitalized expression of economic value of holdings, for the economic value of holdings is dependent upon their net annual return. If the former is unascertainable so is the latter. For we are agreed that even in the rare instances that dependable market quotations for land exist, such quotations may be widely divorced from economic values.

In short, no reliable assessment of the economic value of agricultural land in Palestine expressed in money, whether in the form of income or capital, is practicable for the simple reason that the necessary data is neither existent nor obtainable at present. Monetary expressions of annual or of capital value could no doubt be produced: but they would at best be (as in Egypt) relative values cast into absolute form.

At bottom capital and annual values are different

expressions/

expressions of the same thing, and I do not imagine that the bulk of the peasantry really differentiate between them. Thus exchange and partition of land are capital transactions, but the majority of the innumerable dealings of this sort that occur in villages are governed (if not solely determined) by the net annual return to be anticipated from the parcels affected. For the real value of a holding to a peasant is naturally measured by the net annual return that he expects to obtain from it. Useful as our conceptions of capital and income are in civilised finance, the differentiation is not necessary for purposes of assessment of agricultural land in Palestine. It will be cheaper and better at this stage to aim at relative valuation only and follow ordinary village practice in arriving at it. No difficulty occurs in conducting the innumerable village valuations connected with the exchange and partition of land which occur daily throughout Palestine, owing to failure to discriminate between capital and annual values. And no serious difficulty need be experienced on this account in assessing the relative taxable capacity of blocks, with satisfaction to the people and with ample fiscal accuracy, if the duty is entrusted to competent officers working in the field in conjunction with the village elders.

Section 15. I have suggested in my accompanying Note, that classification of the land into a limited number of categories is not the best method of procedure. It is however of course a perfectly practicable expedient.

Section 16. You suggest earlier that numerous minor exceptions should be made in the ordinary operation of the land tax law with a view to stimulating improvements by remissions of taxation. In the present section you suggest that a major exception should be made for the purpose of allowing

the/

-5-

the assessment of land that has been improved to be increased before the normal time. Both for simplicity of administration and for public convenience and contentment it is I think most desirable that the operation of the land tax shall be as simple and free from exceptions as possible. One of the great benefits to be gained by the introduction of a land tax is the creation of a stable tax demand reviewed at regular stated periods only. The proposed temporary assessment both cuts at the root of this stability, and removes an incentive to the improvement of poorly developed land which falls naturally within the four corners of normal procedure and which no one is likely to resent. It is true that in Egypt the expedient of a temporary assessment was adopted as a means of eluding the general provision that assessment should stand for 30 years. But not only is 30 years too long to maintain a fixed assessment anywhere; but further in Egypt during these 30 years an agricultural revolution was being effected at great public expense by the progressive conversion of the country from basin to perennial irrigation.

Section 17. As you know, I think 10 years preferable to 12. After 15 the Egyptian assessment had become seriously uneven as between cultivator and cultivator, and yielded much less than fairly due, even in areas which had been perennially irrigated throughout.

Section 18. There should be no need for any quarternary revision of block assessments. During the next few years it should be possible to assess blocks definitely for the first ten or twelve year period of the land tax (whether distributed by block or by parcel) just as easily as at any subsequent date. Settlement of rights (as I have often said) is neither a necessary preliminary nor an assistance of any sort to
assessment. /

assessment. There should not be the slightest need to repeat the cost and labour of assessment in four years' time.

Section 19. I see no more reason for temporary tax rates than for temporary assessments of taxable capacity. Presumably no decision will be come to regarding the tax rate until at least the taxable capacity of the whole plain area has been assessed (i.e. about the end of 1929); when this assessment is complete the tax rates that will bring in the same maximum, mean and minimum revenues from the same area as the present tithe and werko can be calculated. The maximum statutory land tax rate could then be safely fixed and the Block land tax applied forthwith throughout the plains and thenceforward advanced progressively on the heels of assessment. The parcel land tax could be instituted immediately in the villages in which settlement of rights had been completed and elsewhere could replace the Block land tax village by village, pari passu with the settlement of rights.

The change from the Block land tax to the Parcel land tax merely requires the distribution of the tax demand on the block among the parcels comprising it. It should involve no alteration whatever in assessment, tax rate, tax demand on the individual, or yield to the Treasury.

Section 23. I suggest that you should be content to let the revision of the taxation of village buildings stand over until you have put the taxation of (a) towns and townships, and (b) agricultural land, on to a proper basis. There will only be a certain amount of money and energy available, and I suggest that it should not be diverted to a less fruitful and less important field.

In Egypt the built-over area of the village is untaxed, simply because of the cost and trouble entailed are disproportionate. A slight addition to the land tax rate would

allow/

-7-

allow the same course to be followed in Palestine without loss of revenue and with substantial justice, since the largest landowners as a rule have the best houses, and provision could readily be made to tax houses of any importance exceptionally where the owners did not pay an adequate amount of land tax to justify exemption from village house tax.

(Sgd) ERNEST M. DOWSON.

5.06

PALESTINE.

**GOVERNMENT OFFICES,
JERUSALEM.**

DESPATCH NO. 311
REFERENCE NO. 6464/29

17th April, 1930.

Enclosure

My Lord,

    I have the honour to forward for Your Lordship's information a memorandum by the Commissioner of Lands on the economic condition of farmers in Palestine.

2.   I considered this memorandum in Executive Council and decided to appoint a Committee to investigate and report on the matter, in accordance with the following terms of reference:

"   To examine into the economic condition of agriculturists and the fiscal measures of Government in relation thereto, and to make recommendations".

3.   The Committee, which has already begun its work, is composed as follows:-

Mr. W.J. Johnson, O.B.E., Deputy Treasurer.	Chairman.
Mr. R.E.H. Crosbie, O.B.E., Assistant District Commissioner, Southern District.	Member.
An Area Officer nominated by the District Commissioner in whose district the Committee is sitting from time to time.	Member.

I have the honour to be,
My Lord,
Your Lordship's most obedient,
humble servant,

J.R. Chancellor.

HIGH COMMISSIONER
FOR PALESTINE.

The Right Hon'ble. Lord Passfield, P.C.,
His Majesty's Principal Secretary of State
for the Colonies.

Enclosure.

Memorandum
by
The Commissioner of Lands.

The Arab farmers economic condition.

(i) From my knowledge of the Arab cultivators acquired during a period of six years in the Southern and Northern Districts, I am of opinion that the two burdens which weigh most heavily on the cultivator are:-

   (a) excessive taxation; and
   (b) indebtedness to Government and to money lenders.

(ii) Some measure of relief has been provided by the substitution of the Commuted Tithe for the annual assessment of crops, but while this measure avoids the loss of grain from various causes during estimation operations covering several months each year which the cultivator was formerly subject to and because during those operations he was unable to dispose of his crops at the time when the best prices might have been obtained, the rate of the tithe is still too high. 10% of the gross produce amounts to at least 35% of the net produce. This is an unduly high tax for a farmer to pay and accounts very largely for his unhappy economic situation. In addition he also has to pay the Werko Tax.

(iii) /

-2-

(iii) His indebtedness is due to a number of causes; The effects of the great war; the high prices demanded by Government for grain and animals advanced as loans from 1918 onwards; excessive taxation; and the improvident nature of the fellah.

(iv) It is hoped that the Land Tax, when it is introduced, will materially relieve the agricultural population of excessive taxation, but the burden of his present indebtedness would appear to require the serious attention of the Government.

(v) The situation of the Jewish cultivator is less unhappy than that of the Arab only because he is able to obtain financial assistance from various Jewish agencies; but his advantage over the Arab is perhaps more apparent than real, because if he does obtain such assistance to pay off arrears of tithes and agricultural loan instalments and for the purchase of seed etc., it makes no difference in his indebtedness, for it merely means that instead of being in debt to Government or to a money lender, he is indebted to a Jewish agency.

(vi) It is submitted that Government should consider the advisability of appointing some Commission to inquire exhaustively into the economic situation of Arab and Jewish farmers with a view to ascertaining whether there are any grounds for a "write off"

of arrears/

—3—

of arrears of tithes, taxes and agricultural loan instalments; for the reduction of the rate of Commuted Tithe from 10% to say 8%; to provide material which would enable Government to decide on the question of the exemption of small holdings when the Land Tax is introduced; and generally on the measures to adopt for the agricultural development of the country and the relief and support of the cultivator.

(Signed) A. Abramson.
COMMISSIONER OF LANDS.

21st February, 1930.

5.07

HIGH COMMISSIONER FOR PALESTINE,
JERUSALEM.

DESPATCH NO. 618
REFERENCE NO.6464/29

July, 1930.

My Lord,

      I have the honour to refer to the High
No 15 Commissioner's despatch No.311 of the 17th April
last and to Your Lordship's despatch No.388 of the
No. 21. 28th May, on the subject of the appointment of a
Committee to inquire into the economic condition
of agriculturists and the fiscal measures of
Government in relation thereto, and to enclose
two copies of the report of the Committee.

    2.   The report contains statistical information
respecting 104 Arab villages representing a total
population of 136,044, and a total area of 1,247,581
dunums. It also contains statistical information
respecting 7 Jewish agricultural settlements
representing a total population of 4,185 and a total
area of 47,698 dunums. The total number of villages
in Palestine according to the census of 1922 is 844,
the total rural population (excluding the Bedu)
according to vital statistics is 481,828, and the
total cultivable area, excluding the Beersheba
Sub-District, according to the estimates of the
Commissioner of Lands, is 10,592,000 dunums. The

The Right Honourable Lord Passfield, P.C.,
  His Majesty's Principal Secretary of State
      for the Colonies.

inquiries/

−2−

inquiries of the Committee have covered a sufficiently wide field; and their recommendations are the weightier by reason of the unanimous agreement of the Area Officers throughout Palestine.

3. The High Commissioner has already addressed Your Lordship in his telegram No.185 of the 21st June regarding the reduction of the tithe, and in his despatches No.572 of the 21st June and No.599 of the 28th June regarding the measures to restore the home market for wheat and olive oil and the issue of agricultural loans. The High Commissioner has further addressed Your Lordship on these matters in his telegram No.195 of the 29th June; and in my telegram No.199 of the 2nd July, I have recommended the imposition of an import duty on sesame seed. I trust that Your Lordship will approve these recommendations and that I may be able to make an early announcement.

No.1. on 77304/30.
No.6/30 on 77304/30
No.11 on 77034/30
No.7. on 77304
No.8. on 77304

4. Your Lordship has already informed the High Commissioner in telegram No.179 of the 30th June of the acceptance by Mr.Strickland of the proposal that he should visit Palestine for the purpose of advising this Government on the establishment of Village Co-operative Bodies.

No.5 on 77299

5. Your Lordship will doubtless take the opportunity of the High Commissioner's presence in England to discuss with him the further recommendations of the Committee, particularly those in connexion with the appointment of an expert on Income Tax assessments, the reduction of the tithe to $7\frac{1}{2}\%$ in 1931, and the increase in the rate of Urban Property Tax in 1931 to meet the deficit on the tithe.

In view/

In view of the urgent necessity for reducing the taxes borne by the rural population, I consider that the recommendations of the Committee for alternative taxation are the only practical means of replacing the diminished revenue from the rural population.

6. The Chairman has brought to my notice the good work done by Mr. R.E.H. Crosbie, O.B.E., in the collection of village statistics, in which he was ably assisted by Mr. Mousa Nassir, Administrative Officer, Jaffa, and in his general assistance in framing the report; and by Mr. J.C. Gress and Mr. V.N. Levi of the Treasury, who have acted as Joint Secretaries to the Committee, in the compilation of statistics and the preparation of the report. I consider that great credit is due to the Committee under the Chairmanship of Mr. Johnson, for their careful and comprehensive report to which they have devoted much time and thought. The report is of considerable value to Government.

7. I have forwarded a copy of the Committee's report to Sir John Chancellor, and have also given a copy to Sir John Hope Simpson.

I have the honour to be,
My Lord,
Your Lordship's most obedient,
humble servant,

OFFICER ADMINISTERING THE GOVERNMENT.

REPORT OF COMMITTEE

ON

THE ECONOMIC CONDITION OF AGRICULTURISTS

AND

THE FISCAL MEASURES OF GOVERNMENT IN RELATION THERETO.

THE TREASURY,
    JERUSALEM.   3RD JULY, 1930.

(i)

EXTRACT FROM OFFICIAL GAZETTE No.258
1ST MAY, 1930.

NOTICE.

APPOINTMENT OF COMMITTEE.

It is hereby notified that the High Commissioner has appointed a Committee of the undermentioned officers to examine into the economic condition of agriculturists and the fiscal measures of Government in relation thereto; and to make recommendations:-

    W.J. Johnson, Esq., O.B.E.,
    Deputy Treasurer   Chairman.

    R.E.H. Crosbie, Esq., O.B.E.,
    Assistant District
    Commissioner, Southern
    District   Member.

    An Area Officer nominated by the
    District Commissioner in whose
    District the Committee is sitting.

Mr. J. Gress and Mr. V.N. Levi of the Treasury will act as joint secretaries to the Committee.

                                  (sgd) E. MILLS

                              ACTING CHIEF SECRETARY.

22nd April, 1930.

(ii)

PERSONNEL OF THE COMMITTEE.

W.J. Johnson, Esq., O.B.E., Deputy Treasurer	Chairman
R.E.H. Crosbie, Esq., O.B.E., Assistant District Commissioner, Southern District	)
L. Andrews, Esq., O.B.E., Area Officer, Nazareth Area	)
A.T.O. Lees, Esq., Area Officer, Haifa Area	)
M. Bailey, Esq., Area Officer, Nablus Area	) Members
J.H.H. Pollock, Esq., Area Officer, West Area, Southern District	)
* W.J. Miller, Esq., O.B.E., Area Officer, East Area, Southern District	)
G.F. Sulman, Esq., M.C., Area Officer, Jerusalem Division	)
J.C. Gress, Esq., Senior Assistant Treasurer	) Joint) Secretaries
V.N. Levi, Esq., Junior Assistant Treasurer	)

* Was absent from Palestine at the
time the report was drafted.

(iii)

TABLE OF CONTENTS.

	Para.	Page
INTRODUCTORY	1 to 3	1 and 2
GENERAL INFORMATION	4 to 7	2 to 6
THE ARAB VILLAGE QUESTIONNAIRE	8 to 49	6 to 41
Statistics	8 to 10	6 and 7
<u>Aggregate gross income</u>	11 to 24	8 to 20
Declared gross income from 104 village	11	8
Gross income from cultivation of 104 villages on basis of commuted tithe figures	12	
Difference between declared gross income and commuted tithe figures	13	9 to 11
Comparison of declared average yield per dunam of field crops and yield on basis of commuted tithe figures	14	11 and 12
Other selected production figures	15	12 and 13
Percentages of areas and values of crops	16	13 and 14
Comparison of income from average dunam of field crops with rents	17	15 and 16
Revised gross income from fruit trees	18 to 20	16 to 18
Revised gross income from stock, poultry and dairy produce	21 to 23	18 and 19
Revised gross income from all sources	24	20
<u>Average cost of production per unit</u>	25 to 29	20 to 25
Declared costs of production of 100 dunams of field crops	25	20
Revised costs of production	26	21 to 23
Cost of production of trees ignored	27	23 and 24

TABLE OF CONTENTS (cont'd).   (iv)

	Para.	Page
Cost of production of stock ignored	28	24
Cost of production excludes labour of the farmer and his family	29	25
Inclusion of allowance for rent	30	25
<u>Average Net Return</u>	31 to 33	25 to 28
Average net return from 100 dunams of field crops	31	26
Average net return from 100 dunams of all kinds of land	32	26
Average net return is not true profit	33	27 and 28
<u>Average Cost of Living</u>		
Declared cost of living of a family of six	34	28
Revised cost of living of a family of six	35	28 and 29
Addition for family share of communal expenditure	36	28 and 29
<u>Average and minimum holdings</u>	38 to 42	30 to 33
Declared holdings of 104 villages	38	30
Average holding per family	40 and 41	32
Minimum holding	42	32 and 33
<u>Average family income</u>	43	33 and 34
Income from Agriculture and from other internal and external village sources		
<u>Surplus produce for disposal</u>	44 and 45	34 to 36
<u>The burden of Taxation</u>	46	36 to 38
<u>General position of villages</u>	47 to 49	38 to 41
JEWISH AGRICULTURAL SETTLEMENTS	50 to 63	41 to 51
<u>General Information</u>	50 to 52	41 to 43
Gross income		
Income from cultivation	53	43 and 44

TABLE OF CONTENTS (cont'd). (v)

	Para.	Page
Productivity and distribution of principal field crops	54	44 to 47
Numbers of stock of six settlements	55	47 and 48
Gross income from all sources of six settlements	56	48 and 49
Cost of production		
Costs of production per 100 dunams for two P I C A settlements and Rehoboth	57	49 and 50
Net income cannot be determined for mixed farms	58	50
Cost of living	59 to 62	50 to 53
Net income from cultivation	63	54 and 55
GENERAL CONCLUSIONS	64 to 73	55 to 72
Local supply and imports of principal marketable commodities	64	55 to 57
General Conditions of Arab farming	65	57 to 60
Financial situation of the Arab farmer prior to 1929	66	60 to 62
Burden of taxation on the Arab farmer	67	62 to 64
Present financial situation of the Arab farmer	68	64 to 66
The Musha'a system of land tenure	69 and 70	66 to 69
Financial situation of the Jewish farmer prior to 1929	71	69 and 70
Burden of taxation on the Jewish farmer	72	70 and 71
Present financial situation of the Jewish farmer	73	71
RECOMMENDATIONS	74 to 88	72 to 87
Necessity of a Marketing Board and of Village Co-operative Bodies	74 and 75	72 to 74
Income Tax and Land Tax	76 and 77	74 to 77

TABLE OF CONTENTS (cont'd).　　　(vi)

	Para.	Page
Graduated income tax	76	74
Practical difficulties	76	74
Low land tax	76	74
Abolition of animal tax	76	74
Income tax expert	76	76
<u>Interim measures for partial relief of rural Tax-payer</u>	78 to 81	77 to 80
Direct taxes of urban and rural populations	78	77 and 78
Reduction on tithe and increase of urban property tax from January 1st, 1931	79	78 and 79
Recommendations for using proceeds of income tax	80	79
Reduction of tithe in 1930	81	77 to 80
<u>Credit facilities</u>	82 and 83	80 to 82
Co-operative groups	82	81
Issue by Government of short term loans for the coming season	83	82
<u>Development of foreign markets for Palestine produce</u>	84	82 and 83
<u>Protective duties against foreign imports of Agricultural produce into Palestine</u>	85 to 87	83 to 88
Licensing of wheat and flour imports and increase of import duties	85	84
Prohibition of the importation of unrefined olive oil	86	85 and 86
Protective duty on sesame seed	87	86
<u>Abolition of Musha'a System of Tenure</u>	88	86 and 87
The possibility of expediting land settlement	88	87
Compulsory partition of Musha'a villages	88	87

TABLE OF CONTENTS (cont'd). (vii)

	Para.	Page
SUMMARY OF RECOMMENDATIONS	89	88 to 90
CONCLUSION	90 and 91	91

APPENDIX A.

List of 104 Arab villages in respect of which the questionnaire was completed

SCHEDULE OF STATISTICAL TABLES IN TEXT.

Serial Number	Contents	Reference to Paragraph of Report	Page
I	Cultivable Area of Palestine	4	3
II	104 Questionnaire Villages	8	6
III	Population and Areas of 104 Villages	9	7
IV	Declared Gross Income from all sources of 104 Villages	11	8
V	Revised Gross Income from Cultivation of 104 Villages	12	9
VI	Declared Produce in kind and value	13	10
VII	Commuted Tithe figures of Produce in kind and value	13	10-11
VIII	Declared Productivity per dunom	14	11-12
IX	Productivity per dunom on Commuted Tithe figures	14	12
X	Comparison of various figures of Productivity	15	13
XI	Percentages of area and value for various crops and average gross income from 100 dunoms field crops (on commuted Tithe figures)	16	14
XII	Number of trees of 104 Villages	18	17
XIII	Revised Gross Income from fruit trees of 104 Villages	18	17
XIV	Numbers of Stock of 104 Villages	21	18
XV	Revised Gross Income from Stock of 104 Villages	23	19
XVI	Revised Gross Income from all sources of 104 Villages	24	20
XVII	Declared Average Cost of Production of 100 dunoms field crops	25	21
XVIII	Revised Cost of Production of 100 dunoms field crops	26	23
XIX	Average Net Return from 100 dunoms field crops	31	26
XX	Average Net Return from 100 dunoms all kinds of land	32	27

SCHEDULE OF STATISTICAL TABLES IN TEXT (Continued)

Serial Number	Contents	Reference to Paragraph of Report	Page
XXI	Declared Cost of Living of family of six	34	28
XXII	Revised Cost of Living of family of six	35	29
XXIII	Declared Holdings of 104 Villages according to Ownership	38	30
XXIV	Declared Holdings of 104 Villages according to Size	39	31
XXV	Average Holding per family	40	32
XXVI	Total Net Income of 21,066 families	43	33
XXVII	Surplus Produce for disposal of 104 Villages	44	34
XXVIII	Percentage of Taxation on Net Return from Use of Land	46	36 and 37
XXIX	Percentage of Taxation on Income from Ownership	46	37
XXX	Percentage of Taxation on Gross Income from Agriculture	46	38
XXXI	Total Income and Expenditure of 104 Villages	47	38
XXXII	Capacity of Payment of individual Villages	48	40
XXXIII	Seven representative Jewish agricultural settlements and Population	50	41 and 42
XXXIV	Areas of seven Jewish Agricultural settlements	51	43
XXXV	Income from Cultivation of six Jewish settlements	53	44
XXXVI	Yield in Kilos per dunom of principal crops in six settlements	54	44 and 45
XXXVII	Produce in kind and value of six settlements	54	45 and 46
XXXVIII	Percentages of area and value for various crops and average income from 100 dunoms field crops	54	46 and 47
XXXIX	Numbers of Stock and Poultry of six settlements	55	48
XL	Gross Income from all sources of six Jewish settlements	56	48 and 49

SCHEDULE OF STATISTICAL TABLES IN TEXT (Continued) (x)

Serial Number	Contents	Reference to Paragraph of Report	Page
XLI	Costs of Production in three Jewish Settlements	57	50
XLII	Cost of Living of a family or member of a group in six Settlements	59	51
XLIII	Communal expenses, taxes and rent per family or member of a group in six Settlements	59	51 and 52
XLIV	Balance from Gross Income of a family or member of a group after meeting cost of living and other essential expenditure; but excluding costs of production	60	52
XLV	Expenditure on Social and Cultural requirements and interest on debt, excluding settlement loans, per family or member of a group in six Settlements	61	53
XLVI	Estimate by Mr. M. Smilansky, Jewish Farmers' Federation, of Income and Expenditure of a mixed farm of 100 dunoms	63	54
XLVII	Estimate by Mr. M. Smilansky of net return from principal plantation produce	63	55
XLVIII	Comparative table of estimates of percentage of relative cultivated areas of Musha'a and Mafruz land in 1923 and 104 Arab Questionnaire Villages	69	66

THE TREASURY,
JERUSALEM.

Sir,

    We have the honour to refer to your letter No.6464/29 of the 6th April, 1930, appointing us a Committee "to examine into the economic condition of agriculturists and the fiscal measures of Government in relation thereto; and to make recommendations".

2.   After discussing the subject of our enquiry with the Commissioner of Lands, the Acting Director of Agriculture and others the Committee met at Nablus and formulated a village questionnaire. The Committee then visited several villages in the Nablus, Tulkarem and Jenin Sub-Districts for the purposes of testing the practicability of the questionnaire. The questionnaire was drawn up in a form suitable for recording available village information. For instance, while it was possible to estimate the gross produce of the village it was only possible to ascertain the cost of cultivation per dunam and the cost of living per family. We thought that more correct information would be obtainable by adapting the questionnaire to the

The Chief Secretary,
    Government of Palestine.

2.

information that could readily be produced by villagers themselves. It was decided to choose at least one hundred representative villages and that the questionnaire should be filled up personally by Palestinian District Officers, under the supervision of the Area Officer, after consultation with the Mukhtars and Elders of each village in the village itself. It was also decided that the Bedu area and villages mainly cultivating citrous fruits, melons, grapes, etc. should not be taken into consideration as the Committee's investigation into the economic condition of agriculturists was of a general and not a specialised nature. For Jewish statistics the Committee applied for information to the Executive of the Jewish Agency for Palestine, the Palestine Jewish Colonisation Association and the Farmers' Federation which are understood to represent all types of Jewish agriculture.

3. In the meantime the Committee visited the towns and certain representative Jewish and German Colonies, and took evidence from cultivators, landlords, money-lenders, industrialists and from others interested in agriculture.

GENERAL INFORMATION

4. The Commissioner of Lands estimates the total cultivable area of Palestine as approximately

3.

12,233,000 dunams of which approximately 6,857,000 dunams are in valleys and plains and 5,376,000 are in the hills. Topographically Palestine is divided into seven districts as under:-

TABLE I

CULTIVABLE AREA OF PALESTINE

	Dunams
(1) Hills of Galilee and Judea	5,376,000
(2) Plains - (a) Maritime Plain from Ras el Nakura to Gaza (b) Plain of Esdraelon (c) Valley of Jezreel (d) Jordan Valley (e) Huleh	5,216,000
	10,592,000
(3) Plains of Beersheba Sub-District	1,641,000
Total	12,233,000

5. The hills of Galilee and Judea are frequently referred to as the mountainous region or the plateau region of Palestine. The Judean Hills rise from the lower desert hills of Beersheba and continue northwards for some 90 kilometres to the Plain of Esdraelon. The Galilean Hills are situated north of the Plain of Esdraelon and extend beyond the Syrian frontier. The two hilly regions of Judea and Galilee are separated by the Plain of Esdraelon. The eastern slopes

4.

of the Judean Hills are treeless, and the hills themselves and the western slopes are generally denuded of all trees except olive trees and a few figs and apricots. A great part of the region is desolate and stony; but the small wadis and valleys are very fertile and are excellent for cereal cultivation.

6. The Maritime Plain, or as it is sometimes called the Coastal Plain, runs from Ras el Nakura in the north to Gaza in the south. At Mount Carmel near Haifa the Plain is only a few hundred yards in width, and south of Carmel it widens to some two or three kilometres for about 30 kilometres until it reaches Benjamina, after which there is a gradual increase in width to 16 kilometres at Jaffa, 30 kilometres at Askelon and 50 kilometres at Gaza. The eastern side of the Plain has extensive olive groves along the foothills. There are large orchards in certain agricultural centres and richly developed agricultural districts near Jaffa. Otherwise the Plain is used for the growing of cereals, sesame and melons without irrigation, although extensive irrigation works in the region of the Auja are in prospect. Between Benjamina and Jaffa there are large swamps owing to obstruction in the lower courses of the large streams from the western slopes of the mountainous region which traverse the Plain towards the Mediterranean Sea.

5.

Between Jaffa and Rafa there are some 380,000 dunams of sand dunes in addition to swamps. The Plain of Esdraelon and the Valley of Jezreel may be considered together and as extending from the Mediterranean Sea eastward to the Ghor.. The Plain of Esdraelon divides the hills of Galilee in the north from the hills of Judea in the south, and is considered the most fertile part of Palestine and especially suitable for cereal cultivation. The Ghor or Jordan Valley is a natural depression stretching from Tiberias in the north to the Dead Sea in the south with a width varying from 1½ kilometres in the north to 20 kilometres at Jericho. Owing to climatic conditions and the alkalinity of the soil it is doubtful whether it can support a large agricultural population. The Huleh District lies in the valley north-east of Safad and Tiberias and is fertile. The Huleh marsh lying near the Lake covers an area not less than 52,000 dunams. The plains of the Beersheba Sub-District include very extensive areas of cultivable land, but low rainfall is a great drawback to agriculture without irrigation, and the unencouraging prospects of water in quantity make irrigation problematical.

7. The total number of villages in Palestine according to the Census of 1922, on which vital statistics are based is 844. The census shows

6.

a total population of 757,182 of which the rural population, excluding tribal areas, number 389,534. Vital statistics based on that census figure show a total rural population at the end of 1929 of 481,828 or a natural increase of 23.7% over the recorded census of 1922, including recorded immigration, while replies to the information requested in the Committee's questionnaire show an average increase in the rural population of 33.1/3%.

THE ARAB VILLAGE QUESTIONNAIRE

8.   The village questionnaire was completed by the following numbers of Arab villages:-

TABLE II

104 QUESTIONNAIRE VILLAGES

	Number of Villages
Nazareth Area	24
Haifa Area	20
Nablus Area	22
West Area, Southern District	8
East Area, Southern District	16
Jerusalem Division	14
Total	104

The names of the villages are set out in Appendix A.

7.

9. The following table shows the distribution of cultivable land and population among these villages:-

TABLE III

POPULATION AND AREAS OF 104 VILLAGES

Number of Villages	104
<u>Population</u> - as stated by villagers	136,044
Number of families - as stated by villagers	23,573
<u>Population</u> - on vital statistics of Department of Health	126,398
Number of families of six - on vital statistics of Department of Health	21,066
<u>Cultivable area in dunams</u> -	
as given by villagers:	
Field Crops	948,756
Fruit Trees and Fallow	220,570
Uncultivated	78,255
	1,247,581

10. It has been assumed that the differences between the total cultivated areas and the areas cultivated with cereals may be assigned to fruit trees and fallow lands. In default of information it is not possible to distinguish between the two. In drawing up the various tables of this report

8.

an attempt was made to distinguish among hills, plains and foothills, but as the results were not very illuminating the attempt was abandoned.

Aggregate Gross Income.

11. The aggregate gross income of one hundred and four representative villages is stated to be £P.544,881, derived from the following sources:-

TABLE IV

DECLARED GROSS INCOME FROM ALL SOURCES FROM 104 VILLAGES

	£P.	£P.
Cultivation -		
Field Crops		301,999
Fruit Trees -		
Olive	54,377	
Other	19,710	74,087
Total income from Cultivation		376,086
Stock, Dairy Produce, Poultry, etc.		55,357
Total Agriculture		431,443
Other Village Sources		14,112
Transport and Labour outside the village		99,326
Total Income from all sources	£P.	544,881

12. The declared gross annual income of £P.376,086 from the cultivation of the soil is

9.

considerably underestimated. If the commuted tithe is taken as a basis and allowance is made for 15% under-estimation in the assessment, the gross income from this source will be as shown below:-

TABLE V

REVISED GROSS INCOME FROM CULTIVATION
OF 104 VILLAGES

	£P.	£P.
Field Crops		483,600
Trees:		
Olive	32,400	
Other	45,000	77,400
Total Income from Cultivation	£P.	561,000

13. The following two tables show that the difference in the results of Tables IV and V is largely attributable to the different prices at which the produce in kind has been valued. The replies to the questionnaire, though purporting to quote average prices, clearly reflect the depressed prices now prevailing, while the commuted tithe is based on the higher prices of previous years:-

10.

TABLE VI

DECLARED PRODUCE IN KIND AND VALUE

Crops	Total Produce in Tons	Value £P.	Average price per Ton £P.Mils
Winter Crops			
Wheat	16,874	144,647	8.572
Barley	9,142	42,591	4.659
Qatani	3,201	22,824	7.130
Other	-	11,167	-
Total	-	221,229	-
Summer Crops			
Dura	9,617	45,748	4.757
Simsim	1,155	19,301	16.710
Melons (number	1,405,680	4,555	-
Other	-	11,166	-
Total	-	80,770	-
Total	-	301,999	-

TABLE VII

COMMUTED TITHE FIGURES OF PRODUCE IN KIND AND VALUE

Crops	Total Produce in Tons	Value £P.	Average Price per Ton £P.Mils
Winter Crops			
Wheat	24,673	279,638	11.333
Carried forward		279,638	

11.

	Tons	£P.	£P.Mils
Brought forward		279,638	
Barley	8,525	62,587	7.342
Qatani	4,725	41,526	8.789
Other	-	6,242	-
Total	-	389,993	-
Summer Crops			
Dura	8,036	61,477	7.650
Simsim	989	23,008	23.264
Melons (number)	1,509,168	2,881	-
Other	-	6,241	-
Total	-	93,607	-
Total	-	483,600	-

14. It is of interest also to show the average yield per dunam of the principal crops, on the declared and on the commuted tithe figures for produce in kind. In default of any other data, the figures for areas given in the answers to the questionnaire have been used in both tables.

TABLE VIII
DECLARED PRODUCTIVITY PER DUNAM

Crop	Area	Gross Produce	Average yield per dunam
	Dunams	Tons	Kilos
Wheat	352,425	16,874	48
Barley	144,085	9,142	63

12.

	Dunams	Tons	Kilos
Qatani	92,148	3,201	35
Dura	216,720	9,617	44
Simsim	113,257	1,155	10
Melons	10,746	(number) 1,405,680	(number) 131
Other Crops	19,375	Tons 4,422	Kilos 228

TABLE IX

PRODUCTIVITY PER DUNAM ON
COMMUTED TITHE FIGURES

Crop	Area	Gross Produce	Average yield per dunam
	Dunams	Tons	Kilos
Wheat	352,425	24,673	70
Barley	144,085	8,525	59
Qatani	92,148	4,725	51
Dura	216,720	8,036	37
Simsim	113,257	989	9
Melons	10,746	(number) 1,509,168	(number) 140
Other Crops	19,375	Tons 1,234	Kilos 64

15. The productivity figures thus obtained may be compared with productivity figures obtained from other sources. The figures quoted show the averages obtained from selected persons at the

13.

meetings held by the Committee in various centres; an average of the official estimates given by the Director of Agriculture for each Sub-District excluding Beersheba; and the average of five years' exact records kindly placed at the disposal of the Committee by the Salesian Agricultural School at Bait Jemail. In view of the scientific methods employed at the School, it is natural that their figures should be high.

TABLE X

COMPARISON OF VARIOUS FIGURES OF PRODUCTIVITY

Source	Wheat	Barley	Qatani	Dura	Sesame
(a) Table VIII	48	63	35	44	10
(b) Table IX	70	59	51	37	9
(c) Selected Evidence	57	54	58	54	25
(d) Official Estimates	67	74	61	65	39
(e) Bait Jemal Records	86	129	79	74	

16. The following table shows the percentages of the cultivated area assigned to the various crops, and the percentages of the total value derived from them. It will be observed that the winter crop accounts for 63% of the area cultivated, and for 81%

14.

of the total value of crops. From the total area in dunams and the total value of the produce shown in this table, it may be calculated that the average gross income from 100 dunams of field crops is £P.51:-

TABLE XI

PERCENTAGES OF AREA AND VALUE FOR VARIOUS CROPS AND AVERAGE GROSS INCOME FROM 100 DUNAMS FIELD CROPS

Crop	Area in Dunams	Percentage of Total Area	Value of Crops	Percentage of Total Value
	Dunams	%	£P.	%
Winter Crops				
Wheat	352,425	37	279,638	58
Barley	144,085	15	62,587	13
Qatani	92,148	10	41,526	9
Other	9,688	1	6,242	1
Total	598,346	63	389,993	81
Summer Crops				
Dura	216,720	23	61,477	13
Simsim	113,257	12	23,008	4
Melons	10,746	1	2,881	1
Other	9,687	1	6,241	1
Total	350,410	37	93,607	19
Total	948,756	100	483,600	100
Average income from	100		51	

15.

17.   The figure of approximately 500 mils per dunam for the gross income from an average dunam of field crops may be checked by an examination of rents. The usual arrangement is that the tenant pays the landlord in kind a proportion of the gross produce of the land. The proportion may be one-fifth, one-fourth, one-third less the appropriate share of the tithe (i.e. 33.1/3% less 3.1/3%), two-fifths less the share of the tithe, or one half less the share of the tithe and perhaps less a share of the expenses. There are also various modifications. The commonest rent, however, would appear to be 30% of the gross produce, and the next commonest, 25%. The other arrangements apply to exceptionally poor or exceptionally good land. It is desirable to note that the figures quoted show the actual proportion of rent received by the landlord. The nominal rents have been adjusted since the Commuted Tithe Ordinance charged the landlord with the payment of tithe. Thus a landlord who used to receive 33.1/3% of the gross produce and to pay out of it the odd 3.1/3% as his share of tithe now receives 40% and pays the whole tithe of 10%; but his net receipts for rent in either case are 30%. With these terms may be compared the money rents which are beginning to appear in most parts of the country. They range from about 50 mils to 250 mils per dunam, but the most usual figures

16.

seem to be 100 mils and 150 mils per dunam. We have said that the commonest proportion of rent in kind is 30%. If the annual value of the average dunam is 500 mils, as we have estimated, this 30% is worth 150 mils, which corresponds with the last figure quoted for money rents. Such figures of their receipts from rent as were given by landowners suggest rather a lower productivity of the dunam, but we are of opinion that their figures, though purporting to be based on the past, were influenced by the present low prices. It may be added that in various places the tithe on an average dunam was estimated by villagers at something under 50 mils. As there is little doubt that the assessed tithe has in general been rather less than a true tenth, this estimate also supports the view that the yield of an average dunam is worth (at the prices quoted) about 500 mils per dunam.

18. The figures for the produce of fruit trees, both on the basis of the answers to the questionnaire and on that of the commuted tithe figures, are incredibly low. It has always been known that the estimated figures for fruit trees were highly speculative. Investigation has shown that the average yield of an olive tree over a period of two years (to allow for the major and minor crops of alternate years) is not less than $3\frac{1}{2}$ kilogrammes of oil (representing some

17.

17½ kilogrammes of fruit). The average price for olive oil during the period on which commuted tithe was based was 53 mils per kilogramme. The average yield of oil from an olive tree is therefore worth some 185 mils per annum. The produce of other fruit trees can hardly average less than two-thirds of this amount, say 125 mils per annum. These figures are confirmed by the Director, Department of Agriculture. The numbers of olives and other fruit trees, as shown in the questionnaire. are as follows; and as the number of trees is easy to ascertain and there is no reason for villagers to exaggerate it, the figures may be accepted as approximately correct:-

TABLE XII

NUMBER OF TREES OF 104 VILLAGES

Olives	582,951
Other	896,525
Total	1,479,476

19. At the prices quoted, the values are as follows:-

TABLE XIII

GROSS INCOME FROM FRUIT TREES OF 104 VILLAGES

		£P.
Olives		107,846
Other		112,066
Total Income from Trees	£P.	219,912

18.

20. It may conveniently be noted here that, as olive trees are usually planted 9 or 10 to the dunam, an average dunam of olive trees is worth not less than £P.1.750 per annum. A good grove in full bearing is worth more.

21. The figures for stock and dairy produce are also unduly low. Our investigations show that the annual produce of an average flock of sheep in wool, milk or samneh, and meat works out at some 600 mils per head; that of an average herd of goats at some 400 mils. It may be noted that the rate of 48 mils per head of each for animal tax, which must originally have represented a tithe, falls between the two figures. The figures accord also with the common (though not universal) opinion that the annual value of a goat is not much more than half that of a sheep. As milch cows are comparatively few, it has been difficult to determine the annual income from them, but we consider that £P.2.500 would be a conservative figure. The answers to the questionnaires show the following numbers:-

TABLE XIV

NUMBERS OF STOCK OF 104 VILLAGES

Milch Cows	7,935
Sheep	46,824
Goats	81,972

19.

22. It was not possible to ascertain through the questionnaire the number of fowls in each village, because the Arab farmer leaves poultry-farming to the women and does not regard it as a serious source of income. It may reasonably be assumed, however, that on the average there are 10 hens on a holding of 100 dunams. On the whole area of 1,247,581 dunams under discussion, the number of hens would at this rate amount to some 125,000 which represents an average of about 6 fowls for each of the 21,000 families. The Manager of the Stud Farm informs us that a low average bird at the Farm produces 250 mils per annum. If we take half this figure for the farmer's fowls, the 10 fowls on a 100 dunam holding give an income of £P.1.250 per annum. This represents a total of some £P.15,000. We therefore make a further addition of £P.15,000 to the income from stock, dairy produce, etc.

23. At the figures given, the values are as follows:-

TABLE XV

GROSS INCOME FROM STOCK OF 104 VILLAGES

	£P.
Milch Cows	19,837
Sheep	28,094
Goats	32,789
Poultry	15,000
Total	95,720

20.

24. We are now in a position to draw up a revised table of gross income for the one hundred and four villages:-

TABLE XVI

REVISED GROSS INCOME FROM ALL SOURCES OF 104 VILLAGES

	£P.	£P.
Cultivation		
Field Crops		483,600
Fruit Trees -		
Olive	107,846	
Other	112,066	219,912
Total income from Cultivation		703,512
Stock, Dairy Produce, Poultry, etc.		95,720
Total Agriculture		799,232
Other Village Sources		14,112
Transport and Labour outside the village		99,326
Total Income from all sources	£P.	912,670

Average Cost of Production per Unit.

25. As it was impossible for villagers to give any idea of the total costs of production for the field crops of the village, it was necessary to base the enquiry on the costs of production for the common but variable unit, the feddan. The figures obtained were adjusted to a definite unit of 100 dunams. The adjustment of fixed expenses in this

21.

manner is of course inaccurate, but the amounts involved are so small that the inaccuracy is immaterial in the rough estimate which is all that can be attempted. We have excluded altogether the cost of such labour as may be performed by an average family of six persons, since any theoretical payments on this score return to the family in the shape of wages. The figures thus derived from the answers to the questionnaire are set forth below:-

TABLE XVII

DECLARED AVERAGE COST OF PRODUCTION OF 100 DUNAMS FIELD CROPS

	£P.
Annual share of capital expenditure on animals	6
Implements	1
Forage for plough animals	7
Seed	6
Hired labour	12
Transport to threshing floor	2
Total	34

26. The figure for the annual share of the cost of animals appears to be high. For an ox the average farmer does not pay more than £P.8, and he probably sells it to a butcher at the end of four years for half the cost price. The annual

22.

share of the cost of an ox is therefore £P.1; and for the yoke of oxen required to plough 100 dunams, £P.2. It is difficult to distinguish between the capital and the annual expenditure on the simple implements used by the farmer. We consider that the figure of £P.1 per annum will adequately cover purchases, replacements and repairs. The farmer seldom gives his ox more than "tibn" and such grazing as he can obtain except during the period - say, four months - when he is actually ploughing. The estimate of £P.7 for forage for a yoke of oxen, on the basis of the commuted tithe prices, therefore appears to us reasonable. The amount of seed required is approximately 10 kilogrammes per dunam for winter crops, and 1 kilogramme per dunam for summer crops. With the actual distribution of crops and at the commuted tithe prices recorded in Table VII, the cost of seed works out to some £P.6.500 per annum. It is extremely difficult to estimate the cost of hired labour. We think that the best approximation is to suppose that the average family can do all the work of the holding except for the bulk of the harvesting of winter crops. We do not think that the payment for this service could exceed 10% of the crop thus harvested. It is seen from Table XI that the winter crop is worth 81% of the total value of all crops. Thus for an average 100 dunams the winter crop is worth some £P.40.

23.

Allowing for the part of the harvesting done by the family, we assess hired labour at £P.3.500 per 100 dunams. The village figure of £P.2 for transport from the fields to the threshing floor we are prepared to accept. If the farmer does his own transport, the additional cost of forage is likely to exceed this sum. We are now in a position to construct a revised table of costs:-

TABLE XVIII

REVISED COSTS OF PRODUCTION OF 100 DUNAMS FIELD CROP

	£P.
Annual share of cost of plough animals	2.000
Implements	1.000
Forage for plough animals	7.000
Seed	6.500
Hired Labour	3.500
Transport to Village	2.000
Total £P.	22.000

27. It is difficult to compile any statement of the cost of production of trees. On the lines we have adopted, we exclude the cost of any labour that the average family may be expected to perform. According to the statistics of the Department of Health the one hundred and four villages under

24.

consideration have a population of 21,066 families of six persons. As the total number of fruit trees is 1,479,476 the average number of fruit trees owned by a family is about 70, which represents about 7 dunams. The ploughing and picking for such a holding is well within the capacity of the average family. For the pressing of olives few figures have been given. This is perhaps because the owner of the press sometimes takes the refuse of the olives after pressing as payment. Sometimes, however, the payment takes the form of a proportion of the oil. Oxen and implements for ploughing are normally already in the possession of the family for cultivating their cereal land. On the whole it seems to us best to ignore the costs of production for trees.

28. An estimate of the costs of production of cows, sheep and goats represents a similar difficulty. It appears that the average family has about 2 sheep and 4 goats, while only one family in three possesses a cow. We must therefore ignore any payments to shepherds, and we think it best to ignore also any costs for feeding and watering the animals.

29. It is important to stress the point that the present enquiry does not aim at the costing of the different stages and the various types of agriculture. All that it is required to ascertain

25.

is the amount of net income that the farmer will have to meet his cost of living and other personal expenses. Hence, the value of his own labour and that of his family is excluded from the costs of production, because any theoretical payments on this score return to the family in the form of wages.

30. In addition to the costs of production already discussed, allowance must be made for rent. This allowance must equally be made when the farmer owns his own land. As has already been recorded, our investigations have led us to the conclusion that the commonest rate of rent in Palestine is 30% of the gross produce from cultivation. We have therefore adopted this figure for our calculations.in subsequent tables.

Average Net Return.

31. The net return from 100 dunams of land under field crops may now be calculated. It is interesting to note that the net return is almost equal to the rent. The general though not universal opinion of the country confirms this relation, which happens also to be the relation now adopted for income tax purposes in England.

26.

TABLE XIX

AVERAGE NET RETURN FROM 100 DUNAMS FIELD CROPS

	£P.
Average gross income	51
Average costs of production	22
	29
Rent (at 30% of gross income)	15
Average net return £P.	14

32. We may also present a more complete picture of an average general holding of 100 dunams including the calculated proportion of gross return from fruit trees and stock. The costs of production are the same as in Table XVIII since the cost of producing olives and stock is being ignored. The figure for gross income from field crops of course differs from the figure in Table XIX, since a portion of the 100 dunams now under consideration is assigned to fruit trees and fallow or uncultivated land that may be used for grazing.

TABLE XX

AVERAGE NET RETURN FROM 100 DUNAMS OF ALL KINDS OF LAND

	£P.
Gross Income	
Field Crops	39

27.

	£P.
Brought forward	39
Fruit Trees -	
Olive	9
Other	9
Total from Cultivation	57
Stock, Dairy Produce, Poultry, etc.	7
Total	64
Cost of Production	22
Taxes -	
Tithe	4.5
Werko	1.8
Animal Tax	.5
Total	28.8
Net return to Owner-cultivator	35.2
Rent at 30% of income from cultivation, viz. £P.17, less £P.1.8 Werko paid by the landlord	15.2
Net return to Tenant	20

33. It must be repeated that the net return shown in Table XX does not represent a true net profit, since no account has been taken of the labour of the farmer and his family. The net return indicates only the amount of income which the farmer of a 100 dunams has to meet his cost

28.

of living and other personal expenses.

Average Cost of Living.

34. The principal items of the cost of living of a village family are wheat and dura, olives and olive oil, lentils, vegetables, dairy produce and clothes. The replies to the questionnaire show the following averages:-

TABLE XXI

DECLARED COST OF LIVING OF
FAMILY OF SIX

	£P.
Wheat and Dura	12
Olives and Olive Oil	3
Other village produce	4
Other necessaries not of village origin	5
Clothing	14
Total	38

35. We do not feel competent to discuss the correct figure for the cost of living of an average family. We therefore aim merely at ascertaining the actual expenditure of an average family. The figure of £P.12 for wheat and dura is excessive. The price of a ton of wheat is £P.11, and an allowance of one ton of wheat for a family of six exceeds the

29.

162 kilogrammes per person in Greece which is the highest figure we have seen quoted. As the usual practice in this country is to mix a certain proportion of dura with the wheat, the actual expenditure for this item may be reduced to £P.10. The next two items we are prepared to accept. The figure for necessaries not of village origin is obviously elastic and varies with the financial position of the family. We consider that in point of fact it does not exceed £P.3. Similarly we consider that the actual expenditure on clothing does not exceed £P.5. The revised results are show below:-

TABLE XXII

REVISED COST OF LIVING OF
FAMILY OF SIX

	£P.
Wheat and Dura	10
Olives and Olive Oil	3
Other village produce	4
Other necessaries not of village origin	3
Clothing	5
Total	25

36. To this figure must be added approximately £P.1 for the family share of communal expenditure, which includes such items as payments to Imams,

30. ghaffirs and naturs and the cost of entertaining village guests. The full total is therefore £P.26.

37. This total takes no cognisance of debt which works out on the estimates given by villagers to some £P.27 per family. Even the interest at a rate of 30%, which cannot be regarded as unusual, would amount to £P.8 per annum.

Average and Minimum Holdings.

38. The one hundred and four representative villages are reported as having a total population distributed by families and areas as under. The village figures for families have necessarily been used for this section:-

TABLE XXIII

DECLARED HOLDINGS OF 104 VILLAGES
ACCORDING TO OWNERSHIP

Population	136,044
Number of families	23,573
Area under cultivation -	Dunams
Owned by Villagers	797,529
Absentee Landlords	245,275
Leased from other villages	126,522
	1,169,326
Area uncultivated but cultivable	78,255
Total	1,247,581

31.

39. The figures shown in Table XXIV are expressed in feddans. It was impossible to obtain the size of holdings in dunams since the dunam is not a unit in common village use. The area of the feddan varies from twenty four dunams at Rameh in the Acre Sub-District to the feddan "rumi", or double feddan of three hundred dunams in Burka in the Nablus District, but the feddan most used is between 100 and 160 dunams, and 120 dunams may be regarded as a middle figure. A feddan (mashi) originally represented the area that one man could plough himself with one yoke of oxen during the course of the year. It now tends rather to represent an average holding in the locality concerned. The 23,573 familes are shown in the following categories:-

TABLE XXIV

DECLARED HOLDINGS OF 104 VILLAGES
ACCORDING TO SIZE

Owner-Occupiers living exclusively on their holding -	
Over two feddans	3,873
Between one and two feddans	1,604
Owner-Occupiers who also work as labourers -	
Between one and two feddans	1,657
Under one feddan	8,396
Trees only	1,103
Labourers	6,940
Total	23,573

32.

40. The distribution of 797,529 dunams of cultivated land owned by the villages, excluding the land of absentee owners, among 15,530 families owning land gives the average holding per family as under. There is no record of the holdings of tenant farmers cultivating 245,275 dunams owned by absentee landlords and 126,522 dunams leased from other villages:-

TABLE XXV

AVERAGE HOLDING PER FAMILY

	Dunams
Of cultivated Area	51
Of uncultivated Area	5
Total	56

41. On the average holding of 56 dunams at which we have arrived, the net return per annum of the tenant amounts, on the proportion of Table XX, only to £P.11. It is obvious that this amount does not suffice for the maintenance of an average family, the minimum cost of which has been estimated at £P.26.

42. To provide the minimum cost of living for a family, a holding of 75 dunams seems to be necessary for an owner-cultivator, while a tenant requires 130 dunams. The small holder or tenant

33.

who has not the necessary minimum holding must supplement his income either by hiring himself out as a labourer inside or outside the village, or by engaging in transport work, in charcoal or lime-kiln burning or some such occupation.

Average Family Income.

43. To ascertain whether in point of fact the average family does secure a livelihood, it is necessary to determine the average share of the 21,066 families in the total net income of the one hundred and four villages. In the calculation of net return from agriculture, the cost of hired labour for harvesting and transport were deducted from the gross income, because the individual farmer has to pay these expenses. But the amounts thus paid out by the farmer are received by other villagers in the form of wages or transport charges. Figures for the receipts from hired labour and from transport must therefore be included in the total of the 21,066 families. Similarly rent, except on the 245,275 dunams owned by absentee landlords, and on 126,522 dunams leased from other villages - a total of 371,797 dunams - must be included.

TABLE XXVI

TOTAL NET INCOME OF 21,066 FAMILIES
AND AVERAGE PER FAMILY

	£P.
Net return from agriculture (at £P.20 per 100 dunams - Table XX)	249,516
Carried forward	249,516

34.

	£P.
Brought forward	249,516
Receipts from -	
Rent	148,157
Hired labour (at £P.3.5 per 100 dunams)	43,665
Transport (at £P.2 per 100 dunams)	24,952
Other village sources	14,112
Transport and labour outside village	99,326
Total	579,728
Average for 21,066 families	£P.27.5

Surplus Produce for disposal.

44. The replies to the village questionnaire indicate that the village produce of these one hundred and four villages surplus to village requirements which is put on the market for disposal is as under. The total value of this surplus produce is £P.106,000, and it has not been possible to obtain any information regarding surplus stock put on the market for disposal:-

TABLE XXVII

SURPLUS PRODUCE FOR DISPOSAL OF 104 VILLAGES

	Tons
Wheat	3,807
Barley	1,295
Qatani	316

35.

	Tons
Dura	3,325
Simsim	723
Tobacco	131
Vegetables	565
Olive Oil	706
Fruits other than olives	238
Melons	Number 613,000

45.   It is difficult to reconcile this surplus produce with the gross produce less the produce retained for human and animal consumption in the village, nor does the surplus produce necessarily represent this surplus. In a great many cases the declared surplus finds its way on to the market through the money-lender who takes what he can from the threshing floor for the part settlement of his debts and often leaves the cultivator insufficient produce for seed or subsistence. Thus the cultivator has again to borrow later from the money-lender, who is often at the same time a grain merchant, his seed and subsistence in kind. In most cases also the villager has to dispose of a part of his crop for the payment of taxes, for the purchase of implements for cultivation and articles of food

36.

and clothing which he does not himself produce,
and for purchase from or barter with other
villages when his own produce is deficient of
village requirements.

The Burden of taxation.

46.   With the figures now available, it is
possible to show the proportion of taxation on the
income from the use of land in the form of the
net return and from the ownership of land in the
form of rent.   The former will show the proportion
that tithe and animal tax constitute of net income;
the latter, the percentage that werko constitutes
of rent.   In order to give an idea of the total
burden of taxation, it is necessary to show the
two percentages on a common basis.   Advantage has
therefore been taken of the fact that rent is
estimated at 30% of gross income to show the percentage
that werko, tithe and animal tax constitute of gross
income.

TABLE XXVIII

PERCENTAGE OF TAXATION ON NET RETURN
FROM USE OF LAND

	£P.
Total Income from Agriculture (Table XVI)	799,232
Cost of Production (at £P.22 per 100 dunams - Table XVIII)	274,468
Rent (at 30% of gross income from cultivation)	211,054
	485,522

37.

	£P.	£P.
Net Return		313,710
Taxes (Actual):		
Tithes	53,034	
Animal Tax	6,460	59,494
Percentage of total Tithe and Animal Tax of Net Return		% 19

TABLE XXIX

PERCENTAGE OF TAXATION ON INCOME
FROM OWNERSHIP

	£P.
Rent	211,054
Total Werko (Actual)	21,955
Percentage of total Werko of Rent	% 10,4

38.

TABLE XXX

PERCENTAGE OF TAXATION ON GROSS INCOME FROM AGRICULTURE

	£P.
Gross Income from Agriculture	799,232
Total Werko, Tithe, and Animal Tax (Actual)	81,449
Percentage of total taxes of Gross Income	% 10.2

General Position of Villages.

47. While it is necessary to consider the economic condition of agriculture from the point of view of the return per average holding and the income per average family, it is also essential to view the matter from the point of view of the one hundred and four villages as a whole and of the individual villages. For this purpose, internal transactions such as the hire of labour and transport charges, may be ignored. Similarly rent, except on the 245,275 dunams owned by absentee landlords, and on 126,522 dunams leased from other villages - a total of 371,797 dunams - may be ignored. The financial position of the one hundred and four villages in total, based on the figures already shown but excluding internal village income and expenditure, is consolidated in the following statement:-

39.

TABLE XXI

TOTAL INCOME AND EXPENDITURE OF 104 VILLAGES

	£P.
Income from Agriculture (Table XVI)	799,232
Other Income	113,438
	912,670
Cost of Production –	
Seed and Forage	168,423
Implements and annual share of cost of plough animals	37,427
	205,850
Balance	706,820
Cost of Living –	
Village Produce	358,122
Other requirements for living and clothing	168,528
Share of Communal Expenses	21,066
	547,716
Balance	159,104
Taxes (Actual)	81,449
Rent payable outside village	62,897
	144,346
Balance	14,758
Interest on debt averaging £P.27 per family at the rate of £P.8 per family	168,528

40.

48.   The following table shows the number of villages able to meet the various categories of expenditure from their gross income after the costs of production have been met. The figures for the individual villages have been adjusted in proportion to the adjustments we have made in the totals:-

TABLE XXXII

CAPACITY OF PAYMENT OF INDIVIDUAL VILLAGES

	Total of 104 Villages
Cost of living (with share of communal expenses)	84
Cost of living and Taxes	70
Cost of living, Taxes and Rent	56
Cost of living, Taxes, Rent and Interest on Debt	31

49.   We feel, however, that though the figures for the one hundred and four villages as a whole are not very far from the truth, it would be unwise to attach undue importance to the figures of individual villages, which have sometimes been obviously incorrect. We think that it may safely be assumed that, with very rare exceptions, every village can provide its own subsistence, even if the standard of living may fall slightly below the

41.

figure we have estimated. The farmer is often – perhaps habitually – short of ready cash, but there is no evidence that he or his family are ever without sufficient food for their subsistence. The table may rather be regarded more generally as showing how few villages can fully meet their annual liabilities in an average year.

JEWISH AGRICULTURAL SETTLEMENTS

General Information.

50. For a picture of Jewish agriculture we have relied on the statistics forwarded by the Palestine Jewish Colonisation Association, the Executive of the Jewish Agency for Palestine and the Farmers' Federation for the representative agricultural settlements shown below. The figures for the various types differ so greatly that it has seemed wiser to show them separately instead of merely summarising the results:-

TABLE XXXIII

SEVEN REPRESENTATIVE JEWISH AGRICULTURAL SETTLEMENTS AND POPULATION

Sub-District	Settlement	Owner of Land	Population
Tiberias	Yavneel	Palestine Jewish Colonisation Association	422
	Kinnereth	do.	48
			470

42.

Nazareth	Nahalal	Jewish National Fund x	691
	Ginegar	do.	64
	Hasharon	do.	35
Beisan	Beth-Alpha	do.	135
			925
Ramleh	Rehoboth	Individual	2,790
		Total	4,185

x The Executive of the Jewish Agency for Palestine control these settlements.

51.   The two Palestine Jewish Colonisation Association settlements are mainly devoted to field crops, though Kinnereth obtains a considerable portion of its income from bananas and vegetables. Yavneel is unirrigated, while Kinnereth is irrigated. The feature of the four Zionist settlements is mixed farming. About half of their income is derived from stock and dairy produce. In Nahalal each settler has a holding of 100 dunams; in the remaining three settlements of this group all land is held and worked in common. Rehoboth is mainly devoted to plantations. A number of the settlers own considerable property, but 239 out of the 599 families that constitute the population are Yemenites with an extremely low standard of living. Table XXXIV shows the areas of these settlements.

43.

TABLE XXXIV

AREAS OF SEVEN JEWISH AGRICULTURAL SETTLEMENTS

Settlement	Field Crops	Fruit Trees	Cultivable but Uncultivated	Total
	Dunams	Dunams	Dunams	Dunams
Yavneel	10,000	500	3,500	14,000
Kinnereth	756	14	800	1,570
	10,756	514	4,300	15,570
Nahalal	5,383	2,492	-	7,875[a]
Ginegar	2,258	-	742	3,000
Hasharon	1,563	-	2,187	3,750
Beth-Alpha	2,265	190	-	2,455
	11,469	2,682	2,929	17,080
Rehoboth	350	14,698	-	15,048
Total	22,575	17,894	7,229	47,698

a. Including 1,125 dunams leased.

52. Such figures as were given for Rehoboth do not lend themselves to the form of tabulation we have adopted. They are therefore recorded separately after the other settlements have been dealt with.

Gross Income.

53. The following tables show the gross income

44.

derived by the various settlements from cultivation:-

TABLE XXXV

INCOME FROM CULTIVATION OF SIX JEWISH SETTLEMENTS

Settlement	Field Crops	Fruit Trees	Total Income from cultivation
	£P.	£P.	£P.
Yavneel	5,744	150	5,894
Kinnereth	1,393	560	1,953
	7,137	710	7,847
Nahalal	6,709	560	7,269
Ginegar	1,960	46	2,006
Hasharon	1,351	-	1,351
Beth-Alpha	4,153	335	4,488
	14,173	941	15,114

54. The following three tables show the total productivity per dunam of the principal crops and the percentages of the cultivated area assigned to the various crops and of the total value from them:-

TABLE XXXVI

YIELD IN KILOS PER DUNAM OF PRINCIPAL CROPS

	Wheat	Barley	Maize	Green Maize	Vetches and Forage	Vegetables
P.I.C.A. (2 Settlements)	111	177	-	-	1,180	-
Nahalal	110	154	107	5,175	3,270	1,000

45.

| Ginegar, Hasharon and Beth-Alpha | 109 | 153 | 130 | 2,118 | 3,200 | 403 |

TABLE XXXVII

PRODUCE IN KIND AND VALUE OF SIX SETTLEMENTS

Crop	Total Produce in Tons	Value	Average Price per Ton
		£P.	£P.Mils
P.I.C.A. (2 Settlements) -			
Wheat	326	2,609	8.000
Barley	357	1,428	4.000
Maize	-	380	-
Green Maize		-	
Vetches and Forage	3,194	1,780	-.557
Other	-	1,650	-
Total	-	7,847	-
Nahalal -			
Wheat	209	1,843	8,818
Barley	91	592	6,506
Maize	200	1,200	6.000
Green Maize	1,876	1,517	-.809
Vetches and Forage	376	306	-.814
Other	-	1,811	-
Total	-	7,269	-

46.

Ginegar, Hasharon and Beth-Alpha -			
Wheat	188	1,837	9.771
Barley	167	1,372	8.215
Maize	141	1,033	7.326
Green Maize	582	422	-.725
Vetches and Forage	3,380	1,728	-.511
Other	-	1,458	-
Total	-	7,850	-

TABLE XXXVIII

PERCENTAGES OF AREA AND VALUE FOR VARIOUS CROPS AND AVERAGE INCOME FOR 100 DUNAMS FIELD CROPS

Crops	Area	Percentage of Total Area	Value	Percentage of Total Value
	Dunams	%	£P.	%
P.I.C.A. (2 Settlements) -				
Wheat	2,940	30	2,609	34
Barley	2,010	21	1,428	18
Maize	1,270	13	380	5
Vetches and Forage	2,710	28	1,780	22
Other	756	8	1,650	21
Total	9,686	100	7,847	100
Average income from	100	-	81	-

47.

	Dunams	%	£P.	%
Nahalal –				
Wheat	1,898	35	1,843	25
Barley	689	11	592	8
Maize	2,240	42	2,717	38
Vetches and Forage	115	2	306	4
Other	533	10	1,811	25
Total	5,475	100	7,269	100
Average income from	100	–	135	–
Ginegar, Hasharon and Beth-Alpha				
Wheat	1,720	29	1,837	23
Barley	1,095	18	1,372	17
Maize	1,355	22	1,455	19
Vetches and Forage	1,055	18	1,728	22
Other	802	13	1,458	19
Total	6,027	100	7,850	100
Average income from	100	–	130	–

55.   It is also of interest to record the stock belonging to the various settlements from which they directly derive income:-

48.

TABLE XXXIX

NUMBERS OF STOCK AND POULTRY OF SIX SETTLEMENTS

Settlement	Milch Cows	Other Cattle	Sheep and Goats	Poultry
Yavneel	150	-	324	-
Kinnereth	50	-	40	-
	200	-	364	-
Nahalal	240	172	-	14,207
Ginegar	41	22		650
Hasharon	8	10	-	330
Beth-Alpha	146	85	24	489
	435	289	24	15,676
Total	635	289	388	15,676

56.   Table XL shows the total income of the various settlements from all sources:-

TABLE XL

GROSS INCOME FROM ALL SOURCES OF SIX JEWISH SETTLEMENTS

Settlement	Cultivation	Stock, Dairy Produce, Poultry, etc.	Other Sources	Total Gross Income
	£P.	£P.	£P.	£P.
Yavneel	5,894	2,600	-	8,494
Kinnereth	1,953	545	-	2,498
	7,847	3,145	-	10,992

49.

	£P.	£P.	£P.	£P.
Nahalal	7,269	10,777	840	18,886
Ginegar	2,006	2,523	805	5,334
Hasharon	1,351	498	38	1,887
Beth-Alpha	4,488	3,825	560	8,873
	15,114	17,623	2,243	34,980
Total	22,961	20,768	2,243	45,972

Cost of Production.

57. The two Palestine Jewish Colonisation Association settlements estimate the cost of production as shown below. As the Palestine Jewish Colonisation Association authorities lay no restriction on the employment of labour, it is probable that a considerable proportion of the amount shown for labour is paid to labourers from outside the settlement. Mr. Smilansky gives an average figure for 100 dunams at Rehoboth. The Executive of the Jewish Agency for Palestine states that, owing to the internal transfers of values involved, it is impossible to calculate the cost of production for mixed farming. For example, the income from the produce of certain field crops becomes, in the shape of forage, part of the cost of production of dairy produce. They therefore take the view that cost of production is

50.

the difference between the gross income and the total cost of living.

TABLE XLI

COST OF PRODUCTION IN THREE JEWISH SETTLEMENTS

Item of Cost	Yavneel	Kinnereth	Rehoboth
	£P.	£P.	£P.
Forage for Plough Animals	900	140	
Implements	430	70	
Seed	470	25	
Hired labour	2,176	898	-
Total	3,976	1,133	-
Cultivated Area in dunams	10,500	770	15,048
Average per 100 dunams	38	147	25

58. In default of definite cost of production figures for four out of the seven settlements under discussion, any attempt to determine net income must be abandoned.

Cost of Living.

59. The following two tables show the cost of living and the remaining essential expenditure of the various settlements. Expenditure on social and cultural requirements, such as insurance, share in education, books and contributions to societies,

51.

has been excluded as being above the minimum requirements for existence with which alone we are at present concerned. As family expenditure cannot suitably be compared with the expenditure of communal settlements, the unit quoted by each settlement has been retained:-

TABLE XLII

COST OF LIVING OF A FAMILY OR MEMBER OF A GROUP IN SIX JEWISH SETTLEMENTS

Settlement	Unit	Farm Produce	Other requirements	Clothing	Total
		£P.	£P.	£P.	£P.
Yavneel	Family of six persons	26	-	7	33
Kinnereth	do.	27	-	46	73
Nahalal	do.	59	44	22	125
Ginegar	Member of Group	14	14	5	33
Hasharon	do.	15	8	5	28
Beth-Alpha	do.	14	12	4	30

TABLE XLIII

COMMUNAL EXPENSES, TAXES AND RENT PER FAMILY OR MEMBER OF A GROUP IN SIX JEWISH SETTLEMENTS

Settlement	Unit	Communal Expenses	Taxes	Rent	Total
		£P.	£P.	£P.	£P.
Yavneel	Family of six persons	9	9	-	18

52.

Settlement	Unit	£P.	£P.	£P.	£P.
Kinnereth	Family of six persons	18	7	-	25
Nahalal	do.	20	2	6	28
Ginegar	Member of Group	2	2	3	7
Hasharon	do.	4	3	4	11
Beth-Alpha	do.	2	2	2	6

60.   In the next table are shown the balances left out of gross income after the cost of living and other essential expenditure have been met to meet the cost of production and other expenses:-

TABLE XLIV

BALANCE FROM GROSS INCOME OF A FAMILY OR MEMBER
OF A GROUP AFTER MEETING COST OF LIVING
AND OTHER ESSENTIAL EXPENDITURE

Settlement	Unit	Gross Income	Cost of Living	Communal Expenses, Taxes and Rent	Balance to meet cost of production and other expenses
		£P.	£P.	£P.	£P.
Yavneel	Family of six persons	121	33	18	70
Kinnereth	do.	244	73	25	146
Nahalal	do.	164	125	28	11
Ginegar	Member of Group	83	33	7	43
Hasharon	do.	54	28	11	15
Beth Alpha	do.	77	30	6	41

53.

61.   The other expenses have been quoted as follows:-

TABLE XLV

OTHER EXPENDITURE AND INTEREST ON DEBT
PER FAMILY OR MEMBER OF A GROUP

Settlement	Unit	Social and Cultural Expenditure	Approximate Interest on Debt excluding Settlement Loan	Total
		£P.	£P.	£P.
Yavneel	Family of six persons	-	4	4
Kinnereth	do.	-	4	4
Nahalal	do.	25	10	35
Ginegar	Member of Group	16	3	19
Hasharon	do.	14	2	16
Beth Alpha	do.	16	3	19

62.   It is clear that the balances are not always adequate to meet this further expenditure, even without the settlement of loan charges. The loans to Zionist settlers vary from £P.600 - £P.900 per family repayable over a period of 45 to 50 years. We are therefore led to the conclusion that the figures quoted for cost of living and perhaps communal expenses are theoretical rather than actual, and that in practice the expenditure on these heads depends mainly on the amount available after costs of production have been met.

54.

Net Income from Cultivation.

63.   This section may be concluded with a record of the figures given by Mr. Smilansky.

TABLE XLVI

ESTIMATE BY MR. SMILANSKY OF INCOME
AND EXPENDITURE PER 100 DUNAMS
OF MIXED FARM LAND

Average 100 Dunams		Value
		£P.
Income		
Grain	7.4 tons	41.500
Milk	3,400 litres	50.500
Sundries		6.000
Total		98.000
Expenditure	£P.	
Concentrated food	20.750	
Sundries	4.250	25.000
Communal expenses and taxes		24.000
		49.000
Surplus		49.000
Cost of living of family of 5 persons		46.500

55.

TABLE XLVII

ESTIMATE BY MR. SMILANSKY OF NET
INCOME PER DUNAM OF PRINCIPAL
PLANTATION PRODUCE

Per Dunam	Gross Produce	Value	Cost of Production	Net Income
		£P.	£P.	£P.
Oranges	100 boxes [a] / 35 " [b]	30 [c] / 4.500 [c]	15	19.500
Grapes	300 kilos	4.500	2	2.500
Almonds	75 "	3.250	1.500	1.750
Olives	200 "	2.500	1	1.500

a. For export
b. For Egypt and local consumption
c. Price on tree

GENERAL CONCLUSIONS

Local Supply and Imports of principal marketable commodities.

64.   Before examining the financial position of the farmer, it will be of interest to consider the local supply of the principal marketable commodities, and imports of these commodities from abroad. It is unnecessary in this connection to consider oranges and melons with which no imports compete, or tobacco which is protected by a heavy import duty. The average production of wheat in the country is estimated at 115,000 tons per annum. Of this, about 10% is required for seed, leaving a

56.

balance of some 104,000 tons for consumption. The rural population of Palestine including tribal areas is about 97,000 families (at an average of six persons). On the basis accepted in Table XXII, a family of six persons requires about a ton of wheat and dura per annum, dura being mixed with the wheat to make bread. Thus 97,000 tons of wheat, less such quantity as is replaced by dura, are required for the consumption of the rural population, leaving a balance of 7,000 tons, plus the quantity replaced by dura, for the use of the urban population. It is not possible to estimate the proportion of the admixture which varies with the annual crop and the financial situation of the family. As there are still some 56,000 urban families (at the same average of six persons) to be fed, Palestine has to import every year an average of 15,000 tons from Transjordan and Hauran, some 7,000 tons foreign wheat and some 28,000 tons of foreign flour in terms of wheat, a total of some 50,000 tons. The supply of local wheat available for the market constitutes therefore only a small proportion of the total urban requirements, and consequently market prices are mainly determined by imports. In the Beersheba area, the principal commodity is barley instead of wheat. In good years, such as the present, large quantities are available for export. The crop, however, is peculiarly uncertain, and in ordinary years there is little or

57.

no surplus for the market. There are no competitive imports of barley, but there is no export market for any surplus. As regards olives, even in the minor year of the olive cycle, the crop is ample for the needs of the country. There is therefore no need for soap-manufacturers, who, apart from the farmer himself, are the principal consumers of olive oil, to import their requirements from abroad. In spite of the adequacy of the local supply, 2,500 tons of unrefined olive oil and 765 tons of olive oil offaling were imported in 1929. As regards sesame seed, both the exports and the imports in 1929 were approximately 3,500 tons. It would therefore appear that the local producers of sesame oil prefer to import their requirements of sesame seed from abroad. There is no duty at present on imports of sesame seed. Sesame oil does not enter into the question, as the exports of it are small and it is not imported at all. For example, in 1929 the exports were 71 tons, while the imports were nil. Although the crops mentioned are the most important for the country as a whole, it should be added that villages near the large towns are able to derive a considerable income from the sale of vegetables, fruit and dairy produce; but the number of villages thus favourably situated is small.

General conditions of Arab farming.

65.   It may be asked why the Arab farmer does

58.

not increase his wheat cultivation so as to eliminate the need for foreign imports. First, allowance must be made for the fact that whatever the local supply might be, a certain quantity of foreign white flour, estimated at 12,000 - 15,000 tons per annum, would be imported to make bread of fine quality and confectionery. Next, it must be noted that there is no Customs barrier between Palestine and Transjordan or Syria (including Hauran), and that consequently imports from these countries will continue so long as market prices render them profitable. However, the local farmer is quite prepared, with the natural protection due to transport charges, to compete with grain produced on a system similar to his own. His fear is of the grain produced by large scale cultivation in the great wheat centres of the world. There is still a remainder of imports which he might replace by local wheat, but this additional quantity could be raised only by increasing the area under cultivation or by more intensive cultivation. Palestine is not a large country containing vast tracts of land suitable for economical mass production of cereals or vast grazing lands for flocks and herds. There is little cultivable land which remains uncultivated except in the plains of Beersheba, the Jordan Valley and the Huleh Area all of which require large capital expenditure for irrigation and improvement; and it is yet to be proved whether from the point of

59.

view of profitable agriculture alone, the expenditure
of large sums of capital on these lands is justifiable.
The cultivable land of Palestine is impoverished,
and the cultivator has not the necessary means to
undertake its improvement. Moreover, the present
system of farming seems to be designed primarily
to meet the needs of the farmer's own family, and
does not attempt to cater either for the local or
the foreign market. To effect any radical change
would be a matter of time and careful direction.
The principal difficulty here, as in most other
countries, is the general lack of organisation of
cultivation and of marketing, and the reluctance
of credit institutions to finance agriculturists.
There is a great need for the training of cultivators
in simple and economical methods of cultivation.
Intermittent efforts in a small way have been made
by Government in this direction by the establishment
of experimental stations and village plots, and
Jewish Training Institutions have done much; but
their influence over the bulk of the country is not
felt. Little has been done in spite of the example
of Jewish Societies to consolidate or create markets
for local produce. The cultivator has no credit
facilities to save him from the necessity of resort
to money-lenders. In consequence, he is unable
to choose and to await the best market, because the
bulk of his crop is seized by the money-lender, as

60.

soon as it appears on the threshing floor, in settlement of loans at usurious rates of interest. Having thus lost the bulk of his crop, the farmer has again to apply to the money-lender, who is often a grain merchant, for seed for the following season and for the means of subsistence of his family. He needs credit facilities - within his capacity to repay - to enable him to avoid this disastrous arrangement. He can then be taught to market his produce in the most economic way. In other words the foremost need of the agricultural industry is rationalisation. The claims of agriculture, which provides the fundamental necessaries of human and animal existence, cannot be overlooked. The rural population, which forms the bulk of the indigenous population, could not easily be industrialised even if there were industries to absorb it. It is therefore essential to secure to this rural population in its present occupation at least the minimum of subsistence.

Financial situation of the Arab farmer prior to 1929.

66. We may now turn to the financial situation of the Arab farmer. In the absence of reliable data, it has been difficult to check the information provided in the answers to the questionnaire. But whatever may be thought of individual items, it is the view of the Committee that, up till the middle of 1929, the net income of the average agricultural

61.

family has been between £P.25 and £P.30, and that the family has contrived to live on this income. It is clear, however, that there must have been many families less favourably situated, who have been obliged either to lower their standard of living or to fall into debt. The figures quoted for debt indicate that recourse has often been had to the latter alternative. Part of this debt is doubtless due to improvidence and extravagance, but the bulk of it must have gone to pay for costs of production, cost of living, and part payment of capital and of interest on previous debts. Little of it appears to have been devoted to capital improvements. If the average debt of the 21,066 families is uniform over the whole country, the total debt amounts to some £P.2,000,000. It is interesting to note that the security for such a debt would be covered by the sum of the values of the annual produce of the country and of the agricultural stock. The position appears to have been similar before the War, except that the sums involved were much smaller. During the War and for a few years after it, prices were very high. The farmer as a rule seems to have cleared off his debts and to have become comparatively prosperous. His standard of living improved accordingly. Unfortunately, he came to look upon the abnormal war-time prices as normal, and when prices began to fall to their natural level, it took time for him to adjust his

62.

outlook or his standard of living to meet the changed conditions. Consequently he began again to borrow, and more heavily than before, while the money-lender was imprudent enough to advance unduly large sums. Whenever the time came for repayment the farmer was unable to pay more than a fraction of the amount due, and was obliged to renew the bulk of the loan at an exorbitant rate of interest. A rate of 30% per annum is perhaps the commonest, but 50% for three months is not unusual. The result is that many farmers now owe sums that are quite beyond their capacity to pay. In justice to the money-lender it must be recognised that, in default of other sources of credit, he has performed a certain service to agriculture; and that, from an economic standpoint the inadequate security for his loans justified relatively high rates of interest. For many of the transactions of money-lenders, however, no justification can be offered.

Burden of taxation on the Arab farmer.

67.   The next point for consideration is the taxation of the agriculturist, which comprises werko tax, tithe and animal tax. The werko tax (£P.111,835) on land and buildings is mainly based on a pre-war assessment and its distribution is very unequal. The tithe (£P.247,949) since its commutation no longer varies with the quantities and prices of the farmer's produce, and as the

63.

amount of this tax is comparatively high, its inelasticity is a serious matter. The animal tax (£P.35,303) is primitive. In Table XXIX it has been seen that the owner-cultivator of rural property pays in werko, as owner, 10.4% of the rental value of his property. But he also pays, as cultivator, 19% of his net income from the use of land. Table XXX shows that the combined payments represent 10.2% of his gross income, which (if rent be 30% of gross income) is equivalent to 34% of the rental value of his property. This percentage may be compared with the percentages paid by owners of urban property in werko tax, when the property is not subject to tithe, or in urban property tax. The werko tax on urban property is in general 10 per mille (excluding additions) of capital value. If capital value be converted to annual value at the official rate of 6% (equivalent to some 17 years' purchase), the payment becomes one-sixth of the annual rental value. The maximum payment under the Urban Property Tax Ordinance is 10% of rental value. The werko assessment is known to be defective, and experience has shown that when werko has been replaced by urban property tax, the latter tax of some 9% on net annual values yields nearly as much as the werko tax on a nominally higher basis. The comparison may therefore be said to lie between the farmer paying

64.

taxes to an amount equivalent to 34% of his rent, and the urban owner of immovable property paying less than 10%. There is no direct taxation in urban areas to counter-balance the 19% of net income paid by the cultivator in tithe and animal tax.

Present financial situation of the Arab farmer.

68.   All the arguments and the figures that have been used hitherto have been based on the average prices for the commuted tithe which have been sufficiently accurate till about a year ago. A fall in the prices of agricultural produce then began, which has continued ever since and has become rapid during the past three or four months. The price of wheat in June, 1929, was about £P.12 a ton; it is now (in June, 1930) £P.6-7. For similar dates, the price of barley has fallen from over £P.6 to £P.3; that of olive oil from £P.77 to £P.40. Other prices have followed suit, and it may be said that the value of agricultural produce is now roughly half of what it was a year ago. The fall in prices appears to be mainly due to world over-production and the dumping of foreign produce which has resulted. The market is glutted, and the farmer is unable to sell his surplus produce. He is particularly affected by the lack of demand for wheat and for olive oil, as these commodities are his principal means of barter, of transactions with money-lenders and of realising cash to pay

65.

tithes and taxes. Similarly the money-lender holds as security more wheat and oil than he can dispose of, and is therefore unwilling to increase his commitments by further advances. As has been pointed out earlier, the supply of local wheat available for the market is very limited, and consequently market prices are easily affected by imports. It may be argued that, as the farmer is unable to sell his wheat, he will be better supplied with seed for the next season and will be able to raise his standard of living by eating a better quality of bread. But this enforced improvement of his standard of living will really be at the expense of his creditors, and will render his position, which is already difficult, little short of desparate. In the appreciation of the financial situation of the farmer, it was emphasized that the figures applied only to the period previous to the middle of 1929. At the present time, when the prices of agricultural produce have fallen approximately by half, his situation is far less favourable. The net income of an average family has now fallen from £P.27.5 to some £P.16.5; the net income of a tenant farmer of 100 dunams has fallen (since some of his expenses are fixed) from £P.20 to some £P.9; while the percentage that tithe and animal tax constitute of the net return from the use of land has risen from 19% to some 32%. It would appear clear that

66.

the farmer's position is serious, and that something must be done to relieve at once his immediate difficulties and in the near future to raise his income to its former level.

The Musha'a System of land tenure.

69.   It remains to consider what is perhaps the greatest obstacle to agricultural progress in Palestine, viz. the musha'a system of land tenure. Under this system the village lands are divided into the requisite number of shares, and each share-holder is allotted the number of shares or the fraction of a share to which he is entitled. At the end of a prescribed period - usually two years, to suit the crop rotation - the shares are re-allotted, and each share-holder moves to a fresh holding. Consequently, no one has any inducement to improve his land; for the fruits of his industry would be reaped by his successor in the holding at the bi-ennial re-allotment, while he himself would probably have to suffer from the negligence of his predecessor in his new holding. The system misses the advantages alike of individualism and of co-operation.   While it remains, it is useless to expect that land will be weeded or fertilised, that trees will be planted, or, in a word, that any development will take place. In addition, legal transactions in respect of musha'a land are difficult, and consequently it

67.

is difficult to raise a loan on the security of a share in musha'a land. The estimates of the relative cultivated areas of musha'a and mafruz land obtained by the Musha'a Land Committee in 1923 for 753 villages, and the estimates obtained by the present Committee for 104 villages (66 in the Northern District, 14 in the Jerusalem Division, and 24 in the Southern District) are summarised in the following table:-

TABLE XLVIII

District	Musha'a Committee				Present Committee			
	Musha'a		Mafruz		Musha'a		Mafruz	
	1000 dunams	%	1000 dunams	%	1000 dunams	%	1000 dunams	%
Northern District	743	37	1279	63	185	29	449	71
Jerusalem Division	22	5	407	95	32	28	83	72
Southern District	1950	80	475	20	292	69	129	31
Total	2715	56	2161	44	509	44	661	56

The later results show a rather lower proportion than the former of musha'a land; but the later result is affected by the large proportion of villages in the Northern District and Jerusalem Division (80 out of 104), where the proportion is much lower than in the Southern District. From a comparison of the two sets of estimates, it may be surmised that something like half of the

68.

cultivable land of the country is musha'a.

70. The large majority of musha'a share-holders would welcome a permanent partition, but the difficulties and expenses of arranging in advance of Land Settlement a partition that could be accepted by the Land Registry are prohibitive. Partition may be effected in either of two eays. First, all the interested parties may execute a deed of partition. The difficulty of securing the consent of each of the interested parties (some of whom may be living in America) is so great as to render this method impracticable. Secondly, any co-owner may apply to the Courts for partition; but it seems probable that he might have to pay the whole cost of survey, and in addition he would bring upon himself and his fellow-owners a number of other expenses. The Musha'a Land Commission recorded that a musha'a share-holder might well have to pay on partition:-

(a) the cost of a certificate of succession (Ilam Shara'i),

(b) 5% of the market value of his land to establish either original registration or subsequent purchase,

(c) survey charges amounting to several pounds,

(d) a registration fee for partition of ½% of the registered werko value of his land, and

(e) in the future, an increase of 100% on his werko.

69.

It is hardly surprising that the partition of musha'a land has not progressed.

Financial situation of the Jewish farmer prior to 1929.

71.   The financial position of the Jewish farmer is in some ways harder to determine even than that of the Arab farmer. As has been noted earlier the Executive of the Jewish Agency for Palestine themselves admitted their inability to offer any direct estimates for costs of production. Further, the figures for interest and amortisation charges on loans for capital expenditure are not available. On the whole, we are of the opinion that the gross income of a Jewish farmer is roughly double that of an Arab farmer with a similar holding. On the other hand, his costs of production and his cost of living are certainly much higher, and it seems doubtful whether his net surplus after meeting the costs of production and the cost of living and similar expenses is much greater than that of the Arab farmer. The initial cost of his holding and the costs of developing it have involved him in an expenditure quite out of proportion to his income; while the Arab farmer has long been established on his land and has incurred little expenditure in developing it. In consequence the Jewish farmer must find large sums for improvements to his holding and for debt charges. On the other hand, Jewish agriculture is highly organised and numerous

70.

facilities exist for obtaining credit. To sum
up, the Jewish farmer is better equipped for the
operations of agriculture than is the Arab farmer,
his standard of living is higher and he enjoys
social and cultural amenities that are unknown
to the Arab farmer. On the other hand, he appears
to be weighed down with a heavy burden of debt
which we have no means of estimating. As much
Jewish agriculture is at present in an experimental
stage, we do not feel prepared to commit ourselves
to any more definite expression of opinion.

Burden of taxation on the Jewish farmer.

72. We may now consider the burden of taxation
on the Jewish farmer. The werko that he pays in the
case of post-war settlements is based on re-assessed
values, and therefore, in spite of his consequent
exemption from the War-time additions to the werko,
his payments are probably relatively heavier than
those of the Arab. On the other hand the Jewish
farmer in the newer settlements probably benefits
from the fact that the commuted tithe was based
on the lower productivity of Arab farming. It is
perhaps easier to appreciate the burden of taxation
on the Jewish farmer by looking at the matter in
a different way. We have estimated that his
gross income which largely determines the present
amount of his taxation is double that of the
Arab farmer of a similar holding. His cost of
living, which represents his net income, is more

71.

than double that of the Arab farmer. It follows that the burden of taxation upon the Jewish farmer in relation to his net income is less than the burden upon the Arab farmer in relation to his. This view is confirmed by the attitude of settlers who gave the Committee to understand that taxation was relatively an unimportant item in their expenditure.

Present financial situation of the Jewish farmer.

73.   It remains to state that the Jewish farmer, like the Arab farmer, has suffered from the recent fall in prices of agricultural produce. In one settlement, however, the Committee was informed that this fall in prices was an advantage, not a disadvantage, because prices of other commodities had also tended to fall, and because at the lower value of his produce the farmer could afford to improve his standard of living. For example, when eggs are expensive the farmer feels obliged to keep them all for the market, but when they are cheap he feels justified in using them for family consumption. We have no evidence, however, that this view is at all common, and we are of opinion that the ordinary Jewish farmer, no less than the Arab farmer, would welcome a rise in the prices of agricultural produce.

72.

RECOMMENDATIONS

<u>Necessity of a Marketing Board and of Village Co-operative Bodies.</u>

74.   From the picture that we have drawn of agriculture in Palestine it is abundantly clear that the net income of the farmer must somehow be increased.   To achieve this result one of two things must be done.   Either the costs of production must be reduced, or the gross income must be increased.   We are satisfied that the methods of Arab agriculture in this country are so primitive that it is impossible to reduce the primary costs of production.   There remains the other alternative. Gross produce may be increased, either by improving the present system of farming or by introducing a better one.   By fertilising the impoverished land, it may be possible to secure a yield of 120 kilogrammes of wheat per dunam where now it is only 60.   By replacing part of the cereal cultivation by plantations - irrigated or unirrigated, or by adopting a system of dairy-farming or mixed farming, the gross income of a holding may be greatly increased; but the danger of over-production must be avoided. It is outside our province to consider which of these or other methods should be adopted, but we are convinced that something must be done, and that Government should be in a position to tell the farmer what he should do.   To this end, it is probable that much experimental work must be done

73.

and that much instruction and, above all, demonstration, must be given; but we strongly deprecate any attempts to produce the desired result which might end in tempting the farmer away from the soil and turning him into a black-coated effendi. There would also appear to be need for something of the nature of a Marketing Board to advise the farmer in the disposal of his produce.

75. Palestine has no facilities for large scale production, and must always be a country of small holders. We consider, however, that some of the advantage of large scale production should be secured by co-operation among the small holders. It may be argued that the mentality of the country is not favourable to co-operation and that such efforts as have been made in this direction have met with scant success. On the other hand, the "kafalah mutasalsilah" (mutual guarantee) is familiar to villagers. We regard the matter as so important that we recommend the appointment of an expert to advise the Government on the methods of achieving this object. An opening might be found in the utilisation of village co-operative bodies, on the lines of the system adopted in Cyprus, to deal with the issue of agricultural loans, to supervise the use of them and to be responsible for their repayment; and the effect of such co-operative action might serve as the thin end of a wedge to open the way to co-operation in the purchase of agricultural requirements, in the improvement of village cultivation and in the marketing of village produce.

74.

We are of opinion that the most efficacious method of dealing with the individual farmer is through the medium of some sort of village co-operative body; and we consider that, whatever difficulties may lie in the way of co-operative action, an effort must be made to surmount them.

Income tax and Land tax.

76. From the figures obtained to show the burden of taxation on agriculture, it is clear that the Arab farmer is paying far more than his share of direct taxation. The most equitable form of direct taxation, in our opinion, is a graduated income tax not only on agriculture but on all classes of income. At present many classes of income entirely escape direct taxation, and some of these classes are far better fitted than is agriculture to bear the burden. It may be added that the idea of income tax is not new to the country as it is in effect only a development of the old "temettu tax". We recognise, however, that the practical difficulties of assessing small incomes from income tax would be almost insuperable. We therefore consider that werko tax and tithe should be replaced by a low land tax designed to secure an equitable share of revenue from small incomes, and that income tax should be levied only on incomes above a certain minimum. To avoid double taxation, any income subject to land tax would of

75.

course be exempted from a corresponding amount of income tax. Animal tax should, we think, be retained for the present to secure a proper contribution from the owners of stock who possess no land of their own but graze their flocks and herds on other land, usually State land. When the income tax is in full operation, the question of retaining or abolishing this tax can be further considered. It is generally accepted that the incidence of direct taxation on immovable property and of indirect taxation on commodities in ordinary use is satisfactorily dispersed over the whole community provided that the former tax is not greater than can easily be paid even in bad years. We are unable to accept the suggestion frequently made that the sacrifice of revenue involved by the substitution of a low land tax for the present tithe and werko should be made good by additional Customs duties. The Customs Tariff is already high and careful examination by those concerned has shown that there is no possibility of substantially increasing the yield from this source. It should further be noted that indirect taxation tends to fall relatively heavier on the poor man than on the rich. Through a land tax and a Customs Tariff small incomes would make their contribution to Government revenue, while income tax would secure a further and progressive contribution from larger incomes. It may be noted

76. that the suggested substitution of a low land tax and an income tax for the present method of taxation would afford relief to agriculturists during the period of development of their land. We are not prepared to share the fears that have been expressed to us from certain quarters that an income tax, though at a reasonable rate, would tend to drive away any considerable amounts of capital that might otherwise have been invested in the country, particularly if the proceeds of the income tax are used to reduce other forms of taxation. The Committee recommends that the services of an official from England with experience in income tax assessment should be obtained for the purpose of advising Government on the introduction of an income tax.

77. A fiscal survey is in progress for the assessment of a fixed land tax on annual value in replacement of the werko tax and the tithe; and the Commissioner of Lands informed the Committee that the fiscal survey would be completed in 1932. It therefore appears that it will not be possible to impose a land tax till then. We recommend, however, that an attempt should be made to introduce the income tax at an earlier date to permit the rectification of present inequalities of taxation between urban and rural areas.

77.

Interim measures for partial relief of rural tax-payer

78.   It is obvious that the introduction of an income tax and, as has been noted, of a land tax must be a matter of time. We have therefore considered an interim measure for the partial relief of the rural tax-payer. The comparison between their payments at the present time is shown below:-

	Urban Population £P.	Rural Population £P.
Werko Tax	28,000	112,000
Urban Property Tax	91,000	-
Animal Tax	1,000	35,000
Commuted Tithe	11,000	243,000
Tithe	-	5,000
Total	131,000	395,000

These will shortly be adjusted as follows:-

Urban Population £P.		Rural Population £P.	
Urban Property Tax	119,000	Werko	112,000
Animal Tax	1,000	Animal Tax	35,000
Commuted Tithe	11,000	Commuted Tithe	248,000
Total	131,000		395,000

79.   The urban property tax represents something under 10% of the annual value of immovable property

78.

in urban areas. With the addition of the payments for animal tax and for commuted tithe this proportion is slightly increased. The proportion remains, however, far below the 34% of rental value which has been estimated for rural taxation. In principle, therefore, we think that the commuted tithe should be reduced to such a rate that the total burden would be equally divided between the two sections of the population, so that each should pay at the rate of 22%. To achieve this object, however, it would be necessary to increase the rate of urban property tax by more than 100%, since the urban population would also benefit slightly by the reduction of commuted tithe. Such an increase in one step we feel to be out of the question. We therefore recommend that as a partial measure the tithe should from 1st January, 1931, be reduced by one quarter to $7\frac{1}{2}$%, and that the rate of urban property tax should be increased to meet the deficit. The resulting position would be as follows:-

	Urban Population £P.		Rural Population £P.
Urban Property Tax (at about 15%)	183,800	Werko	112,000
Animal Tax	1,000	Animal Tax	35,000
Commuted Tithe	8,200	Commuted Tithe (at $7\frac{1}{2}$%)	186,000
Total	193,000		333,000
		Total £P.526,000	

79.

On this arrangement, the total revenue would remain unaltered, but the rural population would be relieved to the amount of £P.62,000, while the urban population would make up the difference. As incomes below a certain minimum are exempted from urban property tax, it is improbable that the addition to this tax would cause any serious hardship.

80. We further recommend that the proceeds of the income tax, as soon as they become available, should be used first to reduce the commuted tithe to such a rate that the rate of taxation on rural and urban areas would be equal, and then to reduce this equal rate on both sections to the level of the future low land tax.

81. We have yet a further recommendation to make. The position of the agriculturist at the present time seems to us so serious that it cannot await the relief proposed for next year. We have already recorded that the prices of winter crops have fallen some 50% since the corresponding date last year, and that even at these low prices there is no demand for them. In consequence the farmer is unable to pay his tithe. We therefore recommend that the portion of commuted tithe based on winter crops should in 1930 be reduced from 10% to 5%. As the tithe on winter crops represent at least two-thirds of the total tithe, this reduction would

80.

be tantamount to a reduction of the whole commuted tithe from 10% to 6.2/3%. The sacrifice of tithe revenue involved is estimated, on the basis of average collections, at some £P.70,000. It is estimated that if the tithe had been collected on the old system, the loss resulting from the lower prices of cereals would have been approximately that sum. It is important that, if these proposals are approved, immediate action should be taken, since the first instalment of the tithe will very shortly fall due. We also recommend that consideration should later be given to the further reduction of the commuted tithe in 1930 on that portion of the commuted tithe based on summer crops should the prices of summer crops remain low.

Credit facilities.

82. The Committee hesitates to recommend the provision by Government aid of credit facilities for agriculturists, since it has been shown that the average farmer is hardly in a position to repay any loan from net profits. There are, however, farmers with incomes sufficiently above the average to leave a margin for repayments, who need advances to tide them over to the next harvest, or to enable them to improve their land. There are others who though their incomes do not for the moment leave any margin for repayment could increase their incomes sufficiently to permit of repayment if they could

81.

find the necessary funds for improving their cultivation or to free themselves from a burden of debt at high interest. These classes would benefit by credit facilities, but as a rule only their fellow-villagers would be in a position to know if they were suitable persons to receive loans. We recommend therefore that Government should provide credit facilities, but that loans should normally be given through the medium of a village group of a co-operative nature, which would be responsible for the issue, control and repayment of the loans. Apart from the issue of loans for agricultural purposes, we see no objection to the issue through these groups of loans for the repayment of loans from money-lenders at usurious rates, provided that adequate security is offered for such loans. It is essential that loans for improvement should be for comparatively long periods and at a low rate of interest. It would sometimes be necessary to require as a condition for a loan that the borrower should undertake prescribed improvements to his land of a nature to enable him to repay the loan in due course. We therefore recommend that the Government should take steps to organise co-operative groups for dealing with village loans and to finance these groups. Care should of course be taken to avoid competition with local banks and other credit institutions.

83.   It is obvious that time is needed to organise and to finance village co-operative groups. Meanwhile the economic situation of the farmer calls for immediate relief. We therefore recommend that, as an emergency measure, the Government should issue £P.100,000 in short term loans to small farmers to enable them to cultivate their land in the coming season. Since the failure of demand for agricultural produce, which is the principal cause of the present crisis, has at least ensured that the supply of seed will be ample, we hope that this amount may be sufficient for the purpose indicated, though obviously it will not provide loans to meet the payment of debts to money-lenders nor for any large development schemes.

Development of foreign markets for Palestine Produce.

84.   Various complaints were received that the farmer was greatly handicapped in the marketing of his produce by protective tariffs abroad, especially in Egypt. It is natural that Egypt should want to protect her own home markets in the same way as Palestine is trying to protect hers. The Committee feels that Government should enter into commercial negotiations with Egypt for the entry of Palestine agricultural produce on at least as favourable conditions as existed before the introduction of the new Egyptian Tariff. This is immediately essential as the export of melons to Egypt may be

83.

adversely affected by the increased tariff. We understand that the Department of Agriculture is already negotiating with Egypt with regard to the importation of the coming Palestine melon crop. Every effort should be made in other quarters also to negotiate foreign markets for Palestine agricultural produce on such terms that any reciprocal arrangements may interfere as little as possible with the main Palestine home industries. Difficulties may arise owing to the restriction imposed by the Mandate against discrimination between signatory Powers, but the Mandate permits at least of the establishment of a Customs union among adjacent Arab countries. Negotiations might conveniently be conducted by the Marketing Board which we have suggested.

<u>Protective Duties against foreign imports of agricultural produce into Palestine.</u>

85.   The demand for relief from foreign tariffs is accompanied by a much stronger demand for protective duties against foreign imports of agricultural produce into Palestine. The Committee dislikes protective measures, but feels that the present economic situation is so serious that even this expedient must be tried. We propose that the measures should be applied in the first place only to the principal commodities of wheat, which must of course be accompanied by flour, olive oil and sesame seed. In our opinion protective duties

84.

would not stop the present dumping of foreign wheat, flour and olive oil unless they were high enough entirely to stop importation. The Committee therefore recommends that the importation of foreign wheat and flour should be prohibited except by flour mills or bakeries under licence, and that the present specific duties on wheat and flour should be raised 50%. As the present specific duty on wheat is estimated to be 20 - 25% ad valorem, the new duty would represent some 33.1/3% ad valorem. Licences for importation would be issued by the Customs Authorities in accordance with allotments by the Standing Committee on Commerce and Industry having regard to the requirements for town consumption. Licences would be issued for all consignments now in transit, and after that, allotments would be made at the discretion of the Standing Committee on Commerce and Industry having regard to last year's consumption of foreign wheat and flour and the requirements of any new industries. There are five flour mills which import wheat or mill largely for urban consumption and only a few bakeries import flour direct. It might be necessary to force bakers to use a larger proportion of local flour in the making of bread by restricting importations. The effects of these measures will not be apparent until the local stocks of imported wheat have been absorbed. The questions of sufficiency of supply

and of prices must be carefully watched, and in
view of the large world supply there should be
no difficulty in replenishing the market by removing
the ban on importation should the necessity arise.
Municipalities might use their powers under the
Turkish Law to prevent profiteering by flour-millers
and bakers. Should these measures result in the
importation of foreign wheat via Syria, the Syrian
Government might be approached with a view to their
assimilating their tariff on imported wheat and
flour to that of Palestine, and to their introducing
a system of licences for the export into Palestine
of Syrian wheat and flour. We understand that
importation of certain foreign agricultural produce
is prohibited in France when the local market prices
have fallen below a certain point, and that in
Germany importation is permitted only subject to
the export of a corresponding quantity of the same
kind of produce. We do not think that either of
these methods would be applicable to Palestine wheat,
as there is no export market for it and to determine
the saturation point of the local market would be
difficult.

86. The Committee also recommends the prohibition
of the importation of unrefined olive oil until
further notice. It would be difficult to control
importation by a system of licensing owing to the
large number of importers; and a protective duty
would not be effective unless it were made prohibitive.

86.

As the local produce is suitable and ample for local needs, the Committee recommends the prohibition of importation of unrefined olive oil and that the question of the removal of this ban be considered periodically or when the local price returns to normal. It would, of course, be necessary to admit into Palestine any consignments in transit.

87. It has been noted that the producers of sesame oil appear to prefer imported sesame seed to the local sesame seed. This preference cannot be due to the poor quality of the local sesame seed for we are informed that the local sesame seed is inferior to none. Nor can it be supposed that the quality is too high, since the figures for 1929 show that the average price of imported sesame is rather higher than that of exported sesame. It seems reasonable therefore that the producers should pay for their preference. Accordingly the Committee recommends that an import duty of 3 mils a kilogramme, as advocated by the Standing Committee on Commerce and Industry, should be imposed on sesame seed. It is perhaps desirable to emphasize that this recommendation applies only to sesame seed, not to sesame oil.

Abolition of musha'a system of tenure.

88. We have pointed out earlier that no improvements can take place in something like half the area of the country until the musha'a system

87.

of tenure is abolished. We understand from the
Commissioner of Lands that it is not feasible to
undertake in advance of the general settlement
the sporadic partitioning of musha'a villages
in various parts of the country; and without
the facilities of settlement operations we do not
think that partitioning can satisfactorily be
effected. We are glad to learn, however, from
the same officer that the bulk of the settlement
may perhaps be completed at a far earlier date
than has hitherto been anticipated. We hope that
this possibility will eventualise and that
Government will then take steps compulsorily
to enforce partition of all musha'a villages.
Such a measure of compulsion would be welcomed
by a vast majority of the musha'a share-holders
as enabling them to overcome the obstacle, at
present insurmountable, created by a handful of
objectors. We are convinced that unless this
obstacle to development is removed, and the
development thus made practicable actually occurs,
so that the economic situation of the farmer is
substantially improved, such fiscal measures as
we have recommended must be no more than palliatives
of a disease that they cannot cure.

88.

SUMMARY OF RECOMMENDATIONS

89.   We summarise our recommendations as under:-

(A) Government should carry out experimental work and demonstrations and give instruction to villagers in better methods of farming, and should appoint an Advisory Marketing Board to advise the farmer on the disposal of his products (Para.74).

(B) Establishment of village co-operative bodies to deal with the issue of agricultural loans and later with the purchase of agricultural requirements, the improvement of village cultivation and the marketing of village produce. The appointment of an expert to advise Government on the methods of achieving this object (Para.75).

(C) Replacement of werko tax and tithe by a low land tax on annual value designed to secure an equitable share of revenue from small incomes, and the introduction of a progressive income tax on high incomes from which shall be deducted, to avoid double taxation, an amount corresponding to the land tax.   The appointment of an officer from England with experience in income tax

89.

assessment for the purpose of advising Government on the introduction of an income tax (Paras. 76 and 77).

(D) Consideration should be given to abolition of the animal tax when income tax is in full operation (Para. 76).

(E) Partial relief of the rural tax-payer from the 1st of January, 1931, by the reduction of the commuted tithe by one quarter to 7½%, and the increase in the rate of urban property tax to meet the deficit (Para. 79).

(F) Proceeds of the income tax as soon as they become available to be used first to reduce the commuted tithe to such a rate that the rate of taxation in rural and urban areas shall be equal, and then to reduce this equal rate in both urban and rural areas to the level of the future land tax (Para. 80).

(G) Relief in 1930 of the rural tax-payer by the reduction of the commuted tithe by one-third to 6.2/3%, representing 50% of the portion of the commuted tithe based on winter crops (Para. 81).

(H) Consideration should be given later to the further reduction in 1930 of the commuted tithe in respect of the portion based on

90.

summer crops should the prices of summer crops remain low (Para.81).

(I) Government should provide credit facilities, and loans normally should be issued through the medium of a village group of co-operative nature (Para.82).

(J) As an emergency measure in 1930 Government should issue £P.100,000 in short term loans to small farmers to enable them to cultivate their land in the coming season (Para.83)

(K) Negotiation of commercial treaties for development of foreign markets for Palestine produce (Para.84).

(L) Protection of local agricultural produce against foreign imports into Palestine (Paras.85, 86 and 87) -

   (i) Temporary prohibition of the importation of foreign wheat and flour except by flour mills and bakeries under licence with the object if necessary of forcing bakers to use in the making of bread a larger proportion of flour made from local wheat; and the increase in present specific duties on wheat and flour by 50%

   (ii) Prohibition of the importation of unrefined olive oil until further notice; and

   (iii) Imposition of a specific duty of 3 mils per kilogramme on imported foreign sesame seed.

(M) The partitioning of musha'a land (Para.88).

90. We have endeavoured to confine ourselves to strictly fiscal measures, and have therefore avoided as far as possible all purely technical questions of agriculture. We have felt, however, that our picture of the economic situation would be incomplete if we did not touch in general upon the need for rationalisation of agriculture and also upon the need for partitioning musha'a land. We have therefore ventured to include recommendations on these two matters, which, though not properly of a fiscal nature, are of first-class economic importance.

91. Finally, we desire to record our appreciation of the services of Mr. J.C. Gress and Mr. V.N. Levi of the Treasury who have been Joint Secretaries to the Committee. We desire to pay our tribute to their ability and diligence in the compilation of statistical information and in the preparation of this report.

We have the honour to be,

Sir,

Your obedient Servants,

Acting Treasurer, Chairman.

Assistant District Commissioner,
Southern District.

92.

[signature]
Area Officer, Nazareth Area.

[signature]
Area Officer, Nablus Area.

[signature]
Area Officer, Haifa Area

[signature] [signature]
Senior Assistant Treasurer.   Area Officer, West Area,
  Southern District

[signature] [signature]
Junior Assistant Treasurer.   Area Officer, Jerusalem Division.

3rd July, 1930.

TB.

Appendix A.

LIST OF THE 104 REPRESENTATIVE ARAB VILLAGES.

Nazareth Area (24 Villages).

Beisan Sub-District -

1. Murassas
2. Qumieh
3. Samriyeh
4. Sirreen
5. Taybeh

Nazareth Sub-District -

1. Beineh
2. Iksal
3. Kefr Kenna
4. Mujeidel
5. Reineh
6. Saffouri

Safad Sub-District -

1. Farradeh
2. Fir'im
3. Khalsa
4. Meiroun
5. Na'ameh
6. Ras El-Ahmar
7. Tleil

Tiberias Sub-District -

1. Abediyeh
2. Hittin
3. Kefr Kama
4. Lubieh
5. Mughar
6. Samakh

2.   Appendix A.(cont'd).

Haifa Area (20 Villages).

Acre Sub-District —

1. Bassa
2. Damoun
3. Julis
4. Kufr Yassif
5. Manshieh
6. Mejd El Kroum
7. Rameh
8. Sejour
9. Smeiriyeh
10. Tarshiha

Haifa Sub-District -

1. Arab El-Awadine
2. Arab El-Tawatha
3. Beled El-Sheikh
4. Esfia
5. Ijzim
6. Kannir
7. Kireh Keimoun
8. Kufr Lam
9. Tantourah
10. Tireh

Nablus Area (22 Villages).

Jenin Sub-District -

1. Arrabeh
2. Deir Ghazaleh
3. Jalboun
4. Mughair
5. Silet Daher

3. Appendix A.(cont'd).

<u>Jenin Sub-District (continued)</u> -

   6. Silet Hartieh

   7. Yabad

   8. Zirin

<u>Nablus Sub-District</u> -

   1. Bidia

   2. Burka

   3. Jamain

   4. Tallouza

   5. Telfit

   6. Till

   7. Toubas

<u>Tulkarem Sub-District</u> -

   1. Anebta

   2. Faraon

   3. Irtah

   4. Kakoun

   5. Kalkilia

   6. Rameen

   7. Showeikeh

   <u>West Area, Southern District (8 Villages)</u>.

<u>Jaffa Sub-District</u> -

   1. Beit Dajan

   2. Kefr Ana

   3. Kheiriyeh

   4. Saqieh

<u>Ramleh Sub-District</u> -

   1. Deir Qaddis

   2. Iqzazeh

   3. Kubab

   4. Na'ani

4.   Appendix A.(cont'd).

East Area, Southern District (16 Villages).

Gaza Sub-District -
1. Barbara
2. Dimra
3. Ibdis
4. Isdud
5. Jabalia
6. Kokaba
7. Mesmiyeh El-Kabira
8. Yasour

Hebron Sub-District -
1. Ajjour
2. Beit Jibrin
3. Dahriyeh
4. Dawaymeh
5. Halhul
6. Idna
7. Samu'
8. Yatta

Jerusalem Division (14 Villages).

Bethlehem Sub-District -
1. Beit Fajjar
2. Khader

Jericho Sub-District -
1. Jericho

Jerusalem Sub-District -
1. Ain Karem
2. Aizarieh
3. Ammas
4. Yalo

5. <u>Appendix A.(cont'd)</u>.

<u>Ramallah Sub-District</u> -

1. Ain Yabrud
2. Atara
3. Bait Ello
4. Bait Likia
5. Bait Rima
6. Bir Zait
7. Deir Dibwan

5.08

97060

HIGH COMMISSIONER FOR PALESTINE,
JERUSALEM.

CONFIDENTIAL.
Reference No. F/27/32.

13 August, 1932.

Sir,

    I have the honour to refer to the correspondence ending with my Confidential despatch of the 27th January, 1932, with regard to the appointment of a Committee to consider proposals for the introduction of a Land Tax to replace the House and Land Tax and the Commuted Tithe and to forward herewith, in triplicate, a copy of the Committee's Report.

Enclosure I.

Enclosure II.

    2. I also forward a copy of a minute by the Acting Treasurer setting out the results of a discussion between the Commissioner of Lands, the District Commissioner, Southern District, the Treasurer and the Deputy Treasurer, which I thought it desirable should take place with a view to attaining agreement as far as possible between the officers mainly concerned in respect of the principal recommendations of the Committee; and a statement of the decisions which I took in Executive Council after considering the Report in the light of those results.

Enclosure III.

    3. I shall submit for your consideration in due course the draft of the necessary legislation to give effect to the recommendations in the Report as modified by my decisions in Executive Council.

    I have the honour to be, Sir,
Your most obedient, humble servant,

Arthur Wauchope
HIGH COMMISSIONER
FOR PALESTINE.

The Right Honourable
  Sir Philip Cunliffe-Lister, G.B.E., M.P., etc., etc.,
    His Majesty's Principal Secretary of State
        for the Colonies.

REPORT OF THE RURAL TAXATION COMMITTEE.

Terms of reference.

On December 23rd, 1931, His Excellency the High Commissioner appointed a Committee with the following terms of reference:-

" In view of the inequitable incidence of the present system of taxation on agricultural land, and of the urgent need for its reform, to consider the proposals which have been made to Government for the substitution of a new form of Tax for the existing Werku and Commuted Tithe, and, after taking into account the observations on this subject contained in paragraph 271 of the Report of the Financial Commission, to submit detailed proposals to Government with a view to the introduction of the proposed alteration in the system of taxation at as early a date and over as wide an area as may be found to be feasible."

I. PROCEDURE.

1.   The Committee held its first meeting on January 7th, 1932, and considered the lines on which it should proceed. Provisional agreement on general principles was reached, and outline proposals, covering the major points at issue, were drafted to form a basis for discussion with the public.

2.   The Committee then held a series of meetings in Jerusalem, Jaffa, Haifa, Nablus and Tiberias with representative agriculturists from the respective areas. At the first meeting in each centre, copies of the proposals (in the appropriate languages) were circulated, and a full explanation of their nature was

given orally. Those present were invited to ask questions on any points that were not clear. They were then requested to meet the Committee again about a fortnight later, to furnish certain information desired by the Committee, to express their considered views on the proposals, and to put forward any alternative proposals of their own. At the second series of meetings the Committee went at length into figures of gross yield, costs of production, and relative values of various categories of land; obtained the views of the public on the outline proposals; and heard such other proposals as were put forward.

3. The Committee next met representatives of various public bodies, namely, the Arab Executive and the Muslim Congress, the Palestine Jewish Colonization Association, the Executive of the Jewish Agency and the officially constituted Agricultural Council. The Committee was thus able to obtain information from these different bodies, and to ascertain their views.

4. The Committee desires to record its appreciation of the cooperation afforded both by these public bodies and by the various individuals all over the country who devoted much time and trouble to the assistance of the Committee in its investigation. Without this cooperation and assistance the Committee would have had serious difficulty in preparing its report.

5. After completing the public inquiry, the Committee held further meetings to consider its views and to draft its report.

- 3 -

II. BASIC PRINCIPLES.

Replacement of Werku & Tithe by single tax.

6.   The bulk of the present Werku assessments were made a quarter of a century ago, and even when they were new, they were notoriously incorrect. With the lapse of time they have become still more incorrect. Those owners of immovable property who have not registered successions, sales or other transactions, even when such changes have occurred, continue to pay tax on an obsolete and unreliable assessment; while those who have duly registered their transactions have had their properties reassessed and pay on a much higher assessment.

7.   Commuted Tithe is based on annual estimates made in past years of the quantities of crops lying on the threshing-floors of villages or of fruit growing on their trees. Sometimes there was deliberate over-estimation or under-estimation. Sometimes crops were concealed from the estimators. Apart from any considerations of this sort, such estimates must by their nature be unreliable, and the fact that a large number of estimators had to be employed obviated any possibility of uniformity.

8.   Without going into further detail, it is clear that the existing Werku and Commuted Tithe must be inequitable in their incidence. The Committee recommends that both of them should be abolished and replaced by a single form of taxation.

9.   The Arab Executive held that all forms of agricultural taxation should be abolished for a period of twenty years at least, on the ground that in the past agriculture had paid far more than its proper share of taxation. Even a grove-owner with an income of LP.20,000

- 4 -

should be exempt from taxation. Any funds required by Government to replace the loss should be drawn from "Tmettu" and from increased Customs duty. A few individuals adopted the same view, but the great majority of opinion, as ascertained by the Committee, coincided with the opinion of the Committee.

Capital or annual value.

10. The new system of taxation might be based either on the capital value of land or on the value of the annual products of land. The present system affords precedent for either principle. For the purpose of a choice between the two, a capital value calculated at an arbitrary number of year's purchase from net annual value may obviously be ignored, and capital value may be interpreted as meaning market value.

Soil survey.

11. A proposal has been made for a valuation by means of soil survey. The proposal involves no new principle of valuation, but only a method; for a value can be assigned to the chemical constitution of soil only on the basis of the annual products of the soil or of its consequent market value. Experiments arranged by the Commissioner of Lands have shown that this method is much slower, and therefore more costly, than valuation by direct human judgment; and that the results of the two closely correspond. The Committee has found no demand for such a method of valuation, and does not recommend it.

Arbitrary assessment.

12. A proposal has also been made for the so-called arbitrary assessment of different qualities of land. It is immaterial whether the assessment be expressed in terms of money or in index numbers. It is clear that any such assessment would really be based on a rough estimate either of capital or of annual value.

- 5 -

The proposal does not therefore call for separate consideration.

Gross or net annual value.

13. A tax (or, more strictly, a revenue charge) on the annual value of land might be based either on gross or on net annual products. The Committee is of opinion that a tax on gross products is unsatisfactory, as it not only penalizes the cultivator who puts more work or more money into his land, but also obscures the true burden of taxation. Net annual products therefore afford a better basis.

Improved or unimproved value.

14. The new system of taxation might be based either on the present (improved) value or on the unimproved value of land. The Committee is of opinion that it is impracticable, whether by soil survey or other means, to determine the unimproved value of land. Even if it were practicable, the result of adopting such a basis (unless other taxation were introduced as well) would be to tax those who have not means to improve their lands as heavily in terms of money as those who have, and in proportion to their respective incomes much more heavily. The Committee has found no demand from the public for such a system, and has confined itself to consideration of systems based on present values.

Market or net annual value.

15. The choice of a basis of taxation therefore appears to lie between market value and net annual value. The Committee would have preferred to adopt market value as the basis of taxation, since in principle it can be determined directly. Unfortunately it has often happened that the prices paid for land have either been speculative or have been governed by political and sentimental, rather than purely economic, considerations.

To adopt the market value would therefore cause a serious disparity of assessment between districts or sometimes even between adjoining villages. In consequence the Committee is of the opinion that the basis of the new tax should be the net annual value of land; and in this opinion nearly all those consulted have concurred.

Definition of net annual value. 16. The Committee considered the possibility of defining net annual value as rental value, but was again met by practical difficulties. A very small proportion of rents is at present paid in money; and the rents payable in kind (for example, one-third of the gross produce) are so complicated by specially added conditions that it appears impracticable to determine their value. The Committee has therefore considered net annual value to be the balance left after deducting costs of production from the average value of the average gross annual produce of the land.

III. GROSS ANNUAL PRODUCE.

Categories of cultivable land. 17. The average gross annual products and the costs of production obviously differ for various categories of land. The following classification of cultivable land has been adopted with the general agreement of all consulted:-

    A. Fruit Plantations.
        (a) Citrus.
        (b) Bananas.
        (c) Others.
    B. Ground Crops.
        (a) Irrigated.
        (b) Unirrigated.
    C. Planted Forests.

- 7 -

Other categories of rural land and buildings, which have no net annual value under the definition given, will be considered later.

Citrus. 18. Since the vast majority of citrus groves are orange groves, it is generally agreed that in this category only oranges need be considered. Estimates given of the average gross annual products of an orange grove have varied very considerably. Figures as high as 125 cases per dunum, and in some places as low as 30, have been given. The Committee considers that a general average may without substantial injustice be taken for the whole country except the Acre Sub-District. The Committee recommends that the general average should be fixed at 100 cases per dunum, and that for Acre Sub-District at 50. The average price of a case on the basis explained in paragraph 24 below is 200 mils, and this figure has commonly been accepted as correct. The gross assessment of a dunum of citrus grove would therefore be LP.20 for the country as a whole, and LP.10 for Acre Sub-District.

Bananas. 19. An estimate of the gross annual value per dunum of a banana grove is particularly difficult. Experience is limited, the life of a banana grove is short, and, since the export market for bananas has lately been restricted, prices have fallen heavily with the recent increase of groves. Figures as high as 1500 kilogrammes per dunum, and as low as 600, have been given. Some cultivators consider bananas to be in much the same class as oranges, while others consider that they should rank more or less with ground crops. On the whole the Committee considers that a fair assessment would be 900 kilogrammes per dunum, at an average price

- 8 -

of 15 mils per kilogramme, giving a gross annual value of £P.13.500 per dunum. It is generally admitted that it is unnecessary to distinguish different zones for banana groves.

Other fruit plantations.
20. It would not appear reasonable to prescribe a general value per dunum for other fruit plantations. Unlike citrus and bananas, other fruit trees are often not planted in groves, but may be scattered over ground crop land. Hence the number of trees per dunum varies very greatly. In addition, different varieties of fruit trees, with crops of differing values, may be intermingled. On the other hand, it would not appear equitable to ignore them altogether. Fruit trees may be successfully grown on land that for ground crops would be of inferior quality; and thus, for example, a profitable olive grove might escape with a very low assessment as ground crop land. The Committee therefore recommends that the valuers should be given discretion to make a suitable addition to the assessment of a fiscal block in respect of the fruit trees planted on it; but that a maximum assessment per dunum should be prescribed. After consideration of the numerous figures given, the Committee recommends that the maximum assessment should be one and a half times the maximum assessment for ground crop land which is recommended in paragraph 22 below.

Irrigated ground crops.
21. Land irrigated by natural flow of water is planted with vegetables, forage or ordinary ground crops. The values of these crops respectively are roughly 300%, 150% and 75% of the value of the ground crop from the best unirrigated land. Since frequent changes of crop occur, it is essential for practical reasons to fix a flat rate. The Committee recommends

- 9 -

that irrigated ground crop land should be assessed at one and a half times the maximum assessment of un-irrigated ground crop land, which is recommended in paragraph 22 below.

Unirrigated ground crops.

22. The Committee considered the possibility of prescribing a fixed number of classes of ground crop land, and a fixed assessment for each. Various sections of the public were inclined to think that a division into good, medium and poor land would be adequate, but the experiments that have been made by the Commissioner of Lands indicate that at the least eight classes would be required. With so many classes, any advantages there may be in a rigid classification would disappear. The Committee next considered whether the valuation should be made on the basis of wheat productivity. So rigid a basis appears to be undesirable. The Committee therefore recommends that the valuers should be given full discretion in assessing the gross annual value of ground crop land, provided that the assessment per dunum should not exceed a prescribed maximum. The Committee considers that the highest yield obtainable with the ordinary methods of agriculture in Palestine amounts to 80 kilogrammes of wheat. Any excess over this quantity would be due to improved methods of cultivation involving costs of production above the normal proportion. In consideration of the extra expenditure, the assessment should not be increased. The average price of wheat on the basis to be explained in paragraph 24 below is 10 mils per kilo. The maximum assessment of gross annual value that should be permitted would therefore be 800 mils per dunum. It has been found that approximately the same figure is reached if the calculation is made on a

- 10 -

a two year rotation of wheat and dura and wheat and sesame, instead of on wheat alone.

Planted forests.

23. It is impossible to calculate the gross annual value of planted forest lands. At the same time, it is clear that they have some gross annual value, and there would appear to be no reason why they should not be taxed like other categories of land. In order to encourage afforestation, the Committee recommends that merely a nominal assessment should be placed upon land planted with forests, and that this nominal assessment should be fixed at 5 mils per dunum.

Conversion prices.

24. To calculate gross annual value from gross annual products, the Committee has selected the average of the harvest-time prices for the five years 1927 to 1931, as quoted from his lists of wholesale market prices by the Director of Agriculture and Forests. This period comprises two years of good prices, one of medium prices and two of low prices, and should therefore yield as equitable an average as it is possible in this time of unstable prices to obtain. Certain crops are harvested only during specific months of the year; others yield throughout the year. Harvest-time for the former class therefore covers only a limited number of months, while harvest-time for the latter must be regarded as covering the whole year. Since the majority of cultivators have to dispose of their products at harvest-time, it appears just to consider only the harvest-time prices of the respective products instead of the prices over the whole year, which effect the merchant rather than the cultivator.

IV. COSTS OF PRODUCTION.

Definition. 25. The Committee has considered the costs of production to include the annual cost of labour and of material required for the cultivation of various categories of land, and the annual provision to be made for amortization of capital outlay and interest on capital. The cost of maintenance of the farmer and his family has been excluded from the costs of production.

Determination. 26. The Committee has heard much detailed evidence on the costs of production. Agricultural experts have given figures of what the costs ought to be to ensure proper cultivation; practical agriculturists in different parts of the country have given widely differing figures of what they actually expend. The Committee has aimed at ascertaining the average actual expenditure rather than the ideal expenditure, but, in order not to prejudice the progressive cultivator, has thought it proper to take a somewhat lenient view. On these lines the Committee has come to the conclusion that the full annual cost of production (as defined in paragraph 25 above) for citrus and bananas and for best quality ground crops is about two-thirds of the gross annual value. The cost for other fruit trees is rather less than two-thirds, and that for lower qualities of ground crops rather more. Since these estimates cannot hope to be more than very rough, the Committee recommends that the cost of production for all categories should be considered to be **two-thirds** of the gross annual value.

V. NET ANNUAL VALUE.

Table. 27. By deduction of the percentage allowed for costs of production from the estimates of average gross

- 12 -

annual value, the following table of average net annual values is obtained:

Category	Gross Annual Value. LP.	Costs of Production LP.	Net Annual Value. LP.
A. Citrus (a) Acre Sub-Dist.	10.000	6.666	3.300
(b) Rest of country	20.000	13.333	6.600
B. Bananas.	13.500	9.000	4.500
C. Maximum for other fruit plantations.	1.200	-.800	-.400
D. Irrigated ground crops.	1.200	-.800	-.400
E. Maximum for unirrigated ground crops.	-.800	-.534	-.260
F. Planted Forests.	-	-	-.005 (nominal)

As the figures for gross annual value and for costs of production are obviously only approximate, the figures for net annual value have been rounded off.

Comparison with rent.

28. The Committee has estimated that net annual value is one-third of gross annual value. It will be noted that the commonest rent of ground crop land bears the same proportion to gross produce. As plantations are not rented, it is not possible to make a similar comparison with their net annual value.

Index numbers.

29. It has been proposed that a series of index numbers (from 1 upwards or from 100 downwards) should be calculated for the various categories from their respective annual values, and that, if assessments were to be altered on account of a change in the level of prices, the proportions of these index numbers should be maintained. Since a fall in the price of ground crops might be accompanied by a rise in the price of citrus fruit, or the reverse might occur, it is clear that such an arrangement would be inequitable.

- 13 -

VI. OTHER CATEGORIES OF RURAL LAND.

Classification.

30. Consideration must now be given to other categories of rural land and buildings, which have no net annual value under the definition given. They may be classified as follows :-

A. Natural forest land.
   (a) owned individually or in determinate shares;
   (b) owned by a village in indeterminate shares;
        (1) registered "matruke";
        (2) other.

B. Uncultivable land.
   (a) owned individually or in determinate shares;
   (b) owned by a village in indeterminate shares;
        (1) registered "matruke";
        (2) other.

C. Village areas.
   (a) possessing urban services and amenities;
   (b) not possessing urban services and amenities.

D. Buildings outside village areas.
   (a) residential or agricultural;
   (b) industrial.

Natural forests.

31. It is impossible to calculate the gross or the net annual value of natural forest lands, but it is clear that they have a value. The Committee therefore considers that in principle they should be taxed, like planted forests, on a nominal assessment of 5 mils per dunum. This principle should be applied to natural forests owned by individuals or by groups of individuals where each has a determinate share.

32. Usually, however, natural forests belong either to Government, when obviously they cannot be taxed, or in indeterminate shares to whole villages. In the latter case, they are either registered as

- 14 -

"village metruke" or are not so registered. Lands registered as "village metruke" have always been exempt from taxation. The Committee considers that it would be undesirable to depart from this long established practice, and recommends that the existing exemption should continue and that therefore no assessment should be made.

33. Natural forest lands that are not registered as "village metruke" should in theory be taxed; but it does not appear possible to determine on what individuals or in what proportions the tax should be levied. The Committee therefore finds itself obliged to recommend that such lands should be left unassessed. The anomaly will disappear after land settlement, when all natural forest lands will be registered as individual property, or as "village metruke", or as state domain. Meanwhile it is not serious; for the total amount of a nominal assessment would be small, and the villagers pay license fees for specific privileges on natural forest lands.

Unculti- 34. The next category comprises marshes, rocky
vable land. areas and moving sand dunes, which are definitely uncultivable by ordinary methods of agriculture. Such lands, however, have a value either as grazing grounds or on account of their potentialities for development by means of considerable capital outlay. In principle, therefore, the Committee recommends a nominal assessment of 5 mils per dunum on uncultivable lands. In accordance with the recommendation concerning natural forests, this principle should be applied to uncultivable land owned by individuals or in determinate shares.

Village 35. In accordance, again, with the recommendations
metruke.

- 15 -

concerning natural forests, registered "village metruke" should not be assessed, while other uncultivable lands used in common by villages must perforce be left unassessed. This anomaly also will disappear after land settlement.

Urbanized village areas. 36. The question of built-on areas in villages has next to be considered. These may be divided into two classes. A limited number of them closely resemble urban areas, and the residents enjoy many of the public services and other amenities of an urban area. The Committee recommends that such areas should be declared urban areas under the Urban Property Tax Ordinance. A special rate should be fixed, under that Ordinance, for farm buildings other than dwelling houses.

Rural village areas. 37. In other built-on village areas, whether they contain scattered homesteads or closely built houses, the residents enjoy little or nothing in the way of urban amenities. The Committee recommends that, in all areas that have not expressly been declared urban areas, buildings should be ignored and that a uniform assessment per dunum should be arbitrarily imposed on each built-on plot. This arbitrary assessment should be five times the maximum assessment for ground crop land, i.e. LP.1.300 mils per dunum.

Prescription of village area. 38. The Committee further recommends that, for practical convenience, a "village area" should be prescribed by Order in each village, and that to all land within this area the special assessment per dunum should be applied.

Buildings outside "village areas". 39. It remains to consider buildings outside the prescribed "village area". These are usually residential or agricultural, but may sometimes be industrial.

- 16 -

The Committee recommends that the residential or agricultural buildings should be ignored, like those within the "village area", and that, for practical convenience, the plots on which they are built should be assessed at the same valuation per dunum as that of the fiscal block in which they are situated.

Industrial buildings. 40. Industrial buildings in rural areas, i.e. in areas that have not expressly been declared urban areas, should be treated differently. Since it will not normally be possible to determine the rental value of such buildings, the Committee recommends that they should be assessed with regard (a) to the size, materials and state of repair of the property and the amenities and the value of the site, and (b) to the use to which the property is put; provided that no account should be taken of any plant or machinery in or on the property. This recommendation follows the terms of section 5, subsection 3, of the Urban Property Tax Ordinance.

VII. VALUATION.

Fiscal blocks. 41. Owing to the "musha'" system, which prevails or has at some time prevailed throughout most of the country, agricultural practice has divided cultivable land into blocks of approximately equal fertility (known in the north as "mawaqia" and in the south as "qitaat"). Under the "musha'" system, not only had each owner holdings in various blocks, but also at each periodical repartition he had to exchange these holdings for others in the same blocks respectively. Each owner was therefore vitally interested in securing that the classification of the land was as accurate as possible, and in addition he had a very accurate idea of the relative values of the land in the different blocks. Thus the experience of

- 17 -

many past generations has provided material of unsurpassable reliability which may conveniently be used for purposes of valuation. The Committee recommends that these blocks should be utilized as valuation units, i.e. as fiscal blocks, and that an assessment per dunum should be made for each.

Official valuers & Appeal Commissions.

42. In the course of his experiments, the Commissioner of Lands has actually adopted this system, and fiscal blocks comprising nearly 4,000,000 dunums of land have been determined, surveyed and valued according to productivity by officers of Government. These operations are still in progress. The Committee is of opinion that the whole valuation should be carried out by official valuers. This system assures greater uniformity and is much quicker and cheaper than valuation by local commissions. In view of the amount of valuation work that has already been done, the Committee recommends that the valuation should be completed on the present lines. The interests of the public should be protected by provision for an appeal to a Commission on which the public would be represented. The Committee recommends that in each District one or more Appeal Commissions should be constituted. These Commissions should be appointed by the High Commissioner and should be composed of an Assistant District Commissioner, as Chairman, one other official member and one unofficial member. After a preliminary objection to the original official valuer, an appeal should lie to one of these Commissions.

Fruit plantations (other than citrus and bananas).

43. For practical reasons, a special arrangement is necessary for valuing fruit plantations other than citrus and bananas. As has already been pointed out, trees may be planted close together or wide apart; there may be isolated trees on ground crop land. Thus the number of trees per dunum may vary greatly. There may

- 18 -

be different varieties of trees in the same fiscal block, - and, indeed, in as small an area as one dunum. To survey or to count the trees would involve time and trouble quite out of proportion to the result. The Committee therefore recommends that, when the valuers come to a fiscal block in which fruit trees other than citrus and bananas are planted, they should first assess the land at its ground crop value per dunum, and should then assess a value per dunum to be added to this land valuation in respect of the trees planted on it. It has been recommended (paragraph 20) that the total valuation per dunum of the block should not exceed one and a half times the maximum value per dunum prescribed for ground crop land.

VIII. REVALUATION AND REVISION.

General revaluation of land.

44. The average produce (in kind) per dunum of the various categories of land respectively is likely to remain the same for an indefinite period; or, if any increase occurs, it is likely to be offset by a corresponding increase in the costs of production. Hence, unless some unforeseen revolution in agricultural practice should occur, a general revaluation in the field of fiscal blocks should be required only at lengthy intervals, to rectify any deficiencies in the annual revision recommended in paragraph 46 below. The Committee recommends that the High Commissioner in Council should be empowered to order such a general revaluation in the field when he deems it to be necessary.

General revaluation of conversion prices.

45. On the other hand, it is probable that fluctuations in prices of crops will occur, and that it may be desirable to substitute different conversion prices for those now proposed. Such a revaluation in

- 19 -

money would be a mechanical operation that could be performed in the office. Since it is clearly desirable for a cultivator to be able to foresee his liabilities for some time ahead, such changes should not be more frequent than is necessary. The Committee recommends that the price level should be considered by Government every five years, and that, if necessary, revaluation in money should be carried out.

Annual revision. 46. There would, however, be frequent changes in ownership and in the category of specific parcels of land. The Committee recommends that an annual revision should be made to ascertain and to record such changes.

IX. RATES.

Uniform or different. 47. The rate of tax might be uniform for all categories of land, or different rates might be levied. The difference in assessment provides for the difference in net annual value, but it is probable that the owners of the more valuable crops will be more able to bear the burden of taxation than the owners of less valuable crops. The Committee recommends that the High Commissioner should be empowered to prescribe different rates for different categories; and suggests that, in the first instance, different rates should be levied on (a) village areas (which have not been declared urban areas), (b) citrus and banana groves, (c) other categories.

Period. 48. Reference has been made above (in paragraph 45) to the need of the cultivator to know for some years ahead what taxes he will have to pay. The Committee recommends that the rates of taxation should be fixed for periods of five years, at the same times as the money valuation is fixed.

X. INCIDENCE.

Reputed owner.

49. The Committee recommends that the liability for the tax should rest with the reputed owner. The term "reputed owner" should be defined to include a lessee (or a sub-lessee), other than a lessee (or a sub-lessee) of Government land, who has a registered lease for a period of not less than three years. If a lessee fails to pay the tax, the Government should then have recourse to the owner.

Tenants of Government land.

50. The case of tenants of Government land calls for special consideration. Hitherto these tenants have normally paid rent and Commuted Tithe, but it would appear illogical that Government property should be assessed for the new tax. The Committee therefore recommends that no lessee (or sub-lessee) of Government land should be liable for the tax, but that <u>in principle</u> his rent should be increased to compensate for the abolition of the Commuted Tithe. When tenants have hitherto paid a negotiated rent, the necessary adjustment of rent should be made by the Director of Lands.

"Mudawara" lands.

51. Tenants of "mudawara" lands have hitherto paid rent in the form of a Rental Tithe equal in amount to the Commuted Tithe. Effectively, therefore, they have paid, in consideration of their tenancy of Government land, twice the Commuted Tithe. The Committee recommends that, when the new tax is introduced, such tenants should pay as rent twice the amount that they would have paid in tax had they been owners of the land, but should not be liable for the tax.

XI. INTERNAL DISTRIBUTION.

Post-Settlement.

52. As soon as the area of fiscal block, the valuation per dunum of the block and the rate of

- 21 -

tax are determined, the total tax on the fiscal block can be calculated. In villages where settlement is completed, the process can be carried a step further and the tax can be calculated for each individual owner.

Pre-Settlement. 53. In villages where settlement has not yet been completed, provision must be made for the internal distribution of the tax on the fiscal block. The Committee recommends that the distribution should be effected by Village Committees subject to the approval of the District Commissioner. If the lands are divided ("mafruz"), the distribution should be based roughly on area, determined according to the local custom of each village by ropes, rods or other means. If the lands are undivided (mushaa") the distribution should be based on shares. When there is an additional tax on a block in respect of the fruit trees other than citrus and bananas planted in it (paragraph 20), the additional tax should be distributed among the owners of such trees in accordance with their value as determined by the Village Committee.

XII COLLECTION.

Official tax-collectors. 54. Werku is collected by official tax-collectors, and accounts for individual tax-payers are kept in the various revenue offices. Commuted Tithe is collected (in first instance) by mukhtars on behalf of their respective villages, but no general provision has been made for the maintenance in revenue offices of individual Tithe accounts. It is important that, when a revised system of taxation is introduced, records should be adequately kept; and this will never be achieved through the medium of unsalaried and illiterate mukhtars. The

- 22 -

The Committee therefore recommends that the collection of the new tax should be undertaken entirely by Government officials. If the number of tax-collectors were increased, a tax collector might be placed in charge of a group of villages and might also perform official duties other than tax collection in connection with his group.

XIII. EXEMPTIONS AND REMISSIONS.

Plantations. 55. From time to time areas of ground crop land are converted into plantations. Capital expenditure is involved in the transformation, and until the trees come into bearing, the owner obtains little or no return for his outlay. In principle, therefore, it would appear reasonable to exempt the owner of the new plantation from taxation for a prescribed period. In practice, however, the Committee considers that such exemption is necessary only in respect of new citrus groves. Banana groves begin to yield during the second year; and thus the unprofitable period is so short that the payment of tax for this period does not constitute a real hardship. The exemption of fruit trees other than citrus and bananas would, for the reasons already explained (in paragraphs 20 and 43), present grave practical difficulties. Since the allowance proposed for cost of production in respect of such trees is admittedly generous, there would appear to be small injustice in making no provision for their exemption. The Committee therefore recommends that citrus groves, and citrus groves only, should be granted exemption during the period before they come into bearing, and that the prescribed period for such exemption should be six years. It should be incumbent upon the owner to give such notice as may be prescribed of the change

- 23 -

to citrus cultivation and of the approximate area affected; and in default of such notice he should lose the privilege of exemption.

Uncultivable land. 56. Similar exemption might be accorded when genuinely uncultivable land is brought under cultivation. This has been regarded (in paragraph 34) as comprising marsh, rock or moving sand. The Committee recommends that, if the High Commissioner is satisfied that a genuine reclamation of marsh land is being effected, he should have power to grant exemption for the period of the reclamation and for such subsequent period as in the circumstances he deems fit. Rocky land or moving sand would be planted either with ground crops or with plantations. Ground crops would yield an immediate return, while for plantations no period of exemption has been considered necessary.

No other exemptions. 57. Provision has now been proposed for the exemption of citrus groves before they come into bearing, and, for practical reasons, of natural forests and uncultivated land in indeterminate ownership. Village areas declared to be urban areas (paragraph 36) would naturally be eligible for the exemptions provided in the Urban Property Tax Ordinance. The Committee recommends that no further statutory provision for exemption should be made.

Remissions. 58. On the other hand some provision must be made for specific remissions in case of emergency. The Committee considers, however, that they should be limited as far as possible; and recommends that the High Commissioner should be empowered to grant remission only when he is satisfied that the disaster which has caused the emergency:-

- 24 -

    (a) is widespread;

    (b) is due to unavoidable natural causes such as drought, locusts or field mice;

    (c) has caused a loss amounting to not less than two-thirds of the average crop of the fiscal block for which remission is asked.

Any remission, in whole or in part, that may be granted, should be applied to specified fiscal blocks.

XIV. APPLICATION.

59.   The Committee recommends that the new system of taxation should be applied in the first instance to the Sub-Districts of Jaffa, Ramle and Gaza, where land settlement operations are in progress, in order that the system may be tested both in its interim and in its final form. If the tests are satisfactory, the system should then be extended to all areas where fiscal blocks have been determined and valued. In the area to which the new system is then applied, the proportion that the new tax constitutes of the sum of the Tithe and the Werku previously paid should be calculated, and the sum of the Tithe and the Werku payable in other areas should be adjusted in this proportion. Subsequently, the system should be extended progressively to the rest of the country.

XV. ABOLITION OF ANIMAL TAX.

60.   The great majority of persons who pay Animal Tax already pay Werku and Commuted Tithe, and would pay the new tax if it were introduced. The Animal Tax is a primitive tax unsuitable to the requirements of a progressive country, and affords continual opportunities

- 25 -

for malpractice. The total amount of revenue derived from it is not large in proportion to that derived from Werku and Commuted Tithe. The Committee recommends that Animal Tax (as well as Werku and Commuted Tithe) should be abolished, and suggests that the abolition should take effect when the new tax is applied to the Sub-Districts of Jaffa, Ramle and Gaza.

XVI. WAQF INTERESTS.

61. The Waqf authorities are entitled to the Tithe derived from certain lands. If the new tax is introduced, provision must be made to meet such claims as they may have. The Committee recommends that Government should negociate with the Waqf authorities for the commutation of their tithe interests.

XVII. AMOUNT OF THE TAX.

62. In the foregoing paragraphs the Committee has tried to elaborate a system of rural taxation that should be as equitable as possible in its incidence. It is obvious, however, that no system of assessment can be satisfactory if the rate of taxation is too high. The Committee recommends that the maximum rate that may be prescribed in respect of the new tax upon rural property should always be the same as the maximum rate prescribed in section 5(1) of the Urban Property Tax Ordinance for urban property. The rates actually prescribed in any year for most categories of rural land should be less than the rates actually prescribed in that year by an Order under the Urban Property Tax Ordinance. The Committee is of opinion that the early

- 26 -

adoption of these recommendations with regard to the incidence and the rates of rural taxation would afford a much needed relief to agriculture in Palestine.

     A. ABRAMSON - CHAIRMAN.

     R.E.H. CROSBIE - MEMBER.

     L. ANDREWS - MEMBER.

Jerusalem 14th March, 1932.

- 27 -

I N D E X.

Section.	Paragraph.		Page.
		Terms of reference.	
I		PROCEDURE.	
II		BASIC PRINCIPLES...	
		Replacement of Werku and Tithe by single tax	
	10	Capital or annual value ...	
	11	Soil survey.	
	12	Arbitrary assessment.	
	13	Gross or net annual value... ...	
	14	Improved or unimproved value	
	15	Market or net annual value.	
	16	Definition of net annual value.	
III		GROSS ANNUAL PRODUCE.	
	17	Categories of cultivable land.	
	18	Citrus	
	19	Bananas.	
	20	Other fruit plantations	
	21	Irrigated ground crops ...	
	22	Unirrigated ground crops	9
	23	Planted forests	10
	24	Conversion prices.	
IV		COSTS OF PRODUCTION ...	11
	25	Definition.	
	26	Determination.	
		NET ANNUAL VALUE.	
	27	Table.	
	28	Comparison with rent ...	
	29	Index numbers.	
		OTHER CATEGORIES OF RURAL LAND...	13
		Classification.	

Section.	Paragraph.		Page.
	31	Natural forests.	
	34	Uncultivable land ...	
	35	Village metruke.	
	36	Urbanized village areas	
	37	Rural village areas.	
	38	Prescription of village area.	
	39	Buildings outside village areas.	
	40	Industrial buildings	1.
VII		VALUATION.	
	41	Fiscal blocks.	
	42	Official valuers & Appeal Commissions	
	43	Fruit plantations (other than citrus and bananas).	
VIII		REVALUATION AND REVISION	
	44	General revaluation of land.	
	45	General revaluation of conversion prices.	
	46	Annual revision	19
		RATES.	
	47	Uniform or different.	
	48	Period.	
		INCIDENCE	20
	49	Reputed owner.	
	50	Tenants of Government land.	
	51	Mudeware lands.	
		INTERNAL DISTRIBUTION.	
	52	Post-Settlement.	
	53	Pre-Settlement	
XII		COLLECTION.	
	54	Official tax-collectors.	

- 29 -

Section.	Paragraph.		Page.
XIII		EXEMPTIONS AND REMISSIONS ...	22
	55	Plantations.	
	56	Uncultivable land	23
	57	No other exemptions.	
	58	Remissions.	
XIV	59	APPLICATION	24
XV	60	ABOLITION OF ANIMAL TAX.	
XVI	61	WAQF INTERESTS	25
XVII	62	AMOUNT OF THE TAX.	

ENCLOSURE No .... TO PALESTINE DESPATCH
Date

Enclosure II.

COPY.

554(794)4615.   20th June, 1932.

Chief Secretary.

Subject: Recommendations of Rural Taxation Committee.

I set out below the results of the discussion between the Commissioner of Lands, the District Commissioner, Southern District, and this Department on the principal recommendations of the Rural Taxation Committee:-

Recommendations of Rural Taxation Committee.	Results of discussion with Treasurer.
Basis of Tax.	
(1) The existing Werko Tax in rural areas (based on capital value of immovable property) and Commuted Tithe (based on the average village assessment of tithe on the produce of the soil) to be replaced by a single form of taxation on the net annual value of land represented by the balance left after deducting costs of production from the average value of the average gross annual produce of the land.	(1) The Treasurer is of opinion that - (a) There should be two distinct forms of tax under one Ordinance as under:- Part I - A tax per dunum on the landowner's interest, based on the estimated annual rental of the land and on the estimated annual rental of buildings, varying in rate according to defined categories of land or value of buildings; Part II - A tax per dunum on the cultivator's interest, based on the estimated net annual value of cultivated land, varying in rate according to defined categories. (b) The tax under Part I should not be subject to any remission or rebate on account of poor harvests or prices. It follows that uncultivated land would be taxable only under Part I.

The/

-2-

Recommendations of Rural Taxation Committee.	Results of discussion with Treasurer.
	The agreement arrived at is expressed in the following words:-
	"It was agreed that in principle there was no objection to two distinct forms of land tax under one Ordinance, viz. on annual rental values and on net annual values; that the former should not be subject to any remission or rebate, and that the latter should be subject to rebate or remission as recommended in paragraph 58 of the Committee's report. But it was pointed out that it would be necessary to adopt conventional proportions as between landlords and cultivators which bear relation to annual rental values and net annual values, i.e. annual rental values may have to be taken as the equivalent of net annual values".
Incidence of Tax.	
(2) The liability for the tax should rest with the reputed owner. The term "reputed owner" should be defined to include a lessee (other than a lessee of Government land) who has a registered lease for a period of not less than three years, but Government should have recourse to the owner if the lessee fail to pay the tax. Tenants of Government land should not be liable for the tax but in principle their rent should be increased to compensate for the abolition of the Commuted Tithe. Where tenants have hitherto paid a negotiable rent any necessary adjustment of rent should be made by the Director of Lands.	(2) It was agreed that the reputed owner should be liable for both parts of the tax provided that:- (a) the definition of "reputed owner" is amended so as to provide that after settlement the registered owner shall be liable for the tax; (b) the land-owner shall continue to have a right of indemnity against the cultivator in respect of Part II of the tax as provided in Section 19(1) of the Commutation of Tithes Ordinance, 1927; (c) In the event of default by the land-owner payment of the tax under Part I may be demanded from the lessee to the extent of any rental payable by him on the property on which the tax is assessed provided that the liability of the land-owner for the tax is not affected thereby and that the lessee is given a right of indemnity against the land-owner to deduct the tax under Part I paid by him from any rent payable.

-3-

Recommendations of Rural Taxation Committee.

Village Assessment.

(3) The determination of the total assessment of village lands and buildings to be as under -

(a) To accept as valuation units or fiscal blocks the existing divisions of cultivable land of the village into land of approximate equal fertility, known in the north as "mawaquia" and in the south as "quitaat";

(b) To ascertain by survey the area of each fiscal block:

(c) To assess the net annual value of each block of cultivable land on the lines actually adopted by the Commissioner of Lands in test operations and on the basis of the figures of net annual value and maximum net annual value per dunum assigned to categories as shewn in paragraph 27 of the Report;

(d) To adopt -

  (i) a nominal assessment per dunum for natural forest land and uncultivable land;

  (ii) an arbitrary assessment per dunum for rural village areas;

  (iii) the principles of the Urban Property Tax for urbanised village areas and industrial buildings in other village areas, with a special rate for farm buildings other than dwelling houses.

(e) Valuation to be undertaken by official valuers subject to appeal to a Commission on which the public would be represented.

Results of discussion with Treasurer.

(3) The Treasurer does not agree with the proposals for the assessment of the net annual value of fiscal blocks. In his opinion the method of assessment should be simple and should avoid such detail as may afford to cultivators grounds for appeal which may be difficult to resist. The Treasurer supports the proposal for ascertaining the total area of land of the various categories shewn in paragraphs 17 and 30 of the Committee's Report (supplemented if necessary by additional sub-categories based on productivity for ground crops land and fruit plantations) and fixing rates of tax for the various categories according to conventional proportions as between land-owners and cultivators which shall bear relation to annual rental values and net annual values. The rates for each part of the tax would be calculated having regard to the relation of rental value to net annual value, and for each category having regard to the total area of each category and the relation between rental values and net annual values of each category. The Commissioner of Lands and the District Commissioner, Southern District, agree that the proposal is practicable but prefer the system recommended by the Commission. It is therefore a matter of choice for Government.

—4—

| Recommendations of Rural Taxation Committee. | Results of discussion with Treasurer. |

Apportionment of Tax.

(4) The apportionment of the village assessment among reputed owners of land in the village to be made —

(a) In villages where settlement has not yet been completed —

   (i) Mafruz lands roughly on area;

   (ii) Musha'a lands on shares;

   (iii) additional tax on fruit trees other than citrus and bananas) in accordance with the value of the trees;

(b) In villages where settlement is completed, according to the area held by each individual owner in the fiscal block.

(4) The Treasurer makes no observations on the Committee's recommendations; but the Deputy Treasurer states that there is no objection to the recommendations except that following the Treasurer's observations under (3) above it follows that after settlement the tax would be divided among individual owners according to the area of land held by each in the several categories.

Collection of Tax.

(5) Records of individual tax accounts must be kept, and since Mukhtars are not salaried and many are illiterate, collection should be by tax-collectors.

(5) No remarks. This is a matter of detail.

Exemption of Citrus Groves.

(6) Citrus groves to be exempt pending bearing, i.e. for six years. It should be incumbent upon owner to declare change of cultivation from ground crop to citrus and approximate area affected.

(6) Citrus groves should not be exempt from the tax under Part I, i.e. on rentals. In regard to Part II, pending bearing, the tax should be paid on the ground crop value of the land.

-5-

| Recommendations of Rural Taxation Committee. | Results of discussion with Treasurer. |

Experimental Application.

(7) The new system (Land Tax) to be applied in the first instance to Jaffa, Ramleh and Gaza Sub-Districts in order to test the method of distribution. If tests prove satisfactory, the system should be extended to all areas covered by the fiscal survey at the time of enactment of Ordinance, and in other areas, pending the application of the Land Tax, the sum of the Tithe and Werko to be adjusted in the proportion that the new tax constitutes to the aggregate of the Tithe and Werko previously paid in the areas to which the tax is applied.

(7) The Treasurer deprecates the introduction of tax measures experimentally and is unable to advise any new tax measure until estimates of the revenue likely to be received under the new tax and the cost of re-valuation and revision have been prepared in sufficient detail and considered by Government.

Animal Tax.

(8) Abolition of the Animal Tax.

(8) The Treasurer is of opinion that Animal Tax should be maintained on the ground that the tax seems a proper contribution from owners of stock who possess no land of their own but graze their flocks and herds on other land usually State lands.

Rate of Tax.

(9) Maximum rate which may be prescribed upon rural property should be the same as the maximum rate which may be prescribed for urban property. Actual rates prescribed in rural areas in any year should be less than those prescribed that year in urban areas.

(9) The Treasurer points out that the tax under Part II is in the nature of an income tax, and that there is no tax of like character in urban areas; and that any legislation on the lines proposed by him is temporary only and must of necessity be revised if and when an income tax is introduced.

The revenue receivable under Part I should exceed the present receipts from Werko (rural areas) and the revenue receivable under Part II will doubtless be less than the assessed revenue from Commuted Tithes.

2. I regret the delay in dealing with this matter. The file has been in my possession for about ten days but owing to the Treasurer's departure and other work, I was unfortunately unable to deal with the matter earlier.

(Sgd.) W.J. Johnson.
ACTING TREASURER.

Enclosure III.

Decisions taken by the High Commissioner in Executive Council on the recommendations of the Rural Taxation Committee. 13-7-32.

It was decided by His Excellency in Executive Council that the basic proposals of the Rural Taxation Committee be modified as follows before submission to the Secretary of State.

(1) **Basis of Tax.**

There should be two distinct forms of tax under one Ordinance as under:-

Part I - A tax per dunum on the land-owner's interest, based on the estimated annual rental of the land and on the estimated annual rental of buildings, varying in rate according to defined categories of land or value of buildings;

Part II - A tax per dunum on the cultivator's interest, based on the estimated net annual value of cultivated land, varying in rate according to defined categories.

The tax under Part I should not be subject to any remission or rebate on account of poor harvests or prices, and the tax under Part II should be subject to remission or rebate as recommended in paragraph 58 of the Committee's report.

It follows that uncultivated land would be taxable only under Part I; and it may be necessary to adopt conventional proportions as between landlords and cultivators which bear relation to annual rental values and net annual values, i.e. annual rental values may have to be taken as the equivalent of net annual values.

(2)/

-2-

(2) Incidence of Tax.

The reputed owner should be liable for both parts of the tax provided that:-

(a) the definition of "reputed owner" is amended so as to provide that after settlement the registered owner shall be liable for the tax;

(b) The land-owner shall continue to have a right of indemnity against the cultivator in respect of Part II of the tax as provided in Section 19(1) of the Commutation of Tithes Ordinance, 1927;

(c) in the event of default by the land-owner payment of the tax under Part I may be demanded from the lessee to the extent of any rental payable by him on the property on which the tax is assessed provided that the liability of the land-owner for the tax is not affected thereby and that the lessee is given a right of indemnity against the land-owner to deduct the tax under Part I paid by him from any rent payable.

(3) Village Assessment.

The method of assessment should be simple and should avoid such detail as may afford to cultivators grounds for appeal which may be difficult to resist. The total area of land of the various categories shewn in paragraphs 17 and 30 of the Committee's Report (supplemented if necessary by additional sub-categories based on productivity for ground crops land and fruit plantations) should be ascertained and rates of tax fixed for the various categories according to conventional proportions as between land-owners and cultivators which shall bear relation to annual rental values and net annual values. It was decided that the number of categories should be fixed by the Commissioner of Lands.

The/

-3-

The rates for each part of the tax would be calculated having regard to the relation of rental value to net annual value, and for each category having regard to the total area of each category and the relation between rental values and net annual values of each category.

(4) <u>Apportionment of Tax.</u>

There is no objection to the Committee's recommendation, but after settlement the tax should be divided among individual owners according to the area of land held by each in the several categories.

(5) <u>Exemption of citrus groves.</u>

Citrus groves should not be exempt from the tax under Part I, i.e. on rentals. In regard to Part II, pending bearing, the tax should be paid on the ground crop value of the land.

(6) <u>Experimental Application.</u>

It is not proposed to introduce the tax experimentally as proposed.

(7) <u>Animal Tax.</u>

Animal Tax should be maintained on the ground that the tax seems a proper contribution from owners of stock who possess no land of their own but graze their flocks and herds on other land usually State lands.

At the same time it was decided, /in view of the losses of animals during last winter and the prospect of heavier losses next winter due to the inevitable shortage of grazing and lack of tibbin, that the question of remitting the animal tax for one year (i.e. 1933) should be considered.

(8)./

-4-

(8) Rate of Tax.

The tax under Part II is in the nature of an income tax, and there is no tax of like character in urban areas; and any legislation on the lines proposed is temporary only and must of necessity be revised if and when an income tax is introduced.

The revenue receivable under Part I should exceed the present receipts from Werko (rural areas); and the revenue receivable under Part II will doubtless be less than the assessed revenue from Commuted Tithes.

=======

HIGH COMMISSIONER FOR PALESTINE,
JERUSALEM.

Despatch No. 65x
Reference No. L/65/31.

10 July, 1931.

Enclosures

My Lord,

    I have the honour to refer to the correspondence ending with Your Lordship's despatch No. 108 of the 3rd February with regard to Sir John Hope Simpson's Report on Immigration, Land Settlement and Development in Palestine, and to forward for Your Lordship's information a memorandum, with a covering letter from the Director of Surveys, explaining the method employed by him in arriving at the estimate of cultivable land in Palestine which was accepted by Sir John Hope Simpson for the purpose of the Report.

    2. A copy of the memorandum has been sent to Sir John Hope Simpson.

    I have the honour to be,
    My Lord,
    Your Lordship's most obedient,
    humble servant,

J.R. Chancellor,
HIGH COMMISSIONER
FOR PALESTINE.

The Right Hon'ble LORD PASSFIELD, P.C.,
His Majesty's Principal Secretary of State
    for the Colonies.

Enclosure.

SUR/F/6(a). 9th June, 1931.

Acting Chief Secretary.

Subject : Report of Sir J. Hope Simpson.
         The estimate of cultivable land.

So much critisism in the Press, mostly of a biassed and uninstructed character, has been levelled at my estimate of cultivable land accepted by Sir J. Hope Simpson in 1930, that I had prepared some notes explanatory of the method of estimate for possible use if required by the Government's delegates at Geneva.

I now forward these notes, with regret that they appear too late for this purpose.

But I should like to emphasise the view that the method of estimate employed not only was the best that could be devised with the limited time and means available, but that, if it could be amplified and checks of interpretation added, it would become superior to any other method that could in practice be employed in dealing with a problem which is not amenable to any precise or determinate solution.

(Signed) C.H. Ley.

DIRECTOR OF SURVEYS.

COPY.

Enclosure to despatch No. 654
dated 10 /7/31.

Notes on the Estimate of the amount of
Cultivable Land in the Hill Areas as
given in Sir J. Hope Simpson's Report,
1930.

1. **Advantage of Vertical Photography.**

It is the well established experience of the Survey Department that all estimates by eye on the ground, owing probably to physiological causes in which the influences of perspective, colouring, strain, etc. enter, are liable to be misleading, and more particularly to exaggerate the accumulated area of a large number of small patches to the prejudice of the less evident matrix or background on which these are lying, the extent of which tends to become camouflaged.

This defect rapidly becomes more serious as the area which is the subject of an estimate increases, and it has been found necessary even with experienced surveyors to limit the area of open hill country in any single estimate to a maximum of 300 dunums, or about 60 acres.

Any estimate by ground inspection must therefore be based upon a reasonably accurate representation in plan of a skeleton mosaic of the boundaries of blocks of land the items of which do not at the most exceed 300 dunums in extent. Such a representation and estimate is being executed by the 1/10000 survey now proceeding in the hills, but this undertaking takes years to complete, and, owing to the defect mentioned, can at best only give approximate results.

The alternative presents itself of estimation

on/

on the basis of vertical photography from an aeroplane, in which each photograph of the resulting photo-mosaic is divided by a grid into a number of small squares, each of which is separately scrutinised under a lens and evaluated.

The method has the immense advantages of speed, of being based upon a meticulously complete representation of the ground in plan, and of being practically free from the particular class of defect mentioned. On the other hand, unless time admits of checks upon the ground, there is liability to errors of interpretation of the detail shown upon the less clear parts of the photos.

But to be of use such checks of interpretation on the ground should be sufficiently numerous, and skilled staff must be available. The time and means actually available for the estimate asked for by Sir J. Hope Simpson were quite insufficient for the carrying out of any such checks.

Nevertheless, the unrivalled experience of the Survey Department of the topography of the country, the general excellence of the photographs, the fact that individual detail could usually be separated and classified, and the clarity of definition in the case of all the larger areas of wholly cultivated or wholly uncultivable land, undoubtedly establish the method as a good one over the areas covered by the photographs.

(2) *Effect of the Limits imposed*.

A period of about three months was available for the estimate, photographic material and all other resources, including aeroplanes and staff, were extremely limited, and it became essential to restrict

the/

-3-

the flights to a comparatively small portion of the hill-area, and to cut out localities already so sufficiently known as to have approximate values directly assigned to them.

(3) <u>Cartographic boundaries of the uninhabited area.</u>

The large area of the steep eastern counterscarp overlooking the Jordan Valley, uninhabited since antiquity, only used for occasional grazing, and, by general concensus and report, a wilderness useless for agricultural settlement or development, was clearly indicated for exclusion.

The foot of this counterscarp in the Jordan Valley was generally well defined on the ground and on existing maps, but the upper margin near the hill crest-line of Hebron, Jerusalem and Nablus, needed definition on the map. It is well understood to be generally indicated by the line of most eastern villages on the crest overlooking the valley. The upper boundary was therefore drawn on the map 2 KM. to the east of this line of villages. The whole of this barren area, shown in light yellow on Map 2 of the Appendix to the Report, and termed the uninhabited hill-wilderness, was excluded as uncultivable, and it was considered that any errors that might arise from such definition and classification would be compensated for by the liberal allowance for the cultivable area in foothills included in the coastal plains. That the counterscarp, or any part of it, has been counted twice over in the estimate is, of course, quite untrue, and cannot be read from the Report.

(4)/

-4-

(4) Cartography of the western boundary
of the Inhabited Hills.

On the west of the Judean and Galilean ranges, the common boundary with the coastal plains, of which the survey was incomplete, needed definition on the map.

It was decided that the continuous + 150 metre (500 ft.) contour, which could be drawn on existing maps after check by the heights of triangulation points, should form the boundary for the purposes of the estimate.

It was realised that this definition of hill and plain would probably favour the estimated amount of cultivable land, because it would throw some areas of unsurveyed foothills and rocky escarpments into the category of coastal plain, to which the full percentage of cultivation already obtained by survey in the fertile plains would be assigned.

But it was preferred to hold this probable excess as compensation for any possible under-estimate of the cultivation in the uninhabited eastern wilderness.

(5) The restriction to 10 per cent
of the inhabited hill area.

Although more had been asked for, the number of aeroplane flights had to be restricted to ten, and these were subsequently found to traverse about 10 per cent of the inhabited hill area between the boundaries described.

Now although a valuation on a 10-per cent area-basis may be expected to give considerably less reliable results than one, say, on a 15-per cent area-basis, much depends upon the distribution. Well-distributed samples amounting to 10 per cent of the whole may give better results than less well-distributed samples amounting in the aggregate to 15 per cent.

Good/

Good distribution was aimed at by covering the greatest possible length of country on one bearing from the maximum height at which detail would appear in the photos., and also by selecting the routes so as to provide in the aggregate fair samples of the various types of country, as shown on Map 2 of the Report. The long spur of Mount Carmel was deliberately omitted owing to the known existence there of areas of forest, which, in view of the probable inclusion of forest areas in parts of the flights west of Safad and Hebron, it was considered might unduly weight the effect of forest areas in the result.

The route running due south from Bethlehem was, however, chosen to test the accuracy of the drawn eastern boundary of the inhabited hill area in that region, but the portions of this and of other routes which crossed the cartographic boundaries of the hill area, were not included in the estimate for that area.

The actual point of crossing of the flight into the wilderness south of Bethlehem agreed well with the line which has been drawn on the map.

(6) The absence of ground-control.

The fact that aerial photos are not to constant scale, and need ground-control before correction to uniform scale, is of little importance to the method of estimation.

For the estimate is a purely relative one carried out piecemeal in small squares, in each of which the percentages of cultivable and unciltivable land are separately estimated, using a cardboard template and not employing actual scale measurement. While at a normal height of 2500 metres, or say 8000 feet, the

effect/

-6-

effect of distortion can seldom be serious for purposes of an approximate estimate, its effect on the relative area estimate of a number of small patches in a small area will only contain plus and minus differential errors which are quite negligible in the aggregate. Even if it were not so, the resulting error would by no means operate in favour of the amount of uncultivable land.

(7) Interpretation of the ground detail.

The principal areas of wholly cultivated or wholly uncultivable land clearly appeared on the photos. The former presented the smooth glazed appearance of cleared ground, the latter a granulated texture of different shade in which individual rocks and bushes could be distinguished with the magnifying glass.

In patch cultivation where the patches are less well cleared, the difference was not so clearly pronounced, but a distinction was in nearly all cases apparent. And although the estimate may be thought to be in effect mainly one of the percentage of cultivated as against uncultivated land in each small square, the areas intervening between the cultivated patches were found in the great majority of cases to be rocky. The impression left by analysis of the photographs confirms the general experience of the field surveyors that, with rare exceptions, the cultivated area on the open hillsides between the wadis actually represents the extreme upper limit of the possible cultivable area, as defined on page 21 of the Report, rather than any insufficient development.

It is well known also to the Survey that the

crop/

crop obtainable in patch cultivation on hillsides is very small and, unlike normal cultivation, out of all proportion to the/actual area which produces it.

Yet in the estimate the whole of these extensive localities were given the same weight as the fully cultivable localities.

(8) Trees.

Olive trees were distinguishable on the photos from other trees. Where they were close together, whatever the nature of the intervening ground, the area was classed as cultivable. Only where they were scattered and the intervening ground was of the granulated type characteristic of rocky ground, was an area containing olive trees classed as uncultivable.

Otherwise, and in the case of all other trees, the estimate was made solely on the basis of a close examination of the ground between the trees.

(9) The effect of shadow.

It has been suggested that deep shadows from the walls and steep slopes of hill terraces would exaggerate the apparent area of these uncultivable portions. But the whole amount of terraced cultivation traversed by the flights in which shadow occurred was relatively small, and it was found that in nearly all cases the actual breadth of uncultivable slopes could be well gauged by examination of places on their curved re-entrants where they entered the sunlight.

It was considered that the application which was made of that method had practically eliminated this possible source of error.

(10)/

-8-

(10) **A check from the ground survey.**

For the reasons given above the method itself was considered a good one and doubts as to the results rested chiefly upon the unavoidable restriction of the number of aeroplane flights.

Although a large area of hills has not yet been covered by ground survey, certain figures have recently become available from the 1/10000 survey in the Carmel area, and the comparison of these with the aero-photo estimate of 1930 is of interest.

The area available is roughly a triangle lying between the eastern foot of the Mount Carmel range in the plains of Aesdraelon and Acre, the sea-shore between Cape Carmel and Caesarea on the West, and the line of latitude running East from Caesarea on the South. This triangle comprises in all 754 square kilometres of ground, of which roughly one half falls under the definition as coastal plain, and one half as inhabited hill. Of the hill section the broader and larger southern portion is found to be mostly cultivated, and the smaller northern end mostly forest.

The following table gives the results over this area of the two methods:-

Classification	Estimate of Sir J. Hope Simpson 1930.		1/10000 Survey Estimate 1931.		Difference.
	KM^2	Per Cent	KM^2	Per Cent	Per Cent
Cultivable Land	457.7	60.8	476.9	63.3	- 2.5
Uncultivable Land	296.3	39.2	277.1	36.7	+ 2.5
Total	754.0	100.0	754.0	100.0	∓ 0.0

The result does not indicate the existence of any serious error in either estimate.

(Sgd) C. H. Ley.

Jaffa.
9/6/31.   DIRECTOR OF SURVEYS.

5.09

**HIGH COMMISSIONER FOR PALESTINE,
JERUSALEM.**

Despatch No. 957
Reference No. F/199/31.

September, 1932.

Sir,

With reference to paragraph 2 of my despatch No.305 of the 2nd April, I have the honour to forward for your consideration the report of the Committee which I appointed to enquire into the arrears of werko, tithes and agricultural loans and the causes thereof, and to make recommendations as to the principles that may be applied in writing off or waiving such arrears.

2. The Committee have very properly taken the view that the effort to collect arrears of taxation should not be relaxed, if there was any reasonable probability that, by dint of further investigation and insistence, some part at least might be recovered. They were naturally reluctant, also, to recommend too general an indulgence, knowing that this would in many cases place the honest taxpayer, who has struggled for years to pay off his debts to Government little by little, at a real disadvantage compared with the debtor who had deliberately and consistently avoided his obligations.

It is, however, necessary in my view to face the situation that in the overwhelming majority of instances, apart from those numerous cases in which the debtor is no longer to be found, or the individual

indebtedness/

The Right Honourable
   Sir Philip Cunliffe-Lister, G.B.E., M.P., etc., etc.,
       His Majesty's Principal Secretary of State
                                  for the Colonies.

-2-

indebtedness is unrecorded, there is genuine inability to pay; and that to press for collection would be as unprofitable an expenditure of money, time and trouble to Government as it would be an exasperation to the villagers concerned.

In my telegrams No.113 of the 28th May, 1932, and No.171 of the 10th August, 1932, concerning the reduction and remission of the commuted tithe for 1932, I laid especial emphasis upon the succession of bad agricultural seasons and the increasing poverty of the fellah as arguments in favour of relief. It will hardly be gainsaid that these arguments apply with even greater force to the question of waiving arrears of taxation. In these circumstances I hold that this question should be treated by Government in as generous a spirit as possible, and that debts which it has proved impossible to collect for a considerable period of years, particularly on account of tithes, might well be abandoned.

In the absence of any practical likelihood of recovery, the maintenance of these arrears upon the Government Registers is a constant source of uneasiness to the villagers, harassed as it is by money lenders; and their fear that collections on account of current assessments may be credited by District Commissioners to the liquidation of arrears renders them less ready to meet the demands of tax-collectors, with the result that collections are never up to date.

3. Having examined the recommendations of the Committee in Executive Council in the light of these considerations, I have come to the following conclusions.

(a)/

(a) I am in full agreement with the recommendation to write off all arrears of principal and interest in respect of mule loans, which have for years saddled local cultivators with a burden of debt unmitigated by any commensurate benefits.

(b) I also endorse their recommendations in respect of seed loans issued in 1928 (although in individual cases it may be advisable to remit an amount in excess of the equitable average reduction recommended by the Committee) and in respect of other agricultural loans.

(c) The Committee's recommendation as regards arrears of werko is acceptable: the prospects of collecting arrears of this kind are in general more certain than of collecting arrears of commuted tithes; and there is relatively less excuse for non-payment by defaulters.

(d) For the reasons given in paragraph 17 of their Report, the Committee felt unable to recommend any remission of arrears of tithe. Taking into account, however, the considerations set forth in paragraph 2 of this despatch, as well as the incidence of the fall in market prices to which the Committee themselves draw attention in paragraph 15 of their Report, I am persuaded that there must be some write-off of arrears of tithes. I therefore recommend that all arrears of tithes in respect of the years 1928 and 1929 be now remitted. Although there are no individual accounts of taxpayers it should not be difficult to ascertain the amounts

in/

-4-

in arrear at the 31st December, 1931, in respect of assessments for the years 1930 and 1931, or at any rate for the year 1931; and the difference between these amounts and the total arrears of the village at the 31st December last should be written off. In the absence of individual accounts of taxpayers it is in my opinion useless to carry forward any balance that cannot be distributed among taxpayers; but it is essential that in future Mukhtars should furnish District Commissioners periodically with lists of arrears, and I will cause instructions to be issued accordingly.

Of course. H.D.

4. In summary, my recommendations are to write-off outstanding arrears of revenue under the following Heads of taxation and in the following amounts:-

(1) Mule Loans, 1919		LP. 5,416
(2) Seed Loans, 1929		6,000, approx.
(3) Other Loans (roughly)		25,000
(4) Werko		9,000
(5) (i) Tithes	LP. 9,796	
(ii) Commuted tithe not ascertainable, say	70,000	79,796
		LP. 125,212

5. I shall be grateful for your early approval of these recommendations.

I have the honour to be, Sir,
Your most obedient,
humble servant,

Arthur Wauchope

HIGH COMMISSIONER
FOR PALESTINE.

Report of Committee on Arrears of Werko, Tithes and Agricultural Loans.

The terms of reference of the Committee appointed by His Excellency the High Commissioner as set out in Chief Secretary's letter No.F/199/31 of 2nd February, 1932, were as follows:-

> "To inquire into the Arrears of Werko,
> "Tithes and Agricultural Loans and the
> "causes thereof and to make recommendations
> "as to the principles that may be applied
> "in writing-off or waiving such arrears with
> "due regard to Section 12 of the Collection
> "of Taxes Ordinance,1929, which provides that
> "taxes due shall be a first charge on any
> "immovable property of the defaulter".

2. In this Report the Committee have attempted:

(1) an analysis of the arrears of taxes still outstanding (see paragraphs 3 to 8)

(2) an examination of the three chief causes of arrears of taxes (see paragraphs 9 to 12).

(3) a review of various suggested principles for write-off of arrears of taxes with recommendations of those which the Committee consider practicable and just to apply, (see paragraphs 13 to 20).

(4) an analysis of various forms of agricultural loans in arrears (see paragraphs 21 to 24).

(5) principles recommended to be applied for write-off of agricultural loans (see paragraphs 25 to 28).

Analysis of Arrears of Taxes.

3. Summaries of Assessments, Collections, Remissions and Arrears of Werko, Commuted Tithes and Tithes were obtained from the District Authorities, together with lists of individual cases where remission or exemption from taxation was already authorised and of cases where the taxpayer and the properties were untraceable; and subsequently supplementary information was obtained as to:-

-2-

(1) Collections or remissions in respect of the amounts shown as arrears at 31st December, 1931, effected during the period 1st January to 31st March, 1932;

(2) Werko due by the Orthodox Patriarchate;

(3) Arrears outstanding at 31st December, 1931, in respect of the years 1930 and 1931 for Werko and 1929, 1930 and 1931 for Commuted Tithe (in the case of the Northern District only as the other Districts were unable to divide their arrears according to the years in which they were due).

4. The total arrears recorded in the statements submitted amounted to LP.395,924 at the 31st December, last as under (vide Appendix A).

	Werko LP.	Commuted Tithe LP.	Tithe LP.	Total LP.
Jerusalem District	39,478	14,040	3,539	57,057
Northern District	102,962	117,864	5,203	226,029
Southern District	40,501	71,219	1,118	112,838
	182,941	203,123	9,860	395,924

5. During the first quarter of 1932, however, collections in respect of these arrears amounted to LP.45,174 as under:-

	Werko LP.	Commuted Tithe LP.	Tithe LP.	Total LP.
Jerusalem District	3,457	647	26	4,130
Northern District	14,774	10,145	27	24,946
Southern District	4,554	11,533	11	16,098
	22,785	22,325	64	45,174

-3-

6. The total arrears recorded in para.4 also include the following amounts for which remissions were approved in 1931:-

Commuted Tithe.
LP.

Jerusalem District.

Hebron Sub-District	9,561	
Jerusalem-Bethlehem-Jericho S/D.	77	9,638

Southern District.

Jaffa Sub-District	31,389	31,389
		41,027

and an amount of LP.22,577 due by the Orthodox Patriarchate in respect of Werko which, we understand, is being submitted to arbitration. The distribution of this amount by districts is as follows:-

Jerusalem District	LP.14,381
Northern District	" 590
Southern District	" 7,603
	LP.22,577

7. It is noteworthy that, in the Northern District where tax accounts record assessments and collections separately by years, of the arrears of Werko amounting to LP.102,962, the sum of LP.27,692 relates to the year 1930 and LP.44,895 to the year 1931; and of the arrears of commuted tithe amounting to LP.117,864 the sum of LP.31,300 refers to the year 1929, LP.24,876 to the year 1930 and LP.48,204 to the year 1931.

8. The net arrears of these Taxes after taking into consideration the collections, remissions and the taxes due by the Orthodox Patriarchate referred to in paras.5 and 6 with which the Committee's recommendations deal are as follows:

	Werko LP.	Commuted Tithe LP.	Tithe LP.	Total LP.
Jerusalem District	21,640	3,755	3,513	28,908
Northern District	87,598	107,719	5,176	200,493
Southern District	28,341	28,297	1,107	57,745
	137,579	139,771	9,796	287,146

-4-

Causes of Arrears of Taxes.

9. The Committee found that the three chief causes of these arrears of taxes fell under the following categories.

A. Cases in which there is still doubt as to whether legal exemptions may or may not be applicable.

B. Cases in which both the defaulting taxpayer and property are untraceable.

C. Cases of proved incapacity to pay by a traceable defaulter owing to his property, if any, being undistrainable under Sections 274 (movables) or 294 immovables) of the Ottoman Code of Civil Procedure.

10. The cases reported to the Committee as falling under Categories A and B amount to a sum of LP.17,601 as follows:-

	Werko LP.		Commuted Tithe LP.		Tithe LP.	
	A	B	A	B	A	B
Jerusalem District	6802	2881	–	116	–	534
Northern District	138	2918	7	–	–	386
Southern District	88	2945	–	–	–	786
	7028	8744	7	116	–	1706

It should be noted, however, that no figures were submitted in respect of Haifa Sub-District.

11. The remaining arrears, summarised below, fall, largely in the view of the Committee, under Category C:-

	Werko LP.	Commuted Tithe LP.	Tithe LP.	
Jerusalem District	11,957	3,639	2,979	18,575
Northern District	84,542	107,712	4,790	197,044
Southern District	25,308	28,297	321	53,926
	121,807	139,648	8,090	269,545

Principles for write-off of arrears of taxes.

12. The Committee considered that although these sums may be in large measure uncollectable now owing to the absence of legally distrainable properties it would be difficult to recommend write-off in every case unless the incapacity to pay was permanent. Arrears on Werko may be due to other causes which are dealt with later in this report.

13. A proposal "that all arrears of tithes due in respect of periods prior to 31st December, 1929 should be remitted" was considered in view of the relatively small sum involved. It was realised however that there were certain defaulters who could and should have paid and whose escape now would be a dangerous incentive to future delays.

It is impracticable to deal with specific defaulters since individual accounts have not been kept so that the smallest unit which can be considered for write-off of tithes is the village. Arrears of the tithes from a given village may be due to a variety of causes including the dilatoriness of the mukhtars responsible for collection. The Committee is unable to find any equitable principle on which to base a recommendation for the write-off of arrears of tithes as a whole, or those due from selected villages. Specific cases where exceptional hardships can be proved should in the opinion of the Committee be submitted by District Commissioners and considered by Government on their merits.

14. On consideration of some equitable principle for remission of arrears of commuted tithes it was pointed out that the delay in approval of remissions had given no serious chance of collection during the last two years and that it was therefore wrong to assume that a large percentage of the amount due on Commuted Tithes in respect of the years prior to 1931 is necessarily uncollectable. In the absence of individual taxpayers' accounts it is impossible to assign a given sum as due from a defaulter whose incapacity to pay can be tested.

-6-

15. The Commuted Tithe is an amount fixed in relation to average yields in the past and takes no cognizance of fluctuations in current market prices. As long as both yields and prices showed no violent variations below average figures, collections proceeded normally. Arrears of tithe began to mount seriously after 1928 and it may be argued on the analogy of the reductions since then granted that in view of the fall in market prices, arrears in respect of the period prior to the 31st December 1929 should now be reduced by 50%.

16. The absence of individual accounts would entail the grouping throughout a whole village of all cases of uncollectable ? arrears of commuted tithes due on 31st December 1931, in respect of the years 1928 and 1929 (bearing in mind that with the exception of the Northern District it is impossible to ascertain the outstanding arrears for each year separately).

The recommendations would therefore in any case require to be modified to mean that the total sum to be written-off in any given village, after taking into account remissions already granted, should not exceed 50% of the assessment of Commuted Tithes for that village for the years 1928 and 1929 based on the percentage of remissions subsequently granted for the year 1930.

17. Even if this modified recommendation were adopted, after the maximum for a given village has been written-off, the remaining taxpayers in the same village who owe uncollectable arrears in respect of commuted tithe for 1928 and 1929 could receive no relief. There appears no reasonable method of discriminating between the fortunate defaulters of a village and those whose arrears would be undiminished by write-off. Deductions by equal sums from the arrears of all insolvent defaulters in the village would be as inequitable as writing-off proportional sums. The proposal, therefore, appears impracticable.

> ? i.e. a 50% reduction of arrears would only suffice to cover the arrears owing by villagers who have disappeared. Those who are left would have to pay the full liability to make up the other 50%

18.   With regard to Arrears of Werko, the nature of the Tax implies a property, which can be seized if traceable, unless it is the defaulter's dwelling house, or sufficient miri land to maintain it. In either case a write-off would not be justified. If the property is not traceable the onus of proof of what has become of the property falls on the defaulter. Hence again a write-off would not be justified without detailed examination of the individual circumstances of each defaulting taxpayer.

In some cases neither the defaulter nor the property is traceable. In many sub-districts records of taxpayers were lost during the war and the lists had to be made up from the manuscripts which happened to be still in the hands of the tax-collectors. It is possible therefore that the name of the taxpayer or the description of the property was incorrectly transposed into the official records. The presumption is stronger in cases where no collection at all has been made since the inception of the Civil Government on 1st July, 1920. Even here the identity of the property and of the defaulter may only be disclosed when the whole mosaic of registered parcels in the village are fitted together on completion of Land Settlement.

19.   The Committee cannot, therefore, in view of the arguments set out recommend any wholesale write-off of all arrears of any particular Tax.

The Committee agreed that District Officers should submit through the District Commissioners to Government direct individual cases under the Categories A and B described in paragraph 9 above, with a view to a write-off by Government.

-8-

But how?

In regard to Category C, the Committee suggest that District Officers should make detailed investigations of the means of each individual taxpayer and report on the likelihood of collections and the desirability for a write-off of any arrears due after taking into consideration the particular circumstances in which the taxpayer has been allowed to fall into arrear in the payment of his taxes.

Analysis of Agricultural Loan Arrears.

20.   The total amount of instalments of agricultural loans recorded in the Treasury Registers as in arrears at 31st December, 1931, amounted to LP.63,735 as under (vide Appendix B).

	Loans 1919/ to 1923	Beer-sheba Cultivators 1927	Seed Loans 1928	Agricultural Loans 1930	Total
	LP.	LP.	LP.	LP.	LP.
Jerusalem District	1,239	-	-	-	1,239
Northern District	28,373	-	12,088	10,226	50,687
Southern District	10,529	672	-	608	11,809
Total LP.	40,141	672	12,088	10,834	63,735

21.   During the first quarter of 1932 repayments in respect of the arrears of instalments amounted to LP.1,610 as under:-

	Loans 1919/ to 1923	Beer-sheba Cultivators 1927	Seed Loans 1928	Agricultural Loans 1930	Total
	LP.	LP.	LP.	LP.	LP.
Jerusalem District	12	-	-	-	12
Northern District	67	-	67	151	285
Southern District	1305	8	-	-	1313
	1384	8	67	151	1610

22.   The net arrears of these loans amount to LP.62,125 and may therefore, be summarised as under after deduction of the repayments made in the first quarter, 1932:-

-9-

	Loans 1919/ to 1923	Beer-shoba Cultivators	Seed Loans	Agricultural Loans 1930	Total
	LP.	LP.	LP.	LP.	LP.
Jerusalem District	1,227	-	-	-	1,227
Northern District	28,306	-	12,021	10,075	50,402
Southern District	9,224	664	-	608	10,496
Total	38,757	664	12,021	10,683	62,125

23.   There is in addition to the arrears on account of repayment of instalments of the loans accrued interest on these arrears. It will be realised that interest accrues to the date of payment or part-payment of arrears; and as the majority of the loans have considerably exceeded the period of repayment and accrued interest is calculated to the date of collection there is no record of the actual interest in xx arrear.

24. Mule Loans in 1919. A number of mules that had become unfit for Army purposes were placed on the market for disposal in Egypt and the best mules were sold. At that time agriculture in Palestine was suffering from a dearth of ploughing animals and it was decided by the Military Administration to supply cultivators with the discarded Army mules and to recover the cost in instalments. The remainder of the animals placed on the market in Egypt was sent to Palestine and cultivators purchased the mules at prices varying between LE.50 and LE.60. The animals were old and unfit for agricultural purposes and most of them died within the year of the purchase. The total amount of mule loans issued and the amount of arrears, exclusive of interest, outstanding on the 31st December,1928, 30th June, 1930 and 31st December,1931, are shown in the following table:-

-10-

Sub-District	Total Loans issued in 1919	ARREARS		
		31st Dec. 1928	30th June 1930	31st Dec. 1931
Nazareth	2,446	2,200	2,200	2,196
Tiberias	4,451	3,015	3,013	3,013
Safad	1,692	149	111	111
Beisan	1,600	125	99	96
Total	10,189	5,489	5,423	5,416

Interest accrues on mule loans at the rate of $6\frac{1}{2}\%$ p.a. and for the 3 years from December,1928 to December 1931 an additional amount on account of interest exceeding LP.1000, falls to be paid, while it is observed from the foregoing table that total collections during the period under review amounted to LP.73 only.

In view of the circumstances which attended the issue of these loans and considering that the cultivators derived little benefit from these loans, the Committee feel justified in recommending a write-off of the whole amount, including interest outstanding at the date upon which this recommendation, if accepted, is notified to District Commissioners.

25. <u>Seed Loans 1928.</u> Loans to a total value of LP.19,366 were issued in kind late in 1928 when grain commanded a high market price, and it was agreed at the time with borrowers that loans should be repaid within a period not exceeding one year from the date of issue. When crops were harvested, however, the price of grain had fallen to such an extent that cultivators found difficulty in meeting their obligations. The statement appended shows the value of the seed loans issued and the arrears on 31st December 1930 and the 31st December 1931.

Sub-District	Value of Loans	ARREARS	
		31st Dec. 1930	31st Dec. 1931
	LP.	LP.	LP.
Haifa	1757	1570	1252
Acre	605	52	52
Nazareth	16	16	16
Tiberias	2911	2427	1682
Safad	1592	1548	1536
Nablus	5126	2541	2507
Jenin	3256	1216	1147
Beisane	1603	1460	1396
Jewish Colonies	2500	2500	2500
Total	19366	13330	12088

It will be observed that collections in 1931 are about 9% of the sum outstanding on the 31st December, 1930, but since these loans bear interest at the rate of 5% p.a. the amount collected is barely 4% of the sum due.

On the whole, 38% of the total amount of these loans has been repaid mainly due to collections from Tiberias, Nablus and Jenin; and the Committee feel that it would be unfair to those who have proved to be good payers if they were to recommend remission at this stage.

However, in view of the fact that loans were issued in kind and that undertakings by borrowers were given in terms of money at the high market prices then obtaining, and considering the fall in the market prices when the crops were harvested, the Committee are of the opinion that loans outstanding should be reduced to an amount equal to the value of the grain issued, at the market price at the time the several loans fell due. It is not possible, without further enquiry, to ascertain the extent of the remission recommended; but in any case the Committee consider that interest on the reduced loans should continue to be collected.

-12-

26. In regard to the remaining Agricultural Loans, the Committee considered that no general principle for write-off could be stated having regard to the conditions of the contracts and the fact that writing-off of any loan must have an adverse effect on the recovery of other loans. They considered that all that can be done is to give further time for collection.

27. They agreed that with the exceptions mentioned above arrears of loans should only be written-off when

   (a) the debtor is dead

 or (b) has left the country.

in cases where no guarantors or means of recovery exist; and that District Officers should make detailed investigations on each individual case of arrears, report on the likelihood of collections and the desirability for a write-off having regard to the particular circumstances in which the borrower has been allowed to fall into arrears in the payment of his instalments of the loans.

28. In making these recommendations the Committee has been chiefly concerned in finding principles which will be equitable as between good and bad payers, and which will not encourage evasion of future collections. It has been represented that much more sweeping remissions should be considered on the ground that there is little prospect of these arrears ever being paid within a reasonable term of years or that <u>excessive assessments of taxation constitute</u> the real causes of such arrears.

If such is the case the proper remedy would appear to be to allow the pendulum to swing the other way and to relieve the general burden of taxation rather than to penalise prompt payment. It has been urged again that all outstanding arrears which cannot be recovered within say five years be written-off <u>as in India</u> and other settled dependencies. Such a system undoubtedly encourages vigorous and prompt collection and gives relief from accumulated debts to the State. The Committee consider, however, that to apply such a rule to Palestine would be unsafe and unfair until the machinery of collection is made more effective and until systems of assessment and accounting have been simplified and stabilised over a period of at least a further five years.

Summary of Recommendations.

1. Arrears of tithes prior to 31st December, 1929.

Specific cases of exceptional hardship should be submitted to Government and considered on their merits. (para 13).

2. Arrears of commuted tithe.

Remission impracticable; (para.17).

3. Arrears of Werko.

   (a) Cases in which there is doubt as to whether legal exemption may be applicable should be referred to Government for a decision. (para.19).

   (b) Cases in which both taxpayer and property cannot be traced should be referred individually to Government for decision. In cases where no collections have been made since 1st July, 1920, the Committee consider the arrears may be written off; on completion of Land Settlement for the village. (paras.18 and 19).

   (c) Cases of proved inability to pay should be investigated and referred to Government with a view to writing off the amount; (para.19).

4. Mule Loans 1919.

Arrears outstanding and interest to be written off; (para.24).

5. Seed Loans 1928.

Outstanding loans should be reduced to an amount equal to the quantity of grain issued at the market price of the grain when the several loans fall due, the reduced amount with interest to be collected. (para.25).

6. Other Agricultural Loans.

   (a) Write off of outstanding loans in cases where the debtor is dead or has left the country and there are no means of recovery (para.27).

   (b) In other cases further time should be given for collection (para.26).

Appendix A.

SUMMARY OF ARREARS OF TAXATION AT 31st DECEMBER, 1931.

	Arrears at 31st December 1931				Arrears of Werko in respect of year		Arrears of Commuted Tithe in respect of year			Arrears of Werko due by Greek Orthodox Patriarchate	Collection of Arrears January 1st – 31st March 1932.		
	Werko LP.	Tithes LP.	Commuted Tithe LP.	Total LP.	1930 LP.	1931 LP.	1929 LP.	1930 LP.	1931 LP.	LP.	Werko LP.	Tithes LP.	Commuted Tithes LP.
Jerusalem (including Bethlehem & Jericho	31,902	3,327	2,408	(a) 37,737	District Commissioner reports that information cannot be supplied					14,250	1,717	22	103
Ramallah	5,283	218	601	(a) 6,126						122	1,698	4	327
Hebron	2,223	–	10,911	(a) 13,134						–	42	–	157
Total Jerusalem District	39,478	3,539	14,040	(a) 57,057	–	–	–	–	–	14,361	3,457	26	647
Haifa	34,139	2,331	33,051	69,521	9,371	16,500	10,491	7,134	10,098	418	5,001	–	1,223
Acre	11,755	436	15,618	27,809	3,608	5,918	4,801	2,726	7,001	15	3,422	7	1,983
Safad	8,039	186	9,108	17,333	2,131	3,141	2,614	2,225	3,997	–	1,288	–	952
Tiberias	8,691	193	12,532	21,816	2,611	3,400	3,820	3,245	8,403	102	1,157	–	2,394
Nazareth	18,206	1,022	18,763	37,981	4,789	4,794	5,623	3,031	5,802	45	489	–	560
Beisan	5,425	205	6,316	11,946	1,751	2,250	1,720	1,049	2,240	–	1,109	–	676
Nablus	4,184	408	6,636	11,200	820	3,738	1,074	637	4,021	2	1,102	12	943
Jenin	5,819	87	11,694	17,590	1,744	3,872	1,300	3,087	6,880	8	308	6	979
Tulkarem	6,804	355	4,316	11,475	2,387	3,720	401	–	4,242	–	809	2	554
Total Northern District	102,962	5,203	117,804	226,029	32,602	44,505	31,300	24,070	40,204	590	14,774	27	10,145
Jaffa (including Ramleh)	31,465	820	63,736	96,049	Cannot be supplied. Separately: D.C. Jaffa letter No. 13/20 of 11.4.32		Cannot be supplied Separately: D.C. JAFFA Letter No. 13/20 of 11.4.32			7,008	8,636	3	10,381
Gaza	8,547	80	6,041	15,468						–	990	–	1,102
Beersheba	469	210	642	1,321						8	20	8	40
Total Southern District	40,501	1,118	71,219	112,838	–	–	–	–	–	7,016	4,564	11	11,533
TOTAL	182,941	9,860	203,123	395,924	–	–	–	–	–	22,577	12,795	64	22,325

(a) Includes arrears to 31st March, 1931 and outstanding amounts on account of assessment 1931/32 as at December, 1931.

[Copy is poor in original file, this and following page.]

Appendix B.

STATEMENT SHOWING THE BALANCES OUTSTANDING OF LOANS ISSUED UNDER THE AGRICULTURAL LOANS ORDINANCES, 1930.

	Outstanding arrears at 31st December, 1931				Sums recovered during period 1st January to 31st March, 1932				Net outstanding arrears at 31st March, 1932			
	Prior to 1930	Horseshoe Cultivation Loans	Land Loans 1930	Seed Loans 1930	Loans 1930	Total	Prior to 1930	Horseshoe Cultivation Loans	Seed Loans 1931	1930 Loans	Total	Prior to 1930	Horseshoe Cultivation Loans	Seed Loans 1930	1930 Loans	Total
JERUSALEM DISTRICT												
Jerusalem Sub-District (including Bethlehem & Jericho)	717	–	–	–	–	717	11	–	–	–	11	706	–	–	–	–	706
Ramallah	520	–	–	–	–	520	1	–	–	–	1	519	–	–	–	–	578
Hebron	13	–	–	–	–	13	–	–	–	–	–	13	–	–	–	–	13
	1,250	–	–	–	–	1,250	13	–	–	–	13	1,237	–	–	–	–	1,237
NORTHERN DISTRICT												
Haifa	1,963	–	1,953	1,033	4,949	24	–	24	–	24	1,863	–	1,238	1,033	4,134
Acre	515	–	52	–	567	6	–	–	–	6	513	–	52	–	505
Safad	975	–	1,537	1,304	3,816	–	–	–	–	–	975	–	1,537	1,346	3,518
Tiberias	3,729	–	1,434	1,340	6,703	20	20	–	–	70	3,725	–	1,453	1,846	6,729
Nazareth	14,450	–	16	2,340	14,776	–	5	7	–	–	14,450	–	17	2,348	13,777
Baisan	733	–	306	1,197	2,113	–	3	–	–	303	739	–	1,320	1,078	3,233
Ka'lan	2,000	3,077	–	2,504	5,524	68	4	–	–	–	68	2,000	–	2,504	5,131
Jenin	2,141	–	2,147	–	4,562	–	–	–	–	2,041	–	2,147	–	4,088
Tulkarem	1,024	–	–	–	1,024	–	–	–	–	1,070	–	1,100	2,119
	20,272	–	9,528	20,254	40,827	203	–	50	157	305	20,000	–	9,581	10,000	47,002
Jewish Colonies Northern District	–	2,500	–	2,500	–	–	–	–	–	–	2,500	–	2,500
Total Northern D.	20,270	072	12,108	10,365	49,037	205	1,054	72	157	1,280	20,370	1,054	12,031	12,075	61,402
SOUTHERN DISTRICT												
Jaffa (including Rama leh)	8,875	–	660	660	9,908	6,134	87	–	0,054	0,684	7,570	–	–	806	7,518
Gaza	1,054	–	360	600	2,014	–	–	–	–	1,054	–	860	600	2,514
Beersheba	–	–	–	–	–	–	–	–	–	–	554	–	–	434
TOTAL	10,539	072	–	800	11,069	6,134	87	–	0,054	0,172	10,539	1,054	12,031	2,008	13,496

5.10

PALESTINE.

HIGH COMMISSIONER FOR PALESTINE,
JERUSALEM.

CONFIDENTIAL.

23 February, 1934.

Reference No. CF/264/33.

Sir,

    I have the honour to refer to my Confidential despatch of the 14th December, 1933, and previous correspondence on the subject of rural taxation, and to forward for your consideration the draft of an Ordinance to provide for the taxation of certain lands and buildings in rural areas in accordance with the decisions which I have taken as to the general principles to be followed in this new legislation after exhaustive reconsideration of the proposals with my advisers.

Enclosure I.

    2. In particular I have thought it well to review the proposals in the light of the criticisms of your Economic and Financial Adviser which were brought to my attention, and in the light of the evident desirability of providing for the exemption of the poorest classes of rural property-owners from the payment of the tax.

    At the outset, I had considered the question in Executive Council on the basis of the report of the original Committee and had come to the conclusions set out in Enclosure III in my despatch Confidential A of the 13th August, 1932. A copy of the report of the original Committee also accompanied that despatch.

    Thereafter I appointed a second Committee consisting of the Treasurer as Chairman, the Commissioner of Lands, the District Commissioner, Jerusalem District and the Development

Officer/

The Right Honourable
Sir Philip Cunliffe-Lister, G.B.E., M.P., etc., etc.,
    His Majesty's Principal Secretary of State
            for the Colonies.

-2-

Officer as members, to submit a combined recommendation on all outstanding points, with special reference to the criticisms of Sir John Campbell.

Enclosure II. 3. I enclose a copy of the report of the Committee accompanied by the draft Ordinance forming the first enclosure in this despatch, and a statement of observations on the criticisms of Sir John Campbell; the Committee was unanimous in its recommendations.

The following summary of the recommendations may be found convenient:

(i) The tax to take the form of a single tax levied on owners as a rate per dunum.

(ii) The rate of tax per dunum to vary according to the category of land and to be based approximately on $12\frac{1}{2}\%$ of net annual value of Categories 1, 2, 3, 4; and 10% in other cases.

(iii) Classification of holdings into categories to be made by assessors.

(iv) The tax to be borne by the owner: that is, where the land has been settled, the registered owner; elsewhere the person receiving the rents or profits in such circumstances that he is the reputed owner. In circumstances of dispute, always by the registered owner. In case of lease for more than three years, by the lessee. In case of default, the property to be attachable by Government.

(v)/

-3-

(v) Exemptions to comprise only those enjoyed under the law at present in force. Uncultivable land brought under development, and ground crop land brought under fruit-culture to be taxable under previous category until yielding in new.

(vi) Remission to be granted only where aggregate value of crops in any village falls by one-third or more below average by reason of failure of harvest.

(vii) Waqf land to be liable to the tax, subject to consideration of individual claims with a view to commutation.

(viii) State properties occupied by tenants to be subject to adjusted rental which would include the tax.

(ix) The tax not to be applied experimentally.

(x) The Animal Tax to be abolished, and the new tax to take its place, as well as the place of tithe and werko.

(xi) The rate of tax is intended to produce approximately 1932-33 collections from tithe (including citrus), werko and Animal Tax, or say LP. 250,000.

4. Consideration of the Committee's Report in Executive Council inclined me to the view that the number of categories of land might be reduced; and that the provision for remissions which was suggested in recommendation (vi) was

too/

-4-

too restrictive. But principally, I formed the opinion first that small incomes ought to be immune from taxation; and secondly that the balance of argument was in favour of maintaining the separate enforcement of the Animal Tax.

As regards the exemption of incomes below a certain minimum there are parallels of exemptions of premises possessing less than a certain rental value under the Urban Property Tax Ordinance; and Section 103 of the Municipal Corporations Ordinance, 1933, provides for the waiver of municipal rates on any land or building where its assessment would not produce 100 mils. I fully appreciate that the proposed tax is not strictly an income tax but a "per dunum" tax; basically, however, the rate of tax is determined by the average net income of the category in which the property is classified.

My reasons for maintaining the Animal Tax were that this is the only direct contribution to State revenue by the pastoral population, and that if the tax were abolished in Palestine there would be a standing inducement to stock-owners in neighbouring territories to come over into Palestine during the season of enumeration and collection so as to evade payment.

5. The precise form in which to grant exemption of the poorest classes from the Rural Property Tax was next considered in consultation with District Commissioners. I decided in Executive Council that the law should be so framed as to provide for a set of invariable remissions, as well as for the grant of relief from payment of the tax when circumstances appear to the High Commissioner to demand it. Consequently in addition to empowering the High Commissioner to grant remission in cases of general or partial failure of crops or fall in prices as recommended under paragraph 3(vi) supra - and experience shows that the extent of remission in

such/

such cases must often be very substantial - provision is made in the Schedule to the draft Ordinance for the total exemption from the tax of the three lowest categories of land. I also decided that exemption, when statutorily admissible, should extend to all persons whether heads of families, orphans, minors or owner-cultivators, who as registered and reputed owners were liable to pay the tax; and should extend to unsettled as well as settled areas.

6. As regards the actual degree of exemption, I had to choose between:

(a) exempting all taxpayers in respect of the first 500 mils of assessment; or

(b) reducing or wholly eliminating the tax payable on certain categories of land.

I have reluctantly abandoned the first proposal, for the time being, being advised that it would lead to evasion of payment on a large scale, and was not susceptible of effective control. Land-owners, in the areas in which Land Settlement has not yet been completed, would divide up their property among their children and relatives in order to obtain the greatest possible exemption.

Until the assessment under the new Tax is complete, no close estimate can be formed of the revenue which it will produce: but there is little doubt that the revenue will be substantially less than that from the commuted tithe and werko. If therefore these reduced receipts were to suffer in addition further considerable reduction on account of wide spread evasion, the financial effect might well be serious.

Once, however, assessments are completed, the tax has been applied, and a complete list of taxpayers compiled, I hope that it will be possible to reconsider the proposal whereby all taxpayers would be exempted from the payment of the first 500 mils. The exemption would then only be

applicable/

applicable to persons whose names appeared on the list of taxpayers or to persons whose title to their land had been registered. By this means it should be possible, if not to eliminate evasion, at least to restrict it within very narrow limits.

It is anticipated that the tax will begin to be collected and that a full list of taxpayers will have been compiled by the 1st April, 1935. Until then, in the circumstances, I will defer further consideration of the proposal wholly to exempt the poorest classes from payment of the new tax. In the beginning, therefore, my intention is to grant total immunity in respect of land in categories 14, 15 and 16 of the Classification recommended by the Committee, and to reduce appreciably the rate of those recommended by the Committee for categories 5 to 13 inclusive. I enclose a schedule of the categories, showing the original rates recommended and the rates that I have decided to adopt.

Enclosure III.

I am content, in the changed circumstances, that there should be sixteen categories.

7. I am still engaged in examination of the question of the improvement of the machinery of tax-collection, in the light of the report of a committee set up in January, 1933, and in the light of changes contemplated in the organization of the three Departments of Government which are concerned with the settlement, registration and survey of lands. I forward a copy of the report of this Committee for your information at this juncture.

Enclosure IV.

8. A rough estimate of the total annual assessment of rural taxation under the new system is LP. ~~212,800~~ 497,000 derived as follows:-

* See no. 2.

Tithe assessments in Beersheba sub-district and other Bedu lands (to which the rural property tax would not be made applicable)	L.P. 9,000
Rural Property Tax	150,000
Animal Tax	38,000
	197,000

By way of comparison it may be said that in 1932-33 the total assessment of rural taxes exclusive of remissions was L.P. 425,000, and collections amounted to only L.P. 227,000. Section VIII of the report of the Rural Property Tax Committee, mentioned in the third paragraph of this despatch, suggests that a figure of L.P. 250,000 (or approximately L.P. 208,000 excluding the Animal Tax) would fairly represent the ability of the rural population to pay the new tax. The figure of L.P. 150,000 in the preceding table is the result of exempting low-earning categories of land and the reduced rates. But as citrus cultivation increases and as credit facilities become available and agricultural methods are improved, land will pass from the lower to the higher categories, and the receipts from the new tax will be proportionately enhanced. I do not consider however that any form of fixed land tax is likely to produce appreciably more than L.P. 150,000 in the aggregate bearing in mind the fact that the bulk of rural property for some years to come will be cereal land of low-earning capacity and the necessity for relating the burden of the tax to that on urban property as a percentage of income.

9. The cost of the present machinery of rural taxation (see paragraphs 144, 145 of the report of the Committee mentioned in the seventh paragraph of this despatch) has been calculated at L.P. 29,468. It is estimated that the cost of the initial assessment of the proposed Rural

Property/

-8-

Property Tax will be LP 15,000; and the cost of annual revisions of assessments should not be greater than that of the Commuted Tithe alone, viz. approximately LP 1,500. There should, however, be a considerable saving in the cost of collection of the Rural Property Tax by Mukhtars who will be paid on a percentage basis, instead of, as now, the employment of whole-time tax collectors for the House and Land tax and the payment of Mukhtars on a percentage basis for the collection of the commuted Tithe. I shall however address you further on this matter in connection with the draft Estimates for 1935-36.

     I have the honour to be,
      Sir,
       Your most obedient,
        humble servant,

         Arthur Wauchope
         HIGH COMMISSIONER
         FOR PALESTINE.

REPORT OF THE COMMITTEE APPOINTED BY HIS EXCELLENCY
TO GIVE FURTHER CONSIDERATION TO THE DRAFT ORDINANCE
ON RURAL PROPERTY TAX.

Committee:

    H.J. Johnson, Esq., O.B.E. - Chairman.
    A. Abramson, Esq., C.B.E.)
    J.E.F. Campbell, Esq., O.B.E.) Members.
    L. Andrews, Esq., O.B.E.)

Terms of Reference:

A. To give further consideration to the draft Ordinance on Rural Land Tax with the following duties :-

    (i) to submit a combined recommendation upon all outstanding points upon which it is possible to reach agreement, and

    (ii) to set out for the final decision of His Excellency, the issues upon which the Committee is unable to agree.

B. To study the memorandum written by Sir John Campbell and to submit :-

    (i) agreed recommendations,

    (ii) points on which agreement cannot be reached,

guided throughout by the decisions taken by His Excellency in Executive Council in this regard.

2.

Procedure:

From the start it was apparent that the sentence "guided throughout by the decision taken by His Excellency in Executive Council" appearing in the terms of reference required elucidation since it was not clear whether the decisions taken were intended to be excluded from the scope of the Committee's deliberations.

According to the attached copy of letter No.CF/308/32 dated 8th April, 1933, from the Chief Secretary these decisions are within the purview of the Committee; and the Committee therefore proceeded to examine the application of the rural property tax from the point of view of the decisions taken bearing in mind the memorandum written by Sir John Campbell and they now submit their recommendations.

I. <u>A Single Tax</u>.

The question of taxing the two sources of income from immovable property in rural areas, namely the rent representing the landlord's interest and the net annual yield representing the cultivator's interest was discussed at some length. It was clear that owing to local conditions income from these two sources was dependent largely upon annual gross yields and that in Palestine, where payment in kind for rent and wages is the common form of payment, the absence of crop records made an annual assessment of the value of the gross yield

3.

impracticable. The only practical method of assessing the value of gross annual yield would be to take the average productivity value of the holding at the average market price over a period of years.

In England, where rent in cash is the common form of payment, the net profits of the farmer are conventionally based on rent; but in Palestine rent in cash is the rare exception. In the great majority of cases rent is taken in kind, in proportion varying from 20% to 75% of the gross yield according to the extent by which the landlord assists the tenant in supplying seed, animals, subsistence or paying the tithe. When the tithe was collected in kind rent was usually collected as a percentage of the crop after a tithe of the crop had been taken. The owner therefore in practise paid the tithe as well as the werko tax. The Committee agreed that the tax should take the form of a single tax levied on the owner as a rate per dunum. The Committee realise, however, that the rate at which such a tax will be levied must necessarily be low in order to admit of collection in a bad year, since in a good year the cultivator's improvidence will militate against his saving, while in a bad year he will not possess the wherewithall to pay.

II. **Basis of the Tax**.

In view of the practical difficulties of

4.

meeting objections if net annual value of land were shown on the actual assessment the Committee decided to recommend that a rate of tax per dunum varying according to the category of the land should be shown. It would be necessary therefore to divide the land into classified categories according to the average net annual return of each; and to afford the tax payer the opportunity of objecting to the classification of his holding. Mr. Abramson acquiesces in this view reluctantly because he considers that the tax payer should know the basis of the tax on which his holding is assessed. As to the actual classification, the Committee accept in principle the categories suggested by the Commissioner of Lands, vide Appendix A, and recommend that the classification of holdings into the various categories should be left to Assessors. The rates of tax per dunum have been calculated roughly at 12½% of the net annual value of categories 1, 2, 3 and 4 and at roughly 10% of net annual value of each of the remaining categories as estimated by the Commissioner of Lands.

III. *Incidence of the Tax*.

The Committee agree that the tax should fall on the owner of the land provided that where the property has been subject to settlement the owner shall be the registered owner of the property; and where the property has not been subject to settlement, the owner shall be the person who

ε.

receives the rent and/or profits of the property in such circumstances that he is the reputed owner, whether or not he is in possession or whether or not he is the registered owner, provided always that in the case of dispute the registered owner shall be deemed to be the owner. If the property is let, leased or sub-leased for a term exceeding three years and the lease is registered in the Land Registry, the lessee or sub-lessee of the property or if there be two or more sub-leases the sub-lessee under the last created sub-lease shall be deemed to be the owner instead of the person entitled to the rent and/or profits. However, since land is the object of the tax the Committee recommend that in case of default of the owner as defined, Government should have the power to attach the property.

IV. **Village Assessment and Apportionment.**

Since the tax proposed is to take the form of a rate per dunum varying according to categories into which land is classified, the village assessment becomes relatively simple. The village land will be classified into the various categories by Assessors under the direction of the Commissioner of Lands. Lists by village showing the fiscal block numbers, the names of the Oltas, the number of dunums, the category, the rate of tax per dunum and the total amount of the tax payable by the village will be prepared in the office of the Commissioner of Lands and forwarded to the District Officer concerned for posting in the village for

6.

a period during which objections and appeals may be lodged against the classification.

The total amount of tax payable by the village will then be distributed among tax payers by village committees appointed by the District Commissioner calculated, where settlement is not completed, in the case of Mafrus lands roughly on area, and in the case of Musha' on shares. These lists will be posted for fourteen days during which objections may be lodged. When these objections have been disposed of by the District Officer, the list will be submitted for the District Commissioner's approval.

Where settlement of a village is completed, the Distribution Lists will be prepared in the office of the Commissioner of Lands from the Schedules of Rights and Partition prepared at Land Settlement and according to the actual area of land owned by tax payers in the village. The lists will be forwarded to the District Officer concerned for posting in the villages and for collection.

V. **Exemption.**

The Committee recommend that uncultivable land, by reason of development, and ground crop land brought under fruit trees should on changing category remain liable to the tax appropriate to the former category until such time as such lands begin to yield in the new category.

The Committee next considered whether it

7.

is possible to waive collection of the tax when the amount due by an individual tax payer fell below a certain minimum. It was agreed that such a principle is unusual in a land tax and if applied may lead to systematic evasion; but the Committee agreed to recommend that the aggregate amount of tax payable by any owner in the village should be increased or decreased, as the case may be, to the nearest 5 Mils.

The Committee agreed with the Commissioner of Lands that remission should only be granted in cases where the estimated aggregate value of the crop in any village falls by one-third or more below its average by reason of failure of harvests.

Next, the question as to whether Waqf land should be exempt was considered and it was decided that since the greater portion of the Waqf Tithes had been commuted for a fixed annual payment, Waqf land should be liable to the tax. Individual cases, should any arise, might be treated each on its merits with a view to commutation.

Under existing conditions State Property is exempt from the payment of Werko but the tenant is subject to the payment of the Commuted Tithe and to the payment of a rental which in the majority of cases is equivalent to the Commuted Tithe. The Committee agree that State Properties other than such as are actually occupied by Government, are unoccupied or set aside for a specific public service should be subject to an adjusted rental

6.

which should include the tax. It is realised that wherever the tenant occupier of a State property falls within the definition of owner, he will be liable for the tax.

VI. Experimental Application.

The Committee is agreed that the tax should not be applied experimentally.

(It was explained to the Committee that the previous recommendation was not an experiment as to the application of the tax, but rather an experiment of distribution amongst tax payers as shown in the Schedule of Rights).

VII. Animal Tax.

The animal tax was originally a tithe on the living produce of land and was collected in kind at the rate of one head on every ten heads (vide Young's Corps de Droit Ottoman Vol. V, page 292). It is not of the nature of a grazing fee. It was ascertained by the Committee that grazing fees are not charged and until quite recently the flocks of one village were allowed to graze freely on the lands of another village. By reason of the drought and the consequent insufficiency of pasture villagers now view with disfavour the grazing of flocks belonging to other villages or nomads on their village lands. As a deterrent to flock migration an attempt is being made by villagers to charge a fee on foreign flocks grazing on village lands. The Committee was further

9.

informed that in the great majority of cases, if not in all of them, flock owners possess lands and are liable to the payment of the land tax (Werko). In view of the foregoing explanations the Committee agreed to recommend the abolition of the animal tax and to recommend that the proposed rural land tax should be substituted for the animal tax as well as the tithe and werko. In making this recommendation the Committee is alive to the possibility of an objection being raised on the grounds that during the enumeration in Syria and Trans-Jordan, flocks may migrate to Palestine and thus evade the payment of the tax in those countries. They do not consider, however, that this objection should stand in the way of the general welfare of the Palestinian peasant, nor do they consider the objection insuperable.

VIII. Rate of the Tax.

In order to determine the rate of tax which should be levied it is necessary in the first place to gauge the ability of the tax payer. It is generally recognised that the year 1932-33 was an abnormally bad year for the agriculturist, and following as it does a number of bad years immediately preceding, the Committee considered that it would not be unfair to take actual collections during 1932-33 as a guide to the ability of the rural tax payer. In 1932-33 the total assessment of tithes (irrespective of

10.

remissions), of house and land tax and animal tax amounted to approximately £P.425,000, as under :-

	£P.
Tithe (including citrus)	275,000
House and Land Tax (in rural areas)	112,000
Animal Tax	38,000
Total:	£P.425,000

During 1932-33, however, collections were approximately £P.227,000 as under :-

	£P.
Tithe (including citrus)	100,000
House and Land Tax	85,000
Animal Tax	42,000
Total:	£P.227,000

Thus collections represent roughly 55% of the total assessment.

The Committee realise that a rate per dunum calculated to yield as much as the aggregate assessment of tithes, house and land tax and animal tax would be unduly high and practically impossible to collect. They consider that the assessment should be materially reduced. On the other hand the assessment should be maintained at a figure above actual collections during 1932-33 to ensure collections amounting to £P.227,000 at least. On the basis of figures supplied by the Commissioner of Lands for villages which have been settled

11.

and in which fiscal survey has been completed, it is estimated that the rural property tax if applied to the country as a whole at the rates shown in the enclosed schedule (Appendix A) should produce a total assessment of £P.250,000. It must be pointed out, however, that this estimate has been made by substituting the proposed tax in these villages for existing taxes; and that there is no record of the total number of dunums in the various categories for the whole country.

23rd June, 1933.

ACH.

Appendix A.

RURAL PROPERTY TAX.

Category	Description	Rate of Tax per dunum Mils
1	Citrus (omitting Acre)	825
2	Citrus (Acre Sub-District)	410
3	Bananas	560
4	Village or Colony built-on area or reserved therefor	160
5	1st Grade Irrigated Land and ⚡ 1st Grade Fruit Plantation	40
6	2nd Grade Irrigated Land and ⚡ 2nd Grade Fruit Plantation	35
7	3rd Grade Irrigated Land and ⚡ 3rd Grade Fruit Plantation	30
8	1st Grade Ground Crop Land, ⚡ 4th Grade Fruit Plantations and 4th Grade Irrigated Land	25
9	2nd Grade Ground Crop Land, ⚡ 5th Grade Fruit Plantation and 5th Grade Irrigated Land	20
10	3rd Grade Ground Crop Land, 6th Grade Irrigated Land and ⚡ 6th Grade Fruit Plantation	18
11	4th Grade Ground Crop Land, 7th Grade Irrigated Land and ⚡ 7th Grade Fruit Plantation	15
12	5th Grade Ground Crop Land, 8th Grade Irrigated Land and ⚡ 8th Grade Fruit Plantation	12
13	6th Grade Ground Crop Land, 9th Grade Irrigated Land and ⚡ 9th Grade Fruit Plantation	8
14	7th Grade Ground Crop Land and 10th Grade Irrigated Land	5
15	8th Grade Ground Crop Land	3
16	Forests planted and indigenous uncultivable land	½

⚡ Other than Citrus and Bananas.

AGH.

OBSERVATIONS OF COMMITTEE ON SIR JOHN CAMPBELL'S NOTE ON THE REPORT OF THE RURAL TAXATION COMMITTEE.

General.

The "back ground" of the Committee's recommendations is supplied in Chapters IV and VI of Sir John Hope Simpson's report on Immigration, Land Settlement and Development.

Agricultural property is commonly held by Miri title and ownership is vested in the Government; but the right of possession is granted by Government to private persons in perpetuity subject to certain conditions – the chief of which is continuous cultivation, although Government has in recent years seldom exercised the right of escheat. Approximately half the agricultural land is Mesha'a and is held in common although measures are being taken by Government to partition these lands by agreement among the parties and in exceptional cases through the Courts. No occupancy right exists in favour of the Arab tenant who as a rule holds his land on a three year lease and sometimes on a yearly tenancy terminable at the end of the lease.

The taxes paid by the agriculturalist are the Tithe, Werko, and Animal Tax apart from the indirect taxes upon imported goods which he purchases and fees on registration of land on

2.

transfer or mortgage. The Commuted Tithe replaced in 1928 the tithe payable on the produce of the soil. It is based on the average amount of tithe payable by a village during a period of four years. The tax is apportioned among reputed owners, in the case of divided lands, in the proportion of estimated productivity usually in the terms of wheat; in the case of undivided lands, in the proportion of their respective shares; in tribal areas, in accordance with tribal customs; and, in the case of the produce of fruit trees, usually according to the average amount of tithes payable during a period of four years. As prices and crops have been very poor since the commutation of the tithe, collection has been difficult. The Werko Tax is assessed on the capital value of land and buildings in rural areas and is payable by the owner; the last general assessment was made some thirty-five years ago; but re-assessments are made whenever dispositions in land are registered. The assessment is very uneven and in many districts the original records of assessment have been lost. Animal Tax is a per capita tax on sheep, goats, camels, buffaloes and pigs; excepting camels and buffaloes used solely for ploughing. The Committee now proposes to substitute a Rural Property Tax for the Commuted Tithe, the Werko and the Animal Tax.

Government's present proposal for a Rural Property Tax is for the purpose of re-distributing

3.

the burden of rural taxation in accordance with the ability to pay. The ability of agriculturists to pay taxes is obviously measured, in the case of the landlord, by the rental value or earnings of his capital investment in the property, and, in the case of the cultivator, by his net profits from cultivation after the deduction of rental value. But the actual rental value and net profits from cultivation of each individual holding in rural areas in Palestine cannot be ascertained as rents and wages are usually paid in kind and there are no crop records. Rural property is however easily divided into general categories representing degrees of fertility in respect of which the average net annual value can be estimated.

Principles of Taxation.

It is agreed that "the fundamental principle if things are to work smoothly should be to keep as close as possible to definitely ascertained facts". As explained in the Committee's report fiscal blocks will be formed of land of approximately equal fertility established throughout most of the country by agricultural practice under the "masha'a" system; and it will not be difficult to estimate the <u>relative values</u> of land in the different fiscal blocks. If during the fiscal survey it is found necessary to increase the number of categories where there are appreciable variations in net annual value

4.

of land within a category, this can easily be done without changing the relative value of any of the remaining categories, or new categories can be formed.

Price Basis.

The observations under this head are met by the Committee's recommendation for a general review of conversion prices every five years.

Irrigated land as compared with unirrigated land.

Sir John Campbell is obviously thinking of land irrigated by large irrigation canals with an almost unlimited supply of water, and not of ground-crop land irrigated by the primitive and mechanical handling of water from wells or springs. The Committee's recommendations are based on actual experience of conditions prevaling in Palestine. It will be observed that the schedule of categories provides for ten categories of irrigated land, and that the rate of tax per dunum ranges from 5 mils to 40 mils.

Collection.

It is agreed that "assessments on landowners, if the assessments are reasonable and made under a sound system, practically collect themselve The recommendation for a single fixed tax on landowners at reduced rates is made with the object of making the incidence more equitable and the tax easier of collection.

5.

Rates.

The actual taxes to be collected will be the product of the number of dunams in each category throughout the country and the rate of the tax per dunam of each category. The differences between the rates of tax of categories represents (relative) net annual values of a dunam of land in the various categories.

Incidence.

The separate taxes on the interests of landowners and cultivators, based on the principle of the English Income Tax, is not being proceeded with. The tax now proposed is a single tax on the landowner.

Remission.

The adequacy or otherwise of the provision for remissions depends mainly on the rate of tax; but it is considered that adequate provision has been made for remission in times of poor harvests and low prices.

Experimental Introduction.

The previous recommendation was not an experiment as to the application of the tax, but rather an experiment of distribution amongst tax-payers as shown in the schedule of rights. Experiments have however proved the practicability of the proposals and there is no necessity for any further experimental period.

6.

Character of the Tax.

The "net annual" value referred to by the Committee represented the profits of husbandry upon which the cultivator had to subsist. In any system of income tax this source of income would be taxable. In the same way rent represents income from the ownership of land upon which the landowner subsists. But in any case as it is not now proposed separately to tax the cultivator's net annual income, the argument is irrelevant.

MF.

RURAL PROPERTY TAX ORDINANCE.

SCHEDULE I.

Category	Description	Rate of Tax per dunum Mils
1	Citrus (omitting Acre)	825
2	Citrus (Acre Sub-District)	410
3	Bananas	560
4	Village or Colony built-on area or reserved therefor	160
5 ∅	1st Grade Irrigated Land and 1st Grade Fruit Plantation	20
6 ∅	2nd Grade Irrigated Land and 2nd Grade Fruit Plantation	17
7 ∅	3rd Grade Irrigated Land and 3rd Grade Fruit Plantation	15
8 ∅	1st Grade Ground Crop Land, 4th Grade Fruit Plantation and 4th Grade Irrigated Land	13
9 ∅	2nd Grade Ground Crop Land, 5th Grade Fruit Plantation and 5th Grade Irrigated Land	11
10 ∅	3rd Grade Ground Crop Land, 6th Grade Irrigated Land and 6th Grade Fruit Plantation	9
11 ∅	4th Grade Ground Crop Land, 7th Grade Irrigated Land and 7th Grade Fruit Plantation	
12 ∅	5th Grade Ground Crop Land, 8th Grade Irrigated Land and 8th Grade Fruit Plantation	
13 ∅	6th Grade Ground Crop Land, 9th Grade Irrigated Land and 9th Grade Fruit Plantation	
14	7th Grade Ground Crop Land and 10th Grade Irrigated Land	nil
15	8th Grade Ground Crop Land	nil
16	Forests planted and indigenous uncultivable land	nil

∅ Other than Citrus and Bananas.

RURAL PROPERTY TAX ORDINANCE, 1935.
EXEMPTION OF FRUIT TREES.

Description of Fruit	Stated by Department of Agriculture			Limit of exemption from increased tax from beginning of tax year following planting Recommended
	Self sustaining	Maturity	Length of profitable life	
Oranges ⎫	8th year	13th year	⎫	
Grape Fruit ⎬ Citrus	6th "	12th "	⎬ 40 years	6 years
Lemons ⎭	6th "	10th "	⎭	
Bananas	2nd "	2nd "	6 "	1 year
Almonds	6th "	8th to 10th "	25-30 "	6 years
Vines - Table	4th "	6th "	20-25 "	⎫ 10 years if American Stock and 6 years if other.
Vines - Wine	4th "	6th "	20 "	⎭
Olives	10th "	15th "	50 "	10 years
Figs	6th "	8th "	40 "	6 "
Apricots	6th "	8th "	35 "	6 "
Pomegranates	4th "	4th "	25-30 "	6 years
Dates	12th "	15th "	80 "	12 "
Apples	8th "	12th "	30 "	6 "
Pears	8th "	10th "	20 "	6 "
Plums	6th "	8th "	15-25 "	6 "
Quinces	6th "	8th "	30 "	6 "
Mulberries	6th "	8th "	40 "	6 "
Carub	10th "	12th "	100 "	10 "
Walnuts	10th "	15th "	50 "	10 "
Mixed Fruit Plantations	-	-	-	6 "
Uncultivable Land developed	.	.		6 "

AGH.

ENCLOSURE IV.

REPORT OF THE RURAL TAXATION MACHINERY COMMITTEE.

On the 5th January, 1933, His Excellency the High Commissioner appointed a Committee with the following terms of reference

> "to consider whether the present
> machinery of rural tax assessment
> and collection is so defective as
> to cause loss to the Government or
> injustice to the rural tax payer and,
> if so, to make recommendations for its
> improvement."

His Excellency directed that the Committee should have regard to the fact that a new system of rural taxation would shortly be introduced and that unless there were very grave deficiencies in the present machinery of taxation it would be unwise to introduce changes which would themselves have to be altered in some two years' time. The Committee was also required to bear in mind the importance of the principle that the ratio which the cost of collection of revenue bears to the total revenue collected must be kept as low as possible.

2. In order that the Committee might be in a position to state what defects, if any, there were in the present machinery of taxation and what loss, if any, resulted to Government, or injustice to the rural tax-payer, it was necessary in the first instance to obtain as full information as was available in regard to the machinery in force.

./.

- 2 -

3.   The Committee obtained information from the District Authorities on the existing systems of assessment and collection of the various rural taxes and statistics of the aggregate amounts payable and collected annually of each of those taxes, the staff employed for their assessment and collection and certain details of annual expenditure incurred thereon.

4.   The rural taxes which the Committee considered came within the purview of their inquiry are:-

   The House and Land Tax (WERKO);

   The Tithe and Commuted Tithe ('USHER); and

   The Animal Tax (AGHNAM).

The nature of the rural taxes and their legal bases.

House and Land Tax.

5.   House and Land Tax is levied on MULK and MIRI land and houses and is payable at rates varying from 4 to 10 per mille of the value according to the category of the property.

Additions to this tax, aggregating 41% on buildings and 56% on lands were made from time to time under Ottoman decrees. These additions are still payable, except in the case of buildings and lands re-assessed since 1919.

Tithe and Commuted Tithe.

6.   Tithe was paid on all cultivable land, pasture lands, other than village pasture lands,

./.

and wood lands in the possession of private persons. State Forests, MAHLUL land not regranted, MATRUKA land and land belonging to the State, other than (JIFTLIK) MUDAWWARA land, were exempt.

7. The Tithe, as its name indicates, was supposed to be equal to one tenth of the produce. The Ottoman Government had added various percentages, but these were all abolished by the Tithe Reduction Ordinance, 1925, which provided that from the 1st May 1925, the rate of Tithe on all crops and other produce should be reduced again to 10%.

8. In 1927, the Commutation of Tithes Ordinance was enacted and has since been applied to the whole country.

9. The Commuted Tithe is a fixed annual payment and does not vary with changes of cultivation or with the value of the crop. It corresponds to the average amount of Tithe that was payable by each village or tribe during the four years immediately preceding the application of the Ordinance to the village or tribe.

Animal Tax.

10. The Animal Tax is an amount payable annually on each animal at the following rates:-

Sheep	-	48 mils;
Goats	-	48 mils;
Pigs	-	90 mils;
Camels	-	120 mils;
Buffaloes	-	120 mils.

./.

- 4 -

Animals under one year and camels and buffaloes used solely for ploughing are exempt by an Order dated the 4th April, 1921, and the Animal Tax Ordinance, 1925.

11. The legal bases and authorities for the assessment, collection and remission of the House and Land Tax, the Commuted Tithe and the Animal Tax are enumerated in Appendix I to this Report.

The procedure for the assessment, collection and exemption of rural taxes.

House and Land Tax.

Assessment:

12. The assessment of rural lands for the House and Land Tax, which was carried out under the provisions of the Ottoman Regulations of the 23rd Zul Kidr, 1302, was not based on a survey. It was probably based on the Land Registry record of property but that registration itself was not based on a survey.

13. The assessment was made by assessment committees of four persons, two of whom were appointed by the Council of the NAHIYA and two by the Government. The NAHIYA was a sub-division of a KAZA which itself was a sub-division of a LIWA. A KAZA was equivalent to the present administrative Sub-District and a LIWA to the present administrative District.

14. If the Committee failed to reach an agreement as to the value of a property, a fifth

./.

- 5 -

member was appointed jointly by the Council of the NAHIYA and the Government.

15. The Committee members were not necessarily tax-payers or owners of immovable property. They were presumed to be unbiased experts.

16. No provision appears to have been made for the hearing of objections.

17. The Ottoman Law prescribed a general quinquennial re-assessment of immovable property throughout the country. At that re-assessment, objections were to be allowed. These were to be heard by the Council of the NAHIYA whose decisions were subject to appeal to the Council of the KAZA. No quinquennial re-assessment has, however, been made for more than twenty years.

18. The tribal lands in the Beersheba Sub-District, with the exception of approximately 60,000 dunums, were not assessed by the Ottoman Authorities and are therefore not subject to the tax.

19. The Nebi Rubin and Abu el Fadl tribal lands in the Ramle Sub-district, comprising an area of approximately 27,000 dunums were also never assessed and are not subject to the tax.

20. There are approximately 1,000,000 dunums of tribal lands in the Jerusalem District, situated in the Jordan Valley and to the west of the Dead Sea which were not assessed for the tax as such but are liable to payment of "WERKO MAQTU'", a

./.

- 6 -

fixed commuted property tax, levied in the form of a poll tax on the tribes in this area and is apportioned by each Sheikh among his tribesmen and is collected by him on behalf of Government.

The annual amount of "WERKO MAQTU'" payable is LP.252. The average annual amount collected is LP.210.-

21. The tribal lands in the Northern District are all assessed for the House and Land tax.

22. The lands of a number of villages are reported by District Commissioners to have been originally heavily over-assessed by the Ottoman Authorities.

23. Properties are now assessed for the tax only when

> an addition is made to a building or a new building is erected; or
>
> a property is discovered which has not been registered in the Land Registry and has previously not been subject to the tax.

24. Properties are re-assessed for the tax only when

> a property is the subject of a transaction which is registered in the Land Registry, and the Registrar of Lands or the Revenue Officer considers that the value has been under-stated; or
>
> a building has been considerably damaged; or
>
> an owner claims that the value of his property has decreased since the last assessment, or the Revenue Officer claims that a property has increased in value since the last assessment.

./.

25. The procedure for assessment and re-assessment is identical.

26. In areas where there is a Municipal or Local Council, a Committee is formed consisting of two official members (usually Revenue clerks) and two non-official members appointed by the Municipal or Local Council.

27. Where there is no Municipal or Local Council, the Committee consists of one official member, usually a Revenue clerk, and one non-official member nominated by the village concerned.

28. The Committee, assisted by the MUKHTAR, assesses the value of the property, the owner being granted a period of thirty days within which to object against the assessment if he so desires. The objection is heard by the District Officer, leave being given to appeal against his decision within a further period of fifteen days. The appeal is heard by the District Commissioner or Assistant District Commissioner whose decision is final.

29. When a non-registered property is discovered, or the Land Registrar or the MUDIR MAL considers that the value of a property has been under-stated, an assessment is made by a committee of two official members, usually a Revenue clerk and a Land Registry clerk. Any objection made to the assessment is heard by the District Commissioner whose decision is final.

./.

- 8 -

30. The administrative council of a **NAHIYA** (the MEJLESS NAHIYA) has not been revived since the British Occupation. Under the Palestine Government, the District Officer of a **Sub-district** is presumed to represent the Administrative Council of the KAZA and the District Commissioner and the Assistant District Commissioner the Administrative Council of the LIWA.

31. At the time of the British Occupation, it was found that the retreating Turks had taken away or destroyed a number of tax registers. The inhabitants of each village affected prepared lists at the request of the British military authorities of persons in the village whom they considered to be **tax-payers** and distributed the aggregate amount of the tax known to be due from the village among such persons. It is on those lists that the tax has been demanded in those villages.

32. The tax-payers' register for each village is re-compiled each year in a number of Sub-districts. In other Sub-districts the register is in the nature of a running register over a period of several years and a complete re-compilation is made only when the folios in the register are fully used.

Collection:

33. The House and Land Tax is collected by tax-collectors who are unclassified Government officials.

34. Each Sub-district is divided into a number of collecting zones, each in charge of a tax-collector.

./.

The size of each zone is determined principally by the situation of the villages, the number of tax-payers, the extent of village land, etc.

35. Each tax-collector must provide a fidelity guarantee as security against embezzlement.

36. The tax is payable in one instalment if the amount due is less than LP.2, or in two equal instalments if the amount due is LP.2 or over.

Generally speaking, the collection period is arranged to synchronize with the maturity of the principal crops.

37. A printed counterfoil tax receipt book, serially numbered, is issued to the tax-collector together with lists of tax-payers and the amounts due by them.

38. On arrival at a village, the tax-collector with the assistance of the MUKHTAR notifies tax-payers generally of his presence in the village and calls upon them to pay the taxes due.

39. When a property is owned in common by a number of persons, the tax-collector with the assistance of the MUKHTAR or the village elders, apportions among the several owners the tax payable on the property.

40. If a tax-payer does not reside in the zone in which his land is situated, but resides in the same Sub-district, the tax-collector of the zone in which the tax-payer resides is instructed to collect the tax.

./.

- 10 -

41.   If the tax-payer resides in another Sub-district, the Revenue Officer of that Sub-district is requested to arrange for the tax-collector of the relevant zone to collect the tax.

42..   If any instalment due is not paid, recovery is made under the Collection of Taxes Ordinance, 1929.

43.   Tax-collectors are required to pay in their collections weekly to the Sub-Accountant or to the Bank. When the sum collected amounts to LP.50 or over, it must be paid in immediately.

44.   For the purpose of paying in amounts, the tax-collector prepares a schedule in duplicate stating:-

> The serial number of the tax-payer, the name of the tax-payer and the village in which he resides;
>
> the amount of tax collected;
>
> the number and the date of the receipt issued for the amount received; and
>
> the period in respect of which the tax is paid, i.e. for the current year, or for arrears of tax from previous years.

45.   The schedules are first checked by a revenue clerk against the counterfoil tax receipts and, if found correct, are initialled and handed back to the tax-collector. He then pays in the money collected to the Sub-Accountant or to the Bank. Before the amount is accepted by the Sub-Accountant, the schedule is again checked against the counterfoil receipts.

./.

- 11 -

46. The Sub-Accountant or the Bank issues a cash receipt for the amount paid in, which is then withdrawn from the tax-collector by the revenue clerk against receipt and the amount is entered in the Tax Register by the revenue clerk from the original copy of the schedule. The duplicate copy of the schedule is retained as a supporting document for the Cash Book.

Exemption:

47. Exemptions are granted in accordance with the Resolutions of the Ottoman State Council of June, 1318. These allow for exemption in respect of properties which do not yield revenue and are owned by and are in the use of educational, charitable and religious institutions, or are the residences of priests or nuns or the METAWALLIS of charitable WAQFS.

48. In accordance with a Public Notice of the 18th September, 1932, (published in Official Gazette No.78 of the 1st November, 1922), the exemption of an educational institution is authorised by the District Commissioner on application by the managers on a form which is endorsed by the Revenue Officer and recommended by the Director of Education.

49. For religious and charitable institutions, an application form, introduced during the Military Occupation, is submitted in triplicate by the applicant to the District Officer of the Sub-District containing particulars of the property and stating the ground for claiming exemption.

The property is inspected by a District

./.

Officer who endorses the form and transmits it to the District Commissioner for approval.

50. A number of religious institutions have claimed that their properties are exempt from the tax in accordance with custom or under the terms of a treaty or FIRMAN.

These institutions have refused to pay the tax and in many cases no action has been taken for recovery under the Collection of Taxes Ordinance in the absence of categorial rulings by Government. The amounts due are included in the arrears of tax brought forward from year to year.

Observations by the Committee.
----

51. The main defect in the machinery of assessment, in the opinion of the Committee, is that the assessment operations were not preceded or accompanied by a survey whereby all parcels of land whether in separate or in common ownership were indicated on the ground and plotted on a map.

52. Although the House and Land tax was based originally on parcels of land and the register of tax-payers was related to the Land Registry record of property, it was generally impossible, owing to the absence of a survey, to connect the parcel of land on which the tax was presumed to be payable with a specific piece of land on the ground. Neither was it possible, in the absence of a survey, to know the area of each parcel.

53. The Ottoman Land Registration Law has been generally ignored and the House and Land

- 13 -

Tax register has become a mere register of tax-payers with the amounts of tax due from them but with no definite or identifiable relation to the parcels of land in respect of which the tax is payable.

54. There is also no method at present to ensure that changes of ownership (resulting from sales, exchange and succession) and changes of identity of parcels (due to the breaking up of a parcel by partition or by the sale of only a portion of it) are reported to the Revenue Office or are registered in the Land Registers. The tax registers are thus not even a correct record of the names of tax-payers.

55. The destruction or removal of a number of tax-registers by the Turkish authorities at the time of the British Occupation has caused further confusion.

56. Owing to the absence of machinery for recording changes in the distribution of liability for the tax, the lists of tax-payers prepared for certain villages at the time of the British Occupation are also no longer reliable.

57. As the present assessment is not based on a survey, the Committee are of opinion that many properties must have escaped assessment and many persons are successfully evading liability for the tax.

58. Further, in almost all rural areas, the tax is payable to-day on an assessment made many

./.

- 14 -

years ago.

59. In the cases where dispositions of land have been registered in the Land Registry and the value of the transaction has been correctly stated, the tax has since been payable on that value. It is common knowledge, however, that in a large number of cases the purchase price which was paid was considerably higher than the normal value of the land.

Where this has occurred, the new owner of the land has paid the tax on a recent and high valuation, while his neighbours in an adjoining village or even in the same village, whose lands have not been the subject of a transaction or are the subject of an unregistered transaction, still pay the tax on a low assessment made many years ago. To a small extent, however, this has been corrected by the abolition of the additions to the tax in cases of re-assessment.

60. On the other hand, if the assumption of District Commissioners is correct that the lands of a number of villages were deliberately over-assessed during the original assessment operations, the inhabitants of those villages have been paying for many years a higher sum in taxation than has been properly due from them.

61. The absence of a basic survey for assessment and of adequate measures to provide for notification of all changes of ownership has added considerably to the difficulties of

./.

tax-collectors. Much time is lost in endeavouring to trace persons from whom the tax is due, and in many cases the efforts of the tax-collectors to trace such persons have been unsuccessful.

62. These defects have also added to the work in the Revenue Office and have made it increasingly difficult for the Revenue authorities properly to supervise the work of the tax-collectors and have caused delay and difficulty in applying the Collection of Taxes Ordinance to defaulters.

63. It has been stated in paragraph 50 that a number of religious institutions have refused to pay the tax on the ground that their properties were exempt under the terms of some treaty or FIRMAN. In many cases those institutions have been unable to indicate the properties and the particular treaty or FIRMAN under which exemption was claimed and in such cases Government has hitherto not authorised District Commissioners to take any action to collect the taxes due. Where institutions have indicated the treaty or FIRMAN under which they have claimed exemption and the District Commissioners have not concurred that the claim for exemption was justified and have referred the matter to higher authority, no decision has been obtained from Government in many cases.

64. The amount of tax thus unpaid has swollen the volume of the arrears of unpaid taxation and the absence of instructions or authoritative decisions by Government on the claims

./.

- 16 -

for exemption has been the cause of much embarrassment to the revenue collecting authorities and has added considerably to the labour of the Revenue Office staff in their maintenance or annual re-compilation of the House and Land Tax registers.

65. There is no central authority to supervise the machinery for assessment, collection and accountancy or to ensure uniformity of procedure throughout the country.

66. The Committee are of opinion that the District Administration has recognized its responsibility for the assessment and due collection of taxes but the Revenue Offices are badly staffed.

Many of the present Revenue Office officials are totally unfitted to carry out the duties imposed by a British Mandatory Administration, as they do not possess a knowledge of English or adequate educational qualifications.

67. The Committee also consider that the present MUDIRS MAL are under-graded, having regard to the responsibilities of their office and the experience required for the post.

68. The official members of the Committees for the annual revision of assessments are recruited from the Revenue clerical staff. These officers have neither the time nor the qualifications required for property valuation.

./.

69. The tax-collectors at present employed are, in the opinion of the Committee, under-paid and the majority are insufficiently educated to enable them to perform their duties satisfactorily. In addition, their equipment is not calculated to inspire respect by the tax-payers.

70. The Committee are not satisfied that the best use is made of the available tax collecting staff. For example, tax collectors are diverted for a six weeks enumeration of animals under an obsolescent law which could be performed in a much shorter period.

71. Under the Ottoman Administration, tax-collectors were pensionable officers, and pensions were, in fact, granted to tax-collectors who were retired under the Turkish Pensions Ordinance, 1325, by the present Government up to 1924. Since 1924, however, the grant of pensions under this Ordinance has been discontinued and replaced by gratuities at the rate of one week's pay for each year's service of not more than fifteen years.

72. The Revenue staff includes a number of elderly officials and tax-collectors many of whom have had long periods of service under the Ottoman Government. Several of these are already well over the retiring age but in some cases their services have been retained because of their intimate knowledge of the Ottoman House and Land tax procedure and of persons from whom the tax is rightly due in cases where notification

./.

- 18 -

of changes of ownership due to death and other causes may not have been made to the Revenue Office.

73.   Although District Commissioners have divided their Districts into tax collecting zones, the number and extent of the zones were necessarily governed by the number of collectors available in each District. The Committee are of opinion that, in the absence of a central authority the tax collecting staff, such as it is, has not been distributed between the Districts in due proportion to the relative number of villages and tax-payers in each District, nor the zones arranged to best advantage. The Committee also suspect that the tax collecting staff is inadequate.

74.   The Committee also consider that, owing to the absence of a central authority, it has been difficult for authoritative and well informed advice to be submitted to Government in order to ensure uniformity of procedure, systematic zoning of the country and proportional distribution of the revenue and tax collecting staff between the Districts.

75.   In the opinion of the Committee there would seem to be no doubt that the defects in the machinery for assessment have caused loss to the Government and have resulted in inequality in the incidence of the tax and in injustice to the rural tax-payer, while the defects in the

./.

machinery for collection and accounting have increased the arrears of the tax.

RECOMMENDATIONS OF THE COMMITTEE.

76. As the Committee understands that a new system of rural taxation will probably be introduced within the next two years, they have recommended only such changes which, in their opinion, would not dislocate an already complicated system.

They recommend that the following steps be taken without delay:-

> (i) Government should obtain from the District Commissioners a schedule of all arrears of taxes due from institutions for which exemption is claimed by virtue of a treaty or FIRMAN, for ruling by Government as to which claims should be admitted and which rejected.
>
> (ii) The amount of House and Land tax due from villages which provided tax distribution lists at the time of the British Occupation should be re-distributed by village Committees under the supervision of District Officers.
>
> (iii) The present legislation affecting the pensions of ex-Ottoman members of the Revenue staff should be amended to enable adequate pensions or largely increased gratuities to be granted to officials of long service. The Committee understand that, apart from the District Revenue staff and certain officials in the Judicial Department, there are comparatively few ex-Ottoman Government officials now in the service of the Government.
>
> (iv) When the amending legislation has been enacted, all Revenue officials who are no longer efficient on the ground of age should be retired.
>
> (v) All vacancies in the Revenue Establishment should in future be filled only by officers who have adequate educational qualifications including the knowledge of English.

- 20 -

- (vi) The posts of MUDIRS MAL in the larger Revenue offices should be in Grade M, and all others in Grade N.

- (vii) The official members of the committees for the annual revision of assessments should not be recruited from the Revenue Office staff. Suitable persons should be temporarily appointed as and when required as official members of the committees.

- (viii) Tax-collectors should be placed in a semi-specialized pensionable cadre in old Grade V (LP.96-6-132), similar to Sub-Sanitary Inspectors. A limited number, stationed in the larger Revenue Offices who should perform the duties of District Chief Tax-collectors, should be placed in old Grade IV (LP.144-6-180).

- (ix) Tax-collectors should be provided with uniforms and should be properly equipped with leather pouches and official note books.

- (x) When carrying out seizure duties, tax-collectors should be invariably accompanied by a police escort.

Tithe and Commuted Tithe.

Assessment:

77. The assessment of the tithe was an estimation by estimators of the quantity of produce on the threshing floor or of the crops in the field and was arrived at, more or less, by guess-work.

78. Lists were prepared for each village, of the names of cultivators and the estimated quantity of their crops.

79. Inspectors followed within a short time who examined the lists and satisfied themselves by visual test and occasionally by the threshing of some of the crops, as to the general correctness of the estimation.

./.

- 21 -

80.   The Commuted Tithe is based on the average of the tithe payable in each village in the four last preceding years.

81.   The Commuted Tithe payable by each village is calculated separately for ground crop land and for fruit plantations.

82.   An Assessment Committee is appointed for each village for the distribution of the amount of Commuted Tithe due from the village among the reputed owners of land.

83.   If the ground crop land is held in common ownership (MUSHA'), the Commuted Tithe is distributed by the village Assessment Committee among the owners in proportion to their respective shares. If the land is owned in separate parcels, the Assessment Committee distribute the Commuted Tithe among the owners in accordance with the potential productivity of the land in terms of wheat. The Commuted Tithe on the fruit plantations is distributed among the owners of fruit plantations in proportion to the average amount of tithe payable during the preceding four year period.

        In tribal areas, the distribution is made by the Sheikhs in accordance with tribal custom.

84.   Any objection to the distribution in a village is heard by a Village Revising Committee appointed by the District Commissioner.

85.   Appeals against the decision of the Revising Committee are heard by the District

./.

- 22 -

Commissioner or Assistant District Commissioner whose decisions are final.

86.   Separate distribution schedules of payers of Commuted Tithe are prepared in duplicate by the Assessment Committee for MUSHA' land, for parcelled land and for fruit plantations.

87.   The assessment and distribution of the Rental Tithe is made in the same manner as the Commuted Tithe.

88.   An annual revision is made of the assessment list of the village to provide for a redistribution of the Commuted Tithe on

> parcels which, in whole or part, have changed hands since the previous distribution; or
>
> MUSHA' land which has been partitioned since the previous distribution.

Collection:

89.   The Tithe and Commuted Tithe (and the Rental Tithe in JIFTLIK villages) has always been collected by the MUKHTAR of the village on behalf of Government.

90.   By law, the Tithe was payable by the owner of the land but in practice, prior to the enactment of the Commutation of Tithes Ordinance, it was collected from the cultivator.

91.   When the Tithe was estimated annually, the estimator compiled a tithe-payers' book which was kept by the MUKHTAR of the village who was responsible for the collection of the tithe.

./.

92. The Revenue Office of the Sub-district merely compiled a village Tithe Register in which was entered only the name of the village and the aggregate amount of tithe due on each crop from the village.

93. Under the Commutation of Tithes Ordinance, one copy of the Schedule of Commuted Tithe which is prepared by the Village Committee is kept by the MUKHTAR to enable him to collect the C Commuted Tithe and one copy in the Revenue Office of the Sub-district.

94. In six Sub-districts registers are kept of individual payers of Commuted Tithe. In the remaining Sub-districts the registers show the aggregate amount of Commuted Tithe due from each village or tribe and not the amount due from each person.

95. In the six Sub-districts, any amount collected by the MUKHTAR and paid in to the Sub-Accountant is credited to the individual tithe-payer. In the remaining Sub-districts, any amount collected by him and paid in to the Sub-Accountant is credited to the village as a whole and not to an individual tithe-payer.

96. The following numbers of MUKHTARS were responsible for the collection of the Commuted Tithe in 1932:

        Jerusalem District - 337 Mukhtars,
        Southern District - 369 Mukhtars,
        Northern District - 638 Mukhtars.

./.

97. MUKHTARS for many years received remuneration at the rate of 2% on their collections but since 1932 are now paid a commission of 5% on their collections.

Exemption and Remission:

98. Exemption is granted when land planted with ground (rotation) crops is planted with fruit trees and for certain educational and religious institutions.

99. Remission of Commuted Tithe in whole or in part is granted in the event of a general failure of crops in whole or in part.

100. Recommendations for exemption and remission are made by District Commissioners and are approved by the High Commissioner.

When a general remission is recommended over an extensive area, an inspection is made by the District Officers, Agricultural Assistants and an Inspector of the office of the Commissioner of Lands.

Observations by the Committee.
----

101. After the application of the Commutation of Tithes Ordinance in 1928, the owner was free to dispose of his crop as and when he pleased. He was no longer compelled to run the risk of loss of his crops on the threshing floor and was no longer obliged to incur any expenditure on entertaining estimators and inspectors.

102. The Commuted Tithe, however, was not

based on the average quantity of four years
produce with a redemption price fixed annually,
but it corresponded to the average amount of
tithe that was paid by the village during a
period of four years. As that amount was based
on a redemption price which had been calculated,
not necessarily at the price which the owner
obtained for his produce, but at the market
price of the crop, the inequalities in the price
basis as well as the inaccurate estimation
referred to in paragraphs 77 and 79 were perpetuated
under the Commutation of Tithes Ordinance.

103. The inequalities in the price basis
of crops, which were accentuated by the effect
in Palestine of the world fall of grain prices
since 1930, have been corrected by Government
to a certain extent by remissions in 1930 and
in 1931 and by the reduction in 1932 of the
rate of tithe from 10% to 7½% on all crops
except citrus fruits.

104. In the Sub-districts in which Registers
of individual tithe-payers are not kept, it is
difficult to apply the provisions of the Collection
of Taxes Ordinance to defaulters and to account
satisfactorily for collections.

105. An accumulation of circumstances due
to poor harvests resulting from lack of rain
during the past three or four years, depredations
by field mice and other pests and the high
incidence of the tithe have so seriously and
adversely affected the financial condition of

./.

- 26 -

the rural population that, notwithstanding remissions which have been made by Government in 1930, 1931 and 1932 because of the fall in the price of grain and other remissions because of drought and damage of crops by locusts and field mice, the collection of the Commuted Tithe has recently been extremely low.

RECOMMENDATIONS OF THE COMMITTEE.

106. In view of the proposed introduction of a new system of rural taxation in some two years time, the Committee recommend that

  (i) notwithstanding its obvious deficiencies, no change should be made in the present system of accounting for the Commuted Tithe in the Sub-districts where the Tithe Registers do not contain individual tithe-payers accounts; and

  (ii) no change be made now in the present system of collection of the Commuted Tithe by MUKHTARS.

Animal Tax.

  Assessment and Collection:

107. With the exception of the enumeration of pigs which is carried out in September and the enumeration of the animals of nomadic tribes in Beersheba Sub-District where enumeration and collection are carried out by special officials as and when possible during the year, the enumeration of animals is made once annually during the month of February, on a date prescribed by the Palestine Government in consultation with the Governments of Trans-Jordan, Syria and the Lebanon to prevent evasion.

./.

- 27 -

108. The MUKHTARS of villages and tribes are directed to prepare a list of owners and the number of animals owned by each.

109. Each Sub-district is divided into a number of animal enumerating zones each under the control of a tax-collector acting as an enumerator.

110. Each enumerator counts all the animals in the villages in his zone and issues an Enumeration Bill to every owner.

111. One month later the enumeration in each zone is controlled by a tax-collector from another zone who re-counts the animals in each village. The numbers are compared with the Enumeration Bills and the tax due is immediately collected, a receipt and Control Bill being given to each owner.

112. If animals are found outside a village during enumeration, the tax is immediately collected and a Control Bill and receipt given to the shepherd or owner at the time without waiting for control.

113. Any owner or shepherd found without an Enumeration or Control Bill is considered as having attempted to conceal his animals and a double tax is imposed.

114. On the completion of the whole enumeration and control, the tax-collectors pay in the amount collected.

./.

Observations by the Committee.

115. As the tax is collected at the time of enumeration or control, there should be no arrears of the tax but, for various reasons, small sums remain uncollected but are relatively unimportant.

116. The machinery for the enumeration of animals and collection of the tax would appear to work fairly satisfactorily but, in the opinion of the Committee, the period of the operations could be reduced and the tax-collectors employed on more remunerative work.

117. As not all animals are kept at night in the villages, there may be evasion of enumeration on a small scale. The open frontiers on the south, east and north of the country and between Sub-districts and Districts facilitate, however, evasion on a large scale.

118. But it may be assumed that not many animals escape enumeration and that any loss which is caused to Government is not of serious extent.

RECOMMENDATIONS OF THE COMMITTEE.

119. The Committee recommend that the District Commissioners should arrange for enumeration and control to be completed within a shorter period than is provided for in the Animal Tax Law without risk of evasion and loss of revenue and that the Ottoman Animal Tax Law be amended, if necessary.

./.

- 29 -

Enforcement of Collection.

120.   The tax and tithe payers registers are examined by the District Officers who use their influence with defaulters to obtain payment of the tax and settle dificulties met with by MUDIRS MAL.

121.   Monthly returns of collections are submitted by District Officers to each District Commissioner who investigates the reason for low collections.

122.   General difficulties are discussed at District Commissioners monthly meetings with District Officers or when the District Commissioners or Assistant District Commissioners inspect the work in their Sub-districts.

123.   When the House and Land Tax or Tithe which is due from any person is not paid, action is taken in accordance with the Collection of Taxes Ordinance, 1926.

124.   When the Tithe due is not paid, if individual tithe-payers' accounts are not kept in the Revenue Office, a statement is obtained from the MUKHTAR of the name of the defaulter and the amount unpaid.

125.   If the tax or tithe still remains unpaid after a number of oral demands, a notice is served by a tax-collector on the defaulter requiring him to settle the amount forthwith. If after a further period it remains unpaid, a seizure warrant is issued to the tax-collector

./.

- 30 -

by the District Officer.

126.   The tax-collector then acts as Seizure Officer and, accompanied by a police escort (when available) and the MUKHTAR, calls on the defaulter to pay the amount due. If payment is not made, the Seizure Officer seizes the movable property of the defaulter and makes an inventory of the articles which under the law are subject to seizure. The Seizure Officer estimates the value of the articles seized which are then given into the custody of the MUKHTAR.

127.   If the amount due is not paid by the defaulter within two or three days, the articles seized are sold by public auction.

128.   The MUKHTAR'S fee for the custody of the property, the auctioneer's fee and any transport expenses which may have been incurred by the Seizure Officer are first deducted from the proceeds of the sale. The amount of the tax or tithe due is then taken and any sum left over is given to the defaulter.

129.   Particulars of the sale are entered on a printed form which is signed by the Seizure Officer and counter-signed by the Sub-Accountant.

130.   When no movable property liable to legal seizure is found, or its value is insufficient to cover the amount of tax due, a declaration to that effect is signed by the

./.

- 31 -

Seizure Officer, the MUKHTAR and the police escort, and submitted to the District Officer. Application is then made through the District Commissioner to the Chief Execution Officer for the attachment and sale by public auction of the immovable property of the defaulter.

Observations by the Committee.
----

131.   It has been possible only in rare cases to sell immovable property under the Collection of Taxes Ordinance, 1929. When an immovable property is put up for sale there is seldom any bidding and Government has been generally averse from taking over the property in its own name in lieu of the unpaid tax or tithe, even pending payment of the amount due by the defaulter.

132.   In consequence the volume of unpaid taxes has increased, causing additional labour to the Revenue staff and having a detrimental effect on their morale.

RECOMMENDATIONS OF THE COMMITTEE.

133.   The Committee recommend that, where the public auction of the immovable property of a defaulter does not result in a sale of the property at the market value of similar properties in the village or neighbouring villages, action should at once be taken under Section 9 of the Collection of Taxes Ordinance, No.26 of 1929, to offer the property on an annual lease, in the first place, to the defaulter and, on his

./.

refusal of the lease or his inability to pay the agreed rental, to lease it on an annual lease to some other person. Such leases should not be subject to the provisions of the Protection of Cultivators Ordinance, No.27 of 1929.

At the end of the period prescribed in Section 9 of the Collection of Taxes Ordinance, the property should be registered in the name of the High Commissioner as "Public Lands" within the meaning of Section 13 of Part II of the Palestine Order in Council, 1922.

Comparative figures of assessment and collection and cost of rural taxation machinery.

134.   In 1925 a re-grouping was made of the Sub-Districts of Palestine into three main Administrative Districts each under a District Commissioner as follows:-

Northern District:

Acre.
Safad.
Tiberias.
Nazareth.
Haifa.
Beisan.
Jenin.
Tulkarm.
Nablus.

Jerusalem District:

Ramallah.
Jerusalem.
Jericho.
Bethlehem.

Southern District:

Jaffa.
Ramle.
Hebron.
Gaza.
Beersheba.

The Hebron Sub-district was transferred in 1931 from the Southern District to the Jerusalem

- 33 -

District. The Jerusalem, Jericho and Bethlehem Sub-districts now form one Sub-district.

135.   For the purpose of providing comparative figures of assessments and collections, the Committee have confined themselves to the returns received from District Officers for the years since 1925 as the figures for earlier years are incomplete and differently arranged.

136.   The following is a summary of the annual assessments, remissions and collections:-

House and Land Tax.

Year.	Assessments.	Remissions and exemptions.	Collections.		
			Current.	Arrears	Total
	LP.	LP.	LP.	LP.	LP.
1925	174,554	1,028	138,661	33,949	172,610
1926	196,347	1,530	146,565	34,463	183,028
1927	216,266	2,705	157,774	35,471	193,245
1928	228,895	2,120	132,519	36,277	168,796
1929(x)	149,265	1,080	91,147	87,442	178,589
1930	140,052	895	80,845	49,628	130,473
1931	134,988	3,285	77,419	42,758	120,177
1932	123,727	1,505	61,726	47,352	109,078

(x) From 1929 the House and Land Tax was replaced progressively in urban areas by the Urban Property Tax.

Tithe and Commuted Tithe.

Year.	Assessments.	Remissions and exemptions	Collections.		
			Current.	Arrears	Total
	LP.	LP.	LP.	LP.	LP.
1925	274,249	579	257,449	25,552	283,001
1926	268,324	599	217,431	18,354	235,785
1927	234,835	1,743	153,596	42,213	195,809
1928(x)	255,393	520	132,464	99,129	231,593
1929	276,895	14,644	160,747	91,172	251,919
1930	277,058	60,542	104,586	84,955	189,541
1931	278,639	174,055	17,165	42,845	60,010
1932	214,532	154,211	66,423	40,418	106,841

(x) From 1928, the Tithe was progressively replaced by the Commuted Tithe.

Animal Tax.

Year.	Assessments.	Collections.		
		Current.	Arrears.	Total.
	LP.	LP.	LP.	LP.
1925	39,200	38,906	-	38,906
1926	47,939	47,839	294	48,133
1927	29,160	28,260	-	28,260
1928	35,163	34,963	-	34,963
1929	35,985	35,648	-	35,648
1930	36,582	36,437	37	36,474
1931	41,346	40,946	44	40,990
1932	36,668	36,049	-	36,049

Arrears.

137. Based on the returns from District Officers the increase in volume of the amount of unpaid taxes and tithes would seem to be:-

- 35 -

House and Land Tax.

Arrears brought forward prior to 1925	LP. 12,383	
Aggregate assessments, 1925-1932	LP.1,364,995	LP.1,383,378
Less aggregate remissions, 1925-1932	LP. 14,148	
Aggregate collections, 1925-1932	LP.1,255,996	LP.1,270,144
Arrears carried forward		LP. 113,234

Tithe & Commuted Tithe.

Arrears brought forward prior to 1925	LP. 17,436	
Aggregate assessments, 1925-1932	LP.2,079,925	LP.2,097,361
Less aggregate remissions, 1925-1932	LP. 406,893	
Aggregate collections 1925-1932	LP.1,554,499	LP.1,961,392
Arrears carried forward		LP. 135,909

Animal Tax.

Arrears 1925-1932	LP. 331	
Aggregate assessments, 1925-1932	LP. 302,043	LP. 302,374
Less aggregate collections 1925-1932		LP. 299,423
Arrears carried forward		LP. 2,951

138. The Committee have not been able to reconcile a number of figures in the returns rendered by the District Officers with certain figures obtained from the Treasurer's Office, but they are of opinion that, in the aggregate, the figures obtained from the District Officers generally represent the annual trend of assessments, remissions, collections and arrears and, as such, provide a fair

./.

- 36 -

estimate of the movement of direct rural taxation.

139.   The Committee have not succeeded in obtaining assessment and collection figures of the House and Land Tax for rural areas separately from the figures for towns prior to the application of the Urban Property Tax Ordinance in 1932 to all the towns of Palestine.

140.   It has not been possible to obtain figures of the cost of machinery taxation seperately for each tax, nor to distinguish definitely between the cost for rural taxes and for urban taxes as, in most Sub-districts the same Revenue Office staff is employed for all taxes.

141.   However, from the returns obtained from District Officers, the Committee have calculated what amounts represent approximately the average annual assessments of purely rural taxation, and the average annual collections under normal conditions.

142.   As the Urban Property Tax Ordinance was first applied to all the towns of Palestine in 1932, the House and Land Tax figures for that year must necessarily have been for purely rural areas. In the absence of other information the Committee have selected the figures for 1932 to represent the normal annual amounts of assessment and collection of the rural House and Land Tax.

The Committee have selected the average of the assessments and collections of the tithe during the period 1925 to 1928 to represent the normal annual amounts of assessment and collection of the Commuted Tithe.

./.

- 7 -

In regard to the Animal Tax, the Committee have taken the average of the assessments and collections during the period from 1925 to 1932 as representing the normal annual amounts of assessment and collection.

143. On these bases the normal annual assessments and collections of rural taxation are as follows:-

Tax.	Period of assessment.	Amount of assessment.	Period of collection.	Amount of collection.
House and Land Tax	1932	LP.123,727	1932	LP.169,870
Commuted Tithe	Average of 1925-28	LP.258,200	Average of 1925-28	LP.235,547
Animal Tax	Average of 1925-32	LP. 37,755	Average of 1925-32	LP. 37,420
	Average annual aggregate assessments	LP.419,602	Average annual aggregate collections	LP.303,053

- 3 -

144. The cost of the machinery for purely rural taxation in 1932, based on figures obtained from the District Commissioners is as follows:-

(a) Assessments:

Assessment and re-assessment of rural House and Land Tax.	LP. 713	
Re-distribution of Commuted Tithe.	LP. 780	LP. 1,493

(b) Collections:

Permanent rural tax-collectors	LP. 7,729	
(See Appendix II)		
Temporary rural tax-collectors	LP. 150	LP. 7,879
5% commission to Mukhtars on average annual collections of Tithe & Commuted Tithe (1925-28) amounting to LP.236,547	LP. 11,827	LP. 19,706

(c) Revenue Office Staff
(excluding Sub-Accountants Cashiers and staff engaged on purely urban taxes)   LP. 8,269

Total:-   LP. 29,460

145. The cost of the machinery of rural taxation is thus LP.29,468 for the collection of LP.383,053, which is approximately 7.7% of the collections.

146. The Committee have further compiled from returns received from the District Authorities a Statement (See Appendix III) of the volume of work carried out in 1932 by the Revenue staff on the assessment, collection and accounting of purely rural taxes. In the opinion of the Committee this statement represents fairly an average normal year's

./.

- 30 -

work of the Revenue staff.

147. Before the enactment of the Commutation of Tithes Ordinance in 1927 and the Urban Property Tax and the Land Settlement Ordinances in 1928, the duties of the Revenue Office staff included

> the annual re-compilation of the House and Land Tax registers for towns and rural areas,
>
> the assessment of additional properties and re-assessment of other properties,
>
> the recording of collections of the tax,
>
> the recording of the Animal Tax enumeration and collections,
>
> supervision of the estimation of crops for the Tithe and the maintenance of Village Tithe registers, and
>
> the submission of monthly returns of collections to the District Officers and summaries of those returns to the District Commissioners.

148. After the enactment of those Ordinances the duties of the Revenue Office staff, in addition to those enumerated in the previous paragraph in respect of the House and Land Tax for rural areas and the Animal Tax, included

> the supervision of the original distribution and annual re-distribution of the Commuted Tithe in villages,
>
> the compilation and maintenance of Commuted Tithe registers by village in some Sub-districts and for individual tithe-payers in other Sub-districts,
>
> the maintenance of Urban Tax registers for the towns,
>
> the complicated procedure of "disentanglement" of the House and Land Tax on village lands which were included in the urban areas for the purpose of the Urban Property Tax, and

./.

- 40 -

in the Jaffa and Gaza Revenue Offices

the re-compilation of the House and Land Tax registers of villages in which Land Settlement operations have been completed, and

the compilation and maintenance of registers (by village) of persons from whom Registration, Survey and Court fees were due as a result of Land Settlement operations.

149. Notwithstanding these additional duties and the demands on the staff due to the requirements of a British Mandatory Government, there has been little increase in the establishment in the Revenue Office which is still not much larger than it was in 1920.

150. It will be seen from an examination of the figures in paragraph 137 that the amount of unpaid taxes and tithes has increased from an aggregate sum of LP.36,150 in arrear at the end of 1924 to an aggregate sum of LP.252,154 at the end of 1932.

151. The sum of LP.36,150 carried forward as arrears from 1924 to 1925 is not, in the opinion of the Committee, open to legitimate criticism.

152. The corresponding figure of LP.252,154 carried forward at the end of 1932, is, however, very serious, even, bearing in mind that the figure includes arrears due to a series of agricultural catastrophies since 1929 and also the cumulative arrears of thirteen years of

./.

- 41 -

taxes disputed by religious institutions.

153. This high figure also reflects the burden of indebtedness of villagers to private money-lenders, due partly to the heavy incidence of the Tithe and partly to their own improvidence.

154. But is must be admitted that part of the increase in arrears is due to faulty administration, such as defective assessment procedure, inefficient Revenue clerks and collectors, inadequate supervision etc.

RECOMMENDATIONS OF THE COMMITTEE.

155. The Committee recommend that:

(i) The annual re-compilation of the House and Land Tax registers in certain Sub-districts should be abandoned and that a running register should be used over a number of years until the folios in the register are fully used; and

(ii) instructions be issued for full lists to be submitted by District Commissioners annually to Government with their recommendations for a write-off of all taxes outstanding for a specified period of, say, five years.

GENERAL OBSERVATIONS AND RECOMMENDATIONS.

156. In regard to the villages which District Commissioners state have been originally over-assessed, the Committee are of opinion that a reassessment would involve considerable expense and, in view of the present prices which are paid for land, it may well be that, as a

./.

result of the re-assessment, the amount of tax payable by a village may exceed the present assessment.

The Committee therefore recommend that no re-assessment should now be undertaken but that early steps should be taken by Government to bring the total amount due by each of these villages to the same level as that payable by neighbouring villages and then to re-distribute the reduced tax among tax-payers in the present proportion.

157. The Committee are of opinion that the division of the responsibility for revenue assessment, collection and accounting between the three District Commissioners, the Commissioner of Lands and the Treasurer has resulted in the absence of effective control and in the growth of different and often wrong practices in different parts of Palestine.

The Committee therefore recommend that, without reverting to the re-establishment of a separate Revenue Department similar to that which was abolished in 1923, a single centralized Revenue Controlling Authority should be established, directly responsible for the proper assessment, collection and accounting of all direct taxes including urban taxes.

They venture to suggest that the office of the Commissioner of Lands might be charged with this duty. The office of the

- 43 -

Commissioner of Lands is at present the controlling authority for the Commuted Tithe, for assessment operations under the Urban Property Tax Ordinance and for the fiscal survey of rural areas for the new tax. The Committee are of opinion that, with a small addition to the staff, the Commissioner of Lands office should be able to carry out the duties of a centralized Revenue Controlling Authority.

158. The Committee further recommend that the establishment of such a central authority should not be delayed until the introduction of the new tax referred to in their terms of reference.

159. The Committee have discovered a wide variety of internal regulations and practices between District and District and even between different Sub-districts in the same District. They consider that there should be a standardized practice as regards assessment, collection and accounting for each tax throughout Palestine.

The Committee recommend that the proposed central revenue authority should undertake this standardisation. Whatever accounting system is adopted should be approved by the Treasurer before submission to the High Commissioner.

160. The ratio of the cost of machinery to the average total collections is stated in paragraph 145 to be 7.7%. The Committee are of opinion that this figure is not low in comparison with that in other countries.

./.

- 44 -

On this ground, therefore, the Committee do not feel justified in recommending any increase of revenue staff at present, especially as they anticipate a considerable improvement in the machinery as soon as their recommendations for re-organization are carried into effect.

161. The Committee further recommend that, on the establishment of a central revenue authority, the officer responsible for that control should consider the revision of the permanent establishments of Revenue Offices in all Sub-districts, the re-distribution of the tax-collecting staff and the re-arrangement of the zones as to provide an equal amount of work for each collector and office. If later on increase in the number of tax-collectors or revenue clerks is found necessary, the central revenue authority should submit recommendations to Government with an estimate of the cost. The Committee are informed that Government has already under consideration a small increase of the staff in the Revenue Offices of the Southern District in which House and Land Tax registers must be re-compiled for the villages in which Land Settlement has been completed and Fees registers compiled of Registration, Settlement and Court fees which are due as a result of settlement operations.

./.

162. The Committee recommend that, prior to the replacement of the present taxes by the new tax, the central revenue authority should be invited to formulate proposals for adapting the present machinery of collection and accounting to the new tax.

One of the measures that is envisaged in this connection is the replacement of MUKHTARS by tax-collectors and the abandonment of the present system of payment to them of a percentage of the tithes collected by them. If this be done it will be necessary for Government to consider well in advance what alternative methods are available for remunerating MUKHTARS for the considerable amount of other administrative work which they perform for Government. If no such steps are taken, it will not be possible to retain the services of the MUKHTARS who are a valuable link between Government and the population.

A. ABRAMSON	-	CHAIRMAN.
C.D. HARVEY	-	MEMBER.
E.H. SAMUEL	-	MEMBER.

Jerusalem 22nd June, 1933.

I N D E X.

Paragraph No.	Subject.	Page No.
1	Terms of reference.	1
4	Rural taxes within purview of enquiry	2

NATURE OF RURAL TAXES AND LEGAL BASES.

5	House and Land Tax.	
6	Tithe and Commuted Tithe.	
10	Animal Tax.	3
11	Legal Bases	4

PROCEDURE FOR ASSESSMENT, COLLECTION & EXEMPTION OF RURAL TAXES.

House and Land Tax.

12	Assessment	
33	Collection	8
47	Exemption	11
51	Observations by Committee	12
76	Recommendations of Committee	19

Tithe and Commuted Tithe.

77	Assessment	20
89	Collection	22
98	Exemption & Remission	24
101	Observations by Committee	
106	Recommendations of Committee	26

Animal Tax.

107	Assessment & Collection.	
115	Observations by Committee	28
119	Recommendations of Committee	

./.

Paragraph No.	Subject	Page No.
120	Enforcement of Collection.	29
131	Observations by Committee	31
133	Recommendations of Committee	
134	COMPARATIVE FIGURES OF ASSESSMENT AND COLLECTION AND COST OF RURAL TAXATION MACHINERY.	32
136	Summary of annual assessments, remissions and collections (1925-32)	33
137	Arrears	34
143	Average normal annual assessments and collections.	37
144	Cost of rural taxation machinery.	38
146	Volume of work of Revenue staff in 1932.	
147	Normal duties of revenue office staff	39
150	Increase in volume of arrears from 1924 to 1932	40
155	Recommendations of Committee	41
156	General observations & recommendations	

APPENDIX I.

A. HOUSE AND LAND TAX (WERKO).

ASSESSMENT.

Young Vol. VI p.120.

1. Ottoman Law of 5 Ailka, 1303, (5.8.1886).

2. Regulations for the Collection of Werko Tax of 24.7.1302 and 29.8.1304.

 Art. 5 — Method of assessments in villages and municipalities.

 Art. 6 — Re-assessment every five years, and on application.

 Arts. 7-10 — Objections and appeals.

 Art. 13 — Evasions.

Bent. Vol. II p.371. O.G.No. 3 of 15.8.1919.

3. Notice of 15.11.1918 and Notice No.114 of 15.8.1919 in O.G.No.3.

Imposes Werko Tax with all additions as before 30.9.1914.

Bent. Vol. II p.42. O.G.No. 58 of 1.1.22.

4. Notice dated 5.12.21 on Re-valuation for purposes of House and Land Tax.

Re-valuation of undivided share of Musha' transferred by sale; No re-valuation on gift to heir.

5. Revenue Circular No.56 (3486/Rev.-896) of 29.12.21 amended by Rev. Circular of 31.1.22 (Rev./3486). Valuation of immoveable property for purposes of Werko.

 Art. 4 — Rates of Werko on property:
  (i) not built upon;
  (ii) built upon.

  Additions authorised by Ottoman decrees:
  (a) on buildings — totalling 41% — decrees of 1302, 1315, 1328-29.
  (b) on land — totalling 56% — decrees of 1315, 1330.

6. Revenue Circular No.73 (3486/Rev) of 18.2.22.

 (a) Cancels the additions on land on re-assessment on new valuation.

Bent. Vol. II p.371. O.G.No. 83 of 15.1.23.

7. Notice on House and Land Tax War Surtax of 8.12.22.

 (b) Cancels addition on buildings on property newly re-assessed since 1920.

/8.

- 2 -

8. Revenue Circular No.94 (3486/Rev/C-30) of 7.8.23.

    Re-assessment of property of following categories:
    (i) Lands and Houses transferred;
    (ii) Houses newly built.

O.G.No.115 of 15.5.24.
O.G.No.117 of 15.6.24.
Bent.Vol.I p.402.

9. Werko Tax (and Municipal rate) Validation Ordinance No.19 of 1924.

    Section 2 - Validation of Werko Assessments subsequent to British Occupation.

COLLECTION.

1. Ottoman Regulations for Collection of Werko Tax - of 24.7.1302.

    Art. 12 - Tax Demand Notes and instalments.
    Art. 14 - Delinquents.

Bent.Vol.II p.371.

2. Notice dated 15.11.1918.

    Art. 2   - Instalments and dates of payment.
    Arts. 3 & 4 - Payments on account and receipts.
    Art. 5   - Defaulters.

EXEMPTION.

Young Vol.VI p.120.

1. Irade of 13 Nich, 1303/1887.

    Exemption on property of Royal family, religious and charitable institutions and common pasture land.

2. Ottoman Regulations re collections of Werko of 24.7.1302.

    Art. 6 - Re-assessment on application in case of destruction of property.

3. Imperial Order of 15.1.1307.

    Authority to write-off tax due from indigent persons owning and occupying property whose value does not exceed LP.50.

/4.

- 3 -

4. **Order of Ministry of Finance No. 409 of 20.3.1327.**

   Making the Order of 15.1.1307 applicable to a whole house or to a share thereof.

5. **Imperial Order 187 of 11.7.1308.**

   Exempting Consular and Ambassadorial offices and residences, if registered in name of their Governments.

6. **Imperial Irade - 1320.**

   Resolution of the Financial Committee of the Imperial Privy Council - 14th Rabbi el Awal 1320.

   Exemption to property belonging to religious, benevolent and educational institutions, not producing revenue.

Bent.Vol.II
p.371. O.G.No.
78 of 1.1.22.

7. **Notice on Remission of House and Land Tax on registered educational institutions dated 18.9.22.**

   Exemption to schools and playgrounds owned by educational institutions and used for educational purposes, and not revenue producing.

8. **Treaty of Lausanne.**

   Art.69 - Continues up to financial year 1922-1923 exemptions enjoyed under the capitulations by allied subjects.

9. **Treaty of Mitylene.**

   Grants immunity from taxation to French and to French protected institutions - religious, charitable and educational, both scheduled to Treaty and existing without special authority at the date of Treaty.

/B. THE TITHE

- 4 -

B. THE TITHE.

ASSESSMENT.

Young 1906 -
Vol.V p.310.

1. The Law of 10 Haz.1305 (June 23,1889) as modified by the Law of 1322/1906.

   Art. 1 of Law of 1889 -
   A tithe of 10% on produce of all cultivable land, whether pasture or forest (Miri, Mulk or Waqf).

Young 1906 -
Vol.V p.329.

2. Amending Laws and Regulations.

   Regulations of 24.5.1287 (5.6.1871);
   9.6.1321 (1905);
   9.12.1924 (1878);
   4.1.1295 (1880).

Young Vol.V p.324.

Amending Law of 3 Zilhi 1309 (9.7.1891)

Young 1906 -
Vol.V p.303.

3. Increase in rate.

   By law of 1883 - 1.5%; 1897 - 0.5%;
   1900 - 0.63%; Total - 2.63%.

Bent.Vol.I - p.503. O.G.No. 138 of 1.5.25)

4. Tithe Reduction Ordinance No.10 of 1925.

   Reduction of the rate to 10%.

Bent Vol.II p.81. O.G.No.94 of 1.7.23. O.G. No.215 of 16.7.28.

5. Regulations governing assessment of Tithe of 5.6.23, and Notice on Control and supervision of Tithes of 29.6.28.

   1 - 3 : Commissions & inspectors of Assessments.

   5 : Method of Assessment.

   6 - 7 : Amendment and Notification of Assessment.

COLLECTION.

Bent.Vol.II p.81.

1. Regulations of 5.6.23 - 11, 12, 13, 14, 16.

   Collection, Redemption price, method of payment and Remuneration of Mukhtars.

/EXEMPTION.

- 5 -

EXEMPTION.

Young Vol.V - p.310.
1. **Law of 10 Haz.1305 (23 June 1889).**

    Art.3 - Produce of Mulk land, enclosed and adjoining a house, not exceeding 919 sq. pics - exempt;

    Perishable vegetables, firewood and charcoal - are exempt.

Bent.Vol.II pp.389-390.
2. **Notice of Exemption from Tithe of certain vineyards of 25.9.20.**

    Containing exemption given by Irade of 5.2.1315 to vineyards planted with American Stock for a period of 10 years.

O.G.No.22 of 1.6.20.
3. **Order of May 19, 1920.**

    Exempting bee-hives for 5 years.

O.G. Extraord. of 18.4.25.
4. **Tobacco Ordinance of 1925.**

    Exempting Tobacco plantations.

Bent.Vol.I p.517. O.G. No.181 of 16.2.27.
5. **Cotton Exemption from Tithes - Ordinances of 1925 and 1927.**

    Exempting Cotton cultivation for a period of two years.

C. COMMUTATION OF TITHES.

ASSESSMENT.

No. 49 of 1927 - O.G.No.197 of 16.10.27.
No.27 of 1928 - O.G.No.220 of 1.10.28)
1. **Commutation of Tithes Ordinances,1927-1928.**

    Section 3 - Commutation of Tithes by Order into fixed aggregate amounts.

    Section 5 - Method of Assessment and Distribution by Assessment Committees under supervision of District Commissioner

    Sections 4 & 7 -Assessment and Revision Committees.

    Sections 8 & 10 - Objections and Appeals.

    Section 14- Annual Revision of Assessments.

/2.

An.Vol.II 1927 p.39.	2. Regulations dated 14.2.28 under Section 16 No.49 of 1927.
	1 - Forms to be used.
	3,4 & 6 - Hearing of objections and Appeals.
	5 - Publication of Revised Assessment Lists.
O.G.No.241 of 1.11.29.	3. Regulation under Section 16 dated 28.10.29.
	Correction of average aggregate amount of Commuted Tithe as stated for village by District Commissioners, and distribution.
Official Communiqué No.20/32 of 11.6.32 - O.G. No.315 of 1.9.32.	4. Non-Statutory Notice dated 30.8.32.
	Reduction in rate of Commuted Tithe from 10% to 7½% on all crops except on Citrus.

COLLECTION.

O.G.No.197 of 16.10.27.	1. Commutation of Tithes Ordinance 1927.
	Sections 11, 12 & 13 - Commuted Tithe instalments and recovery.
An.Vol.II of 1927 p.39.	2. Regulations dated 14.2.28.
	Section 8 - Manner in which Commuted Tithe payable: rates of instalments.
	Section 10 - Remuneration to Mukhtars for collection.

EXEMPTION.

O.G.No.197 of 16.10.27.	1. Commutation of Tithes Ordinance 1927.
	Section 18 - Power of High Commissioner to postpone or remit payment of Commuted Tithe.
O.G.No.232 of 1.4.29.	2. Exemption from Tax Ordinance 1929.
	Exemption of land utilised for agricultural research and instruction.

/D. ANIMAL TAX.

- 7 -

D. ANIMAL TAX.

ASSESSMENT.

1. **Aghnam Law 1/14th January 1320/1905.**

   Sections 1 - 14 - Procedure for enumeration and control.

   Sections 10 & 14 - Penalty for evasion.

   Section 18 - Rates of tax.

Young Vol.V p.292.

2. **Ottoman Instruction of 1.10.1903.**

   Rates on certain categories of animals.

3. **Revenue Circular (5956/FR) dated 12.4.20.**

   Imposes tax on animals of tribes crossing the Jordan.

4. **Revenue Circular (3957/Rev) dated 17.12.20.**

   Collection of Tax for 1921/22.

5. **Revenue Circular No.118(3957/Rev-461) of 19.12.22.**

   Per-capita rates for sheep, goats, camels, buffaloes and pigs;

   Date and procedure of enumeration;

   Forms used, and stamp duty.

Bent.Vol.I, p.374
O.Gs. No.109 of
15.2.24 & No.194
of 1.8.25.

6. **Animal Tax Ordinances 1924-25.**

   Prescribes penalty for concealment or removal of animals prior to enumeration.

COLLECTION.

1. **Aghnam Law 1320/1905.**

   Section 15 - Instalments and method of enforcement of collection.

   Section 17 - Remuneration to collectors-enumerators.

2. **Revenue Circular No.118 of 19.12.22.**

   Prescribes rates of collection and rate of remuneration to collectors-enumerators.

/EXEMPTION.

- 8 -

EXEMPTION.

Young Vol.V p.297.

1. **Aghnam Law, 20 Djcm 1305 (3.2.1888).**

    Art.26 - Exemption of flocks bred in Tekios and monasteries, enjoying ab-antiquo exemption.

2. **Revenue Circular No.118 of 19.12.22.**

    Exempting Camels used solely for ploughing.

Bent.Vol.I p.374. O.G. No.144 of 1.8.25.

3. **Animal Tax Ordinances 1924-25.**

    Section 3 - Exemption of buffalos used for ploughing.

APPENDIX II.

STATEMENT OF RURAL TAX COLLECTORS' ESTABLISHMENT.

District.	RURAL			
	No. of Tax Collectors.	Emoluments	Travelling Allowances	Total Cost.
		LP.	LP.	LP.
Northern	24	2,592	936	3,528
Southern	16	1,678	513	2,191
Jerusalem	15	1,650	360	2,010
Total:-	55	5,920	1,809	7,729

5.11

BY AIR MAIL

HIGH COMMISSIONER FOR PALESTINE,
JERUSALEM.

PALESTINE

CONFIDENTIAL

REFERENCE NO. F/105/34

February, 1935.

Sir,

I have the honour to refer to my despatch No. of the 11th February, 1935, forwarding sealed and plain copies of the Rural Property Tax Ordinance No.1 of 1935, and to inform you that the correspondence referred to therein is that ending with your Confidential telegram No.4 of the 2nd January, 1935.

ENCLOSURE I

2. I enclose a statement setting out all the amendments to the draft Ordinance which were approved in Advisory Council prior to its enactment, with the reasons in each case.

3. It will be observed from this statement that the amendments suggested in your Confidential telegram No.4 have been given effect in the following manner.

Section 4(2). I agree that it is necessary to afford security to taxpayers and a provision has accordingly been added to this section to ensure that whenever the Schedule to the Ordinance is varied it will remain unaltered for a period of not less than five years from the date at which the variation takes effect.

THE RIGHT HONOURABLE
  SIR PHILIP CUNLIFFE-LISTER, G.B.E., M.P., etc., etc.,
    HIS MAJESTY'S PRINCIPAL SECRETARY OF STATE
                        FOR THE COLONIES.

2.

Section 11(2). The obscurity in the reference in this sub-section to the inclusion of the names of persons in the valuation list has been met by amending section 8 (1)(b) by inserting the words "and the names of the owners".

Section 14(b). The references to the sub-section of section 12 have been deleted.

Section 18(1)(a). The words "member of a" have been inserted in the last line of the proviso.

Section 38. The first sub-section has been divided into two sub-sections and the second of these now limits the liability of an agent to the extent of the amount of any monies collected by the agent on behalf of the owner.

4. I gave careful thought to the suggestion in your telegram, relating to section 21, that sections 23 and 24 should be enlarged so as to enable objection to be made to a District Commissioner in respect of distribution lists prepared by himself. I came to the conclusion that it was neither necessary nor desirable to introduce machinery which might have the effect of further lengthening the process of preparation of the distribution lists by consideration of objections presented to the District Commissioner against distribution lists prepared by him; particularly as it is intended that the District Commissioner should only prepare the list in the eventuality of a Tax Distribution Committee failing to prepare it prior to the date prescribed by the District Officer.

Moreover, under section 24, the District Commissioner himself decides appeals from decisions on objections under section 22, and it would appear to me to be impracticable to provide effectively for any further revising authorities

3.

for the purposes of the Ordinance.

3. It will be recollected that a similar provision exists in Section 5 of the Commutation of Tithes (Amendment) Ordinance, 1928, which is now being replaced in those areas to which the Rural Property Tax Ordinance has been applied; and the Commissioner of Lands was of the opinion that the same procedure might reasonably be followed in regard to the Rural Property Tax as no hardship had been caused by the operation of Section 5 of the Commutation of Tithes (Amendment) Ordinance, 1928, which reads as follows:-

" 5. Where an Assessment Committee appointed by the District Commissioner under section 4 or section 14 of the principal Ordinance fails, after notice from the District Commissioner, to carry out the assessment prescribed herein or the revision of the list of the reputed owners, the District Commissioner shall prepare or revise the assessment list, and apportion the tithes in accordance with the provisions of this Ordinance, and no appeal shall lie from his apportionment. "

6. I was advised, however, that to prevent ambiguity regarding the procedure to be followed with respect to the preparation of distribution lists, the following words should be inserted at the end of section 18(3)(b):- "and "no objection shall be heard to any such list". This addition was accordingly made.

7. I considered in Advisory Council a number of amendments designed to give effect to the representations of the Jewish Agency, set out in the accompanying copy of a letter

ENCLOSURE II dated the 9th January, 1935, that the definition of owners should be amended so as to include tenants holding land on long-term leases. This is a matter which raises difficult

4.

and complicated issues and requires careful examination; I therefore decided not to delay the promulgation of the Ordinance on this account but to exclude the proposed amendments for the time being and to give further consideration to the particular case of tenants of Jewish colonizing agencies who hold their lands on virtually perpetual leases. I shall accordingly address you in due course as to the need, if any, for amending the Ordinance in this respect.

ENCLOSURE III
ENCLOSURE IV

8. I forward, at this opportunity, the memorandum by the Law Officers on the draft Ordinance, as it was published as a Bill, together with a note on the comments enclosed in your Confidential despatch of the 7th August, 1934, which were made by your legal advisers on the first draft Ordinance prepared by the Commissioner of Lands. It is regretted that, through an oversight, these documents were not submitted with my despatch Confidential (B) of the 12th December, 1934.

9. I take this opportunity of informing you that the printing of the various notices and registers required in connection with the enforcement of the Rural Property Tax is likely to involve a greater expenditure than was anticipated and that it will probably be necessary, in the circumstances, to seek your authority for the expenditure of funds additional to the vote of LP. 8000 sanctioned in your telegram No.7 of the 9th January, 1935.

I have the honour to be,
Sir,
Your most obedient,
humble servant,

Arthur Wauchope

HIGH COMMISSIONER FOR PALESTINE.

APPENDIX.

ENCLOSURE I

RURAL PROPERTY TAX BILL.

Amendments passed in Advisory Council, 14th January, 1935.

Amendments	Reasons
Clause 2.	
Definition of "House and Land Tax". The Meqtu Ijara Zamin has been added.	It was decided by the Committee appointed by His Excellency the Officer Administering the Government to report on exemption from Customs and Taxation that the Meqtu Ijara Zamin made payable under the Franco-Turkish Agreement of 1913 in respect of miri properties exempt from Verko is the same Mukata Tax as the Badl Ushr and is collected at the same rate. The variation in nomenclature is determined by the category of the land. The Committee therefore recommended that, since the Badl Ushr has been abolished in those areas in which the Urban Property Tax Ordinance has been applied, whereas the Meqtu Ijara Zamin is still collected in those areas, steps should be taken to remove this inconsistency in the Rural Property Tax Ordinance and to abolish the Meqtu Ijara Zamin.
Definition of "Industrial building". (1) Read "an" for "the" before "official valuer" in second line of definition.	The Commissioner of Lands has explained that it was uncertain whether he would be able to allocate regions to official valuers. This amendment entailed similar consequential amendments in line 2 of the proviso to this definition and in the following sections:- Section 8(2) line 4. Section 10(b) line 4. Section 11(1) line 3. Section 11(2) line 3. Section 12(2) line 2, and line 8 "such" for "the" before "official valuer". Section 14(a) line 2 of paragraphs (a) and (b). Section 26, line 1 and lines 4 and 5 (deletion of words "in respect of the region allocated to him").
(2) After "undertaking" in line 5, insert "in which mechanically driven machinery is used".	The Commissioner of Lands wished to bring the definition of "industrial building" into line with the definition appearing in Rules made under the Urban Property Tax Ordinance. (See Gazette of the 1st August, 1928).

-2-

Amendments	Reasons
Definition of "owner"	
(i) Sub-paragraphs (a) and (b): for "subject to settlement" read "settled".	A definition of the term "settled" was substituted for the definition of the term "subject to settlement".
(ii) Delete the definition of "Settlement" and insert the following definition of "Settled":	
"Settled" used with reference to land means any land included in a schedule of rights or shhedule of partition posted in accordance with the provisions of the Land Settlement Ordinance, 1928. "	
Clause 4(2) add the following proviso:	
" Provided that each time the High Commissioner-in-Council shall vary the schedule under this sub-section the schedule as so waried shall remain unaltered for a period of not less than five years from the date from which any such variation shall take effect."	This amendment gives effect to the Secretary of State's recommendation in his Confidential telegram of the 2nd January, 1935.
Clause 6.	
(i) Sub-section (3), (ii),(iii) and (iv), before the words "such plantation" insert the words "the commencement of".	This amendment was inserted for the sake of clarity.
(ii) Sub-section (7), lines 1 and 7, after "plantation" insert "or crop".	It was considered that the word "plantation" in isolation might be interpreted to refer to fruit plantations only.
Clause 7.	
Delete "and may in any such Order or by a subsequent Order under this Section, allocate regions to such official valuers".	Both this and the following amendment are for the same reason as the substitution of 'an' for 'the' before 'official valuer' in Section 2 above, and themselves necessitate a similar amendment in Section 26(1) lines 4 and 5.

Amendments	Reasons
Clause 8.	
(i) Sub-section (1) line 3, delete "in respect of the region allocated to him".	
(ii) Sub-section (1)(b) line 4, after "the annual value" insert "and the names of the owners".	Secretary of State's amendment.
(iii) Sub-section (2) line 4, read "an" for "the", in line 5 read "who" for "he", and in line 7 read "stamped" for "signed".	For reasons of administrative convenience, the Director of Surveys recommended that maps should be stamped and not signed.
Clause 14, line 2 delete "(1)(a)" after "section 12", and line 2, delete "(1)(b)(i)" after "section 12".	Secretary of State's amendment.
Clause 16.	
Sub-section (1) line 8, "this" for "the".	
Clause 18.	
(i) Delete proviso to sub-section (1)(a) and insert the following:- "Provided that the District Commissioner may appoint any person to be a member of a tax distribution committee notwithstanding that such person is not an inhabitant of the village if such person is an owner of land within the village, or the representative of such person whether such representative be an inhabitant of the village or not."	This amendment gives effect to a proposal made in Advisory Council by the District Commissioner, Southern District, and is intended to remove an ambiguity in the proviso. At the same time it gives effect to an amendment proposed by the Secretary of State.
(ii) Sub-section (3)(b), line 3, after "may prepare such list" insert "and no objection shall be heard to any such list".	See covering despatch.
Clause 20.	
(i) Marginal note read "Distribution list to be open to inspection" for "Posting of distribution list".	The Commissioner of Lands wished this amendment to be introduced for the practical reason that in general there were no facilities in villages for the posting of Distribution Lists. They would therefore be made public by being circulated to mukhtars.
(ii) Line 3 read "made available for inspection" for "posted".	

-4-

Amendments	Reasons
	This amendment entailed consequential amendments in the following sections: Section 21(ii) (1). Section 22(2) line 7. Section 24(4) line 4. Section 25 line 5. Section 29 line 5. Section 30(a)(ii) line 2.

Clause 28.

(i) Delete sub-paragraph (1) and insert sub-paragraphs (1) and (2) as follows:-   Secretary of State's amendment.

"(1) The rural property tax shall be a first charge on the property in respect of which it is payable and no transaction relating to such property shall be entered in any Government register until the rural property tax thereon has been paid.

"(2) Without prejudice to the provisions of section 32 of this Ordinance, if the owner of any property in respect of which the rural property tax is payable is absent from Palestine the said tax shall be payable by and may be recovered from the agent, if any, of any such owner to the extent of the amount of any moneys collected by the agent on behalf of such owner provided always the owner shall remain liable to the Government for the payment of the rural property tax".

(ii) Renumber sub-section (2) and (3) as (3) and (4).

(iii) (4) line 1 read "Ordinance" for "section".

Schedule:

The expression "4th/5th Grade Fruit Plantation" is brought into line with the asterisk in each case.

PCL/5/35.

ENCLOSURE II.

9th January, 1935.

The Chief Secretary,
    Government Offices,
        Jerusalem.

Sir,

        I have the honour to refer to the Rural Property Tax Bill, 1934, published for information in the Palestine Gazette of December 13, 1934, and to submit herewith the observations of the Jewish Agency on the measure.

2.   In presenting its observations, the Executive of the Jewish Agency desires to express its gratification at the comprehensive reform of the system of rural taxation which it is proposed to effect by the present Ordinance. It notes with satisfaction that a consolidated land tax is to be substituted for the antiquated and dual system hitherto in force. It has had occasion, in the past, to draw attention to the defects of a system of taxation based on gross income, thereby penalising exertion and investment, and it is gratified to observe that the new system would appear to be based on net income. It further welcomes the introduction of the principle of the exemption of newly cultivated land for a period of years from the increase of the new tax, though, as will be submitted in the course of this memorandum, the application of the principle does not, in its view, meet all the requirements of the actual

                              situation/

-2-

situation. The amendments to the draft which the Jewish Agency would propose refer to a number of points affecting both the material sections and the procedure to be introduced under the terms of the Ordinance.

3. With regard to the interpretations embodied in Section 2 of the Bill a most important point arises in connection with the interpretation of the term "owner" contained in the Section. It will be recalled that until the Commutation of Tithes Ordinance of December 16, 1927, the liability for the payment of the Osher rested exclusively on the tenant. The Commutation of Tithes Ordinance altered this and shifted the burden of responsibility to the reputed owner of the land. The Jewish colonising agencies have for years past strongly urged the restoration of the former practice but have usually met with the reply that the proper time for raising the question would arrive when the new consolidated rural property tax would be introduced. The Urban Property Tax (Amendment) Ordinance of November 30, 1929 expressly included in the term "reputed owner" tenants holding a contract for three years and upwards. This provision was regarded as an indication that the proposed consolidated rural tax would also be based on the same principle. The Executive of the Jewish Agency believes that at a certain stage in the history of the present Bill it was contemplated that the principle introduced in regard to the Urban property tax would similarly be applied to the new rural property tax. It is therefore noted with regret that no change in this direction has been effected in the present Bill. The Jewish Agency would desire to point out that the matter is one which affects not a number of individual cases but the entire system
of Jewish/

of Jewish colonisation which is, to a large extent, based on a system of leases granted for life and even of hereditary character. The ownership of the Jewish National Fund and, in certain cases, of the P.I.C.A. is thus purely nominal; their tenants hold possession for life and on their death their heirs automatically step into their possession, unless there be some special reasons to the contrary. There is, therefore, no essential difference between a long-term tenant on land of the Jewish colonising agencies and a peasant settled on land of his own. Hence, it is hardly justifiable to impose forever upon the Jewish colonising agencies the responsibility for the payment of the taxes of those who are in permanent occupation of their land, and to place upon these agencies the difficult task of acting as tax collectors on behalf, as it were, of the fiscal authorities. It is, of course, realised that the land owning companies can protect themselves by inserting into contracts with their tenants a provision concerning the liability of the tenants to refund to them taxes paid on their behalf. It is obvious, however, that there is a fundamental difference between an arrangement under which the tenants have to face the tax collecting agencies of the Government and one under which they have to deal merely with the land-owning companies who, by virtue of their public utility character, may find it difficult to resort to those more stringent methods which the fiscal agencies of Government are at liberty to apply. The inevitable result of this will be that in case of default these companies will suffer financial loss and that funds which are destined

for/

for constructive purposes will be diverted to the payment of the tax arrears of the tenants.

It may in general be urged that it is essential for the development of a sense of civic responsibility among the farming community that its members should be made to feel that the responsibility for the management of their settlements rests in every respect - and not least of all in regard to their fiscal obligations towards the Government of the country on their own shoulders. It is of the utmost importance that the Jewish settlers should feel the burden of that responsibility and that they should not be allowed to think that they can shelter behind the paternal protection of the Jewish land owning companies in respect of their financial obligations to the State.

The Jewish Agency would therefore urge that the definition of the term "owner" under Sub-Section (a) should be qualified in the sense that the actual possessor should be made liable for the tax if the lease is for a period of at least three years, if the land is cultivable and if the leasehold contract is registered.

4. It is further submitted, under the head of interpretations, that the definition contained in Section 2 of an "industrial building" as a building construed and used or intended to be used solely for the purpose of an industrial undertaking, or in connection therewith, may leave room for ambiguities of interpretation inasmuch as there exist, in connection with agricultural enterprise, various forms of activities which may be termed industrial and which are yet merely ancillary to the process of agricultural production

and/

and marketing, such as cowsheds, dairies, packing houses, groats mills, etc. It is therefore suggested that the term "industrial undertaking" be qualified by the addition of the words: "exclusive of industrial undertakings which are ancillary to the normal process of agricultural production and marketing."

5. In regard to the system of exemptions provided for in Section 6 of the Draft Ordinance, the Jewish Agency would urge three amendments :

(a) Apart from the five categories of farming in respect of which exemptions are to be granted for varying periods under the provisions of sub-section 3, it is submitted that with a view to furthering the introduction of intensive methods of cultivation and the promotion of close settlement on the land, as enjoined by the terms of the Palestine Mandate, an exemption should be granted in respect of agricultural enterprise tending in this direction. It may be pointed out that no fiscal relief has been granted in the past years to the new colonisation which, as is generally admitted, has played a most important part in the development of Palestinian agriculture and thereby in the increase of revenue.

The Jewish Agency would submit that advantage should be taken of the present opportunity for initiating a fundamental change in this respect. It may be urged that, in view of the very heavy investments involved in the introduction of more intensive methods of cultivation and the long period which has to elapse before these yield a proportionate return, a general exemption from taxation for a period of ten years be granted in respect of rural lands on which fundamental improvements in the methods of cultivation such as amelioration, irrigation and manuring are being effected, or intensive cultures such as vegetable and green fodder growing are being introduced. Such a measure of relief would be substantially in accord with the principle underlying the exemption granted and reaffirmed in the present Ordinance in respect of vineyards planted with American stock.

(b) In view of the special difficulties with which the citrus industry has to contend in the coastal belt and in the Northern sub-districts, arising from the ill effects of sea-winds and sand in the one case and from heavy soils in the other, it is submitted that an exemption for eighty years be granted for orange groves situated within a belt of ten kilometres from the coast or in any of the five northern sub-districts. In view of the inferior yield in these areas during this initial period such an extended exemption would appear to be fully justified.

(c) With/

-6-

(c) With reference to sub-section 6 it is urged that among the exemptions for which provision is there made, rural hospitals, clinics, dispensaries, school buildings and agricultural and industrial training and experimental centres be included.

6. With reference to the general procedure with regard to valuation and appeals, (sub-section 7 to 15) it is submitted that the example of the Urban Property Tax Ordinance be followed and the valuation itself be entrusted to a Committee consisting of two official and two unofficial members - the Chairman to be an official member with a casting vote and the unofficial members to be appointed from a roll submitted by the local or village council-while the appeals should lie to a committee of three members consisting of two officials and one unofficial member. It is considered that such an arrangement will not only enable the special knowledge possessed by the local community to be effectively utilised in the process of valuation and assessment but is also likely to prove more expeditious inasmuch as it will obviate many appeals.

For the same reasons it is suggested that the preparation of annual supplementary rural property tax rolls and valuation lists shall equally be entrusted to a committee of similar composition.

7. With regard to the Schedule it is desired to make the following observations: The shortness of time and the absence of data on the underlying principles of the division of lands into categories and on the assessment of the tax on them render it difficult to calculate or estimate the proceeds of the tax in comparison with those of the previous forms of taxation. It may, however, be

asserted/

-7-

in general that the Schedule as drafted involves a very marked total increase of agricultural taxation, more particularly on the citrus industry:

    (a) In the first instance it is felt that the rate fixed for category 1(citrus exclusive of the Acre subdistrict) is excessively high having regard to the actual yield of citrus cultivation and to the difficulties of marketing against which the industry has to contend. The Executive of the Jewish Agency would strongly urge that the rate should be fixed at not more than 600 mils per dunam.

    (b) With reference to category 2, it is submitted that the sub-districts of Nazareth, Tiberias, Safad and Beisan should be included with that of Acre in this category. It is difficult to see any economic or agricultural ground for differentiating between the citrus groves situated in the sub-district of Acre and the orange and grapefruit plantations in the Nazareth, Tiberias, Beisan and Safad areas. It is further urged that the rate of tax for citrus cultivation in these sub-districts should not exceed 250 mils per dunam having regard to the soil conditions in these parts and the very high expenditure which has to be incurred for fumigation and scale prevention.

    (c) With reference to Category 3 it is similarly felt that the rate of 560 mils per dunam of bananas is very high taking into account the heavy expenses which the growers have to meet in fighting the effects of plant diseases and of frost which both in Judea and in the Emek frequently destroy the banana crop. It is, therefore, urged that a substantial reduction should be effected in the rate of tax for bananas.

    (d) With regard to building plots attention should be drawn to the fact that in planning Jewish agricultural settlements reserves are created for subsequent developments. It would obviously be unfair if these were to be charged at the rate of building plots. It is submitted that except for buildings in rural areas which are rented, there should be a maximum of one dunam per farm. Attention may be drawn to the fact that in Egypt the built on area in villages is not taxed at all

8. With/

8. With regard to the offences and penalties provided for in Section 36, it is submitted that the penalty of imprisonment not exceeding three months prescribed in Sub-Section 3 for failure to notify changes in the mode of cultivation under Section 5 would appear to be unduly harsh having regard to the nature of the offence. It would seem that the fine prescribed in the Sub-Section would be an adequate deterrent.

9. The Executive of the Jewish Agency trusts that Government will give due consideration to its representations, and that in view of the far reaching character of the proposed reform of rural taxation a sufficient time will be allowed to pass between the submission of this memorandum and the enactment of the Bill to make such consideration possible.

                              I have the honour to be,

                                  Sir,

                            Your obedient servant,

                                M. Shertok

                       EXECUTIVE OF THE JEWISH AGENCY.

ENCLOSURE III.

MEMORANDUM.

Draft Rural Property Tax Ordinance,
Palestine.

1. The original draft Ordinance prepared by the Commissioner of Lands and sent to the Secretary of State under cover of Despatch, Palestine Confidential G. of 23rd February, 1934, had already been superseded by a second draft Ordinance by the Commissioner prior to the arrival of the Secretary of State's Confidential Despatch of the 7th August, 1934, containing the comments of the Secretary of State's Legal Advisers, and therefore not all of those comments were applicable to the draft Ordinance which the law officers here were asked to revise.

2. This Ordinance provides for the introduction into those parts of this Territory not being urban areas within the meaning of the Urban Property Tax Ordinance, 1928, of a tax on land and industrial buildings which will be known as the Rural Property Tax and which will replace in such parts the Ottoman House and Land Tax and Tithe.

3. The Rural Property Tax will be levied on lands at the rates set out in the schedule to the Ordinance in respect of the category within which such lands fall, and on industrial buildings at such rate, not exceeding fifteen per centum of the net annual value of such industrial buildings (vide section 4(1)(b)).

- 2 -

4. The Ordinance is one of partial application, the High Commissioner being, by section 3, empowered to apply it by Order to such area as he may name in such Order. The effect of such an Order will be that, by operation of law, the new tax will replace the old as from the 1st April, next following the date of such Order. It is contemplated that the High Commissioner will make an Order as aforementioned as soon as the Ordinance is promulgated and assuming that such promulgation will take place on or about the first day of December, 1934, the new system of taxation will obtain in the areas described in such Order as from the 1st April, 1935.

5. In the meantime the High Commissioner will have exercised the powers in him vested by section 7 of the Ordinance and appointed official valuers.

Section 8 provides that such official valuers shall "as soon as may be, possible after their appointment, from information to be obtained by them" prepare rural property tax rolls in respect of lands and valuation lists in respect of industrial buildings.

It should be understood, however, that such rolls and lists have already been prepared by the Commissioner of Lands and therefore all that will remain to be done will be to post them in accordance with the provisions of the Ordinance.

6. Fourteen days are then given in order to submit objections to the rolls, and lists (vide section 11). It is then the duty of official valuers to consider such objections and to make such amendments as they may think right.

Provision is made under section 14 for any person aggrieved by a decision of the official valuer to appeal from such decision to appeal committees which the High Commissioner will have appointed under section 13.

7. Appeal Committees will determine all such appeals, and by section 16 of the Ordinance the areas of the categories of the lands of a village and such categories as shown on the Rural Property Tax Roll as finally so determined and the net annual value of industrial buildings within any village as shown on the valuation list also so determined, will provide the data on which the tax will be assessed until revised in the manner provided in the Ordinance.

8. In respect of lands however, the rural property tax roll hereinbefore referred to being merely the record of the division of an area, to which the Ordinance has been applied, into categories and the extent of such categories, the next step will be to apportion the tax amongst owners. This is provided for in sections 18 to 25 inclusive.

9. Provision is made by sections 26 to 29 inclusive for maintaining the rolls and lists up to date.

10. With regard to the memorandum containing the comments of the legal advisers to the Secretary of State referred to in paragraph 2 of the Secretary of State's Confidential despatch dated 7th August, 1934:-

(a) Definition of "industrial undertaking". After consideration it was decided that such a definition was unnecessary in view of the fact that its omission from the Urban Property Tax Ordinance, 1928, had not given rise to any difficulties, and the Commissioner of Lands was averse to its inclusion in the present Ordinance.

(b) Definition of "annual value" in clause 5 of the original draft forwarded to the Secretary of State.

The words "annual value" no longer appear in clause 4 of the present draft, and provision giving the High Commissioner-in-Council power with the approval of the Secretary of State to grant relief where any fall in the value of crops makes it in his opinion expedient so to do has been inserted instead.

With regard to the other criticisms contained in the said memorandum due regard has been given to them in the revision of the draft Ordinance, vide sheet attached hereto.

11. As regards the correspondence with the Treasury referred to in the first paragraph of the above mentioned despatch, the point raised in paragraph 9 of the letter

to the Under Secretary of State dated 14th May, 1934, sub-section 2 of section 4 of the Ordinance now provides that no change can be made in the rates set out in the schedule to the Ordinance until after a date being three years from the first day of April, 1935.

[signature]
A/ATTORNEY GENERAL.

30th October, 1934.

ENCLOSURE IV.

OBSERVATIONS ON COMMENTS MADE BY THE SECRETARY OF STATE'S LEGAL ADVISERS ON FIRST DRAFT OF RURAL PROPERTY TAX ORDINANCE PREPARED BY THE COMMISSIONER OF LANDS.

Clause 2: Definition of "industrial undertaking". In revising the second draft prepared by the Commissioner of Lands, I have not inserted such a definition as he informed me that in his opinion it was unnecessary, and that its omission had not given rise to any difficulties in the administration of the Urban Property Tax Ordinance.

Definition of "owner". In revising the second draft prepared by the Commissioner of Lands the proviso to which the Secretary of State took exception has been transferred to the paragraph dealing with registered and unregistered owners which is its proper place.

The proviso dealing with lessees and sub-lessees in the first draft has with the concurrence of the Commissioner of Lands been omitted from my revision of his second draft.

Clause 3: This clause which is also clause 3 in my revised draft has been completely reworded in order to meet the Secretary of State's point.

Clause 5: (clause 4 in my draft). I consulted the Commissioner of Lands on the question of defining "annual value" and he suggested that it should be omitted and replaced by suitable words giving the High Commissioner power to grant relief where any fall in the value of crops makes it in the opinion of the High Commissioner expedient so to do.

Clause 6(b) - (clause 5(2) in my draft). The Secretary of State's point has been met by providing that notice of commencement of cultivation etc., shall be given to the District Officer.

Clause 6(c) - (clause 6(4) in my draft). This sub-clause has been completely redrafted and I think that the Secretary of State's points have been met.

Clause 6(e) - (clause 5(7) in my draft). This sub-clause has been amended in accordance with the Secretary of State's requirements.

Clause 12. - (clause 8(3) in my draft). This sub-clause has been amended in accordance with the Secretary of State's requirements.

Clause 14(1) - (clause 11(1) of my draft). The names of owners do not appear on the Rural Property Tax Roll. Only categories of land and areas, and this sub-clause has now been suitably redrafted.

Clause 15 - (clause 12 of my draft). This has been completely redrafted and the Secretary of State's objections no longer apply.

Clause 17(1)(b) - (clause 14 of my draft). This has been completely redrafted and the Secretary of State's objections no longer apply.

Clause 17 - (clause 13(3) of my draft). Provision has been made for differences of opinion between members of

- 3 -

appeal committees and for taking evidence on oath in clause 13(2) and (3).

Clause 21(4) - (clause 18(3) of my draft). The words "under the supervision of the District Officer" only have been retained, it is not anticipated that any difficulty is likely to arise in practice.

Clause 25 - (clause 24(5) of my draft). Provision has been inserted for a case to be stated upon a point of law.

Clause 26(a): This clause has been redrafted on the lines of section 61 of the Land Settlement Ordinance, and now provides only for correction of clerical errors.

Clause 26(b): I have deemed it advisable to omit the sub-clause for the reason that it would not be possible to arrange for appeals and objections within the prescribed periods in the event of properties being added to the Valuation List and Distribution List after such lists had been determined.

Clause 27: This was omitted from Commissioner of Land's second draft and therefore does not appear in my draft.

Clause 28: Marginal notes throughout my draft are original.

Clause 33(1) - (clause 37(1) in my draft). The Secretary of State's objections have been met.

Clause 33(4): The Secretary of State's objections have been met.

Clause 37 - (clause 30 in my draft). The Secretary of State's objections have been met.

Clause 38(c) - (proviso to clause 30 in my draft). The Secretary of State's objections have been met.

Clause 39(1) - (clause 32(2) in my draft). The Secretary of State's objections have been met.

Clause 39(3) - (clause 32(3) in my draft). The words "objected to" have been omitted.

L.L.B.

30th October, 1934.

BY AIR MAIL

HIGH COMMISSIONER FOR PALESTINE,
JERUSALEM.

PALESTINE

DESPATCH NO. [A]
REFERENCE NO. F/105/34

11 February, 1935.

Sir,

    With reference to previous correspondence on the subject of the introduction of a Rural Property Tax Ordinance, I have the honour to forward herewith for the signification of His Majesty's pleasure, two sealed and six plain copies of Ordinance No.1 of 1935, entitled "The Rural Property Tax Ordinance".

ENCLOSURES

    I have the honour to be,
    Sir,
    Your most obedient,
    humble servant,

Arthur Wauchope

HIGH COMMISSIONER FOR PALESTINE.

THE RIGHT HONOURABLE
    SIR PHILIP CUNLIFFE-LISTER, G.B.E., M.P., etc., etc.,
        HIS MAJESTY'S PRINCIPAL SECRETARY OF STATE
                FOR THE COLONIES.

The Palestine Gazette

Published by Authority

No. 489   WEDNESDAY, 23RD JANUARY, 1935   GAZETTE EXTRAORDINARY

CONTENTS   *Page*

SUPPLEMENT No. 2.

The following subsidiary legislation is published in Supplement No. 2 which forms part of this Gazette:—

Order, No. 22 of 1935, under the Rural Property Tax Ordinance, 1935, regarding rural property tax - - - - - - - - 57

Order, No. 23 of 1935, under the Rural Property Tax Ordinance, 1935, appointing Official Valuers - - - - - - - 57

Rural Property Tax Rules, 1935, under the Rural Property Tax Ordinance, 1935 - 58

Supplement No. 2.
to the
Palestine Gazette Extraordinary No. 489 of 23rd January, 1935.

RURAL PROPERTY TAX ORDINANCE, 1935.

Order, No. 22 of 1935, by the High Commissioner under section 3 (1)

In exercise of the powers vested in him by sub-section (1) of section 3 of the Rural Property Tax Ordinance, 1935, the High Commissioner is pleased to declare and it is hereby declared that the rural property tax shall be payable annually to the High Commissioner as from the first day of April next following the date of this Order for the use of the territory of Palestine on all lands and industrial buildings comprised within the boundaries of Palestine with the exception of Beersheba Sub-District and areas to which the provisions of the Urban Property Tax Ordinance, 1928, have been applied.

No. 1 of 1935.

By His Excellency's Command,

J. HATHORN HALL
Chief Secretary.

15th January, 1935.
(F/164/34)

RURAL PROPERTY TAX ORDINANCE, 1935.

Order, No. 23 of 1935, by the High Commissioner under section 7.

In exercise of the powers vested in him by section 7 of the Rural Property Tax Ordinance, 1935, the High Commissioner is pleased to appoint and the

— 58 —

undermentioned persons are hereby appointed to be official valuers for the purposes of the Ordinance.

MAURICE CHRISTMAS BENNETT.
RICHARD HUGHES.
PERCIVAL CHARLES FORBES AYLMER-HARRIS.

By His Excellency's Command,

J. HATHORN HALL
Chief Secretary.

15th January, 1935.
(F/164/34)

RURAL PROPERTY TAX ORDINANCE, 1935.

RULES MADE BY THE HIGH COMMISSIONER UNDER SECTION 41.

No. 1 of 1935. IN EXERCISE of the powers vested in him by section 41 of the Rural Property Tax Ordinance, 1935, the High Commissioner has made the following rules:—

Citation. 1. These rules may be cited as the Rural Property Tax Rules, 1935.

Forms. 2. The forms to be used for the purpose of the Ordinance shall be the forms set out in the schedule to these rules.

Where forms may be obtained. 3. Any of the forms set out in the schedule to these rules which are required to be filled in by members of the public may be obtained from the District Office of any Sub-District to which the Ordinance is applied.

Deposit. 4. The deposit referred to in section 15 (2) (a) and section 24 (2) (a) of the Ordinance, shall be two pounds.

Manner in which Distribution List to be made available for inspection. 5. A Distribution List prepared in accordance with sections 18 and 19 of the Ordinance shall be delivered by the District Officer to the Mukhtar who shall make it available for inspection by any person desiring to do so in accordance with any directions which such District Officer may give and the date upon which the District Officer delivers a Distribution List to the Mukhtar hereunder shall be deemed to be the date upon which such list is made available for inspection. In addition a copy of the Distribution List shall be made available for inspection by any person desiring to do so in the District Office of the Sub-District in which the property mentioned in such list is situated and the District Officer shall take all such steps as he may think fit to ensure that all the inhabitants of the village to which such list refers are made aware of the list being available for inspection.

— 59 —

RT/1.

SCHEDULE.

RURAL PROPERTY TAX ORDINANCE, 1935.

Notice of development of land under section 5 (1) and application for Exemption under section 6.

To:
    District Officer,
    _____ Sub-District.

In accordance with the provisions of sub-section (1) of section 5 of the Rural Property Tax Ordinance, 1935, I hereby give you notice of the development, which took place after the first day of April, 1935, of the land described in the schedule hereunder of which I am the owner within the meaning of the Ordinance:—

SCHEDULE.

Village: _____   Name of Owner: _____
                                  (In Block Letters)

Name of $\frac{\text{Block}}{\text{Qita'}}$ _____   Previous condition of land: _____

Block No. _____   (*) Parcel No. _____

Development.

Nature of development: _____
Area: _____ m. ds.   Date of commencement of development: _____
                          Anticipated date of completion of development: _____

Note:—If fruit plantation, including citrus or bananas, s'ate:
Kind of trees: _____   No. of trees per dunum: _____
Remarks:—

I hereby declare that the foregoing particulars are in every respect fully and truly stated to the best of my knowledge and belief, and I apply for exemption in accordance with the provisions of section 6 of the Ordinance.

Countersignature of Mukhtar: _____   Signature of Owner: _____
Date: _____   Date: _____

(*) Applicable to settled lands only.

Note:—This notice shall be sent to the District Officer within three months from the date of the commencement of development.

— 60 —

RT/1A.

RURAL PROPERTY TAX ORDINANCE, 1935.

Notice of development of land under section 6 (3) (I) and application for Exemption under section 6.

To:
    District Officer,
    _____ Sub-District.

In accordance with the provisions of paragraph (I) of the proviso to sub-section (3) of section 6 of the Rural Property Tax Ordinance, 1935, I hereby give you notice of the development, which took place prior to the first day of April, 1935, of land described in the schedule hereunder of which I am the owner within the meaning of the Ordinance :—

SCHEDULE.

Village :_____

Name of $\frac{\text{Block}}{\text{Qita}^*}$ _____

Block No. _____ (*) Parcel No. _____

Name of Owner : _____
(In Block Letters)

Previous condition of land : _____

Development.

Nature of development : _____

Area : _____ m. ds.

Date of commencement of development : _____

Anticipated date of completion of development : _____

Note:—If fruit plantation, including citrus or bananas, state:

Kind of trees : _____   No. of trees per dunum : _____

Remarks :—

I hereby declare that the foregoing particulars are in every respect fully and truly stated to the best of my knowledge and belief, and I apply for exemption in accordance with the provisions of section 6 of the Ordinance.

Countersignature of Mukhtar : _____   Signature of Owner : _____

Date : _____   Date : _____

(*) Applicable to settled lands only.

Note:—This notice shall be sent to the District Officer within three months from the first day of April, 1935.

— 61 —

RT/2.
RURAL PROPERTY TAX ORDINANCE, 1935.

NOTICE of completion of an industrial building or of an addition to an existing industrial building under section 5 (2), or of the commencement of the reconstruction of an industrial building under section 6 (5), which took place on or after the first day of April, 1935, and application for exemption under section 6.

To:
    District Officer,
    _____ Sub-District.

In accordance with the provisions of sub-section (2) of section 5 and/or sub-section (5) of section 6 of the Rural Property Tax Ordinance, 1935, I hereby give you notice of the $\frac{\text{completion}}{\text{commencement of reconstruction}}$ of the undermentioned (*) industrial building of which I am the owner within the meaning of the Rural Property Tax Ordinance, 1935, as described in the schedule hereunder:—

SCHEDULE.

Village: _____

Name of $\frac{\text{Block}}{\text{Qit'a'}}$ _____

Block No. _____

Date of commencement of
construction _____
reconstruction

Date of $\frac{\text{completion}}{\text{occupation}}$ _____

State if $\frac{\text{new}}{\text{reconstruction of}}$ building, or addition to existing building: _____

Name of Owner: _____
(In Block Letters)

Area of Site: _____ sq. ms.

(**) Parcel No. _____

Kind of construction: _____

Nature of Industry: _____

No. of Floors: _____

No. of rooms on each floor: _____

Area of ground
floor space: _____ sq. ms.

I hereby declare that the foregoing particulars are in every respect fully and truly stated to the best of my knowledge and belief, and I apply for exemption in accordance with the provisions of section 6 of the Ordinance.

Countersignature of Mukhtar: _____   Signature of Owner: _____

Date: _____   Date: _____

NOTE:—This notice shall be submitted within three months from the *completion* of an industrial building (section 5 (2)) or within three months from the *commencement of the reconstruction* of an industrial building (section 6 (5)).

    (*) By section 2 of the Ordinance any addition to an industrial building of which the net annual value is in the opinion of an Official Valuer more than LP.90 shall itself be deemed to be an industrial building.
    (**) Applicable to settled lands only.

— 62 —

RT/2A.

RURAL PROPERTY TAX ORDINANCE, 1935.

NOTICE of completion of an industrial building or of an addition to an existing industrial building under section 6 (4) (I) which took place prior to the first day of April, 1935, and application for exemption under section 6.

To:
District Officer,
_____ Sub-District.

In accordance with the provisions of para. (I) of the proviso to sub-section (4) of section 6 of the Rural Property Tax Ordinance, 1935, I hereby give you notice of the $\frac{\text{completion}}{\text{completion of reconstruction}}$ of the undermentioned (*) industrial building of which I am the owner within the meaning of the Rural Property Tax Ordinance, 1935, as described in the schedule hereunder:—

SCHEDULE.

Village: _____

Name of $\frac{\text{Block}}{\text{Qita'}}$ _____

Block No. _____

Date of commencement of
$\frac{\text{construction}}{\text{reconstruction}}$ _____

Date of $\frac{\text{completion}}{\text{occupation}}$ _____

State if $\frac{\text{new}}{\text{reconstruction of}}$ building, or addition to existing building:
_____

Name of Owner: _____
(In Block Letters)

Area of Site _____ sq. ms.

(**) Parcel No. _____

Kind of construction: _____

Nature of Industry: _____

No. of Floors: _____

No. of rooms on each floor: _____

Area of ground
floor space: _____ sq. ms.

I hereby declare that the foregoing particulars are in every respect fully and truly stated to the best of my knowledge and belief, and I apply for exemption in accordance with the provisions of section 6 of the Ordinance.

Countersignature of Mukhtar: _____ Signature of Owner: _____
Date: _____ Date: _____

NOTE:—This notice shall be submitted within three months of the first day of April, 1935,

(*) By section 2 of the Ordinance any addition to an industrial building of which the net annual value is in the opinion of an Official Valuer more than LP.20 shall itself be deemed to be an industrial building.

(**) Applicable to settled lands only.

— 63 —

RT/3.

RURAL PROPERTY TAX ORDINANCE, 1935.

Notice for exemption from Rural Property Tax under section 6 (1)

To:
District Officer.
_____ Sub-District.

In accordance with the provisions of sub-section 1 (a) of section 6 of the Rural Property Tax Ordinance, 1935, I hereby give you particulars of the exemption which I lawfully enjoyed on the 31st day of March, 1935, from $\frac{\text{House and Land Tax and Tithe}}{\text{House and Land Tax/or Tithe}}$ in respect of the land described in the schedule hereunder, of which I am the owner within the meaning of the Ordinance:—

SCHEDULE.

Village: _____   Name of Owner: _____
(In Block Letters).

Name of $\frac{\text{Block}}{\text{Qita'}}$ _____   Area: _____ m. ds _____ sq. ms.

Block No. _____   (*) Parcel No. _____

Particulars of $\frac{\text{Law}}{\text{Treaty}}$ under which $\frac{\text{exemption}}{\text{abatement}}$ enjoyed:—
$\phantom{\text{Particulars of }}\text{Firman}$

Amount of $\frac{\text{exemption}}{\text{abatement}}$ of $\frac{\text{House and Land Tax}}{\text{Tithe}}$: LP._____
$\phantom{\text{Amount of exemption abatement of }}$: LP._____

Remarks:—

I hereby declare that the foregoing particulars are in every respect fully and truly stated to the best of my knowledge and belief, and I apply for such $\frac{\text{exemption}}{\text{abatement}}$ as may be prescribed in accordance with the provisions of sub-section (1) of section 6 of the Ordinance.

Date: _____   Signature of Owner: _____

$\phantom{\text{Date: _____   }}$Address: _____

(*) Applicable to settled lands only.

RURAL PROPERTY TAX ORDINANCE, 1935.
VALUATION AND SUPPLEMENTARY VALUATION LIST FOR INDUSTRIAL BUILDINGS.

Sub-District _____

Village _____

Serial No. of Valuation List _____

Block		Parcel Number (in settled lands)	Description of Property	Names of Owners	Register		Previous assessment	Net Annual Value				
Serial Number	Name Number				Volume	Folio		of Official Valuer		Revised Assessment of Appeal Committee		
							L.P.	L.P.	Initial and date	L.P.	Initial and date	

I hereby certify that this List was duly posted this _____ day of _____ 193__

Signature _____
    OFFICIAL VALUER

Date _____
    DISTRICT OFFICER

Signature _____
    CHAIRMAN
    APPEAL COMMITTEE

Date _____

RT/5

RURAL PROPERTY TAX ORDINANCE, 1935.

RURAL PROPERTY TAX ROLL FOR VILLAGE____________

Sub-District:__________ Page__________

Block No.	Name of Block or locality	Total Area of Block m. ds.	Category Number and Area (Metric dunums and square metres)																	Ground crop category of land planted with fruit trees	Remarks
			1 Area	2 Area	3 Area	4 Area	5 Area	6 Area	7 Area	8 Area	9 Area	10 Area	11 Area	12 Area	13 Area	14 Area	15 Area	16 Uncultivated land and forests Area	16 Roads, Railways, Rivers and Lakes Area		
Total area per category in block																					

I certify that this Roll was duly posted, this__________day of__________193...

Signature of the Appeal Committee __________ Signature of Official Valuer __________ District Officer__________

Date. Date__________ __________Sub-District.

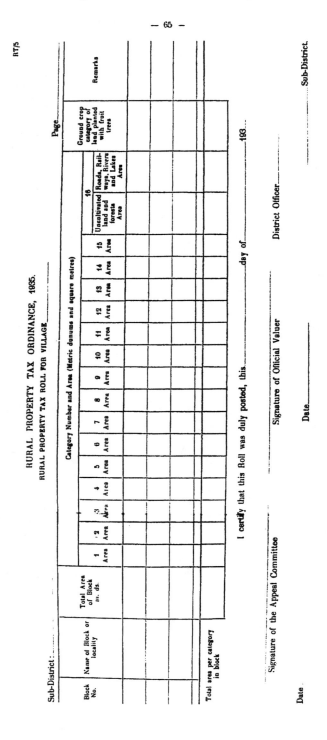

[Page 66 is blank in the original document.]

— 67 —

RT/8.

RURAL PROPERTY TAX ORDINANCE, 1935.

NOTICE of objection to the Rural Property Tax Roll under section 11.

A. *Notice of Objection.*

To:
    Official Valuer, _____
    Through District Officer,
    _____ Sub-District.

In accordance with the provisions of sub-section (1) of section 11 of the Rural Property Tax Ordinance, 1935, I hereby object to the Rural Property Tax Roll posted in the village of _____ on the _____ day of _____ 193__, in respect of the land described in the schedule hereunder:—

SCHEDULE.

Village: _____
Name of $\frac{Block}{Oita}$ _____

Block No. _____

Category (ries) as stated in R.P.T. Roll to which objection refers: _____

Category No. _____
Category No. _____

The grounds of my objection and the particulars in support of such grounds are as follows:—

    In respect of Category No. _____
    In respect of Category No. _____
    In respect of Category No. _____

and I desire that the category (ries) of land be corrected as follows:—

Category No. as stated in R.P. Tax Roll.	To be corrected to Category No.
Category No. _____	Category No. _____
Category No. _____	Category No. _____
Category No. _____	Category No. _____

This _____ day of _____ 193__,

    Signature: _____

    Address: _____

NOTE:—A separate form must be submitted, in duplicate, in respect of each Block, and must be submitted within 14 days from the date of the posting of the Rural Property Tax Roll

— 68 —

B. *Decision of Official Valuer.*

Mr. _____

Village _____

(*) In accordance with the provisions of section 12 of the Ordinance I have to inform you that I have considered the above objection and after making all due enquiries I consider it to be without foundation. I shall make no amendment to the rural property tax roll in pursuance of your objection.

(*) I have to inform you that I have considered the above objection and after making all due enquiries I have made the following decision: _____

_____

Date: _____

Signature: _____

Official Valuer.

(*) Delete whichever does not apply.

RT/7.

RURAL PROPERTY TAX ORDINANCE, 1935.

Notice of objection to the Valuation List under section 11.

A. *Notice of Objection.*

To:
 Official Valuer, _____
 Through District Officer,
 _____ Sub-District.

In accordance with the provisions of sub-section (2) of section 11 of the Rural Property Tax Ordinance, 1935, I hereby object to the Valuation List posted in the village of _____ on the _____ day of _____ 193___, in respect of the industrial building described in the schedule hereunder:—

SCHEDULE.

Block Number	Name of Block Qita'	Serial No. in Valuation List	Description of Property	Name of Owner	Net Annual Value LP. Mils

— 69 —

The grounds of my objection and the particulars in support of such grounds are as follows:—

Section 11 (2). _____
_____
_____

and I desire that the Valuation List in respect of the above building be corrected as follows:—

Name of Owner: _____

Net Annual Value: LP. _____

Signature: _____

Date: _____ Address: _____

NOTE:—A separate form must be submitted, in duplicate, in respect of each industrial building, and must be submitted within 14 days from the date of the posting of the Valuation List.

B. *Decision of Official Valuer.*

(*) In accordance with the provisions of para. (b) (i) of the proviso to subsection (1) of section 12 of the Ordinance, I have to inform you that I have considered the above objection and after making all due enquiries I consider it to be without foundation. I shall make no amendment to the Valuation List in pursuance of your objection.

(*) I have to inform you that I have considered the above objection, and after making all due enquiries I have decided to make the following amendment to the Valuation List: _____
_____
_____

Signature: _____

Date: _____ *Official Valuer.*

(*) Delete whichever does not apply.

— 70 —

RT/8.

RURAL PROPERTY TAX ORDINANCE, 1935.

NOTICE of hearing of objection to Valuation List under section 12 (1) (b) (ii).

To:
  (*) Mr. _____
       _____
          (Address)
       _____

I have to inform you that I have considered your objection, dated _____, to the Valuation List in respect of the industrial building under Serial No. _____ in the village of _____, and after making all due enquiries consider it to be sufficiently well founded to warrant further consideration. I shall hear the objection at _____ on the _____ day of _____ 193__, at which you may appear. Please note that I have given notice to the undermentioned persons, that is to say:—

       _____
       _____
       _____

who I think may be affected by your objection.

                    Signature: _____

Date: _____
                                   Official Valuer.

Copy to:
  (*) Mr. _____
       _____
          (Address)

who may, if he wishes, be present at such hearing.

(*)NOTE:—You are warned in accordance with section 12 (1) (c) that on failure to attend as directed, a decision on the objection may, in your absence, be made as may be deemed right.

— 71 —

RT/9.

RURAL PROPERTY TAX ORDINANCE, 1935.

Notice of appeal from decision of Official Valuer under section 14 (a) or (b).

To:
    The Chairman of the
        Appeal Committee,
    Through District Officer,
        _____ Sub-District.

I hereby appeal against the decision of the Official Valuer, dated_____, copy of which is attached, given by him in respect of my objection to the Rural Property Tax Roll.
    Valuation List.

Date: _____

Signature: _____
Address: _____

Note:—This form must be submitted, in duplicate, within 14 days of the date of the decision of the Official Valuer.

RT/10.

RURAL PROPERTY TAX ORDINANCE, 1935.

Notice of appeal from decision of Official Valuer under section 14 (c).

To:
    The Chairman of the Appeal Committee,
    Through District Officer,
        _____Sub-District.

I hereby appeal against:—

(*) (a) the alteration of the assessment of the industrial building described in the schedule hereunder of which I am the owner within the meaning of the Ordinance, made by the Official Valuer as a result of an objection made by Mr._____

— 72 —

(*) (b) the inclusion of my name as owner of the industrial building described in the schedule hereunder made by the Official Valuer as a result of an objection made by Mr._____

SCHEDULE.

Name of Sub-District	Name of Village	Block Number	Name of Block Qita'	Serial No. in Valuation List

The grounds of my appeal and the particulars in support of such grounds are as follows: _____
_____
_____

and I desire that the correction in the Valuation List in respect of the above building as made by the Official Valuer be amended as follows:_____
_____

Date:_____   Signature:_____

                            Address:_____

(*) Delete whichever ground is inapplicable.

NOTE:—This form must be submitted, in duplicate, within 14 days from the date of the decision of the Official Valuer.

RT/11.

RURAL PROPERTY TAX ORDINANCE, 1935.

NOTICE of hearing of appeal under section 15 (1).

To:
   Mr. _____
        _____
        (Address)

Please note that your appeal, dated_____, against the decision of the Official Valuer in respect of the Rural Property Tax Roll Block No._____ in the Valuation List Serial No.

— 73 —

village of ———— will be heard by the Appeal Committee at ————
(place), on ———— at ———— a.m./p.m.

You are hereby required in accordance with section 15 (2) to pay forthwith to the District Officer, ———— Sub-District, the sum of Two Pounds as deposit on account of costs, and you are hereby notified under section 15 (2) (a) that on failure to pay such amount prior to the abovementioned date of hearing, your appeal will not be heard.

You are hereby warned, in accordance with section 15 (2) (b) that on your failure to attend as directed, a decision on the appeal may, in your absence, be made as may be deemed right.

Date: ————————   Signature: ————————
Chairman of Appeal Committee.

Copy to: Official Valuer.

RT/12.

RURAL PROPERTY TAX ORDINANCE, 1935.

Notice of amount of Rural Property Tax for distribution under section 18.

To:
   Tax Distribution Committee,
   ———————— Village.

(a) In accordance with the provisions of sub-section (2) of section 18 of the Ordinance, I hereby give you notice that the amount of Rural Property Tax payable in respect of the non-settled lands of your village as on 31st day of March, 193————, is £P.———— mils, as set out in detail in the schedule attached hereto, and

(b) In accordance with the provisions of sub-section (3) of section 18 of the Ordinance the date prior to which the Distribution List in respect of the Blocks in the said schedule shall be completed shall be the ———— day of ———— 193————, and you

— 74 —

are hereby warned that on failure to complete the Distribution List prior to the date specified, the District Commissioner may prepare the Distribution List, and no objection will be heard to any such List.

Date : _____   Signature : _____
                                    District Officer,
                                    _____ *Sub-District.*

(Delete if not applicable).

NOTE :—The Distribution List of the tax payable on the lands of your village which were "settled" on 31st day of March, 193_____, will be prepared by the District Officer of your Sub-District, in accordance with section 19 of this Ordinance.

SCHEDULE.

Amount of Rural Property Tax for distribution by the Tax Distribution Committee for the village of_____ in the _____ Sub-District.

Block Number	Category Number	Amount of Tax LP. Mils

RT/14.

RURAL PROPERTY TAX ORDINANCE, 1935.

NOTICE of objection to the Distribution List under section 21.

A. *Notice of Objection.*

To :
  (*) District Officer,
    _____ Sub-District.

To :
  (*) Tax Distribution Committee,
    _____ Village,
    Through District Officer,
    _____ Sub-District.

In accordance with the provisions of section 21 of the Rural Property Tax Ordinance, 1935, I hereby object to the Distribution List on which my name

— 75 —

appears, prepared by you in respect of the lands in the Block(s) of the _____ village, as scheduled hereunder:—

SCHEDULE.

Block No.	Name of Block Qita'	Serial No. §	No. of Parcel in settled lands.	Name of Owner	Area of Parcel. m. ds.	Amount of Rural Property Tax. LP. Mils.

The grounds of my objection, and the particulars in support of such grounds are as follows:— _____

_____

and I desire that the Distribution List in respect of the lands described in the above schedule be corrected as follows:—

Serial No.	Name of Owner.	Area of Parcel m. ds.	Amount of Rural Property Tax. LP. Mils.

Signature: _____

Dated: _____   Address: _____

(*) Delete whichever does not apply.

(§) A separate line must be used for each serial number.

Note:—This form must be submitted, in duplicate, within 14 days from the day upon which the Distribution List is made available for inspection.

— 76 —

B. Decision of District Officer. / Distribution Committee.

(*) In accordance with the provisions of para. (a) of sub-section (1) of section 22 of the Ordinance I/we have to inform you that I/we have considered the above objection and after making all due enquiries, I/we consider it to be without foundation. I/We have decided to make no amendment / have decided not to request the District Officer to make any amendment to the Distribution List in pursuance thereof.

(*) I have to inform you that I/we have considered the above objection, and after making all due enquiries I/we have decided to amend the Distribution List as follows: —

Serial No.	Name of Owner	Area of Parcel m. ds.	Amount of Rural Property Tax LP. Mils.

Date :_____   Signature :_____
                                District Officer,
                                _____ Sub-District.

                   _____ Tax Distribution Committee.

(*) Delete whichever does not apply.

RT/15.

RURAL PROPERTY TAX ORDINANCE, 1935.

Notice of hearing of objection to Distribution List under section 22 (1) (b).

To :
   Mr. _____
      _____
      (Address)

I have to inform you that I/we have considered your objection, dated_____, to the Distribution List for the village of _____ and after making all due enquiries consider it to be sufficiently well founded to warrant further consideration.

— 77 —

I/we will hear the objection at _____ (place) on the _____ day of _____ 193___, at which you may appear.

Please note that I/we have given notice to the undermentioned person (s), that is to say:—

_____
_____
_____

who may be affected by your objection.

Signature: _____

District Officer,
_____ *Sub-District.*

Date: _____

_____ *Tax Distribution Committee.*

Copy to: Mr. _____ Address _____
Copy to: Mr. _____ Address _____
Copy to: Mr. _____ Address _____

who may, if he wishes, be present at such hearing.

NOTE:—You are warned in accordance with section 22 (1) (c) that on failure to attend as directed a decision on the objection may, in your absence, be made as may be deemed right.

RT/16.

RURAL PROPERTY TAX ORDINANCE, 1935.

NOTICE of appeal from decision of District Officer or Tax Distribution Committee under section 23.

To:
The District Commissioner,
_____ District.

I hereby appeal against the decision of the $\frac{\text{District Officer}}{\text{Tax Distribution Committee}}$ dated

— 78 —

_____copy of which is attached, given by $\frac{him}{them}$ in respect of my objection to the Distribution List, copy of which is also attached.

Date: _____

Signature: _____

Address: _____

NOTE:—This form must be submitted, in duplicate, within 14 days from the date of the decision of the District Officer.
Tax Distribution Committee.

RT/17.

RURAL PROPERTY TAX ORDINANCE, 1935.

NOTICE of appeal under section 23 by person aggrieved by reason of decision made on objection by another person.

To:
District Commissioner,
_____ District.

I hereby appeal against the decision of the $\frac{\text{District Officer}}{\text{Tax Distribution Committee}}$ dated _____ given by $\frac{him}{them}$ in respect of the objection to the Distribution List, dated _____, made by Mr. _____ of _____ whereby I am affected.

Date: _____

Signature: _____

Address: _____

NOTE:—This form must be submitted, in duplicate, within 14 days from the date of the decision of the District Officer.
Tax Distribution Committee.

— 79 —

PT/18.

RURAL PROPERTY TAX ORDINANCE, 1935.

Notice of hearing of appeal under section 24 (1).

To:
    Mr._____

    _____
        (Address)

    Please note that your appeal, dated_____, against the decision of the District Officer / Tax Distribution Committee in respect of the Distribution List for the village of_____ will be heard by me at_____(place) on_____ at_____ a.m./p.m.

    You are hereby required in accordance with section 24 (2) (a) to pay forthwith to the District Officer,_____ Sub-District the sum of Two Pounds as a deposit on account of costs, and you are hereby notified that on failure to pay such amount prior to the above mentioned date of hearing your appeal will not be heard.

    You are hereby warned in accordance with section 24 (2) (b) that on your failure to attend as directed, a decision on the appeal may, in your absence, be made as may be deemed right.

Date:_____   Signature:_____

District Commissioner,
_____*District.*

Copy to: District Officer. / Tax Distribution Committee. } Respondents.

— 80 —

RT/19.

RURAL PROPERTY TAX ORDINANCE, 1935.

Notice for preparation of Supplementary Valuation List under section 26 (2).

To:
    Official Valuer,_____
      Through District Officer,
          _____Sub-District.

Please note that in my opinion the Net Annual Value of the industrial building in the village of_____ described in the schedule hereunder of which I am the owner within my Sub-District has decreased/increased by more than 20 per cent and should be included in the Supplementary Valuation List, in respect of the year commencing first day of April, 193____.

SCHEDULE.

Village :_____   Name of Owner:_____
                                (In Block Letters).

Name of Block/Qita' _____   Area of Site:_____ sq. ms.

             (*) Parcel No._____

Block No._____   Kind of construction:_____

                         Nature of Industry :_____

                         No. of Floors :_____

                         No. of rooms on each flloor :_____

                         Area of ground floor space :_____ sq. ms.

In my opinion the present Net Annual Value of the above mentioned industrial building is LP._____

Date:_____   Signature of Owner :_____

                                      Address :_____

Date :_____   Signature :_____

                                            District Officer,
                                          _____*Sub-District.*

(*) Applicable to settled lands only.

— 81 —

RT/20.

RURAL PROPERTY TAX ORDINANCE, 1935.

Notice of change of ownership under section 31 (1).

To:
District Officer,
_____ Sub-District.

(*) I, _____ of _____ being the owner of the $\frac{\text{land}}{\text{industrial building}}$ described in the schedule hereunder, hereby give you notice that on the _____ day of _____ 193___, I disposed thereof to _____ of _____ by way of _____.

(*) I, _____ of _____ have to inform you that I became the owner of the $\frac{\text{land}}{\text{industrial building}}$ described in the schedule hereunder by way of succession from _____ of _____ on the _____ day of _____ 193___.

SCHEDULE.

Sub-District	Village	Block No / Name	Serial No. (if any) in Distribution List / Valuatn. List	Parcel No. (if in 'settled' lands).	Particulars of Registration		
					Vol.	Folio.	Date

Date: _____

Signature: _____

Address: _____

(*) Delete whichever does not apply.

By His Excellency's Command,

J. HATHORN HALL
Chief Secretary.

23rd January, 1935.
(F/164/34)

Section 6: Memoranda on the Settlement of Title to Land, 1927–1934

6.01

PALESTINE.   **GOVERNMENT OFFICES,**
                                                   JERUSALEM.

Despatch No. 534   8th April, 1927.
Reference No. 5076/27.

        I have the honour to inform you that after careful consideration of questions connected with the tenure of land and cognate matters such as reform of the system of inland revenue I am persuaded of the necessity for creating an appointment to be known as Commissioner of Lands.

    2. I transmit a memorandum prepared by Sir E.M. Dowson, K.B.E., on the matter. As you are aware, Sir Ernest Dowson and I have had under consideration for some months the whole question of the policy of this Government in relation to the search and recognition of titles to real estate; the best means of ascertaining the present ownership of real estate; and preparation of an unimpeachable record of titles; and the measures necessary for basing the fiscal system of inland revenue upon interests in real estate.

    3. In my judgment the time has now come when consultation must issue in practical activity and as a first step I accept Sir Ernest Dowson's advice that a Commissioner of Lands be appointed. Sir Ernest Dowson has in the enclosed memorandum indicated the functions of the office and the duties of the officer holding it. I am in general agreement with Sir Ernest Dowson in these matters and suggest that the character of the office may be described in the

                                                          following/

The Right Honourable L.C.M.S. AMERY, P.C., M.P.,
    His Majesty's Principal Secretary of State
                          for the Colonies.

-2-

following manner:-

(a) <u>Relations to Government</u>.

The Commissioner of Lands will be the principal adviser of Government in all matters affecting general Land Policy and will superintend the execution of measures of land reform approved by Government. He will be in direct control of land settlement and will be closely associated in the preparation of fiscal reforms which have as their object the taxation of interests in real estate. As Commissioner of Lands he will be required to be present at Executive Council when matters with which he is concerned are under discussion. He will be appointed a member of the Advisory Council.

(b)   The present Directors of Land Registries and Surveys will remain in executive charge of their respective Departments but will be subordinate to the Commissioner of Lands in matters of Departmental policy affecting the execution of land reforms and settlement work, and will be required to keep him fully informed of all branches of their departmental activities.

4. I propose to give effect to the recommendations in paragraph 3 of the memorandum and to arrange accommodation for the Commissioner of Lands in the Central Government Offices in order to facilitate regular intercourse between him and the Chief Secretary and other principal officers of the Government. But I am interpreting Sir E. Dowson's recommendations in paragraph 4 in the spirit of paragraph 6, as I am averse from the immediate creation of a new department with a large independent Secretariat.

5./

-3-

5. I suggest for your consideration that the terms of the appointment of Commissioner of Lands shall be as follows:-

The appointment will be permanent and pensionable and classified in Grade B (i.e. Salary £1400 plus £200 Expatriation Allowance plus Cost of Living Allowance). Allowances will be paid in accordance with the Regulations of Government.

6. I also suggest for your consideration that the appointment in these terms be offered to Mr. A. Abramson, O.B.E., at present District Commissioner of the Northern District. He has special abilities which combined with his natural vigour, mental and physical, and his local knowledge and experience make him, in my opinion, fully competent to carry out the work of this important office. I have ascertained that he would be prepared to accept the appointment on these terms but he asked at first for an assurance that after reaching the retiring age about five years hence he might be retained in the service in order to carry the work further towards completion. Although I think it may well be in the public interest to retain Mr. Abramson's services for a further period I told him that I did not consider that an assurance to this effect could properly be given him.

He has since waived his request that his retention in the service till the age of 60 should be assured him but he has intimated that, if he is offered the post, he would take up the work in the hope that he would

be/

-4-

be allowed to see it through to successful completion.

I have the honour to be,

Sir,

Your most obedient,

humble servant,

[signature]

HIGH COMMISSIONER.

LAND TENURE AND TAXATION IN PALESTINE.

Memorandum on the appointment of Commissioner of Lands

PREAMBLE :   In the covering memorandum to my Report on the Land System in Palestine submitted in December 1925 after a brief statement of certain evil consequences of the failure of the Land Registries to function I said (p.5)

> "If these and other prevailing defects are to be remedied the reform must be planned and executed as a united whole. So far the (cures of these evils) have for the most part been treated as separate questions, instead of a compound of closely inter-related problems which must be attacked as a connected whole."

In sections 10 and 11 (p.15 et seq.) of the report itself, after illustrating the ineffective pursuit of reform since November 1918 I said

> "The principal lesson to be learnt ..... is the necessity for thoroughly considered and concerted action ..... To continue to pursue reform without having examined its basis, on no comprehensive plan, and through the unco-ordinated efforts of sections of the public service whose views are focussed on their own departmental fields, is to continue to spend money and effort to no useful purpose ..... (The) solution (of the problem) calls for the earnest attention of the Central Government itself, not only in digesting reports but in the detailed planning and execution of reform .... Such exercise by Government itself of general direction and unifying control of reform is perfectly compatible with its decentralized execution. But decentralized execution of a comprehensive scheme of reform is a radically different thing from the disconnected sectional efforts which have hitherto held the field."

2.   In the series of meetings which I came out from England to attend last Spring, the outlines of a comprehensive scheme of reform were accepted, embodied in Despatch No.447 dated the 22nd of April 1926 to the Secretary of State, and in due course approved. I am asked in the present note to outline the reasons calling for the appointment of a permanent Commissioner of Lands and the conditions under which he could, in my opinion, successfully discharge responsibility for the establishment of the necessary reforms. The subject is complex and detailed and the present note is hurriedly written, and is neither as exhaustive nor as concise as I would wish: but I think it covers all the more essential points.

P.T.O.

-2-

3.
Functions and position of Commissioner of Lands.

The appointment of Commissioner of Lands is needed to rectify two radical defects which have so far neutralized the repeated efforts that have been made since 1918 to make some effective progress with reform of land tenure and taxation in Palestine. These two defects are (1) absence of any unified direction and control of such reform: (2) detachment of the Central Administration from the conduct and progress of the various measures attempted

The Commissioner of Lands should not be a detached super-departmental chief, but one of the most senior executive officers of the Central Administration itself specially appointed to concentrate on the execution of an exceptionally complex task on behalf of the High Commissioner-in-Council. To secure the assured liaison with the Executive Council that is essential, I strongly recommend the formal adoption of the procedure proposed by the Chief Secretary whereby the attendance of the Commissioner of Lands at meetings of Council is required whenever questions affecting land are dealt with. As a senior officer of the Central Administration the Commissioner of Lands should occupy offices in the Central Government Building, and thus be afforded the same opportunities for continuous intercourse and the same access to all correspondence and records as his colleagues. He should also be made a member of the Advisory Council.
If the Commissioner of Lands is not effectively associated with the Central Administration the latter will never keep the intimate connection with the conduct of reform that is necessary; while he himself will tend to become either a mere post office or a supernumerary departmental head.

4. The offices of the Commissioner of Lands should constitute (1) the clearing house and general intelligence office of the Administration for all land questions and (11) a single centre for the direction and execution of land policy. Papers concerning land problems should be passed to this office as a matter of routine. If such papers call for the consideration of any other office (e.g. Treasury or Attorney General's office) or Department (e.g. Agriculture) or of the Central Administration as such (in the person of the Chief Secretary or the High Commissioner) it will be the duty of the Commissioner of Lands to secure such consideration after due examination and elucidation. If such papers call for action in accordance with current policy or practice he should initiate such action.

P.T.O.

-3-

4 (Cont'd)

On the intelligence side it will be the function of the office to ensure more particularly that all data required to enable the Central Administration to keep touch with the conduct and progress of reform are trustworthy, intelligible, up-to-date and promptly available. These data for the most part can be better kept by the service directly concerned (e.g. Survey, Land Registry, or Settlement Officer): but key maps and graphic diagrams illustrating the progress of all operations must be maintained in the office of the Commissioner of Lands himself.

In his capacity as the officer charged on behalf of the Central Administration with the unified direction and execution of land reform the Commissioner of Lands must have undivided responsibility for the conduct and progress of land reform and must wield complete authority over the public services (Survey, Land Registries and Land Settlement) whose main duty is to co-operate in the establishment of such reform. Neither the responsibility nor the authority of the Commissioner of Lands should be watered down by enforced association with any standing council or committee.

5. I myself in 1924 suggested that the general execution of reform might perhaps tentatively be undertaken by a Standing Committee presided over by the Chief Secretary and composed of representatives of the services whose work required unified direction. This suggestion was dictated by my own and the general reluctance to subordinate to anyone else two public services (Survey and Land Registries) which have so far enjoyed departmental status directly under the Chief Secretary. The proposal was admittedly an unsatisfactory compromise. It would fasten direct responsibility for the execution of reform upon the Chief Secretary, who has the time neither to learn nor to direct the work effectively. This suggestion has now been definitely rejected by the Chief Secretary as unworkable, and I entirely concur with his judgment. The proposal was worth consideration if only to test whether the unified direction of reform could be undertaken by the Central Administration without re-inforcement, even in the loose and spasmodic way suggested. The answer is unequivocal, that the unified direction of control must be exercised by a special officer able to concentrate wholly upon it: but it is not worth making this appointment, unless such officer assumes full responsibility for, and is in complete executive charge of, the work.

P.T.O.

-4-

Position of executive services principally charged with the execution of reform.

6. The efforts of three executive branches of the public services require to be effectively co-ordinated, the Survey, the Land Registries and the Land Settlement branch now in course of formation. The general reluctance to do anything to lower the status or restrict the independence of the two former services has been mentioned; but the need for common direction is patent and must be paramount. But such direction cannot be achieved by half measures: nor will half measures be any less productive of difficulty and irritation in the long run.

Subject however to the responsibility of the Commissioner of Lands for the conduct of land reform being complete and his authority over the public services concerned unquestioned, everything possible should be done on the one hand to refrain from any unnecessary inroad on their present independence and status and on the other to stimulate their energies and encourage their pride in their work. Thus while unity of direction must be both competent and effectively maintained, it must be reconciled with the minimum of internal interference with the two valuable and experienced services that exist. Such interferences would deflect the Commissioner of Lands from the important duties for which he is really needed; while even unity of direction would be dearly purchased by loss of departmental efficiency and keenness.
The necessity for unobtrusive central direction applies to settlement work as well as to the established services, as it is a cardinal condition of success that each British Settlement Officer shall be the outstanding figure within his own sphere and in his own Settlement Area. Such Officers must of course conform to central guidance and instructions; but the responsibility for their decisions will be their own and appeal from them will lie, not to the Commissioner of Lands, but to such court as may be ordained.
Briefly I conceive it to be the duty of the Commissioner of Lands to ensure that a common policy and plan and common principles are applied, that **services** under his direction are properly equipped and **looked** after, that all necessary outside assistance is forthcoming, and that adequate progress is maintained throughout; but that it is his part so long as he obtains keen and single minded response to his direction to keep his post and himself deliberately in the background. And I conceive it to be the duty of the public services concerned to accept loyally the necessity for unity of direction, to sink entirely in the public interest any reluctance they may feel to be brought under such direction, and to work keenly and wholeheartedly for its success and for the successful establishment of whatever general plan and policy may be laid down.

P.T.O.

7. The necessity that the Commissioner of Lands should not overshadow or outshine the public services placed under his direction is a second reason why his offices should be situated at the Headquarters of the Central Administration. If, as so far suggested, the Commissioner of Lands is located in the building at present occupied by the Land Registries and State Domain services he will not only be cut off from touch with the Central Administration, but he will over-shadow the present departmental chief to the latter's natural chagrin and to the grave detriment of the proper work of them both.

Although the Survey, the Land Registries and the Settlement Organization are the services primarily entrusted with the establishment of the necessary reforms the willing and effective co-operation of other branches of the public service, more particularly of the Judicial Department and of the District Administration, has naturally also to be assumed.

Concentration of Director of Lands on reform of Land Registries.

8. The failure of the Ottoman system of land tenure and taxation dates from the very inception of the Land Code, some seventy years ago, and was an inevitable result of inability to devise and operate a record which unambiguously links registered rights with the parcel of land affected and embodies all transfers of, or changes in, such rights as they occur. This is the abiding cause of the failure of the Ottoman System of land administration, otherwise for the most part well suited to the traditions and needs of the people. This is therefore the fundamental failure to be redeemed, and the most perfect Land Settlement will be wasted if it is not redeemed. It is the particular duty of the Director of Lands (in his capacity as Director of Land Registries) to discharge this task and establish a sound Land Registry throughout Palestine progressively with the march of Land Settlement.

There is a natural tendency to consider the initial settlement of rights over the land as the critical operation of the projected reforms. Such settlement certainly presents serious difficulties which look larger to the imagination than those to be surmounted in establishing a sound land register. But the former more apparent difficulties are much less formidable in fact, if sensibly and systematically attacked, than the less obvious difficulties confronting the perpetual maintenance after settlement of a complete, intelligible, accurate and up-to-date record of all important rights over the land throughout the whole country.

P.T.O.

8 (Cont'd)

The Turks themselves were quite capable of carrying out a settlement and had published a law for the purpose which recognized the essential need of conducting investigations in situ and which was workable, although clumsy. Indeed in every country in the course of the every day life of the people rights over land have continuously to be settled de facto if not de jure. Land settlement by the State is merely an effort to do the same thing systematically and better; but it is evidently unjustifiable for the State to attempt a standard of settlement which cannot be subsequently maintained. And if the standard of the settlement is good, it can only be subsequently maintained by means of a reliable record of all future changes as they occur.

This involves the creation and perpetual maintenance throughout the whole country of a complex system of book-keeping conducted by an honest, competent and highly organized staff. While this presents no insuperable difficulty if undertaken gradually as it must be, it is a severer task than the carrying out of the most thorough and exhaustive series of investigations that can be dealt and done with seriatim.

9. I have for some time urged that the present association in the person of the same officer of responsibility for both (a) the impartial administration of the Land Registers and (b) the partisan defence of the claims of the State as a landowner in conflict with those of private persons, is vicious in principle and inexpedient. Without reviving these issues in the abstract here, I am bound in the present connection again to say that the Director of Lands is far too over-loaded.

The direction of the Land Registries during the inception and consolidation of reform will demand the undivided attention of the head of that service. And I feel most strongly that if he cannot be promptly relieved at least of all responsibility for and connection with the conduct of litigation on behalf of the State, he can neither reasonably nor fairly be expected to carry out punctually and successfully his part in the establishment of the projected reforms.

Settlement
Operations. 10. Settlement operations should be under the direct control of the Commissioner of Lands subject, as previously stated, to the necessity of ensuring that each British Settlement Officer shall be the outstanding figure in his own settlement area. As I have repeatedly emphasized the success of settlement operations will depend upon the quality of the individual Settlement Officers entrusted with the work. The principal Settlement Officers should be picked British Officers who know Arabic and the life of the rural community well, are accustomed to dealing with villagers and have demonstrated their ability to win their confidence, who possess good judgment and good health, and are active and industrious. There are a limited number of officers in the Administration whose employment as Settlement Officers is to be recommended; and the charge of Settlement Operations should strictly be confined to them. The use of unsuitable men or discards from the Administration should be unequivocably ruled out. It is much better to slow down the work than employ indifferent Settlement Officers.

-7-

11. The promulgation of the "Correction of Land Registers Ordinance 1925" makes the question of the settlement of the Jewish and German colonies a matter of some immediate urgency. This ordinance provides (a) for the cessation of the use of unofficial Colony registers hitherto kept, (b) empowers the Director of Lands to transform unofficial titles recorded in those Colony registers into official titles, and (c) reserves power to redetermine those titles without prejudice in the course of settlement.

It is obviously advisable wherever possible to avoid the inconclusive stage of transforming unsatisfactory unofficial titles into unsatisfactory official titles, and to proceed immediately to a definite settlement and dependable official registration. And although this could not be done for all the colonies affected at once, there are a number in which the preliminary survey operations are (or will shortly be) concluded, and in which settlement operations could be undertaken next Autumn. Settlement in the German Colonies could be carried out by the regular Settlement Officer for the area in which such colonies are situated; but settlement of the Jewish Colonies requires a British Officer of character and standing with a knowledge of Hebrew and of Jewish law and customs, with ability to win the confidence and co-operation of the Jewish Colonies and with sufficient prestige to get his rulings respected. As I have represented several times previously, there is only one Officer in Palestine with the qualities mentioned and he should be entrusted with settlement in the Jewish Colonies at least during the opening years of the work.

12. Settlement work is not popular in the service. It will make high demands upon an officer's capacity and character, it will be conducted under conditions of personal discomfort and of separation from an officer's family, it will remove the man from routine work and regular roster of administrative service. At the same time the best men are needed, and good work cannot be expected from them if they are coerced. They must be attracted by the important nature of the public service rendered, and by the conditions and prospects attaching to it. And more particularly, as I have emphasized elsewhere, they should be well found in camp equipment, transport and other facilities, and given a generous special duty allowance while posted to Settlement work.

P.T.O.

Considerations
connected with
the selection
of the Commissioner
of Lands.

13. The selection of the actual officer to be appointed Commissioner of Lands presents evident difficulties. Upon the occasion of my three days visit in 1923 I hoped that unity might be attainable by a re-arrangement of duties, viz, by entrusting the Director of Surveys with the conduct of reform and by letting the Director of Lands concentrate on the custody and development of State property: but no such easy solution is feasible. Each of these two officers has an exacting part to play in the establishment of reform, which will demand his exclusive attention. Nor could either be justly or successfully subordinated to the other. And neither is at present of the weight and standing in the service to take the place in the Central Administration and in the country that is required.

The selection of a permanent Commissioner of Lands is in practice restricted to (a) an outsider with special knowledge of the inter-related problems of survey, settlement, registration and taxation of land, or (b) a local officer without such special knowledge.

To bring in another outsider and entrust him with the general direction of reform is not to be recommended, even if such an outsider is found both qualified and available. I have now been connected with the question of land reform in Palestine since November 1923, I have got to know well most of the individuals who will participate in the execution of the proposed measures, I have gradually been steeped in the local aspects and conditions of the problem. And after consideration and discussion which has now lasted over three years my proposals have to a great extent been accepted and are beginning to be translated into action. Much of this ground would have to be covered a second time if another newcomer came; and in the meantime progress would again be stayed. It is also extremely unlikely that such a new comer would be found who was available at once and combined the special qualifications mentioned with the personal qualities needed. And the appointment of any unknown man to so difficult a post would at best be a hazardous and for some time a doubtful experiment.

P.T.O.

- 4 -

14. There is in my opinion no doubt at all that the best course is the appointment, as from about the beginning of next October, of the most senior local officer available. He will be very fully acquainted with the character of the problem and with local conditions. He will know the men with whom he will have to work and they will know him. He will appreciate the sacrifices that individuals or services may be called upon to make in the public interests and they on their side will be more likely to pull loyally together under a well known colleague than under a stranger. And, perhaps most important of all, the Government will really know the man they are getting and he the task he is taking up.

It is during the critical period of reform, which must be anticipated to extend at least over the first two years of settlement (Oct.1927 - Sct. 1929), that the most valuable experience is to be obtained and that success must be won. It is therefore important that the officer who is to be permanently responsible for the general conduct of the work shall be in charge from the outset of actual settlement operations. But it is evidently also at this time, particularly during the first few months that the Commissioner of Lands will most need the help of special knowledge and previous experience of the various problems to be dealt with.

I think the satisfaction of this need vital to the success of the work and that the obvious way to meet it is for me to remain associated with the conduct of reform, to such extent and in such manner as may be deemed advisable, until the Commissioner of Lands can dispense with this assistance. The minimum measure of such assistance that I think is needed is that I should come out again next Winter for 3 or 4 months, be kept in close touch by post with the work thereafter in case I am again needed for a month or two the following Winter or until such time as the Commissioner of Lands is satisfied that he no longer needs this assistance.

15. I have not discussed either survey or fiscal operations in this note. The principal need of the Survey is increase of staff and equipment and all possible measure of assistance from Government to press on with its work.

Fiscal measures in connection with Land Reform will be discussed in the note which I have been asked to prepare on the abolition of the tithe. Nor have I entered into any details of the staff and equipment either of the office of the Commissioner of Lands himself or of the Settlement parties in the field, as these have already been outlined in previous notes or in the provisional estimates for the nine months ending 31st December 1927 which I have already submitted.

not/ And I have/thought it necessary to suggest the methods by which my various proposals if adopted should be implemented but it would no doubt be necessary to specify either by special ordinance or in the Land Settlement Law the position and responsibilities of the Commissioner of Lands.

Copy.

HIGH COMMISSIONER'S OFFICE.
JERUSALEM.

January 18th, 1927.

Dear Shuckburgh,

File 22865 ME.
(N.7.)

    In continuation of my letter of last week in connection with the appointment of Commr. of Lands, I enclose you my comments on Sir E. Dowson's memorandum.

    I have had some estimates of cost run out but they have to be reviewed by the Trasurer.

    If after having read what I have sent you, you think I should send in an official despatch I will do so on receipt of either a telegram or letter from you.

    Yours

    (Sgd.) Plumer.

Copy.

Notes on Sir E. Dowson's Memorandum recommending the appointment of Commr. of Lands.

Para. 3.   I agree that there should be a Commissioner of Lands, and that he should be a Senior Executive Officer - that he should not be a member of the Executive Council but should attend all meetings of the Ex.C. whenever questions affecting lands are dealt with. He should be a member of the Advisory Council.

Para. 4.   This rules out the suggestion that he should be President of a Lands Commission, or Committee, and I agree.

Para. 6.   The relation between the Commissioner of Lands and the Director of Lands.

Surveys must be carefully regulated on the principle outlined by Sir E.D.

Para. 9.   We shall have to consider relieving the Director of Lands of the work he is involved in at present in connection with litigation.

Para. 11.   Settlement in the German and Jewish Colonies should be undertaken without delay.

Para. 12.   "Settlement" Officers must be selected carefully, and treated liberally.

It is clear that in measures of reform of the system of inland revenue, since activity will be in the direction of taking a land value, the Commissioner of Lands must be clearly associated with the revenue authorities in order to faciltate the determination of

(a) the individual taxpayer and

(b) the amount of tax he should pay on his interest in the lands.

(Initld.) P.

6.02

EXPLANATORY NOTE
on the
LAND SETTLEMENT ORDINANCE.

The Ordinance is partly based on the Sudan Land Settlement Law which has been in operation there for a number of years, and has been found to work satisfactorily. The conditions in Palestine with regard to title to land are in many ways similar to those that obtained in the Sudan, save that there did not exist in the Sudan prior to the Settlement any Government Land Registers; and the scheme of settlement which is proposed in Palestine is modelled generally/on the scheme which has been employed in the Sudan for many years.

The following Sections of the Ordinance call for some special explanation :-

Section 6. The purpose of this clause is to prevent actions being brought in the Civil Courts and Land Courts concerning land which is the subject of settlement. It would be embarrassing to the settlement operations if disputes about the land were being considered by the ordinary Courts at the same time that a Settlement Officer was dealing with rights in the whole village.

Section 10. A Settlement Officer is given the powers of the Land Court, and also of a Civil Magistrate, because he should be enabled to deal with

disputes/

- 2 -

disputes as to title and also as to possession of land. The former matters are within the jurisdiction of the Land Court; the latter within the jurisdiction of the Magistrate.

Section 11. The Sudan scheme of settlement provides for a Kadi being a member of the Settlement authority; and the Ottoman Provisional Law concerning cadastral survey contained a similar provision. It will be necessary in Palestine that a Kadi should be available to give certificates and attestations as to succession and other matters of personal status of Moslems, and the judicial authority in matters of personal status of other Communities available to give similar assistance in relation to questions of the rights of non-Moslems; but it is not proposed that the religious judges shall form a regular part of the Settlement authority.

Section 12. The powers of the District Commissioner under the Survey Ordinance, which are vested in the Settlement Officer, include requiring any owner or occupier of land to demarcate his land, to clear his boundaries, and to provide labour.

Sections 13-15. These are original provisions designed to secure the cooperation of the Village authorities in the work of settlement. The Village Settlement Committee will receive legal personality for the purposes of the settlement.

Section/

Section 22. This provision has been adopted from the Sudan Law, where it is found to be of great use.

Section 23. It is desired to prevent the parcellation of land after the settlement operations have begun, because any such transactions would be likely to cause confusion. Partition will be undertaken on the application either of an individual or of a majority of the undivided owners after the Settlement Officer has established the rights of the co-owners. The proviso at the end of the clause covers a case where the parcellation which has not yet been registered, but which has been acted upon in the Village, and works satisfactorily may be adopted as the basis of settlement.

Section 27(5). The Land Courts Ordinance invests the Land Court with certain powers in cases of arbitration which are different from those of the Civil Court over an arbitration under the Arbitration Ordinance, 1926. It is considered that those provisions are more suitable for the purposes of Land Settlement in the application of the general rules of the Arbitration Ordinance.

Section 28. Where the Government claims the ownership of Miri land, for example, on the ground of escheat or of State Domain, it must obtain a record of its rights in the Schedule of Rights and
the/

the registration of the land in its name in the same way as any other claimant; but the rights of the Government to land which is Mewat, that is, waste land which is not cultivated or occupied, or to Metrukeh, that is, land used for a public purpose such as roads, need not be claimed by the Government in the settlement because all land in a village area to which individual claimants do not establish a title will be registered as Government land.

Section 33 is based upon a provision in the Sudan Law. In the Sudan and in Palestine one of the great difficulties in securing a proper registration of title is that land is held in undivided shares of barflingly large fractions which not infrequently run to seven figures. Those fractions have no real value, and it is proposed that in their place the rights shall be recorded in a definite figure of integral metres. It is proposed, also, that very small fragments of land of no substantial value should not be the subject of registration, and the owner of such fragments will be required to transfer his share to a neighbouring owner; or in the case of undivided land to the owner or owners of the more considerable shares.

Section 41. There is a similar provision in the Sudan Law. On account of the confusion of the old Ottoman Land Registers, it is necessary to

protect/

protect the Government against failure to deal with any plot of land which may be recorded in those Ottoman Registers, but as to which no claim is established during the settlement by the person claiming under the Ottoman registration.

Section 42. It is the intention that when the new Registers are established, they will supersede all previous registration and all rights which are claimed under unregistered documents, save in the cases which are dealt with in Sections 52 ff.

Sections 43 and 44 follow the provisions of the existing Land Transfer Ordinance which was introduced when the Land Registry Offices were opened in 1920.

Section 49. Following the scheme of the Sudan Law, it is proposed that an appeal from a decision of the Settlement Officer as to title shall lie only by leave either of the Settlement Officer himself or of the President of the Land Court which will hear appeals from him.

Section 55. A large part of the village land in southern Palestine is held in undivided ownership, and it is hoped that one of the effects of the settlement will be to secure the division of the land into individual holdings. It is intended that partition shall form a separate operation of settlement to be carried out after the rights of the co-owners have been determined.

The/

- 6 -

The system of partition will be that prescribed in the Ottoman Law with some modification. Partition will not be compulsory save in a special case where the High Commissioner so directs, but it will be carried out where the owners of at least two-thirds of the shares in the land desire it.

Section 62. It is proposed that the fees shall be fixed by Regulation so that they may be more easily amended in circumstances which indicate that changes should be made.

Subsection (2) is inserted in order to make it clear that no fees shall be payable on account of the unregistered transactions upon which a claimant bases his title. It is notorious that throughout the country those unregistered transactions have taken place regularly both before and since the Occupation, and in order that people may cooperate in the settlement, they must be assured that they will not have to pay any charges to the Government on account of them.

Section 63. This provision is introduced in order to encourage applications for partition.

Section 64. It is considered equitable that the fee in respect of registration should not be charged against persons who have already a title registered in the Government Registers; but a fee to cover the cost of survey which would form part

of/

- 7 -

of the settlement may be charged. The owner of the land will be greatly benefited by having an assured survey plan of his land.

                (Sgd.) N. Bentwich.
                ATTORNEY GENERAL.

6.03

Report on the progress

of

land reforms in Palestine

1923-30

Submitted November 1930

Bowyers Field,
Wrotham,
Kent.
November, 1930.

To His Excellency
The High Commissioner.

Excellency,

Progress in land reforms, 1923-1930.

I have the honour to submit as requested by you when I visited Palestine in May last, a report on the progress that has been made in the execution of the various measures of land reform with which I have been connected. As my time in Palestine was very short, and as I was not well at the time, I postponed the preparation of this report until I had had a further opportunity of discussing certain aspects of the work with the Commissioner of Lands, Mr. Abramson, in England this autumn.

To appreciate the progress made to date and what still remains to be done, it is necessary to summarize briefly the position as it existed when I first visited Palestine for three days in November 1923 at the invitation of Sir Herbert Samuel as well as the steps subsequently taken. My original impressions were outlined in a letter dated the 9th. November of that year to the then Chief Secretary, the late Sir Gilbert Clayton. This was followed up on the 7th. December following by some fuller "Notes on Land Tax, Cadastral Survey and Land Settlement."

In June 1924 the Colonial Office advised me that the Palestine Government wished to give effect to my proposals and would like me to visit Palestine again to study the problem more fully. I was in Palestine from November to the end of March 1925. I was able on this occasion to visit all parts of the country and discuss the questions at issue with the principal officers of Government and with a number of representative members of the public. My previous conclusions were confirmed and the results of my enquiries were embodied in three papers which were submitted to the Under Secretary of State for the Colonies in December 1925. These papers were entitled (i) a Memorandum, and (ii) a Report, on the Land system, and (iii) a Preliminary Study of the Land Tenure.

In January 1926, Field Marshal Lord Plumer, then High Commissioner, asked me to come out to Palestine to consult with him and his advisers as to the practical application of my general recommendations. I went to Palestine the following month where my recommendations were subjected to close criticism in seven meetings with His Excellency in Executive Council during March. These recommendations were then outlined in Despatch No.447 dated 22nd. April 1926 addressed by His Excellency to the Secretary of State for the Colonies and in due course were approved. I remained in Palestine until July and came out again from November till the following July at Lord Plumer's request.

This approval in the summer of 1926 marked the crossing of the line between investigation and action: but no practical progress was possible until funds were available, until an administrative co-ordination of the services that were to participate had been effected, until Settlement and Valuation Officers had been appointed, until equipment was available, and until the necessary legislation had been promulgated. The winter-summer season 1926-27 was occupied with discussions on all these points and with such preparatory work as was practicable in the meantime.

Mr. Abramson was appointed Commissioner of Lands on the 7th. November 1927, but the general execution of the reforms was effectively initiated in the Spring of 1928 when funds for the purpose were first provided. Two previously selected British Settlement Officers were appointed. The Land Settlement Ordinance was promulgated in May and the Urban Property Tax Ordinance in July.

November 1923 to the Summer of 1926 was therefore occupied with investigations and discussions which eventually resulted in the adoption of the general programme of land reform recommended. November 1926 to the Spring of 1928 were occupied with preparatory measures of one sort or another. Fortunately the Survey, the one service which could not be improvised, was already organised, equipped and ready, and had several years essential preparatory work in hand. In the field of Land Registration methods of record were revised and such further preparations as were possible made. In the field of settlement of rights, Mr. Lowick did most valuable preliminary work both on the ground and in studying the problems of land tenure.

So that although the execution of the programme of land reform was not initiated effectively as such until the Spring of 1928 and its subsequent progress as a co-ordinated whole must be judged from that date, it must also be realized that such progress has been immeasureably facilitated and accelerated by the long period of previous discussion and preparation.

I will now endeavour to outline the principal evils originally diagnosed, the measures in due course wholly or tentatively approved, the general progress made to date, and the more important issues which still await decision.

- 3 -

2. **PRINCIPAL EVILS.** The principal evils requiring remedy were adjudged to be:

(i) that the land law of the country was an unintelligible compost of the original Ottoman laws, provisional laws, judgments of various tribunals, Sultanic firmans, administrative orders having the force of law overlaid by a further amalgam of post-war Proclamations, Public orders, Orders-in-Council, judgments of various civil and religious courts, Ordinances, Amending Ordinances, and Orders and Regulations under these.

(ii) that while the operation of the basic land law and of the existing taxes on immovable property depended on the operation of the Land Registers, those registers were incomplete, unreliable and often unintelligible.

(iii) that the existing tithe on agricultural products (ushr) was excessive in amount, economically vicious in principle and operated most vexatiously and inequitably.

(iv) that owing to the failure of the Land Registers and to the omission of reassessments the existing taxes on immovable property (werko and musaqafat) had become for the most part arbitrary imposts, adding to the tithe in rural areas and securing an inadequate return from urban areas.

(v) that again owing to the failure of the Land Registers there was no security of rights to land, no basis for economical borrowing for agricultural needs, and unceasing encroachments both on public and private domain.

(vi) that the periodic re-apportionment of village lands, so widely practised in accordance with the system known as mesha', was a most serious handicap on the economic development of the country and the improvement of the position of the peasantry.

(vii) that no effective measures had so far been taken to remedy these evils because the essentially associated problems mentioned had never been considered or dealt with in any thorough manner as a whole. The Departments concerned, more particularly the Land Registries and the Survey, had been left to pursue reform piece-meal without general direction or a common objective.

(viii) that the existing subordination of the Land Registry and of the Public Domain of the State to a common Department was both contrary to the public interest and administratively undesirable.

3. MEASURES OF REFORM.

Among the more important measures of reform approved or initiated were:

(i) A thorough and authoritative review of the land tenure as it existed in law and in practice.

(ii) The creation of the Office of Commissioner of Lands to be filled by a senior officer of Government who would be charged with the general execution and control of the reforms as a whole.

(iii) The execution of a systematic settlement of rights to land.

(iv) The permanent allotment of land held in mesha' as a regular part of this settlement.

(v) The appointment of selected British District Officers to carry out this settlement in co-operation with the Survey and the Land Registries under the general control of the Commissioner of Lands. These officers were to be granted judicial powers for the purpose, subject to suitable provisions for appeal from their decisions.

(vi) The immediate execution as an advanced part of settlement operations of a survey and valuation of village land by "blocks" to enable a land tax to replace the existing tithe and werko at an early date. The survey is briefly termed the Block Survey.

(vii) The survey and valuation of immovable property in the principal towns to enable a complete re-assessment of such property to be carried out as soon as possible.

(viii) The appointment of two experienced officers to the Commissioner of Lands' Office to undertake the valuation of land and buildings for fiscal purposes.

(ix) The thorough reform of the existing system of Land Registration on agreed upon lines.

Details of these recommendations are set forth or were summarized in numerous discussions, letters and memoranda. Among these may be mentioned "Notes on the abolition of the tithe and the establishment of a Land Tax in Palestine", (April, 1928).

The Memoranda of a Conference held at Government Offices, Jerusalem on 21st. February 1927 summarize the general position and future expectations of the more important measures of reform towards the close of my advisory mission.

4. AMENDMENT AND CODIFICATION OF LAND LAW.

A preliminary study and explanatory statement of the existing law was undertaken by Mr. F.M. Goadly and Mrs. Moses Dukhan and was issued in a comprehensive statement towards the end of 1927. This statement clarified a good many points and provided Settlement Officers with an invaluable commentary. It also furnished the preliminary basis for the comprehensive amendment and codification of the law without which the maintenance of the settlement would at best be unduly troublesome and costly, and at worst might be impracticable.

It has, however, been agreed that such amendment and codification must be reached by progressive stages. The judgments of the Land Courts have not been systematically reported, but the experience of the Judges should provide invaluable material for revision of the law. A number of points of practical importance on which the law was silent, ambiguous, obsolete, contradictory, or impracticable had been noted by the Director of Lands on the operation of the Land Registries. Messrs. Goadly and Dukhan raised a number of questions. Many others would appear in the process of settlement.

So far it has not been possible to do very much. A number of amendments of importance to the operation of the Land Registries have I understand been embodied in the Land Registration Ordinance 1929. A draft short Land Law Amendment Ordinance has been prepared dealing with some further points. Now that two years practical experience of systematic settlement of rights is available I suggest that this part of the work should be attacked more vigorously and systematically.

5. **CO-ORDINATION AND CENTRAL DIRECTION OF REFORM.**

The most effective single measure of advance that has been effected is the establishment of the Office of Commissioner of Lands on the general lines recommended in my Memorandum on the subject addressed to the High Commissioner in January 1927. (See Appendix). The creation of this Office has secured the unified direction and co-ordinated execution of the necessary reforms, which were previously lacking. It has provided the Central Administration, through the medium of a Senior Officer situated at Headquarters, with effective general control and regular touch with the work. And this useful and effective control has been accompanied by a surrender of control of details, which was usually ineffective and frequently irritating.

This summer, for the first time since I was originally consulted on the subject, it has been possible to discuss the reforms as a whole with an executive officer whose duty and concern they wholly and effectively were. Previously discussions had necessarily to be conducted with Committees of some sort summoned ad hoc or primarily devoted to other ends, or alternatively with series of individual officers, very much interested, but without direct responsibility for the execution of the work, and without either the opportunity or the continual touch with the public services concerned that was needed to unite them into an effective and unselfish team.

Most understandably these services were opposed to the measures that I advised to achieve this end. These measures necessarily involved some surrender of previous independence and some apparent loss of status. But the principal apprehension was the danger that essential technical requirements might be sacrificed to administrative or political exigencies through lack of appreciation of such requirements.

My admiration was aroused on my recent visit to Palestine by the way in which these services have buried their feelings and fears in pursuit of the general interest. I cannot speak too highly of the restraint and public spirit with which all the officers concerned have co-operated, and are co-operating, to create an organization which combines unity of central direction and co-ordinated execution of a common plan with effective freedom and decentralized management of the component parts. The appreciation that was expressed to me of the sympathy and understanding with which the Commissioner of Land has discharged his difficult functions was as striking a tribute to the speakers themselves as to him.

Far from having lost status, the prestige of the services concerned has mounted with the increasing appreciation of their value which has resulted. With time and further experience the combination should become even closer and more effective. But such improved organization and closer co-operation should be in response to circumstances and the free recognition of its mutual and public advantage by the responsible officers concerned. No risk should be run of damaging or discouraging the remarkable team spirit that has been invoked and displayed.

6. GENERAL PROGRESS OF FISCAL REFORMS. In view of the necessarily slow progress of settlement of rights to land it was recommended that an advanced programme of survey and valuation of land and buildings should be undertaken for fiscal purposes (§§ 13 and 14 Report December 1925). These proposals were subjected to discussion and consideration during 1926, and at a Conference held in Jerusalem on the 19th. January 1927 it was formally agreed that reassessment of land and buildings for taxation was desirable. At this Conference I was asked to go into the question of urban reassessment in detail with the

- 9 -

District Commissioners and a number of other officers of Government directly interested. Three meetings followed in which a detailed scheme was agreed upon. This was submitted to Government on the 30th. March of the same year and constituted the basis of the procedure adopted in due course.

The Urban Property Tax Ordinance was promulgated in July 1928. The progress made in the execution of this Ordinance since its promulgation has been remarkable, and all parties concerned are to be congratulated on a very fine effort. At the time of writing the work has been completed in Jerusalem, Jaffa with Tel Aviv, Ramleh, Lydda, Gaza, Tulkarem, Bersen, Tiberias, Nablus and Haifa. I did not have time to examine the actual work when I was in Palestine this spring; nor did there appear any occasion for me to do so, as I understand its success is not questioned.

The corresponding measure of fiscal reform recommended for adoption in rural areas, pending the completion of settlement of rights to land, was a Block land tax. This necessitated a subdivision of all village areas into blocks composed of land of approximately uniform quality, followed by a systematic survey and valuation of such blocks. Such a sub-division of village areas into blocks already existed to a large extent.

The progress made with the Block Survey has fallen short of the expectation expressed in the Conference held at Government Offices in Jerusalem on 21st. February 1927 with regard to my proposals generally, in preparation for Sir John Shuckburgh's approaching visit to Palestine. The delay is primarily due to the special effort required to complete the maps needed for the urban re-assesaments just mentioned. To a lesser extent it is due to the recent riots and the diversion of officers from their normal duties which followed. The delay is most regrettable; but was unavoidable if the no less urgent work of urban re-assessment was to be disposed of first, a procedure which cannot be reasonably criticized.

Considerable doubts were also felt by a number of the officers of the Central Administration as to the advisability of abandoning the tithe and as to the practicability of my proposals for the valuation of blocks of village land for fiscal purposes. And when I left Palestine in July 1927 the appointment of the two officers whom I had recommended to be charged with such valuation was still under consideration.

Since their appointment these officers have done admirable work and shown that it is quite practicable to carry out the block valuation of village lands on the general lines proposed. A glance at the accompanying map will show the progress that has already been made in the valuation of fiscal blocks. However I understand that this valuation has so far only been authorized as a basis for land registration fees.

It will be noted that my original recommendation to establish a Block land tax was made nearly five years ago. A decision on a proposal of this nature necessarily required careful consideration and time; particularly as there was so strong a body of opinion in favour of maintaining the tithe and completing settlement of rights before introducing any form of land-tax. But it is disappointing to think that if a decision could have been come to more quickly, the work could easily have been completed and the tithe in all its forms have been a thing of the past.

Now that the methods of valuation have been subjected to prolonged trial in the field and that both urban re-assessment and the Beisan land settlement are approaching completion the way appears to be clear for a concentration upon the rapid execution of the Block Survey and Valuation throughout the country.

Experience has now shown (i) that it is quite practicable to carry out a valuation of rural areas by blocks of village land and (ii) that the distribution by villagers of an aggregate

- 11 -

tax among themselves works smoothly. I venture to submit that the Government should now definitely adopt this block valuation as the basis of future land taxation, that they have ample material on which to decide all immediately important matters of principle in connexion with such taxation, and that they should forthwith put in the forefront of their programme of land and fiscal reform, the early substitution of a Block land tax for the remnants of the old medley of Ottoman taxation of land - the tithe, the werko and the animal tax - which still survive. No measure of reform appears to me to be so pressing and important.

7. A decisive step in mitigation of the evils of the tithe was taken by the promulgation of the "Commutation of Tithes Ordinance 1927" following the recommendations of the majority of a Committee set up in the previous year to study the question. A measure on these lines had been advocated for a number of years by nearly all District Officers. While I considered that the evils of the tithe were glaring, and steps towards its abolition were long overdue, I thought Tithe Commutation too uncertain a measure to be generally applied without any previous trial. But the advocates of immediate and general commutation of the tithe by villages have been fully justified by its success in removing the grosser evils of tithe collection.

But although the commutation of the tithe has removed the worst abuses of tithe collection, the resulting commutations are necessarily based upon grouped perpetuations of the previous indefensible individual assessments. And tithe commutation has not touched the no less glaring defects of the surviving Ottoman land tax (werko). It was for these reasons that I recommended the earliest possible establishment of a Block land tax.

The Commissioners of Lands advises me that the present distribution of the commuted tithe among the landholders of villages is well understood, is working smoothly, and has shown itself readily susceptible of the annual corrections necessitated by transfers and transmissions of holdings. While recognizing, as he has always done, that the basis of the computation is grossly defective, he is inclined to think that the method of distribution by village units had better be left as it is until it can be replaced by direct dealings between Government and the individual taxpayer, following the settlement of rights to land.

My own proposal was that Block distribution should be substituted as an interim measure for Village distribution. In principle Block distribution is fairer than Village distribution; but it is better to maintain the former until individual assessments can be introduced if there are good grounds for thinking that there will be greater risk of confusion than of advantage resulting in practice from this change. If Village distribution is finally adjudged to be preferable, the introduction of the Block Land tax will to some extent be simplified. For it will only be necessary to adopt the total assessments of the blocks of which the village lands are comprised, as the new aggregate village assessment in lieu of the commuted tithe.

Equitable individual incidence cannot be secured under any scheme of land taxation until the necessarily slow march of settlement of rights permits it; but, as I have repeatedly urged, the substitution of equitable and economic assessment of a land tax is in no way dependent upon such settlement. There is no justification for perpetuating two unrelated evils if one is immediately remediable, particularly as that one is unquestionably the source of the greater hardship and inequality.

8.   I have hitherto hesitated to include the animal tax (kôda) among the fiscal remnants of the old Ottoman administration

- 13 -

that could be promptly replaced by the Block land-tax; but the Commissioner of Lands is of opinion that, with the exception of the Beersheba District, the majority of flocks are grazed on land that would be readily and justly subject to land-tax, either as cultivable land or specifically as pasture. The disappearance of this awkward minor impost would be a relief to landowners and also to the Administration, if its fiscal effect can be fairly secured by embodiment in the new land tax. Provision would no doubt have to be made for dealing with truly nomadic and immigrant flocks, as well as for grazing on public domain.

9. VARIATIONS FROM THE SIMPLE BLOCK SYSTEM.

The practical advantage of the Block system is that it provides a stable framework within which the ever-changing parcels of property can be conveniently grouped both for registration and for fiscal purposes. Throughout a large portion of the maritime plain there will probably be no difficulty in sub-dividing the land into continuous blocks for both these purposes. And there is an obvious convenience if only one sub-division of the smallest administrative units (villages) is formed.

But in territory occupied by fruit groves and gardens, the variations in the economic value of the land may be too marked to allow this, and it may therefore be necessary again to subdivide the more stable Registration Block for fiscal purposes. This will not be a serious complication. And of course No difficulty will be occasioned in the alternative case of several adjoining Registration Blocks being equally assessed. Indeed this may be expected to occur fairly frequently everywhere.

In the hill areas the position will not be as straightforward and simple, but the problem does not differ in kind. The Registration Block should again constitute the stable sub-division of the village, and it should as far as possible be designed to include land of closely equal economic value. But in the hill areas cultivation is bound to be patchy and discontinuous throughout many blocks, while the size and shape of the blocks may be

- 14 -

expected to vary much more than in the plains. And here again marked variations in the economic value of the land may require frequent sub-division of blocks for fiscal purposes. Although such variations from the simpler form of the block system introduce no change in principle, they will make its application considerably less simple in the areas in which they occur. This arises from the more complicated conditions to be dealt with in such areas, not from any lack of adaptability of the block system.

It is none the less advisable that more experience both of Block Survey and Valuation should be gained in the hill areas than is at present available. This is desirable both to avoid delay when the hill areas have to be dealt with in the mass, and because the Government should have some initial knowledge of the relative values and extent of cultivable land in at least one typical hill area to enable them to estimate the probable yield of different rates of land tax.

10. **VALUATION SCALE.** I understand that some hesitation still exists as to the best method of expressing the relative values of Blocks for purposes of assessment, and that the present inclination is to think that the adoption of a scale of capital values will be most convenient. The importance of the point may perhaps be exaggerated, since a reasonably assessed land-tax should operate quite well however the basic valuations are expressed. I am also reluctant to urge my own views unduly upon officers who by now have had an unrivalled practical experience of the issues in Palestine. But I submit for the consideration of these officers that, whatever scale they may find most convenient for purposes of initial working, it is advisable to view the scale to be finally adopted for general use from the standpoint of the taxpaying public. And in a country in which the prices paid for land have been so much inflated by considerations of sentiment it is

preferable to adopt a scale for fiscal purposes which cannot be confounded with the absolute values of the moment at all.

I have previously represented that whatever theories may be spun about a land tax, such a tax, when levied on a predominantly agricultural community, is in effect an income tax on the net revenues derived from the land taxed. If a landholder is required by the State to pay x mils per annum as land tax on his holding that sum will in sober fact be a charge on the net annual income derived from that holding, although in Palestine such income will commonly not be completely, if at all, expressible in monetary form. The relative economic value of every block of land in, or adjoining, their village is known to all villagers. And such values adjudged from the standpoint of those who live by the land by no means reflect agricultural productivity alone. But these lands rarely come into a free financial market in their income earning capacity, nor, as said, is such income earning capacity ordinarily expressible in currency at all. Consequently a monetary scale purporting to express either (i) the revenue earning or (ii) the capital value of the majority of the blocks of village lands in Palestine is bound to be divorced from the realities of the situation and, as such, both an unreliable basis for taxation and one that invites attack. Of the two the former appears to me to be preferable (a) because a monetary expression of the net annual return from the land is at least some approximation to a reality, and (b) because it represents an attempt to express the actual thing taxed in the terms in which the tax is taken. Whereas the notion of capital value, when applied to the majority of the village lands in Palestine, is little more than a financial fiction. And even were this not so, and were the lump sum values of the village blocks really estimable in terms of cash, we should be little further advanced.

For the levy of an annual tax on a capital sum is a purely arbitrary proceeding unless the capital valuation is continually adjusted to reflect the annual yield, as in the case of capital invested in stocks and shares. For example, no British Government in its senses would annually tax £1,000 sunk in 3½% Conversion Loan the same amount as £1,000 sunk in 5% Conversion Loan. In other words given equal security it is the annual yield, which should determine capital values for any basis of annual taxation. And it is out of such annual yield that the taxpayer has actually to pay the tax. Since therefore the annual yield is the real touchstone, it is surely both misleading and unreal to adopt a scale of fictitious capital values as a basis for land taxation.

It appears to me that the net annual return of the land under normal conditions constitutes the only reasonable basis to be arrived at for a land tax under the primitive economic conditions still so widely prevalent in Palestine. Although, with careful and detailed enquiry, such annual return could no doubt be expressed in a monetary form which was a workable approximation to the truth; it has none the less to be recognized that it could never be more than such an approximation. The taxpayer would probably never appreciate the deep difference between monetary terminology used to express such approximate assessments, and the precise tax payments he would be required to make in cash. He would be sure to think that both should be equally precise.

In my opinion it is much better to abandon an appearance of exactness which can rarely be approached in assessment, and which will always be open to genuine misconception as well as malevolent misrepresentation.

11.   It has now been sufficiently established that all cultivators know the relative economic value of every block of land in, or adjoining, their villages from their own standpoint of value. And the standpoint of value accepted by the taxpayer himself is the least contentious and probably the best economically. These blocks are already graded by villagers for purposes of allotment of land among themselves. The practice is probably

also taken advantage of in the distribution of the commuted tithe. The grading has doubtless hitherto been crude and confined to the village concerned but the basic idea is already familiar and the extension of the same procedure to the country at large would provide both a less provocative and a more elastic basis of assessment than any monetary expression of values. This procedure would be less provocative, because although village communities would agree as to the relative value of various blocks of land, it must be anticipated that their apprehensions and opposition would be provoked by any monetary assessment of the incomes they derive therefrom or of the prices they should ask in the event of sale. The procedure would be more elastic, because, although relative values will change with changing conditions they will not be affected to anything like the extent of absolute money values, by variations in the value of money or in the demand for land.

I have previously represented that a long and delicately graduated scale would be needed to express equitably the assessments of blocks for land tax from one end of Palestine to another. Although this would require more careful adjustment between one locality and another in the first place, than a scale that purported to represent absolute values, this careful adjustment to a generally applicable standard would add greatly to the reliability of the work as a whole in the long run. Moreover now that preliminary valuation has been carried out over a considerable area, and so much practical experience of the work has been acquired, there should be no serious difficulty in translating the valuations that have been provisionally arrived at, into terms of the purely proportional scale of values that I recommended.

The important objective is an assessment of the relative values of the blocks of village land throughout the country which is substantially equitable and is accepted by the mass of the people as such. As soon as this objective is achieved over reasonably wide and representative areas it will be a simple matter (a) to calculate the general scale of land tax that would be needed to produce the same revenue as the existing taxes, and (b) to decide how far this scale of taxation is economically justifiable.

12. **USE OF LAND TAX AS AN INSTRUMENT OF AGRICULTURAL IMPROVEMENT.** I understand that the employment of the land tax as an instrument of agricultural improvement is still advocated. While the greatest sympathy must be felt with the object in view, I feel that I should repeat my previous warnings against any attempt to secure this object by fiscal remissions. Artificial stimuli to particular forms of economic development are dangerous and uncertain weapons, which are apt to operate in quite unexpected ways. In Iraq a similar impulse led to remissions of tax with a view to encouraging the erection of pumps. There has been an enormous speculative erection of pumps there of recent years, largely financed on borrowed money. The remission of tax mentioned has helped to promote many unsound pump-fed undertakings, which in their earlier years showed a profit even on the growth of primitive crops, because world prices were advantageous, because the pumps were new, and because working expenses were not representative. From the point of view of the country at large the gross result has been to add to the flood of inferior cereals, for which there is no market, at the cost of widespread indebtedness and a large volume of tax remission. It would have been far better for Agriculture, for the Treasury and for the majority of those concerned if they had not been artificially encouraged to embark upon this false el Dorado. Now, with some reason, those involved hold Government responsible, and ask for further special assistance.

- 19 -

It is not suggested that the "beneficial improvements" which it is sought to encourage by fiscal remissions in Palestine are of similar gravity, but the underlying dangers and objections to all such hot-house policies are the same in kind if not in degree everywhere. A slower development, which accommodates itself without artificial shelter to actual economic conditions, is much healthier and more stable. And no responsibility rests in such cases on the State for stimulating enterprises which may prove unprofitable.

All good husbandry, whether of land or of other sources of wealth, requires the expenditure of thought, labour and material. It is immaterial whether this expenditure is applied from current resources or derived from previous savings. Such expenditure may take any of the eighteen forms of beneficial improvement tabulated by the Department of Agriculture or of innumerable others. The incentive in all cases is the enhanced return expected from the land, or other source of wealth exploited. If that incentive is inadequate ought the State to try and tempt the taxpayer to embark upon an expenditure of whose economic justification he is so doubtful? And even if it were possible to discriminate with unerring judgment in favour of specified improvements, how is that discrimination to be assessed in terms of tax remission, equitably and to the satisfaction of those who do not benefit to the same extent as the favoured individual, or at all? Solid remissions of tax would be required to induce the taxpayer to incur expenditure from which he was doubtful of obtaining a suitable return. No such inducement is needed at all, when he is satisfied on this point.

To summarize: a considerable artificial stimulus would be needed to produce any appreciable effect on the agricultural development of the country as a whole; this stimulus would operate principally in the economically doubtful marginal cases; it would be provided at the cost of the general mass of taxpayers whose taxation would have to be maintained at a higher level than would otherwise be necessary; its application would greatly increase the labour and costs of administration, both initially and permanently, and would thereby operate again to raise the general level of taxation.

I do not suggest that expenditure on what are judged to be beneficial improvements should be penalized by being treated either immediately, or at all, as necessarily productive and taxable. On the contrary I think it would be justifiable and desirable to defer for a reasonable, even a generous, period, any increased assessment on lands on account of an increased return clearly produced by specific measures of development (e.g. planting fruit groves, building water channels), or even by good husbandry of a less obvious nature. Such deferment of increased assessment on an enhanced return that has already been obtained, could be applied as a regular and routine measure. It has none of the objections inseparable from any system of granting rebates of taxation as inducements to the taxpayer to undertake measures whose economic justification is uncertain.

It will be a sufficiently difficult and delicate task to apply and administer a land-tax equitably and to the general satisfaction as the purely fiscal measure that, I venture to think, it should be. Any features, however attractive, which tend to raise the general level of taxation; to obscure the simplicity, and therefore, the equity of assessment; to add to the expense of administration; or to complicate, and consequently further retard, the introduction of the fundamental reform should, in my opinion, be excluded from all immediate consideration.

The immediate objectives are (i) the reduction and equalization of the existing burden of taxation on the land and (ii) the early substitution of simple, and palpably, equitable methods of assessment and collection for those in force. Whatever views may be held as to the advisability of further refinements later, consideration of such refinements should at least be postponed until this essential task has been successfully accomplished.

13. **SETTLEMENT OF RIGHTS TO LAND.** Systematic settlement of rights to land has made an excellent start. It was always recognized that progress was bound to be slow at first, while the details of procedure were being tested under actual field conditions in Palestine, and while all officers concerned were gaining personal experience of the work and establishing contact with the people. The lessons learnt in the initial period have already borne valuable fruit in actual or prospective elimination of clerical work and simplification of procedure generally.

I had a good, if brief, opportunity of seeing the work on the field last May. The Government can be satisfied that it is going on well and improving daily. Two points that call for special notice are (i) the success which has attended the training of, and the devolution of preliminary settlement operations to, Palestinian Assistant Settlement Officers, and (ii) the general recognition of the discretion and competence with which the two Principal Settlement Officers have exercised their judicial functions. A map is attached illustrating the progress of settlement operations to date.

14. In the numerous discussions which preceded the adoption of the general programme of land reform under consideration, it was frequently pointed out that experience elsewhere, and the known conditions of the local problem alike, indicated that the settlement

- 22 -

of ninety per cent. of the property parcels would present little difficulty, if investigations were carried out on the spot in the presence of the villagers and other interested parties, by officers who knew the language and were in touch with local customs and feeling. This anticipation has now been verified over a sufficiently wide and diverse area to confirm its general validity.

The Commissioner of Lands represents that this opens up the possibility of extending the benefits of settlement and effective registration of rights to the bulk of the country at a greatly accelerated rate. Such settlement and registration could now be organized to proceed in two waves instead of one. An advanced wave would deal, as rapidly as conditions permitted, with the majority of parcels which present no serious difficulty, leaving the few which required fuller enquiry to be settled afterwards.

The parcels would all have to be defined and the new registers be fully written up at the first stage. The position of the minority of parcels left unsettled between the first and the second stage might be somewhat awkward; but they would be in some respects better, and in no respect worse, situated than they would otherwise have been. And in any case some temporary awkwardness in the records of a minority of the parcels is worth putting up with to facilitate the rapid settlement of the majority. And the fact that accelerated settlement would be practicable in the case of all easily settled parcels and might be greatly retarded in difficult cases, or when conflicting claims were stubbornly maintained, would tend to encourage compromises and resorts to arbitration in the early stage. This psychological stimulus to voluntary agreement, would probably affect the speed, and consequently the cost, of the settlement as a whole very powerfully.

15.   It must, however, be recognized that a scheme which, broadly speaking, aims at settling ninety per cent. of the land much more rapidly, is bound to involve a considerable acceleration of expenditure. The economic and administrative benefits of the settlement would be reaped much earlier; the total cost of settlement would be appreciably, probably greatly, reduced; but the annual charge would be considerably increased during the initial years of the scheme.

    As regards the investigation of rights, this forward shift of cost would be small in relation to the accelerated results; because the acceleration would only apply to the ninety per cent. of easily, and therefore cheaply, settled cases. As regards registration, this shift in cost would be the same as if the complete settlement of rights was equally accelerated, as the new registers affected would have to be opened and fully written up in either case. No saving in cost would arise because the entries affecting ten per cent. of the parcels were subject to settlement later. But the resulting acceleration in the cost of introducing an effective system of registration, would to some extent be balanced by a corresponding closure of the old registers. And the working cost of the new records would be legitimately covered by the fees paid for the service rendered. Neither in the field of investigation, nor in that of registration should there be much practical difficulty in applying the Advanced Scheme.

    It is the Survey side of the scheme that is the critical one, both executively and financially, as the Commissioner of Lands fully appreciates. The cadastral work would have to be just as complete for Advanced Settlement under the scheme, as for fully completed settlement; since all parcels would have to be defined and surveyed whether settled then and there, or not. It requires suitable recruits, men and time to train them, and the provision of equipment, as well as additional funds to expand a complicated technical service without lowering its quality. Since the inception of the present reforms on the field, the Survey of Palestine has responded successfully to heavy demands, and care must be exercised not to increase these demands too rapidly. And above all nothing should be allowed to interfere with the early completion of the Block Survey.

16. But although the general establishment of a land tax is the more immediately urgent, as it is the more immediately realizable, reform, it must nevertheless be recognized that the execution of a cadastral survey and systematic settlement of rights is long overdue. The need for these measures was appreciated by the Turks before the war, and a law to give effect to them was enacted in 1913. British Military Proclamations recognized the same need, as the Civil Administration has done consistently ever since. From 1919 a series of advisers, of whom I was the latest, were called into consultation on the subject. But an effective decision to proceed was not taken until 1926, and the work was not actually begun on the field until 1928. Owing, no doubt, to the intricacy of the issues and their multifarious reactions, all countries are slow in embarking upon comprehensive land reforms, however fully the need for such reforms is recognized. Judged by such comparative standards, the Palestine Government has been exceptionally prompt. Nevertheless absolutely there is a tangle of many years standing to unravel before public and private rights to, and obligations arising from, the land are defined and tenure is secure. In a country in which the operation of the land law depends upon an effective State record of rights, the State evidently has a special responsibility to make and keep this record reliable. And this responsibility is not lessened when a considerable revenue has been steadily derived from the operation of the admittedly unreliable records still in general use.

There are therefore strong reasons for adopting the Advanced Settlement scheme suggested by the Commissioner of Lands if, and when, the Survey can be provided with the necessary funds and is in a position to accelerate cadastral work, without lowering its quality and without retarding the block survey. The details of the scheme have still to be worked out; but it is unquestionably feasible. If adopted, it should appreciably reduce the cost of settlement of rights to land as a whole, as well as greatly reducing the period within which the benefits of that settlement reach the majority of landholders and cultivators.

17. MESHA'. The periodic redistribution of land held by a clan or village group among members of the group, known locally as the mesha' system, is a common expedient of primitive communities. The practice has generally tended to disappear before the requirements of better cultivation; but is still widely prevalent in Palestine. Thus the Committee set up to study the question in 1922 put the proportion of cultivated land in the country subject to mesha' at 55%. This Committee unanimously recommended the abolition of mesha' and the permanent allotment of the land held under it: but the Government had doubts as to the practicability and advisability of this course, in view of the great extent of the practice, its similitude of co-operation, and the difficulty of carrying out the permanent allotment equitably. My own view was that the mesha' system was a most serious obstacle to the economic development of the country, but that essentially it was part of the confusion and uncertainty of rights to land generally prevailing, and should be dealt with as part of the systematic investigation and settlement of such rights that I advocated. This course was in due course adopted and the permanent allotment of the land held in mesha' has proceeded smoothly as an intrinsic part of this settlement, with incontestably beneficial results. Indeed so much is this

permanent allotment generally welcomed and demanded by the people, that the Commissioner of Lands is anxious to devise measures whereby it can be greatly accelerated.

While clear as to the desirability of such acceleration the Commissioner of Lands was far from having formulated any concrete measures with this objective, when he invited my opinion on the matter. So that my observations can only be of a general nature and may be beside the mark by now. When he spoke to me he was considering the possibility and desirability of carrying out the permanent allotment of mesha' in two main operations in advance of systematic settlement of rights. The two operations in view were: (a) investigation and settlement by suitable officers of the extent of mesha' holdings, the names of the shareholders, and the numbers and/or fractions of shares held; and (b) the permanent allotment of the land adjudged to be affected in accordance with these shares by the shareholders themselves.

Great as is the economic desirability of bringing mesha' to as rapid an end as possible, and unavoidable as measures of this sort may be if the progress of systematic settlement cannot be accelerated, it must be recognized that they would amount to an anticipation of the settlement in respect of a certain type of claim. The settlement would thereby cease to be a systematic and comprehensive and become a piecemeal operation instead. No isolated investigations of claims that certain areas have been held under a particular practice can be relied upon to be either equitable or final, although no doubt in a great many cases such partial operations would substantially survive review when subject to final settlement. It must also be remembered that actual experience at Beisan and elsewhere shows, as indeed is to be expected, that distribution by the interested parties themselves tends to favour, sometimes very markedly, the stronger or socially more prominent members of the shareholding group. And although prompter permanent allotment may be well worth purchasing at the cost of some imperfection, such imperfection should not involve a lowering of the general equity of the settlement as a whole at the expense of the poorer and weaker.

If the Advanced Settlement scheme is favourably considered and is likely to be put into operation as soon as opportunity allows, there will be less demand for a separate attempt to accelerate the permanent allotment of mesha'. Accelerated settlement of claims to mesha' shares would be more equitably and more conclusively effected as part of the advanced wave of the general settlement, than as a series of isolated undertakings. And the actual allotment of shares on the ground would be carried out by impartial officers and competent technical operations instead of in haphazard ways, while the results would be incorporated there and then in the cadastral survey. The desirability of accelerating the permanent distribution of mesha' is therefore an added reason for adopting the Advanced Settlement scheme: but great as this desirability is it should not tempt Government to dissociate the settlement of claims based upon the practice of mesha' from the systematic and comprehensive settlement of rights to land that is now being undertaken.

18. Reference should perhaps also be made here to the difficulty which, I understand, still exists to the permanent allotment of mesha' of the type classified briefly as Zakûr. In theory this type of mesha' involves the periodic redistribution of the land among all the male members of the community concerned, from the newest born to the most senile, who chance to be alive at the critical day and hour. It may be hoped that such legal difficulty as exists to the abolition of this type of mesha' may soon be surmounted, for in substance there is no more justification for perpetuating the injurious practice in this particular

form than in others. All the varieties of mesha' were originally adopted by the communities concerned, at their own sweet will, under the stress of primitive social and agricultural conditions which are now rapidly passing. And they are all inconsistent with enacted law and a serious obstacle to economic development. The essential thing in the general interest, both of the communities immediately concerned and of the country as a whole, is to remove this obstacle, with substantial fairness to the families and individuals who have definite assessable claims, actual or prospective, to shares to-day. It is neither practicable nor desirable to endeavour to safeguard hypothetical individual claims that might arise under unknown future conditions if the system were to be perpetuated. The equitable allotment of land claimed to have been hitherto held and periodically redistributed under the Takur type of mesha', may involve more study and require fuller powers than that of other types; but, given such study and such powers, it will present no insuperable or even serious difficulty, to the experienced Settlement Officers who are now available.

19. REGISTRATION OF RIGHTS TO LAND.

I had only a brief opportunity last May of seeing the progress made in introducing a reformed system of registration of rights to land following on the systematic settlement of such rights now in progress: but what I saw was most encouraging and satisfactory. My observations here only refer to this reformed system which at present necessarily applies only to a fraction of the country.

The foundations of an effective system of land registration are (i) a good cadastral survey rigorously maintained to date, whereby the parcels of property affected are accurately defined, and (ii) the legal instruments by virtue of which the rights that are registered are created, transferred, transmitted, modified or annulled. The Land Registers should mirror the resulting rights from day to day faithfully and economically. The execution and maintenance of the cadastral survey and the custody of the necessary records are the business of the Survey of Palestine, and call for no comment here. The filing and care of the authoritative legal instruments in the Land Registry is soundly planned and organized; but this branch of the records is gravely hampered by the varieties in shape and form of legal instrument still permitted.

I understand that while Government is agreed that the present arrangements are unsatisfactory, it is considered that the requisite uniformity should be secured by request rather than by order. To maintain an elaborately detailed register of rights to land and to insist upon its use while hesitating to require that the instruments governing these rights shall be embodied on sheets of paper of satisfactory quality and reasonable size is surely somewhat absurd? To seek to satisfy this need by persuasion is to subject the public interest to the whims of the cranky and obstructive. To leave the public free to continue to present the heterogeneous documents customary in the past, is to impede the efficient working of the Land Registry gratuitously, to increase the size of the equipment and of the storage space needed, and thereby to increase the difficulty and cost of administration appreciably and avoidably. The issue may appear to be of negligible importance to the inexperienced; but in practice, as any good administrator knows, it is upon details of this sort that rapidity, efficiency and economy of working largely depend. Nor is it any more difficult to require the public to use paper of specified size and permanence when dealing in land than to require them to use specified forms in innumerable other operations in which economy, efficiency and despatch of business demand it (e.g. when sending telegrams and money orders). And it would be a simple matter for Government to supply standard sheets for the purpose for a small charge through any convenient agencies.

I venture to suggest that the Government is not only fully justified in prescribing the use of documents of definite quality and size; but that it has a duty to do so, if risks of error, waste of time and waste of money are avoided thereby. I see that the Chief Justice agrees that the proposed regulation is necessary and that he is prepared to take steps to ensure that the Courts will comply with it themselves and require advocates and others to do so. I hope that the initial hesitation of the Administration to authorize the measure may, upon fuller consideration, be overcome.

20. The two most important pre-requisites to the successful operation of a Land Register are probably the adoption (i) of a simple and unambiguous numeration of property-parcels, and (ii) of a simple but sufficient machinery for the perpetual routine incorporation of property-mutations in the joint cartographical and written record. In the construction and operation of the register the two most essential features are (a) to allot a separate folio to each property parcel and record all rights to such parcel thereon, and (b) to bind or file these folios in loose-leaf form. Only by conforming to these requirements can this protean record be always kept in orderly sequence, completely up to date, completely free from obsolete matter, and be economically handled and economically stored. These two requirements have also been complied with; but I understand that there is still some reluctance definitely to abandon the more familiar rigidly bound register.

I was originally led, with certain colleagues, to advocate the use of a loose-leaf Land Register in Egypt in 1919 by our realization, from a study of the difficulties of various Land Registries there and elsewhere, that only a completely elastic record could be efficiently and economically maintained. The grounds for this conclusion have been set out more fully by myself and one of those colleagues elsewhere, and they will, I hope, be found sufficiently convincing. Moreover these conclusions have been quite independently confirmed by the experience of H.M.Land Registry in London. H.M.Chief Registrar appreciated a number of years ago the obstacle to prompt, efficient and economical working created by the use of rigidly bound registers. He abandoned them and substituted separated card folios for each property unit. This innovation, which it will be noted carries elasticity even beyond the loose-leaf register, has been completely justified on all the three counts mentioned. A Committee set up by the Lord Chancellor has recently reported "that the system as at present organized is working smoothly and efficiently and to the satisfaction of those whom it affects."* The value and significance of this finding is enhanced to those acquainted with the chequered history of Land Registration in England during the last hundred years, by the far-reaching change whose accomplishment it records. This change is, of course, far from being solely due to the introduction of elastic records; but it would certainly not have been achieved if rigidly bound registers had been adhered to.

The difference between, what may be termed, the loose-leaf and the card-index form of elastic record is primarily a matter of alternative containing receptacles - a book cover or a drawer - and the administrative consequences of each form. Under the conditions prevailing in Palestine, the former appears to me to be preferable; but the respective advantages and disadvantages of each form deserve careful consideration. And important as the difference between these two forms of elastic

*Report of the Land Registration Committee Cond.3564. 1930.

record are, they are insignificant in comparison with the gulf that separates them both from the rigidly bound register. A reversion to the trammels of this bulky and unadaptable vehicle of record would be an unthinkably retrograde step.

21. The Land Register folio adopted in Palestine is somewhat smaller than the Swiss and Egyptian models, on which it was based. Further consideration has suggested the advisability of reducing it still further, which can be done without any inconvenience or loss of efficiency by having recourse to continuation sheets as, and when needed. Since such continuation folios would only be needed for the minority of the parcels the resulting economy in register covers, folios and storage space should be very great. The amended size of folio and a continuation sheet have been illustrated elsewhere.

22. A matter that should not be overlooked is provision for the reconstruction of the records in the event of partial or complete loss or destruction. The initial settlement of rights to land throughout Palestine and the subsequent building up of an authoritative Land Register thereon is necessarily a long and a costly undertaking. Adequate precautions should be taken to ensure against any considerable loss of this painfully acquired record, by fire or otherwise. The most obvious and the most effective of such precautions is the duplication of the primary documents and the storage of these duplicates apart from the originals, preferably in a fireproof building constructed and sited to avoid earthquake effect. As this point has been frequently emphasized and has been discussed more fully elsewhere it need not be entered into further here.

23. But I venture to think that the matter calling most imperatively for the re-consideration of the Government in

connexion with land registration is the scale of fees. Owing to the failure of the government of the country in the past to provide the efficient land registration service that the Land Code assumes to exist, a costly and laborious inquest of all rights to land has been necessitated. This work will be thrown away, and muddle in due course succeed to muddle, unless the results achieved by this inquest are kept up to date effectively hereafter, village by village, and parcel by parcel, through the medium of the reformed land registration system now in course of establishment.

After years of disregard of the law by the public and government alike, it is not to be supposed that the former will be readily brought to co-operate in the systematic registration of rights to land that will be required, if the reforms now in progress are to take root and become established. It is true that if the law is rigidly applied and enforced the necessity to register all major rights to land should gradually be brought home to the public: but this rigid application and enforcement will not be easy while the law itself remains as unsatisfactory as it is, particularly in regard to the transmission of rights on death. It is also true that, if an efficient Land Registry service is progressively introduced, and if all other branches of the Administration co-operate, it should be possible systematically to track, and bring to book administratively, those who fail to register. But when all is said and done it is not desirable, it may not be possible, and it will certainly be troublesome and costly, to dragoon the land holding public into taking advantage of a measure that, properly presented and administered, is intrinsically beneficial and should be attractive in itself.

In other words it is highly important, if not indeed essential, to secure the spontaneous co-operation of those concerned, if the great effort that is now being made to construct and maintain a reliable record of rights to land throughout Palestine is to be successful. To secure such co-operation two conditions should be satisfied: (a) the service given, and the protection afforded, by the Land Registries must be good; and (b) the fees charged must be as low as possible.

The measures that are now in train may be expected to provide good service and effective protection of registered rights; but the fees charged should be strictly related to the cost of the service and not employed as a means of taxation as at present. I have frequently urged the necessity of this reform; but it has always been represented that the Government could not afford to lose the revenue derived from this source; and that the charges levied must be regarded primarily as of the nature of stamp duties on land transactions and not as fees.

I have not got the figures for the last three years, but those returned for six and a half financial years, 1920-27, which were discussed at the Conference held on the 21st. February, 1927 at Jerusalem, were, expressed in thousands:

	Total	Average per annum
Expenditure	L.E. 96.3	L.E. 14.8
Receipts	L.E. 386.5	L.E. 59.5
Registered transactions	49.8	7.7

On this showing the average payment demanded upon registration during this period was four times the cost of the service rendered.

24. If it is thought necessary to impose stamp duties on land transactions in Palestine, at least a clear distinction should be made, as in England, between such stamp-duties and the costs of registration. But it is obviously immaterial to the mass of land-holders, whether the sums they are required to pay upon

registration of rights to land are termed stamp-duties or fees or an amalgam of both. Unless these sums are light they will act as an equally effective deterrent to registration under any name.

So I venture again to plead that the whole principle of tacking stamp duties - whether covertly or overtly - on to land registration fees in Palestine is unsound, and that if the landholding public is to be brought to value, and to co-operate in, the maintenance of the new Register, the payments demanded upon registration should be strictly regarded as fees payable for the services rendered and be governed solely by the aggregate cost of those services.

I realize the facility with which revenue has hitherto been raised through the medium of land registration charges; but it must be remembered that only a fraction of the land, and of the proceedings affecting it, have hitherto been registered, and these have preponderantly concerned the richer parties and larger scale transactions for which the protection of the register has in effect been sought voluntarily, and probably without much regard to the charges made. A similar tolerance can hardly be expected from the great mass of landholders when required to register all rights compulsorily.

And the benefit of a clear title, which it is the main object of the settlement to confer on every landholder, will be considerably attenuated if he is to be taxed whenever he wishes to raise money for improvements; or to consolidate his holdings by judicious exchanges, purchases and sales; or to portion out his parcel among his children; or indeed to dispose of that parcel in any way.

I earnestly submit that it will go far towards jeopardizing both the benefits, and the practicability of maintaining, the settlement of rights, if land registration fees are to continue to be utilized as an instrument of taxation.

26.   On the other hand it is equitable in principle and not unduly onerous in practice, that the cost of the services rendered should be borne by those who directly benefit. The application of the principle no doubt presents some difficulty, since it is impossible to discriminate rigidly between the cost of registering rights to land and the cost of certain public services performed at the same time. A practical compromise, which I suggest is equitable and would be understood, would be to recover the annual cost of maintaining the land registries and the cadastral survey, after settlement from land registration fees. But the maintenance of the cadastral survey must not be confused with its execution, which is an integral part of the settlement of rights. Until recently there has been no cadastral survey to maintain; but such maintenance is an essential part of the current machinery of any effective system of land registration, and this must be recognized in any reasonable assessment of the cost of such registration.

Properly a share in the cost of the other branches of the Survey should also be allocated to land registration; but these branches primarily serve a general purpose and are fairly chargeable to the general revenues of the State. Indeed there are equally strong, if not stronger, grounds on which the general revenues of the State should bear a proportion of the whole costs of land registration. For the Land Register will be the foundation of the Land tax and the Urban property tax records; and indeed should embody those records, if fully and effectively utilized. As however the registered landholder will benefit indirectly from other public services, the compromise suggested earlier appears on balance to be a reasonable one. It will however be appreciated that consideration of the scale of land registration fees cannot be divorced from consideration of the other public charges that registered proprietors will have to meet. Thus, if the general level of land and/or urban property tax is low, the direct costs of land registration should certainly be fully recovered in fees. If on the other hand those tax levels are high, there is justification for considering that the State as a whole should share in, or even possibly entirely meet, the cost of maintaining the fundamental record.

26. **SEPARATION OF CONTROL OF LAND REGISTRIES FROM THAT OF PUBLIC DOMAIN.** I feel that I should also briefly re-affirm the great desirability of separating the control of the Land Registries from the control of Public Domain. The maintenance of the reformed Land Register day by day throughout the whole country will be the most difficult part of the present reforms, not so much intrinsically, as because it will necessitate a very high level of widespread and detailed administration. For many years to come this task will demand the undivided energies of the officer in charge of the service. And on grounds of principle, as well as of administrative efficiency, it is most undesirable that this officer, who ought to be regarded by all as the strictly impartial recorder of rights to land, should be also charged with the incompatible duty of maintaining the claims of the State to land and house property in opposition to members of the public.

The undesirability of this combination of functions was not disputed; but it was considered impracticable to separate them in advance of the general settlement of rights to land, owing to the confusion and inextricability of the existing records. The Attorney-General however took over the presentation and defence of such claims in the Courts in 1927, and thus removed the most objectionable feature of this association of duties.

Now that the general settlement of rights has been in progress for two years, is proceeding smoothly and may possibly be accelerated, I venture to suggest that the time has come when a further move towards the definite separation of these two functions should be made. The progress of settlement will simplify the problem enormously by deciding definitely what land is Public Domain and what is not. So that there seems no reason why every parcel of land thus adjudged to be Public Domain, should not be handed over to the control of some suitable branch of the public service as soon as registration formalities have been completed. Already portions of the Public Domain utilized by the State Railway are in the custody of that Department; while, I believe, the Public Works Department has charge of the land occupied by public roads. Similarly, stretches of forest or potential forest, sand dune areas, public watercourses, waste areas of marsh or of mountain-top, could be placed in the custody of the Department of Agriculture, of the District Administration, or of whatever service is primarily concerned, or can be most conveniently entrusted with, the exploitation, protection or control of each particular area.

These services could maintain the boundaries of their particular stretches of public domain against encroachment and trespass, and utilize these areas more effectively and economically than any general Land Department could do. At the same time the Commissioner of Lands and the Director of Land Registries would be relieved of this unmanageable and invidious task, be able to concentrate upon their special duties, and be able to adopt that entirely detached and impartial attitude towards all land disputes that is so eminently desirable. For it will be appreciated that the majority of the landholding public in Palestine would have difficulty in understanding or crediting the possibility of an impartial Land Registry under the general control of a Commissioner of Lands who was constantly obliged to adopt a partisan attitude in land disputes. Indeed, it is very probable that they will not discriminate between the two offices at all.

27. **CONCLUDING OBSERVATIONS.** I have now endeavoured to touch on the points which appeared to me to be of most immediate concern, either as a result of my brief inspection in May last or of my even briefer conversations with the Commissioner of Lands this autumn in England. My observations necessarily apply mainly to those aspects of the work which still call for further consideration and decision by Government, rather than to those which are proceeding well. So I should perhaps repeat that a most useful organization has been created and a most promising start made. Secure tenure and moderate and equitably distributed land taxation are the primary conditions of agricultural prosperity in Palestine as elsewhere. After a number of years of preparatory discussion, the attainment of these objectives is now in sight and can be secured within a relatively short period, provided the present programme of land reform can be tenaciously maintained, and if possible accelerated. But there is an obvious danger, in times of great difficulty like the present, that effort may be diverted from digging these humdrum foundations of economic prosperity to the premature erection of the upper courses. Among such upper courses, perhaps I may instance the provision of cheap agricultural credit, since the lack of such credit was among the existing evils initially mentioned. Given security of tenure, as well as moderate and equitably distributed taxation, cheap agricultural credit will follow. Nothing will produce it in the absence of those conditions. Nor is the provision of such credit even intrinsically as important; for, whereas security of tenure and moderate and equitably distributed taxation is a direct benefit to all who make their living from the land, cheap credit will only benefit the minority who have the character and the intelligence to employ it advantageously.

No one will contest the potential value of cheap credit, nor of many other ways in which agricultural prosperity can be stimulated. I am only venturing here to offer a warning against any dislocation of the nicely adjusted sequence of administrative, executive, technical and judicial operations which are now in operation. The efficiency, economy and rapidity of these operations can be relied upon to increase steadily, as experience is gained and combination is perfected, provided the organization as a whole can be allowed to adhere to a far-reaching programme or merely to adapt such a programme progressively so to achieve better results. Nothing will exercise so deleterious an effect upon the execution of the main reforms under review, as the introduction of unexpected alterations into the general programme, especially if these occur repeatedly.

I venture to mention this danger simply because the far-reaching effect of such alterations may not at first sight be apparent to Government, and it may be somewhat difficult for the Commissioner of Lands to anticipate their effect fully beforehand.

       I have the honour to be,
        Excellency,
        Your obedient servant,

(Sg) Ernest M. Dowson

APPENDIX.

EXTRACT from MEMORANDUM on the appointment of Commissioner of Lands, submitted to H.E. the High Commissioner on the 11th. January, 1927.

PREAMBLE.

In the covering memorandum to my Report on the Land System in Palestine submitted in December 1925 after a brief statement of certain evil consequences of the failure of the Land Registries to function I said (p.5):-

"If these and other prevailing defects are to be remedied the reform must be planned and executed as a united whole. So far the (cures of these evils) have for the most part been treated as separate questions, instead of a compound of closely inter-related problems which must be attacked as a connected whole."

In sections 10 and 11 (p.15 et seq.) of the report itself, after illustrating the ineffective pursuit of reform since November 1918 I said

"The principal lesson to be learnt .... is the necessity for thoroughly considered and concerted action .... To continue to pursue reform without having examined its basis, on no comprehensive plan, and through the unco-ordinated efforts of sections of public service whose views are focussed on their own departmental fields, is to continue to expend money and effort to no useful purpose .... (The) solution (of the problem) calls for the earnest attention of the Central Government itself, not only in digesting reports but in the detailed planning and execution of reform .... Such exercise by Government itself of general direction and unifying control of reform is perfectly compatible with its decentralized execution. But decentralized execution of a comprehensive scheme of reform is a radically different thing from the disconnected sectional efforts which have hitherto held the field."

2. In the series of meetings which I came out from England to attend last Spring, the outlines of a comprehensive scheme of reform were accepted, embodied in Despatch No.447 dated the 22nd. of April, 1926 to the Secretary of State, and in due course approved. I am asked in the present note to outline the reasons calling for the appointment of a permanent Commissioner of Lands and the conditions under which he could, in my opinion, successfully discharge responsibility for the establishment of the necessary reforms. The subject is complex and detailed and the present note is hurriedly written, and is neither as exhaustive nor as concise as I would wish: but I think it covers all the more essential points.

3. FUNCTIONS AND POSITION OF COMMISSIONER OF LANDS.

The appointment of Commissioner of Lands is needed to rectify two radical defects which have so far neutralized the repeated efforts that have been made since 1918 to make some effective progress with reform of land tenure and taxation in Palestine. These two defects are (1) absence of any unified direction and control of such reform: (2) detachment of the Central Administration from the conduct and progress of the various measures attempted.

- 2 -

The Commissioner of Lands should not be a detached super-departmental chief, but one of the most senior executive officers of the Central Administration itself specially appointed to concentrate on the execution of an exceptionally complex task on behalf of the High Commissioner-in-Council. To secure the assured liaison with the Executive Council that is essential, I strongly recommend the formal adoption of the procedure proposed by the Chief Secretary whereby the attendance of the Commissioner of Lands at meetings of Council is required whenever questions affecting land are dealt with. As a senior officer of the Central Administration the Commissioner of Lands should occupy offices in the Central Government Building, and thus be afforded the same opportunities for continuous intercourse and the same access to all correspondence and records as his colleagues. He should also be made a member of the Advisory Council.

If the Commissioner of Lands is not effectively associated with the Central Administration the latter will never keep the intimate connection with the conduct of reform that is necessary; while he himself will tend to become either a mere post office or a supernumerary departmental head.

4. The offices of the Commissioner of Lands should constitute (1) the clearing house and general intelligence office of the Administration for all land questions and (2) a single centre for the direction and execution of land policy. Papers concerning land problems should be passed to this office as a matter of routine. If such papers call for the consideration of any other office (e.g. Treasury or Attorney General's office) or Department (e.g. Agriculture) or of the Central Administration as such (in the person of the Chief

Secretary or of the High Commissioner) it will be the duty of the Commissioner of Lands to secure such consideration after due examination and elucidation. If such papers call for action in accordance with current policy or practice he should initiate such action.

On the intelligence side it will be the function of the office to ensure more particularly that all data required to enable the Central Administration to keep touch with the conduct and progress of reform are trustworthy, intelligible, up-to-date and promptly available. These data for the most part can be better kept by the service directly concerned (e.g. Survey, Land Registry, or Settlement Officer): but key maps and graphic diagrams illustrating the progress of all operations must be maintained in the office of the Commissioner of Lands himself.

In his capacity as the officer charged on behalf of the Central Administration with the unified direction and execution of land reform the Commissioner of Lands must have undivided responsibility for the conduct and progress of land reform and must wield complete authority over the public service (Survey, Land Registries and Land Settlement) whose main duty is to co-operate in the establishment of such reform. Neither the responsibility nor the authority of the Commissioner of Lands should be watered down by enforced association with any standing council or committee.

5. I myself in 1924 suggested that the general execution of reform might perhaps tentatively be undertaken by a Standing Committee presided over by the Chief Secretary and composed of representatives of the services whose work required unified direction. This suggestion was dictated by my own and the general reluctance to subordinate to anyone else two public services (Survey and Land Registries) which have so far

enjoyed departmental status directly under the Chief Secretary. The proposal was admittedly an unsatisfactory compromise. It would fasten direct responsibility for the execution of reform upon the Chief Secretary, who has the time neither to learn nor to direct the work effectively. This suggestion has now been definitely rejected by the Chief Secretary as unworkable, and I entirely concur with his judgment. The proposal was worth consideration if only to test whether the unified direction of reform could be undertaken by the Central Administration without reinforcement, even in the loose and spasmodic way suggested. The answer is unequivocal, that the unified direction of control must be exercised by a special officer able to concentrate wholly upon it: but it is not worth making this appointment, unless such officer assumes full responsibility for, and is in complete executive charge of, the work.

6. POSITION OF EXECUTIVE SERVICES PRINCIPALLY CHARGED WITH THE EXECUTION OF REFORM.

The efforts of three executive branches of the public services concerned require to be effectively co-ordinated: the Survey, the Land Registries and the Land Settlement branch now in course of formation. The general reluctance to do anything to lower the status or restrict the independence of the two former services has been mentioned: but the need for common direction is patent and must be paramount. But such direction cannot be achieved by half measures: nor will half measures be any less productive of difficulty and irritation in the long run.

Subject however to the responsibility of the Commissioner of Lands for the conduct of land reform being complete and his authority over the public services concerned unquestioned, everything possible should be done on the one hand to refrain from any unnecessary inroad on their present independence and status and on the other to stimulate their energies and encourage their pride in their work. Thus while unity of direction must be both competent and effectively maintained, it must be reconciled with the minimum of internal interference with the two valuable and experienced services that exist. Such interferences would deflect the Commissioner of Lands from the important duties for which he is really needed; while even unity of direction would be dearly purchased by loss of departmental efficiency and keenness.

The necessity for unobtrusive central direction applies to settlement work as well as to the established services, as it is a cardinal condition of success that each British Settlement Officer shall be the outstanding figure within his own sphere and in his own Settlement Area. Such Officers must of course conform to central guidance and instructions, but the responsibility for their decisions will be their own and appeal from them will lie, not to the Commissioner of Lands, but to such Court as may be ordained.

Briefly I conceive it to be the duty of the Commissioner of Lands to ensure that a common policy and plan and common principles are applied, that services under his direction are properly equipped and looked after, that all necessary outside assistance is forthcoming, and that adequate progress is maintained throughout; but that it is his part so long as he obtains keen and single-minded response to his direction to keep his post and himself deliberately in the background. And I conceive it to be the duty of the public services concerned to accept loyally the necessity for unity of direction, to sink entirely in the public interest any reluctance they may feel to be brought under such direction, and to work keenly and wholeheartedly for its success and for the successful establishment of whatever general plan and policy may be laid down.

7. The necessity that the Commissioner of Lands should not overshadow or outshine the public services placed under his direction is a second reason why his offices should be situated at the Headquarters of the Central Administration. If, as so far suggested, the Commissioner of Lands is located in the building at present occupied by the Land Registries and State Domain services he will not only be cut off from touch with the Central Administration, but he will over-shadow the present departmental chief to the latter's natural chagrin and to the grave detriment of the proper work of them both.

Although the Survey, the Land Registries and the Settlement Organization are the services primarily entrusted with the establishment of the necessary reforms the willing and effective co-operation of other branches of the public service, more particularly of the Judicial Department and of the District Administration, has naturally also to be assumed.

6.04

CHAPTER 5.—LANDS DEPARTMENT, COMMISSIONER OF LANDS, AND SURVEY DEPARTMENT.

32. The operations of the Lands Department, the Commissioner of Lands, and the Survey Department, are closely inter-related and to some extent all these departments are under the control of the Commissioner of Lands.

34

(A) Land Registries.

33. In 1858 the Ottoman Government established a Department of Land Registries for the purpose of compiling and maintaining a record of all estates and transactions in immovable property. The record was primarily personal and not territorial. In the absence of a cadastral survey no attempt was or could be made to mark on the ground the area of land to which each transaction related. Moreover, though registration was by law compulsory, it was not in fact enforced and much land remained unregistered and was held in virtue of private and primitively drawn contracts. During the campaign in Palestine many of the registers were removed by the Turkish military authorities and the registries were closed till October, 1920, when the Land Registries Department was established, which took over all the functions of the Ottoman Department (Daftar Khakani). The present Department of Lands dates from 1922 when the Department of Land Registries and the Land Department and Land Commission, which were created in 1920 for the purpose of controlling state domains and advising the Government on matters of land policy, were amalgamated.

34. The duties of the Land Registry are to record all transactions in immovable property. The Registrar is responsible for seeing that the parties to a disposition have a good title, and all title deeds are examined and all documents evidencing transactions are prepared by thirteen district Land Registry Offices. Cases in which difficult questions arise are referred for scrutiny to the headquarters office ; as also cases where the value of the land exceeds £P.5000 if it is situated in a town, and £P.3000 if it is agricultural. The department also deals with all applications* under the Correction of Land Registers Ordinance of 1926 which provides for the investigation of the unofficial registers in which much land was recorded under the Ottoman regime, and for the incorporation of the entries in the official register of titles. The registration of a transaction or of an entry in an unofficial register does not give the person in whose name the land is registered any title to the land. It is merely evidence, which may be rebutted, of ownership. The staff of the department consists of a Director, an Assistant Director, five inspectors styled Land Officers, 16 Registrars, and 37 clerks. The cost in 1930 was £P.17,045 and the revenue amounted to £P.67,758. Most of the revenue was realized from sales of lands by Arabs to Jews, and accordingly the receipts during future years will depend very largely on the extent to which such sales continue.

---

*Except applications relating to land in villages in which settlement operations are proceeding.

35

(B) **Settlement Department.**

Objects and Procedure.

35. At present, therefore, the Land Registers do not contain records of the ownership of land throughout the country. The Turkish registers were very incomplete and even now a large number of the transactions are not registered. Accordingly in 1928 a Land Settlement Ordinance was passed for the settlement of all claims to land and the registration of titles thereto. The operations under this Ordinance fall into four stages :—

(a) *Survey.*—The lands of the villages are divided into blocks of convenient size called "registration blocks." Registration block plans are prepared and on each plan are marked the parcels claimed by individuals.

(b) *Preliminary investigation of claims.*—Assistant Settlement Officers proceed to the village, record all claims and counter-claims, ascertain from claimants and counter-claimants the grounds on which claims are based, obtain the necessary supporting documents with names of witnesses and other relevant information, and then prepare schedules of claims for the registration block which are posted in the village for a prescribed period. During this period additional claims or counter-claims may be lodged.

(c) *Final investigation of claims and deciding of disputes.*—The memoranda of claims prepared by the Assistant Settlement Officers are checked in the Settlement Office and the Settlement Officer then proceeds to the village, decides to what extent he can admit claims to which there is no counter-claim (a claim is not accepted merely because it is undisputed ; in all such cases there is a careful, indeed elaborate examination of documentary evidence) and when there is a counter-claim hears the dispute and gives his decision. The schedule of rights for each registration block is then completed and posted for the prescribed period in the village. During the period of posting, appeals against the Settlement Officer's decision may be filed in the Land Court or the District Court. The Survey Department prepares final registration block plans in accordance with the orders of the Settlement Officers.

(d) *Registration of title after the expiry of the period of posting.*—The schedule of rights with its accompanying registration block plan is forwarded to the Land Registry of the sub-district in which the village is situated and the parcels are entered in a register which is in the form associated with the name of Torrens. The person in whose name a parcel is registered is entitled to a certificate of registration and registration confers a title which is indefeasible except when it is shown that the registration was procured by fraud.

36. A good deal of the land in Palestine is held under the form of tenure known as Meshaa ; the ownership is undivided but for purposes of cultivation the land is periodically distributed amongst the owners. The Settlement Officer may partition such land if in the public interests the High Commissioner so directs, and the Commissioner of Lands has recently proposed that all Meshaa land should be partitioned during the course of settlement.

Cost.

37. The progress of settlement operations has hitherto been slow and the cost has been high. Settlement has been entirely completed in twenty villages and is proceeding in another twenty and the cost (excluding survey expenses) works out at £P·8 per 100 dunums,* for the villages so far completed. For 1931 the cost of settlement (again excluding survey expenses) will be about £20,000, or about £6 per 100 dunums for the area likely to be settled during the year. If this rate were to be maintained the settlement of all titles would not be completed under at least thirty years and the total cost on the Commissioner of Lands' estimate of the area to be settled (which however is much higher than that of Sir John Hope Simpson) would exceed £P.1,000,000. It takes time, however, to organize a new department and to train its officers, and the work of the department was seriously delayed by the riots of 1929. Moreover the Commissioner of Lands has submitted proposals which he believes will enable the work to proceed more rapidly than at present. These include :—

(1) Exclusion of the built-over area in villages in which the sites for buildings and the buildings themselves are of value and their assessment to an urban tax as in the case of towns to which the Urban Property Tax has been applied.

(2) registration in the case of the built-over area in other villages only of properties for which kushans (title deeds) are held.

(3) the speedier registration of undisputed claims to parcels. Under the procedure now in force no parcels are registered until all disputes have been decided.

(4) Substitution of a fee at a flat rate per dunum on agricultural land and at a fixed rate per parcel on built-on land instead of at an *ad valorem* rate. The computation of fees on the basis now prescribed is a slow, laborious, and costly operation.

(5) Enhanced fees in disputed cases with the object of eliminating ill-founded claims.

---

*A dunum is a quarter of an acre.

37

(6) An amendment of the Land Law which will make it unnecessary to register separately land and buildings, and eliminate the numerous disputes between heirs which the present Ottoman Law encourages.

3. On the assumption that these proposals are accepted, that the area to be settled does not exceed Sir John Hope Simpson's estimate of the cultivable area of the country, and that the number of field parties is raised from nine to eighteen, the Commissioner of Lands thinks that settlement operations might be completed by 1942 except as regards disputed claims for the hearing of which Settlement Officers would have to be retained for some years longer. The following table shows the estimated cost of settlement operations on this basis during the next eleven years :—

	£P.
1932	21,816
1933	23,717
1934	27,627
1935	29,880
1936	29,982
1937	30,582
1938	31,132
1939	31,782
1940	32,332
1941	33,032
1942	32,982

To this must be added :—

(1) The cost of the three Settlement Officers, who will be engaged after 1942 in hearing the disputed claims not decided by that date : it is impossible to estimate the number of years for which they would be required : such information as is available, however, suggests that it might be five to seven : the cost for each year will be £P.6,152 ;

(2) The cost of the survey : the Director of Surveys has submitted an estimate* which shows that the proportion of the total expenditure of this department, which is assignable to settlement operations, amounts to £P.468,000, but this sum will be reduced by £P.100,000 if proposals (1) and (2) in paragraph 37 are accepted ;

(3) The cost amounting to £P.14,000 of the additional clerks, who will be needed in the Land Registries.

On the credit side there will be the registration fees realized from successful claimants, but for reasons recorded below we do not think that they will yield a large sum.

---

*See Appendix I.

38

NEED FOR SETTLEMENT.

39. We entirely agree with the proposal of the Commissioner of Lands for the exclusion of the built-over area in the villages in which the sites for buildings and the buildings themselves are of value. As regards the built-over area in other villages it has been decided that only schedules of rights and of reputed owners should be prepared, but we can see no reason why, as the Commissioner of Lands proposed in 1929 and would still prefer, these areas should not be altogether excluded. Apart from savings on the staff of the Settlement and Land Registries Departments their exclusion would reduce the cost of the survey shown in Appendix I by £10,000. But even if the Commissioner's views on both these points and his other proposals are accepted, the expenditure to be met will still be very heavy; and the question arises whether it is likely to be justified by the benefits which the settlement will bring in its train. In our discussions with him, the Commissioner of Lands laid stress on the stimulus to the development of land which is said to be hampered by the lack of an accurate record of title. We are not impressed by this argument. The returns supplied by the Lands Department show that every month considerable areas of land are being bought and sold. The sales are not confined to whole villages owned by a single individual; they include portions of villages and estates. It seems clear, therefore, that an owner desirous of selling or mortgaging part of his land can, through the agency of the Lands Department, give a title which in practice at any rate will be regarded as satisfactory. Moreover, the argument, even if valid, would apply only to the plains. Increased facilities for sales and mortgages will do nothing to promote the development of the hill areas; what this part of the country needs is co-operative societies and demonstration plots. There are, however, other and more cogent reasons for completing the settlement. In the first place, disputes regarding land which are a fruitful source of village affrays and litigation will be greatly reduced; secondly, the settlement provides the only satisfactory means of partitioning the Meshaa land and of re-partitioning the land in Mafruz (divided) villages, where the distribution of the parcels is prejudicial to good cultivation. The existence of the Meshaa tenure has been justly described as perhaps the greatest obstacle to agricultural progress. The fellahin are intelligent and industrious, but no cultivator will manure or improve a holding which in a few years will be transferred to another man. Partition can at present be carried out on the application of a shareholder under the orders of a Magistrate, but the cost to the shareholder is exceedingly heavy and applications, therefore, are few. In the Ramleh sub-district we understand that some villages have been unofficially partitioned and not unsuccessfully owing to the active interest taken in the matter by the Area Officer. But Assistant District Commissioners and District Officers, even if invested with powers of compulsion, cannot spare the time necessary for the partitioning of large Meshaa

areas. Moreover, in the Mafruz villages the need for repartitioning is not confined to a few villages. In most of these villages the plots of individuals are scattered throughout the village or consist of long narrow strips which it is impossible to cultivate properly. Without special agency the cultivable area cannot be partitioned on sound principles and the Settlement Officers are clearly the most suitable that can be provided.

CHANGE IN PROCEDURE PROPOSED.

40. We think, however, that the cost of the settlement can be substantially reduced by a change in procedure. Under the Registration of Land Ordinance of 1929, the Settlement Officer grants only a possessory title in certain cases, namely :—

(1) Where the registered owner cannot be traced or makes no claim ;

(2) where the land is registered in the name of one person but another person is in possession in such circumstances that if his possession continues for the period prescribed by law, an action for recovery by the registered owner will be barred.

Thereafter the person registered as owner can recover the land by an action brought within due time, and the rights of persons who are prevented by minority or absence from asserting their claims, are also safeguarded. Subject to such rights and if no action is brought by the registered owner, the person to whom the possessory title has been given is registered as the owner of the land. We suggest that in all cases only possessory titles should be granted, and that the procedure should be as follows :—In a Mafruz (divided) village an undisputed claim should be accepted without enquiry and the claimant should be given a possessory title for the land claimed ; if a claim is disputed, the dispute should be decided on the basis of possession, that is, the claimant who can show that he is in possession of the land in dispute should be registered with a possessory title ; and if for any reason possession cannot be ascertained the Settlement Officer should determine by a summary enquiry the person who is *prima facie* entitled to be in possession and grant him a possessory title. In a Meshaa village undisputed claims to shares should similarly be accepted without enquiry, and when the land is partitioned, the claimant should be given a possessory title for the land assigned to the share claimed ; in the event of a dispute the Settlement Officer should grant a possessory title for the land assigned to a share or shares to the claimant or claimants who can show by the fact of cultivation or by the receipt of rents that he (or they) is (or are) in possession of land corresponding to the shares claimed ; and if for any reason a dispute cannot be settled on this basis, the Settlement Officer should determine by summary enquiry

40

the person or persons *prima facie* entitled to be regarded as owners and grant them possessory titles for the land assigned on partition to the shares in dispute. Thereafter it would be open to any person who claimed the land to bring an action within the period prescribed by law, namely, ten years. But if no such action were brought within due time or subsequently by a person who had a lawful excuse such as minority or absence from the country, the possessory title would become absolute. It is estimated that in 80 per cent. of the claims that are presented there is no dispute ; that in 10 per cent. the dispute is merely regarding boundaries. In only 10 per cent. of the cases is there a real dispute and even of these disputes a substantial proportion are such as would never be brought before the Land Courts. It is safe, therefore, to assume that after the lapse of ten years all but a small fraction of the possessory titles would become absolute.

41. The objections raised against this procedure are :—

(1) That it would make impossible the partition of Meshaa land because in Meshaa villages what is owned is a share and not a particular piece of land.

We are quite unable to follow this argument. It is true that in a Meshaa village what is owned is not a piece of land but a share. But our proposal is not that a possessory title should be granted for a share, but that such a title should be granted for the land assigned on partition to a share. It is also said that claims to additional shares not taken into account in making the partition may be established after the settlement and if that is so, the partition will have to be revised ; but this contingency could be met by providing that claims to additional shares shall be satisfied by monetary compensation from the other owners. This is the remedy provided in Section 60 of the Land Settlement Ordinance when a person succeeds in proving that an entry in the register which cannot be rectified has been obtained by fraud ; and the Commissioner of Lands informed us that an unofficial partition carried out in advance of settlement, which was found by the Settlement Officer to be acceptable, would not be upset because of any additional claims that might be established before him.

(2) That the rights of minors or absentees might be prejudiced.

It is perhaps open to doubt whether under the present procedure also the rights of such persons will not sometimes be overlooked. But, however that may be, we think that this objection is met by our proposal that an action should not be barred by the lapse of time if the complainant can show that he was prevented from bringing it by minority, or absence from the country, or some other lawful excuse.

41

(3) That possessory titles will not be acceptable to the people, more particularly those persons whose lands are already registered in the Land Registries, and that they will therefore decline to co-operate in the settlement proceedings.

It is in our judgment in the last degree improbable that the villagers will take up this attitude. Registration in the Land Registry of land which has not come under settlement does not confer a title. It is merely evidence which may be and sometimes is rebutted. On the other hand, a possessory title would ensure possession of the land unless and until another person established his ownership by an action in the Land Courts; in any such action the person holding a possessory title would be in the position of defendant, and it is on the other party that the burden of proving ownership would rest.

We are unable therefore to see that the procedure which we propose is open to any serious objection.

Cost of New Procedure.

42. The pace at which settlement can proceed is conditioned not only by the procedure of the Settlement Officers but by the out-turn of registration block plans. We are unable to say to what extent by training more men it would be possible for the Survey Department to increase the out-turn, and it may be that the increase could only be secured by a somewhat larger expenditure than a programme spread over a longer period would involve. It is so important that settlement should be accelerated that some additional expenditure on the survey and staff would be justified. But our recommendation will at any rate reduce very substantially the work of the settlement parties since it eliminates the elaborate examination of documents and evidence in undisputed cases and provides, in cases of dispute, for summary inquiry. We are unable to estimate the cost of the staff that will be required if the settlement is carried out on the lines which we have proposed. That can be determined only in the light of experience of the procedure suggested by us. But at any rate it should be possible to complete the settlement by the end of 1942 if not earlier and at an annual cost that will not exceed and may be less than that provided in the Estimates for the current year. There will remain the charges for survey, which will not be less than £P.368,000. This is a large sum, but so far as we can see no appreciable economies under this head are practicable; and against the total expenditure on settlement may fairly be set the excess of income over expenditure, at present £P.50,000 annually, in the Lands Department. The settlement was undertaken in order to complete and correct the registers maintained by the Lands Department which took over the duties of the Ottoman Land Registry; it would have been unnecessary if the Land Registers had contained a full and accurate record of titles to land.

42

Order of Settlement Operations.

43. Mr. Strickland has recommended that the undivided villages should be settled before those which have been legally divided. Whilst agreeing with this recommendation, we think that the areas in which the villages wholly or partly Meshaa are most numerous should be given priority over all others. In villages unofficially partitioned the distribution of the holdings leaves much to be desired but it is at any rate better than in the Meshaa land. Meshaa villages are scattered and time and money would be lost if the settlement parties were required to proceed from one Meshaa village to another; but the parts of the country in which they are chiefly found should be taken in hand as soon as the settlement has been completed in the area where the Settlement Officers are now working.

Fees.

44. Registration and survey fees are at present assessed on an *ad valorem* basis. The following table shows the fees which have become payable in three villages in the Jaffa sub-district.

Village.	Area in dunums.	No. of parcels.	Registration fees payable on settlement. £P.	Survey fees on settlement. £P.	Commuted tithe. £P.	Werko. £P.	Animal tax. £P.
Yazur	22,424	2,680	1·044	812	1·691	494·270	11·082
Salame	13,041	1,790	1·221	378	2·219	657·270	16·475
Beit Dagan	19,427	951	1·069	285	2·581	907·120	16·19[4]

It will be seen that the sums due are very large amounting in the case of Yazur to more than the annual tithe. If fees continue to be assessed on this scale and are realized they will cover a large part of the combined cost of the Survey and Settlement Departments. So far, at any rate in the Jaffa sub-district, no attempt to collect them has been made. When we visited the Jaffa district offices we found that the clerks had been unable to cope with, had indeed abandoned, the task of compiling from the schedules of claims the sums due from each owner. This appears to have been due to a mechanical defect which no doubt is not insuperable. But it is quite certain that an attempt to realize these fees would provoke great resentment and opposition; they are in fact beyond the capacity of the villagers to pay. The fall in prices has made it difficult to collect the tithe, and even before the fall the agricultural population were heavily taxed. The report of the Johnson-Crosbie Committee shows that the net income to owner-cultivators in the Arab villages on 100 dunums of land is only £P.25. Even a much reduced fee therefore would involve great hardship. The Commissioner of Lands suggested last November that only nominal fees or none at all should be charged. We think that in undisputed cases this is the only course practicable. In disputed cases the fees should be as at present those charged in possessory actions in the Magistrates Courts. If only possessory titles are given the higher scale in force in the Land Courts cannot, even if it were possible to collect it, be levied, but we suggest that an effort should be made to collect such fees by means of a Court fee stamp at the time of hearing. Since the object of the settlement is to register all land it is not possible to refuse to hear a claim because the fee is not paid in advance. Parties might however be encouraged to do so by imposing an enhanced fee on successful claimants if the fee were not so paid.

POST SETTLEMENT REGISTRATIOn.

45. If the settlement is to be of permanent value it is essential that all subsequent dispositions and successions should be registered. It is proposed to ensure this (1) by the charging of low fees*; (2) by making invalid and penalizing all unregistered dispositions; (3) by making it obligatory for heirs and legatees to register land within a year of the death of the proprietor; (4) by requiring the Sharia Courts to send copies of succession certificates to the Land Registries; (5) by rewarding persons who bring to light any such dispositions. We do not believe that these measures alone will suffice. It has not been the practice of the people to register successions and there is a long-standing prejudice dating from the Ottoman regime against registration which it may take generations to overcome. In addition to penalties and awards, there must, we think, be an agency charged with the duty of reporting all successions and transactions.

46. It will not be possible to impose this duty on the already overburdened Mukhtar, and we see therefore no alternative to the appointment for a village or group of villages of an official corresponding to the Indian village accountant.† Moreover, there are other and very strong reasons for appointing such a staff. Mr. Strickland has pointed out that in its absence it will be very difficult to carry out his scheme for liquidating the debts of the cultivators. Sir John Hope Simpson has recommended that occupancy rights should be conferred on tenants. There is no reform more urgently needed. Although accurate figures are not available, the Commissioner of Lands believes that about half the land is cultivated by tenants. Rents are already very high, usually 40 per cent. of the gross produce, and the increase of the population which is rapid will drive them still higher. It will be useless to relieve the tenants of their debts or to

---

*We agree that low fees are desirable in settled areas. The reduction in receipts will be offset, it is anticipated, by the registration of more numerous transactions. But we see no case for reducing the registration fees in advance of settlement, nor, indeed, is this contemplated.

†*See* on this point Mr. Strickland's Report, pages 42 and 43.

44

improve methods of cultivation if the only result is to enable the landlords to extract higher rents. And if occupancy rights are to be conferred provision must be made not only for the compilation but for the maintenance of a register of tenants. The cost of a staff of village accountants will not be very great. Allowing for the large area cultivated by owners and the Jewish Agency land for which no register is required, on the average one village accountant should be able to maintain the registers of three or four villages ; the total cost should therefore not exceed £P.14,000 per annum, and against this must be set the extra registration and Sharia Court fees which will eventually be realized.

(c) **Commissioner of Lands, Director of the Lands Department, and their Staff.**

47. Apart from settlement operations the Commissioner of Lands is responsible :—

(a) for the assessment of the Urban Property Tax which has replaced in all municipal areas the Turkish Werko (House and Land Tax) : it is anticipated that the assessment will have been completed in all the towns by the end of this year after which only annual revisions will be required ;

(b) for the demarcation and transfer of State Domains in the Beisan sub-district : this work, too, will be finished before long ;

(c) for the fiscal survey of all rural lands which is being carried out for the purpose of replacing the tithe and werko by a land tax : this involves the survey of all agricultural land, its division in each village into fiscal blocks of approximately equal productivity, and the valuation of each block : it is hoped that the survey will be completed for the plains by the end of 1932 and for the hill areas by the end of 1933.

48. At present there are two officers both in Class 2 who are in charge of the assessments under the Urban Property Tax ; one of them, however, is mainly engaged on the fiscal survey. It is intended, we understand, that both should be retained after the completion of the survey as inspectors of the Urban Property Tax assessments, though the appointment of one is eventually to be made a Class 3 post. We cannot see that the annual revisions of this tax necessitate the employment of two inspectors. We consider that for this purpose one inspector in Class 3 should suffice.

49. There will also, in our opinion, be no justification when the fiscal survey has been completed for retaining in addition to the Commissioner of Lands, a Director of the Lands Department. The annual revisions of the Urban Property Tax involve only routine references to the Commissioner and a wholetime officer is not needed for the supervision of three Settlement Officers and their staff.

45

The officer holding the post of Commissioner of Lands should take over the work of the Director of the Lands Department ; for the detailed inspection of the land registers there is an adequate staff of inspectors ; and the general supervision and control of this Department will not add unduly to the task of the Commissioner of Lands.

50. The Assistant Director of the Lands Department is at present mainly occupied in representing the Government in cases in which the Government claims to be the owner of land before the Settlement and Land Courts. The Attorney-General has now undertaken to relieve him of this work which is clearly not part of the duties of his post. He will then be employed at headquarters in the examination of the more difficult cases referred by the Registrars. As he will have no administrative duties and is not qualified to act for the Commissioner of Lands if and when that officer assumes charge of the Department, a salary of £P.750–950 appears to us excessive. We do not suggest a reduction of the pay of the officer now holding the post but we recommend that when he retires the post of Assistant Director be abolished and that in its place a third post of Land Officer be created, if the volume of work is then more than two Lands Officers can deal with.

6.05

**HIGH COMMISSIONER FOR PALESTINE,
JERUSALEM.**

C O N F I D E N T I A L.

REFERENCE NO. CF/225/31.   24 October, 1931.

Sir,

      I have the honour to refer to Part I, Chapter 5, paragraphs 32 to 50, of the Report of the Financial Commission regarding the Lands Department, the Commissioner of Lands and the Survey Department.

Enclosures I and II.

  2.   After considering in Executive Council the recommendations of the Financial Commission together with the observations submitted thereon by the Commissioner of Lands, copies of which are attached hereto, I have reached the following conclusions:

    (1) that the built-over area in villages in which the sites for buildings and the buildings themselves are of value should be excluded from settlement operations;

    (2) that the built-over area in villages in which the sites for buildings and the buildings themselves are not of value should be excluded from settlement operations;

The Right Honourable J.H. Thomas, P.C., M.P.,
  His Majesty's Principal Secretary of State
                   for the Colonies.

2

(3) that consideration of the Commission's recommendation that Settlement Officers should grant only possessory titles in all cases that come before them should be deferred until the return from leave of Mr. Drayton.

Mr. Drayton is due to return to duty on the 7th November.

(4) that claims to additional shares in _meshaa_ land which are not taken into account when the _meshaa_ land is partitioned, but which are subsequently established, should be settled by the payment of monetary compensation to the claimant by the other co-owners of the _meshaa_ land;

(5) that land settlement operations should be accelerated, and that additional expenditure on survey and staff would on this account be justified if funds are available;

(6) that acceptance of the recommendation of the Commission that areas in which villages wholly or partly _meshaa_ predominate should be given priority of settlement would, as explained by the Commissioner of Lands, disorganise the regular programme of settlement operations and would not therefore be conducive to efficiency and that the recommendation should consequently be rejected;

(7) that the fees for registration and survey in connection with settlement should in all cases be nominal;

3

(8) that fees for the hearing of disputed cases should be as proposed by the Commission in paragraph 44 of their Report if only possessory titles are given, but should be as those charged in the Land Court if indefeasible titles are given.

A decision as to which of these alternatives should be adopted must be deferred until a decision is taken on the question of the type of title which should be granted by Settlement Officers.

(9) that the Commission's recommendation that fees should be collected by a Court Fee stamp at the time of hearing of the case is impracticable and must be rejected;

(10) that the Commission's recommendation that an enhanced fee be imposed on successful claimants if the prescribed fee is not paid at the time of hearing is impracticable and must be rejected;

(11) that the system of village accountant should be established as an experimental measure in areas where settlement has been completed, but that the title "village accountant" is not appropriate to the duties which it is intended to impose upon these officers;

(12) that consideration of the proposed abolition of the two posts of Officers Class 2 employed on inspection of Urban Property Tax assessments and fiscal survey should be deferred until the fiscal survey is completed;

4

(13) that a decision on the question of the amalgamation of the Lands Department and Land Settlement cannot usefully be taken until land settlement has progressed considerably;

(14) that the recommendation of the Commission for the abolition of the post of Assistant Director of Lands, on the retirement of the present holder, should be given consideration at a later date when the occasion for filling this post arises.

3.   I shall address you further in due course when a decision is taken on the points referred to in sub-paragraphs (3) and (8) of the foregoing paragraph.

        I have the honour to be,
          Sir,
        Your most obedient,
          humble servant,

OFFICER ADMINISTERING THE GOVERNMENT.

Enclosure I

Observations on the recommendations
on Land Settlement in the Report of
the O'Donnell Commission Chap. 8
Middle East No. 43 Confidential.

The reasons for the institution of the operations of settlement of title, commonly known as Land Settlement, and a description of the situation which it was devised to alleviate are to be found in the Secretariat files for 1932 and onwards; in the reports submitted by Sir Ernest Dowson during the same period; and in the minutes of conferences held in the office of His Excellency the High Commissioner when the reports of Sir Ernest Dowson were under consideration.

2. The objects of the Ottoman Land Code and of subsequent legislation and of the Ottoman laws of Registration briefly summarised are :-

 (a) A record of ownership, proprietorship and all other rights to land, including mortgages, leases, servitudes and charges;

 (b) A record to form the basis of taxation of land and of obtaining revenue from fees on dispositions; and

 (c) the economic and agricultural development of land from security of tenure based on titles correctly recorded and kept up to date.

3. The objects which it was hoped to attain by registration of title unfortunately were not realised owing among other reasons to the absence

/of any

- 2 -

of any cadastral survey. Because of the absence of any survey, property boundaries were inadequately described and areas of parcels were almost invariably incorrect. Property boundaries were described by the names of the owners of adjacent properties or by some topographical feature such as a tree or a stream which might disappear or change its course, or simply by a hill, or mountain, or watershed divide. It is therefore apparent that no real record existed of the correct boundaries of parcels. This was and still is the cause of quarrels and fights in the villages and of litigation in the courts.

To avoid the payment of registration fees and to evade the payment of VIRKO in many cases dispositions and successions were not registered, so that in course of time the records in the Registers no longer accorded with the facts of ownership.

The record was primarily personal and not territorial and the method of keeping the Registers was in itself confusing as they were not kept village by village on a block or other simple system, but chronologically by village or group of villages. As a result, when an old kushan is presented in support of a claim, long and tedious search must be made among a multitude of records in order to ascertain whether it is the certificate of the last entry or not.

The Land Registers were also rendered of doubtful trustworthiness by the corruption of the officials dealing with transactions previous to and during the Great War and by the loss of many records.

/The

- 3 -

The intention of the Ottoman Government not to permit the continuation of the MUSHA' system had not been carried out. It should be noted that under the Ottoman Code, according to certain authorities, MUSHA' ownership is not a recognised legal form of tenure, although by long custom it had become an established tenure which the Ottoman Government however was desirous to put an end to.

4. Such in general were the reasons why such records as existed were not in so many cases a basis for title or security of tenure, why they could not continue to be used by the Palestine Government as the system of recording transactions or as a basis for the taxation of land and why the economic and agricultural development of land was impeded. On the other hand thousands of persons and many companies, prior to the War and since the re-opening of the Land Registers in 1920, had paid fees and had kept up their records of ownership title and other rights and held full ownership kushans.

5. This was the situation which existed before the institution of Land Settlement based on the block system of cadastral survey and Land Registry records on a territorial system. It should be noted that the objects of Land Settlement are in fact the same as the fundamental objects of the Ottoman Land Code and of the laws of Registration and that in reality no change has been introduced into the substantive laws of the country by the Land Settlement Ordinances. Even the Registration

/of

- 4 -

of Land Ordinance 1929, which is only for application in villages under "Settlement", is merely in the nature of a law of procedure.

6.   Where Settlement operations have been effected, complete Registration Block and parcel plans exist and the New Registers show all rights to a parcel whether of ownership, mortgage, registrable lease, servitude, attachment or other registrable interest.

In the villages already settled, the quarrels formerly so common in respect of interests in land have been reduced to such an extent that they are almost non-existent; and the same is true of litigation before the Magistrates and Land Courts in respect of such areas, with the exception, I believe, of actions in the nature of breach of contract in respect of "private" sales not accepted during settlement operations by judicial decision of the Settlement Officer.

MUSHA' lands have been divided and the provisions for the elimination of parcels below a certain minimum of broadth or area have been applied.

An important result of these operations can be seen in the development of the lands of "settled" villages and in a comparison of their present condition with their former, or with the lands of villages which have not yet been settled.

7.   The authors of the O'Donnell Report have apparently given undue prominence to matters which were mentioned by me more or less incidentally and which they refer to as points on which I laid stress, which was by no means the case. In the two or three conversations which I had with them, we

/discussed

discussed the details of the operations and procedure of Land Settlement rather than its objects or fundamental principles.

8. Judging from their recommendations in paragraphs 40 and 41 of their report, it would seem that they either knew little of, or have disregarded, the Ottoman Land Code which is still the substantive law of the country in regard to immovable property, and that they have not given due regard to the system of land tenure in Palestine; to the Ottoman laws of Registration, and to the Ottoman method of implementing those laws whereby thousands of ownership, not possessory, titles are now held by many persons and companies. They appear to ignore the existing laws pertaining to succession, and the necessity to record not only ownership but also mortgages, leases, servitudes, and other interests in the Registers.

9. If the suggestions in the Report were adopted, confusion would become worse confounded, litigation would increase beyond its already ample bounds and the effect on the economic and agricultural life of the country would be more disastrous than if no settlement of title of any kind had been attempted by the Palestine Government, and if the land registers had continued to show only records of such transactions as might happen to be brought on to them in the incomplete manner in which they were formerly recorded.

10. The proposals in the Report may be briefly summarised as follows :-

/(a)

- 6 -

(a) Basing themselves on the Registration of Land Ordinance, 1929, the authors suggest that, in what is known as MAFRUZ, and is referred to in the Land Settlement Ordinances as "divided land", the result of land settlement operations should be the issue of possessory titles;

(b) in what is known as village MUSHA', or land held in common by the inhabitants of the village, they suggest :-

  (i) Possessory titles should be issued for shares in MUSHA';

  (ii) the partition of the MUSHA' should be effected on the basis of these possessory titles; and

  (iii) when partition has been effected, possessory titles should be issued for the parcels resulting from the partition.

11. The methods suggested by them for ascertaining the persons to whom possessory titles are to be given, briefly described, are :-

(a) Where a claim is made by a person to land or a share in land and it is not disputed, the claim should be accepted without enquiry;

(b) where a claim in MAFRUZ is disputed, the person who can show that he is in possession of the land in dispute should be given a possessory title. If for any reason possession is not clearly evident, a summary inquiry should be held to determine who is PRIMA FACIE entitled to be in possession and a possessory title should be granted to him;

/(c)

- 7 -

(c) where a claim to a share or shares in MUSHA' is disputed, a possessory title should be granted for the land assigned to the share or shares to the person who can show by the fact of cultivation, or by the receipt of rent, that he is in possession of land corresponding to the share claimed. If a dispute cannot be settled on this basis a summary enquiry should be held to determine the person PRIMA FACIE entitled to be regarded as owner of the share or shares and he should be granted a possessory title to the land assigned on partition as equivalent to the shares in dispute; and

(d) while agreeing with a recommendation of Mr. Strickland that MUSHA' villages should be settled before MAFRUZ villages, they think that such parts of the country in which the villages wholly or partly MUSHA' are most numerous should be given priority in settlement.

12. Their suggestions would introduce no essential change in the work of the Survey Department and the present system, which in its main features is as follows would remain :-

(a) Village lands would be divided into Registration blocks by the Department of Surveys;

(b) parcels as demarcated by claimants would be surveyed;

/(c)

- 8 -

 (c) provisional Registration Block plans would be prepared showing the mosaic of parcels within the block, with a list of the persons who claim to be the owners of the parcels demarcated x and surveyed; and

 (d) on completion of enquiries by the Settlement staff and decision by the Settlement Officers of any dispute as to who was or should be in possession, the provisional block plans, amended where necessary in respect of parcel boundaries in accordance with the decisions of the Settlement Officers, would be returned to the Department of Surveys to prepare the final plans.

13. The work of the Settlement staff would be :-

 (a) Examination of parcels on the ground and of the claims of persons to rights thereto;

 (b) compilation of a list of persons as "in possession";

 (c) in the case of a dispute, the settlement of the dispute as to possession, by summary enquiry;

 (d) the checking and revision, if needed, of Registration Block plans and the return of these revised plans to the Director of Surveys for the completion of final plans;

/(e)

- 9 -

(e) preparation of a Schedule to form the basis of entries in the Land Register containing the following details :-

    Registration Block number.

    Parcel number.

    Area of parcel.

    Name of possessor.

    Shares of possessors, if more than one.

    Amount of Survey fee payable.

    Amount of Registration fee payable.

    Amount of fee payable for hearing an action in case of a dispute where the possessor, as decided by the Settlement Officer, had not already paid the hearing fee;

(f) forwarding of the Schedule to the Land Registrar for registration in the Land Registers and for issue of Certificates of possessory title; and

(g) as regard MUSHA', the work of the surveyors and of the "Settlement" staff, in addition to that set forth above, would remain from the point of view of technical procedure essentially in details what it is at present, but the basis of partition would not be a full title to shares neither would full title be granted in respect of the parcels resulting from partition. Both in the case of shares in MUSHA' which for any reason may not be partitioned, and of parcels resulting from partition, only possessory titles would be granted and registered.

/14.

- 10 -

14. In the case of both MAF UZ, and MUSHA' partitioned as a part of settlement operations, the possessory title, if undisputed, in the courts, would ripen into a full title on the expiration of the prescriptive periods for the various categories of land.

15. The merits and advantages of the system may be summarised as follows :-

(a) It would provide a accurate plans, block by block, of the mosaic of parcels at the time of settlement;

(b) in actions in the courts, in respect of land in the villages completed under the system, accurate plans would be available of any parcel in dispute showing its relation to the other parcels in the block or vicinity;

(c) it would replace the present unsatisfactory system of describing in the old Registers the boundaries of parcels by the names of adjacent owners, or by physical or topographical features, often of a temporary or ill-defined nature, such as a tomb, a stone wall, a track, a rock, a mountain, a hill, a valley, a watershed, or a sand dune;

(d) after the period defined by law, a full ownership title would automatically come into force in the absence of judicial action in the interval;

/(e)

- 11 -

    (e) it would confer possessory titles on persons who now have no title of any kind;

    (f) physical partition of MUSHA' land would be made and the shape and size of parcels would be controlled. The partition of MUSHA' based on possessory titles to shares and with only possessory titles for the resultant parcels may possibly be thought an improvement over the land remaining unpartitioned;

    (g) with a temporary increase in Survey and Land Registry staff, settlement on the basis of possessory titles could be more rapidly extended over the whole country than under the present system and at less cost than on the basis of full title.

16. But it is also necessary to examine the implications of the system, the difficulties it would leave unsolved and the objections, legal, economic, practical and political, inherent in the system, or which might reasonably be brought against it.

17. A fundamental point in the system is that a possessory title for physical property would be granted for a certain period and this title in due course, in the absence of legal action against it in the interval, would ripen into a full title.

But the authors of the Report have not defined what they mean by the term "possessory title". It would appear that they have used it in the sense

/in

- 12 -

in the sense in which it is used in the Registration of Land Ordinance 1939. They appear to have overlooked the exceptional nature and the essential purpose of that Ordinance in so far as the grant of possessory title is concerned, which is to grant a person in possession of land as a reputed owner some sort of title better than no title at all, and to make this title ripen into a full title in due course, <u>while at the same time protecting the rights of the registered owner</u>.

18. It should be noted that that Ordinance does not alter the substantive law of the country, but that it is in reality a law of procedure in Settlement operations.

The authors of the Report however would appear to go further and in effect suspend the law of the country in all cases for a period and then have it come into full force again.

If they mean anything else than this by "possessory title" they have not said so and if they do, it would be necessary to alter the fundamental laws of land tenure. In either event the existing rights of owners having full title would be so greatly jeopardised as to render them almost valueless.

19. The authors of the Report appear to deal with land and houses in the physical sense and only with possessory rights thereto. But the Land Code and other land legislation refer to other rights such as mortgages, leases, servitudes, attachments, and the position of occupants of Waqf and Government land. It would appear that these rights,

/about

- 13 -

about which there are as many disputes and as much necessity for settlement and registration on a satisfactory basis as there are in respect of ownership, would either be extinguished or remain in an ambiguous and perilous state.

20. The objections to their suggestions may be more specifically summarised as follows :-

    (a) Whereas the Registration of Land Ordinance, 1929 was enacted as a law of procedure to be used in exceptional cases and in limited circumstances and did not alter the substantive law, their suggestions, if carried into effect, would reverse the situation and the measure which was introduced for exceptional cases would be made the rule, while the substantive law would be applied exceptionally or be in abeyance.

    (b) In "Settlement" villages ownership rights would be ignored by the Settlement Officers and only possessory rights regarded, while in respect of land in adjoining villages which did not happen to be under "Settlement" the Land Courts would acknowledge and grant full ownership titles in actions brought before them.

    (c) Several sets of Registers would have to be maintained concurrently. In areas not settled, the old Registers would remain in force. When the areas were settled under the system suggested, the new Registers would contain a record

- 14 -

of possession only, while the old Registers which would have to be maintained would contain a confused and incomplete record of ownership, mortgages, leases and other rights, as they now do. Then on the expiration of the prescriptive period presumably still newer Registers would be compiled to show the ownership status then existing.

It would then mean also the establishment of some settlement procedure in order to get all other rights then existing, other than ownership, on to the new and final Registers. In other words, the position would be more complicated than it now is and the evil day of dealing with the tangle would have been merely postponed;

(d) persons who are now registered as owners and who hold ownership Kushans, would in effect lose their ownership rights and become possessors only for a period of years. Holders of registered mortgages, leases, servitudes, attachments etc. would not and could not have them registered in the new possessory Registers. In other words, their rights would be extinguished for at least a period and, if they wished to maintain them, they would presumably have to have recourse to the Courts;

(e) the courts, which are already congested with actions, based on the existing (old) Registers, would be overburdened with additional actions arising from gaps in

/the

- 15 -

the new possessory Registers, the decisions of which would necessarily be given at some rather remote date. The congestion of the courts would also act to the prejudice of the actions of a BONA FIDE nature, not caused by or arising out of "Settlement" under the suggested system, in that decisions on such actions would be indefinitely delayed;

(f) rights to mortgages, leases, servitudes, attachments etc. now unregistered and now being officially recorded as a part of "Settlement" procedure would be unprovided for. The de facto holders of such rights would have to have recourse to the courts or continue to rely on unregistered documents or their prowess or influence in quarrels and disputes;

(g) a similar state of affairs would exist in respect of new mortgages, leases, etc. which persons may desire to effect. The Registration of Land Ordinance 1929, specifically and rightly, prohibits the holder of a possessory title from effecting mortgages and leases, because the land is registered in the name of another and the prescriptive period has not passed;

(h) if only possessory titles were granted, the registration of any mortgages, leases, etc. would be impossible, in addition to not being provided for in the suggested

/system

- 16 -

system, and the public finding little or no value in such a title universally applied, would not be inclined to register dispositions based on succession and could not register sales, or transfers other than by succession. Unofficial transfers and transactions would continue at an increased rate and volume. At the end of the period of prescription, the Registers of possessory title would not represent even a record of possession as it would then exist in fact;

(i) the issue of only a possessory title to land assigned on partition of MUSH' would not be sufficient inducement to the possessor to invest money and labour in developing the parcel, so that although by lapse of time his title would become that of ownership, the object of partition would be defeated during the periods of prescription;

(j) the difficulties which at present exist in regard to succession would be considerably increased. After the decease of a person his estate is divided among his heirs. Under the Law the majority of land estates are not subject to dispositions by will. The rights of heirs are defined by the Law of Inheritance to which the idea of "possession", in the sense underlying the O'Donnell suggestions, is foreign. If a "Miri" estate is to be inherited, not in accordance with a share in the ownership or title as defined by the Law of

/Inheritance

- 17 -

Inheritance, but only based on the fact of possession, an increase of quarrels and fights and of litigation must be expected, because no heir would allow another heir to assume, or remain in, possession, thus creating a "title" in his favour to the detriment of the other heirs. Each heir would quite naturally endeavour to secure physical possession of the estate;

(k) there would be increasing loss of revenue to Government by reason of the impossibility of persons to register transfers, the difficulty of registering succession, and the impossibility to register mortgages and leases;

(l) if persons have paid fees under the prevailing system for the registration of title to ownership and other interests in land, it would be unfair to them to replace those titles by titles of less value and to ignore in any way the validity of the record of any other rights registered in their favour, or to burden them with the necessity of litigation or other costly proceedings in order to maintain or re-establish their rights;

(m) mortgages and leases, if made at all, would be made outside the registers. Mortgagees having little real security, would demand higher rates of interest or larger penalties for breach of contract.

/The

- 18 -

The leasing value of land because of the insecurity of title, or the absence of title so far as the actual lessor may be concerned, would be diminished;

(n) the economic and agricultural development of the country would be impeded owing to the insecurity of title and uncertainty of tenure. The mortgage banks and companies, colonization associations, the Jewish National Fund, the Waqf Authorities, landlords and others in a position to grant or receive mortgages, make leases, and in other ways provide for the development of their land, would be paralysed. The whole credit system, in so far as the land is concerned would probably collapse;

(o) the effect on public security would be detrimental, as family, factional, and inter-village quarrels would continue, in contrast to the absence of such in villages already settled under the Settlement Ordinances, 1928-1930;

(p) in the case of Waqf lands, Jewish National Fund lands, and Government "Jiftliks", it is not clear who would be recorded as the possessor. It could not be assumed that the Government, Jewish National Fund, and Waqf Administration would be content with possessory titles for what they already fully own, and it is not clear how the position of the tenants would be regulated or how it could be set forth in a Register of possessory title only, so as to give

/a

- 19 -

a feeling of security as regards occupation rights of land, or ownership rights of buildings and trees not owned or claimed by the Government, Jewish National Fund, or Waqf Administration;

(q) the difficulty of carrying out a development scheme would be considerably increased for it is surely advisable, before incurring expenditure, to know what all the rights pertaining to the land or lands effected by the development scheme are, and not merely the "possessory rights" in whatever sense of the term that expression may be used;

(r) notwithstanding the optimism of the authors in paragraph 41(3) of their Report, it is extremely unlikely that the public would co-operate in a procedure of Settlement which would impair existing ownership titles, would grant only possessory titles, would adversely affect succession rights, and would render the registration of mortgages, leases, etc. impossible.

21. The operations of Land Settlement, as at present conducted, have met with the approval of all classes and sects in the country. The economic, political and other effects of its substitution by the system suggested in the O'Donnell Commission Report should be taken into careful consideration before that system is looked upon with a view to adoption. If its adoption is seriously considered, it is

/suggested

- 20 -

suggested that the opinion of representative men in all walks of life, and in all the organizations interested in land, should first be consulted.

22.   It is agreed however that, if possible, the system of Settlement operations should be revised in order that the operations may proceed more rapidly and therefore with less expenditure of time and money. Had the practice in the early days of Settlement operations in Yazur and Zarnuka been continued, settlement operations would have proceeded more rapidly than has actually been the case.

It was advised however, at the time that the Administrative Instructions were being prepared, that in undisputed claims all documents must be produced in support of the claims and that they must be carefully checked and investigated before such claims could be favourably decided. A claim could not be accepted merely because it was undisputed; in all cases there must be a careful, indeed elaborate, examination of documentary evidence.

This necessitated a minute and careful checking in the field and in the Settlement Offices.

Had this not been advised as imperatively necessary, greater progress would have been made in Settlement operations. The attention of Government has been drawn to this both verbally and in reports.

23.   A simpler procedure which would enable the attainment of the objects of Land Settlement much more speedily than is possible at present and therefore at less cost, should be adopted.

24.   In the first place it should not be forgotten

/that

that the purpose of Land Settlement is to obtain on the Registers a record of all the rights pertaining to land or any share or interest in land.

25. The procedure in outline would remain as it is at present but in the case of undisputed claims it would not be obligatory on the Settlement Field Staff to demand proofs of succession from remote ancestors and an elaborate examination of documentary evidence in support of claims.

The Memorandum of Claim would remain essentially in its present form except that the term "supporting documents" would be amended to "supporting documents presented". All documents in possession of claimants in support of the claims would be collected, not necessarily for the purpose of verifying the claims, but because it is better to have all old Kushans, Certificates of Registration etc. collected rather than to leave them in the hands of persons who may base specious litigation on them in future. But even where documents were not presented, if the claim forms were fully completed in public, sworn to by the claimants and certified as correct by the Village Settlement Committee, then the claims, if undisputed, would not be subject to a meticulous investigation in the sense of "investigation" as used by the Acting Attorney General in his Minute Reference AG.241 dated 3rd December, 1930.

The checking of the claims in the Settlement Office would then be considerably simplified and the subsequent procedure by the Settlement Officer of reading the particulars of the claims publicly in the village itself and of his decisions thereon would minimize the risk of collusion during the earlier proceedings.

/Claims

- 32 -

Claims to a category of land other than ordinary "Miri" or "Matruka" would have to be supported by documents, or by full statements in case documents are alleged to be missing, as to why the land is claimed as Waqf Sahih, Miri Mauqufa or Mulk.

26. An important factor in the acceleration of Settlement procedure would be the abolition of the present very complicated method of calculation of Registration fees due to the system of charging fees AD VALOREM.

If a flat rate per dunum or per parcel were to be charged, the work of computation, which at present is a laborious and lengthy operation, could be done in a fraction of the time now required.

The fees for mortgages and leases might remain unchanged.

No fee should be charged for the registration of the comparatively few possessory titles registered under the Registration of Land Ordinance, 1929. That Ordinance might also usefully be amended to provide for the ripening of a possessory title into a full title at any time before the prescriptive period is over, provided the consent of the registered owner is obtained.

27. Other factors in the acceleration of settlement procedure would be the exclusion of the built-over area in villages in which the sites for buildings and the buildings themselves are of small value and their assessment to an urban tax;

"Settlement" in the case of the built-over areas in other villages only of properties for which Kushans are held;

Compilation of Schedules of Rights for the

- 25 -

undisputed parcels and the undisputed rights in disputed parcels in a Registration Block for entry in the new Registers without awaiting the Settlement of the last dispute in the Block.

28.   These and other amendments of the Land Settlement Ordinance have been suggested by me in letters, memoranda and minutes dating from November 1930 and onwards.

29.   MUSHA' which has been partitioned by order of a Magistrate, and MUSHA' which has been partitioned for a longer period than that of prescription, should be accepted on Settlement and treated as MAFRUZ, with authority for the Settlement Officer to order compensation where he is satisfied that on partition rights to share have been ignored.

30.   The present provisions in the Land Settlement Ordinance provide in some measure for the correction of bad parcellation of MUSHA' from the economic or agricultural point of view.

An additional improvement would be the provision of a clause for the elimination of shares of a smaller value than a stated minimum to be prescribed by order village by village. Or if a large number of heirs or co-owners held many shares of small value in a number of parcels, for the voluntary re-grouping of owners in the different parcels or for their compulsory re-grouping by the Settlement Officer in case of disagreement, or for the elimination of shares of small value.

For instance:- Forty persons own a garden with an area of a dunam and a half, each having shares

/out of

- 24 -

out of a denominator running into millions or thousands of millions.

The shares of each of twenty of the co-owners vary from one mill to fifty mils in value. The same set of owners own in common in addition from a dozen to a score of such small parcels. No useful purpose would be served in recording all the owners and their shares in the New Register.

It would be reasonable to provide for the voluntary or compulsory elimination of shares below a stated value or to re-group owners in parcels in such a manner as to provide shares of not less than the stated value for registration in the name of any one person in any given parcel.

These provisions might be made applicable to all sorts of shares, whether in MAFRUZ, or MUSHA' already partitioned by whatever method, or MUSHA' remaining MUSHA', or MUSHA' to be partitioned as a part of Settlement operations.

31. The amending of the Land Settlement Ordinance and approval of the procedure suggested would permit of considerable acceleration of settlement operations, would enable ownership titles to be granted, would provide for the registration of mortgages, leases, attachments, servitudes and other registrable interests, and would avoid the legal, economic, political and other difficulties inherent in the system suggested by the authors of the O'Donnell Report.

32. In regard to disputed claims, a large proportion are of such a nature that when summary enquiry had been completed, decisions could be made expeditiously and without difficulty which

/would

would permit of ownership titles being granted.

33. The re-arrangement of the staff in accordance with Appendix II attached to my "Forecast of Period required for Settlement of title operations and Estimate of Cost" dated 28th February 1931 submitted to Sir Samuel O'Donnell with copy to the Chief Secretary, would leave Settlement Officers free to deal without difficulty with remaining disputes which may require more than a summary enquiry for their settlement.

34. The suggestion in paragraph 43 of the Report to give priority to areas in which the villages wholly or partly MUSHA' are most numerous, if adopted, would in all probability add to the expense of survey and settlement.

A programme of settlement proceeding outwards from given centres entails a smaller staff, less transport and travel allowances, and is easier to supervise, than a programme of a sporadic nature.

35. The enactment of the Land Registration Ordinance for post-settlement dispositions which was submitted to Government on 27th July, 1931 and which is referred to in paragraph 45 of the Report should be accelerated. A number of villages have been already settled and if the Settlement is to be of permanent value it is essential that there should be provision for all subsequent dispositions and successions to be registered.

36. In regard to the recommendations in paragraphs 49 and 50 of the Report, when I was appointed to the office of Commissioner of Lands, I was informed

/verbally

- 26 -

verbally by Field Marshal the Right Honourable
Viscount Plumer who was then High Commissioner,
by the then Chief Secretary Colonel (now Sir)
George Symes, and by Sir Ernest Dowson, that the
Government envisaged the amalgamation, at as
early a date as conditions would permit, of the
Land Settlement, Survey, Land Registry and Direct
Taxation Departments, as Sections of a combined
Land & Department under the Commissioner of Lands.
Presumably the matter was discussed at conferences in
the office of the High Commissioner and may have been
the subject of Despatches to the Secretary of State
for the Colonies.

<u>COMMISIONER OF LANDS</u>.

<u>Enclosure II.</u>

MEMORANDUM
on the Recommendations of the Financial Commission
in Paragraph 48 of the Report, Middle East No.43,
Confidential.

In paragraph 48 of their Report, the Financial Commission suggest that the employment permanently of two Class 2 officers after the completion of the fiscal survey for a Land Tax and the initial valuations under the Urban Property Tax Ordinance have been completed, would be excessive.

They envisage that all that those officers would then be required to do would be to act as Inspectors of Urban Property Tax Assessments, and for this purpose they suggest that one Inspector in Class 3 would suffice.

2. They do not suggest that the two Class 2 officers are redundant at present, while the initial urban assessment operations and the fiscal survey are in progress, and they make no reference to the additional officer, Mr. Richard Hughes, who is on contract and who is employed temporarily as a Land Valuer because of his intimate knowledge of local conditions and land values.

3. Among other responsibilities attaching at present to the office of the Commissioner of Lands are :-

the assessment of urban properties under the Urban Property Tax Ordinance and the annual revision of those assessments;

the supervision of the annual redistribution of the Commuted Tithe in rural areas;

the fiscal survey for a Land Tax;

the valuation of properties in Settlement villages for the purpose of a Registration Fee.

It is in carrying out these duties that the two Class 2 officers and Mr. Hughes are employed.

4./

-2-

4. The duties for which this office will be responsible in the future will be :-

    the quinquennial revaluation of all properties in urban areas, as well as the annual revision of individual properties;

    when the fiscal survey is completed, the application of a Land Tax in rural areas in substitution of the werko and commuted tithe and the annual revision and periodic revaluation of rural lands;

    the assessment of properties on the lines of the Urban Property Tax Ordinance in villages where the sites and buildings occupying the sites are of value, the annual revision of individual properties in those villages and the periodic revaluation of all properties in such villages.

It has also been suggested that the Commissioner of Lands should be responsible for supervision of the application and collection of all Direct Taxation.

5. It is difficult at this stage to suggest the staff which would be required for the duties enumerated in the previous paragraph, but I am definitely of opinion that one Inspector in Class 3 would not suffice.

6. On the completion of the fiscal survey, the temporary appointment on contract of Mr. Richard Hughes could be terminated, and it may be possible then to dispense with the services of Mr. Aylmer-Harris who would revert to the Treasury from which Department he is at present seconded to my office, but I anticipate that Mr. Bennett's services could not be dispensed with and that in addition to him I should require at least one officer in Class 3.

7. I refer to paragraph 36 of the Memorandum

forwarded/

-3-

forwarded to you with my letter No.LS/2(6) of the 24th of September, 1931. If it is still the intention of Government to form one combined Lands Department under the Commissioner of Lands, with sections for Survey, Land Registration, Land Settlement, Direct Taxation, and land matters generally, as envisaged in 1927 and 1928 by the then High Commissioner, Field Marshal the Right Honourable Viscount Plumer, it is suggested that this may be a suitable time to consider the question and provide for the progressive incorporation of those sections in one Department. The composition of the staff of this office would naturally depend on the responsibilities which would be attached to this office.

(Sgd) A. Abramson.
COMMISSIONER OF LANDS.

6.06

And I think there would be no harm in asking when a suitable opportunity occurs, if Abramson, as Commissioner of Lands, is satisfied (a) that the amendment of the Land Law is being pursued as steadily and systematically as it should be, and (b) that the Land registry staff and methods can be relied upon to maintain the results of the settlement punctually and entirely dependably in the wake of the settlement.

Sooner or later questions of the responsibility for errors in the land registry is bound to arise, and on whom the cost of damages should fall. The risk is slight if the service is good and an indemnity fund can slowly be built up as elsewhere: but any weaknesses in the registers after settlement may take a long time to appear and their financial consequences might be considerable. There is no need to apprehend anything of this sort, but it is as well to be satisfied on the point. The service is, or should be, self supporting and it is much better that a slightly higher scale of fees should be charged than that there should be any inadequacy in personnel or methods.

Yours sincerely,

(Sgd) ERNEST M. DOWSON.

[This is an extract only.]

LS/13(4).   14th September, 1932.

Chief Secretary.

    I refer to your letter No.L/96/32 of the 27th July, 1932 forwarding for my comments a copy of two extracts from a letter addressed to Mr. Hall of the Colonial Office by Sir Ernest Dowson regarding the system of Land Registration in Palestine.

2.   Sir Ernest Dowson is doubtful if the amendment of the Land Law is being pursued as steadily and systematically as it should be;

    his opinion is that it is difficult for the old register service to purge itself of old methods and adopt sensible and effective ones quickly and thoroughly;

    in his view there will be no excuse if the value of the Palestine costly Settlement work is gradually lost again by any defective keeping of the Land Registers afterwards; and

    he suggests asking if the Commissioner of Lands is satisfied :

(a)/

- 2 -

(a) that the amendment of the Land Law is being pursued as steadily and systematically as it should be; and

(b) that the Land Registry staff and methods can be relied upon to maintain the results of the Settlement punctually and entirely dependably in the wake of the Settlement.

3. The Land Settlement and Land Registry staff are thoroughly trained and can be relied upon to carry out Settlement operations satisfactorily and to maintain the New Registers which are opened at Settlement, if adequate means to enable them to do so are provided them. This is not the case at present.

4. The Land Law Amendment Ordinance which provides for certain important and necessary changes in the Ottoman Land Code and which was submitted to Government in 1928, has not yet been enacted.

Amendments of the Land Settlement Ordinance which were submitted to Government in 1930 etc. to provide facilities for more expeditious work and to remove disabilities during Settlement operations, a number of which were approved in principle, have also not yet been enacted.

Both these Amendment Ordinances are essential for the effective, expeditious and economical carrying
out/

out of Settlement and for the proper maintenance of the Register after Settlement.

The Land Registration Ordinance to provide for the maintenance of the results of Settlement punctually and dependably in the wake of Settlement which was submitted to Government in 1929 has not yet been enacted. The absence of such an Ordinance endangers the maintenance of the records in the New Registers, tends to nullify the value of costly Settlement and Survey work and cannot be too strongly deprecated.

5. On the general question of the Land Law, I am of opinion that a dual method of revising the code should be adopted :

> A Committee of judges and lawyers in Palestine should be appointed to submit for consideration a revised comprehensive Land Code suitable for modern conditions in this country;

> pending the completion of this work, amendments of particular articles in the present Land Code, which present difficulties at Settlement and in the Courts, should be submitted to the above Committee and as approved by Government be provided by ad hoc legislation and subsequently incorporated in the revised code.

(Signed) A. Abramson.
COMMISSIONER OF LANDS.

6.07

PALESTINE.

HIGH COMMISSIONER FOR PALESTINE,
JERUSALEM.

DESPATCH No. 448
REFERENCE No. L/111/31.

13 May, 1933.

Sir,

Enclosure I.

I have the honour to forward herewith for your consideration the draft of an Ordinance to provide for the partition of village Musha' lands in advance of Land Settlement, together with an Explanatory Note by the Solicitor-General.

Enclosure II.

2. The draft Ordinance was considered by the High Commissioner in Executive Council before his departure from Palestine and was approved by him.

I have the honour to be,

Sir,

Your most obedient,

humble servant,

[signature]

OFFICER ADMINISTERING
THE GOVERNMENT.

The Right Honourable
    Sir Philip Cunliffe-Lister, G.B.E., M.P., etc., etc.,
        His Majesty's Principal Secretary of State
                for the Colonies.

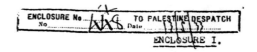

ENCLOSURE I.

An Ordinance to provide for the partition of village Musha' Lands in advance of Land Settlement.

BE IT ENACTED by the High Commissioner for Palestine with the advice of the Advisory Council thereof:-

Short title.

1. This Ordinance may be cited as the Partition of Musha' Lands Ordinance, 1933.

Definitions.

2. In this Ordinance:-

"Commissioner of Lands" means the officer appointed by the High Commissioner to exercise general direction and control over partition of lands under this Ordinance.

"Musha' Lands" means the lands of a village or of a section of a village held in undivided ownership or undivided reputed ownership and periodically distributed for cultivation among the owners or reputed owners of shares in such lands.

"Partition Officer" includes any person duly authorised to act for a Partition Officer for any specified purpose.

"Village" includes a tribal area.

Application for partition of Musha' Lands.	3. Where it is made to appear to the High Commissioner that:-

    (a) the owners or reputed owners of shares in Musha' lands in any area not being part of an area in respect of which a preliminary settlement notice has been published under section 5 of the Land Settlement Ordinance, 1928, or any number of such owners or reputed owners desire to effect a physical partition of such musha' lands and,

    (b) an application has been made to the Commissioner of Lands by one or more of such owners or reputed owners for the appointment of an officer to supervise such partition,

the High Commissioner if he is satisfied that having regard to all the circumstances such partition would be desirable may order that the provisions of this Ordinance shall apply to such musha' lands.

Appointment of Partition Officer.	4. On or after the publication of an Order under Section 3 of this Ordinance (hereinafter called "the Order") the High Commissioner

shall /

– 3 –

shall appoint an officer (hereinafter called a Partition Officer) whose duty it shall be to supervise the partition of the Musha' lands described in the Order.

Partitioning Committees.

5. (1) Upon the application of the Commissioner of Lands, the District Commissioner of the District within which the lands described in the Order are situated shall constitute a committee hereinafter called the Partitioning Committee, and shall determine or vary from time to time the composition of the Committee.

(2) The Partitioning Committee shall be chosen by the District Commissioner from amongst persons nominated by the owners or reputed owners of the shares in the musha' lands described in the Order, and in default of such nomination the District Commissioner shall appoint such persons as he thinks fit as members of the Partitioning Committee.

(3) The Partitioning Committee shall attend and assist in the partitioning of the musha' lands whenever required to do so by the Partition Officer.

- 4 -

Scheme of Partition.

6. The partition shall be carried out in accordance with a scheme agreed to by a majority of the members of the Partitioning Committee and submitted to the Partition Officer, and such scheme shall be subject to the approval of the Commissioner of Lands, regard being had to the area and value of the lands to be partitioned. Provided that the High Commissioner may from time to time by order prescribe the limitation to a minimum or to different minima of the area of any parcel or of the dimensions or breadth of any parcel into which musha' lands may be partitioned under this Ordinance.

General powers of Partition Officer.

7. Subject to the provisions of this Ordinance the Partition Officer in the execution of his duties may:-

(a) issue notices or orders requiring the attendance at any time or place or owners or reputed owners of shares in the musha' lands and of any person whose attendance he may deem necessary for the purposes of the partition,

(b) order the boundaries of any parcel resulting from the partition to be demarcated by the reputed owner thereof in such manner and before such date as he may direct and in default of compliance may cause the boundaries to be marked out at the expense of such person,

(c) impose a penalty of a fine not exceeding £P.2.- in default of compliance with any such notice, order or direction as aforesaid,

(d) dispense with the attendance of any person,

(e) make a copy of any document produced or endorse or stamp such document,

(f) authenticate any document signed or attested before him.

Power of Partition Officer as to boundaries and rights of way.

8. The Partition Officer may in the course of partitioning cause to be demarcated any existing road or path or with the approval of the Commissioner of Lands realign any existing road or path or order the provision of such new roads or paths as may be in the public interest, and cause such new roads or paths to be demarcated.

Duties of Partitioning Committee upon completion of Partition.

9. Upon the completion of the partition of the musha' lands the Partitioning Committee shall submit to the Partition

- 6 -

Officer:-

(a) a list of the parcels resulting from the partition together with the names of the owners or reputed owners of the shares represented by such parcels,

(b) a declaration signed by a majority of the members of the Partitioning Committee to the effect that the parcels resulting from the partition represent the equivalent in value and/or in area of the shares in the lands partitioned.

Effect of Partition.

10. (1) A physical partition of musha' lands made under this Ordinance shall be subject to the approval of the Commissioner of Lands and if so approved shall thereafter be binding upon the owners and reputed owners of the shares represented by the parcels resulting from the partition until such time as a settlement of rights in such parcels shall be effected in accordance with the provisions of the Land Settlement Ordinance, 1928:

Provided that a partition of musha' lands made under this Ordinance shall be without prejudice to the rights of any person claiming any right title or interest in

- 7 -

the lands partitioned.

(2) A partition of musha' lands made under this Ordinance shall not be deemed to be a disposition of immovable property within the meaning of the Land Transfer Ordinance, 1920.

Ottoman Provisional Law of Partition not to apply.	11. The Ottoman Provisional Law concerning partition dated 14 Muharram 1332 A.H. shall not apply to any musha' lands to which the provisions of this Ordinance have been applied.

ENCLOSURE II.

MEMORANDUM.

This Ordinance provides for a physical partition of musha' lands to be made under the supervision of a specially appointed partition officer before a settlement of the rights in the land and registration thereof is effected in accordance with the provisions of the Land Settlement Ordinance, 1928.

Musha lands are lands held in undivided ownership or undivided reputed ownership and periodically distributed for cultivation amongst the owners or reputed owners of shares in the lands.

Hitherto the only practical means of partition have been two, one by the villagers themselves by agreement, and the other through settlement operations which are planned to last over a number of years.

Partition undertaken by the villagers themselves without supervision has not proved entirely satisfactory, and it not infrequently happens that at land settlement the work has to be done again. Under section 51 of the Land Settlement Ordinance, 1928 the High

-2-

Commissioner is empowered to direct a Settlement Officer to carry out the partition of any land held in undivided ownership if such partition is deemed to be in the public interest, but that power relates only to areas included in land settlement operations.

As it is the view of Government that the continued existence of undivided ownership in land is one of the greatest stumbling blocks to agricultural development in Palestine it has been decided to provide by legislation for the physical partition of musha' lands in advance of land settlement.

A physical partition made under the guidance of a partition officer will considerably facilitate and expedite the survey and land settlement operations when in due course the Land Settlement Ordinance is applied to the village.

It has been found in practice that applications are frequently made to the Commissioner of Lands for the assistance of an officer by persons desiring to effect a partition of musha' land in villages situated in sub-districts which have not yet been declared settlement areas, and in villages situated in sub-districts which have been declared settlement areas but to which the provisions of the Land Settlement Ordinance have not yet been applied, and section 3 of the draft Ordinance therefore provides that where such an application is made, the High Commissioner may by order apply the provisions of the Ordinance to the lands in question.

For the purposes of carrying out the partition, a partitioning committee will be appointed from amongst the owners or reputed owners of the shares in the lands to be partitioned and the scheme of partition must be agreed to by a majority of the members of the committee vide clauses 5 and 6.

The partition when completed will be subject to the approval of the Commissioner of Lands, and if so approved, shall thereafter be binding upon the owners and reputed owners of the shares represented by the parcels resulting from the physical partition of the musha' lands until such time as a settlement of rights in such parcels shall be effected in accordance with the Land Settlement Ordinance, vide clause 10.

Pending settlement of rights, it will be possible to register the disposition of shares in the musha' lands in the Land Registry, but the parcels result-

-4-

ing from the partition cannot be so registered until land settlement operations have reached the area concerned, unless the person desiring the registration of a parcel satisfied the Registrar by due process of law that he is the owner of the share which is represented by the parcel, and that the said parcel was allotted to that share at the partition.

The Ottoman Provisional Law of Partition shall cease to apply to any musha' lands to which the provisions of the draft Ordinance have been applied.

SOLICITOR GENERAL

22nd April, 1933.